The Black Child-Savers

The Black Child-Savers

Racial Democracy and
Juvenile Justice

GEOFF K. WARD

The University of Chicago Press
Chicago and London

Geoff K. Ward is assistant professor in the Department of Criminology, Law and Society at the University of California, Irvine.

The University of Chicago Press, Chicago 60637
The University of Chicago Press, Ltd., London
© 2012 by The University of Chicago
All rights reserved. Published 2012.
Printed in the United States of America

21 20 19 18 17 16 15 14 13 12   1 2 3 4 5

ISBN-13: 978-0-226-87316-9 (cloth)
ISBN-13: 978-0-226-87318-3 (paper)
ISBN-10: 0-226-87316-1 (cloth)
ISBN-10: 0-226-87318-8 (paper)

Library of Congress Cataloging-in-Publication Data

Ward, Geoff K.
     The black child-savers : racial democracy and juvenile justice / Geoff K. Ward.
          p.   cm.
     Includes bibliographical references and index.
     ISBN-13: 978-0-226-87316-9 (hardcover : alkaline paper)
     ISBN-10: 0-226-87316-1 (hardcover : alkaline paper)
     ISBN-13: 978-0-226-87318-3 (paperback : alkaline paper)
     ISBN-10: 0-226-87318-8 (paperback : alkaline paper)   1. Juvenile justice, Administration of—United States—History. 2. Discrimination in juvenile justice administration—United States—History. 3. African American children—Legal status, laws, etc.—United States—History. 4. Juvenile courts—United States—History.   I. Title.
HV9104.W37 2012
364.36089'96073—dc23

                                                    2011035702

CONTENTS

ILLUSTRATIONS

FIGURES

TABLES

The Rise and Fall of Jim Crow Juvenile Justice

Over a century after the birth of Jim Crow juvenile justice, this book offers the first detailed account of this peculiar institution and how it collided with black freedom dreams to spawn a long movement on behalf of that entity W. E. B. DuBois called "the immortal child," in a veiled reference to group fate.[1] The project began with a naive interest in documenting the historical significance of race in American juvenile justice. My initial thought was to make a graph, but in the late 1990s that graph expanded to a time line depicting the historical backdrop of racial inequality in this institutional context. That summary was to be embedded in the brief "historical background" section of a contemporary statistical study of race and juvenile justice. The history, I thought, would be the easier part, with my overview of historical race relations based on institutional commitment rates of black youths dating to around 1900—when the juvenile court movement began. Given the scarcity of government and academic sources concerning this racial history, however, even this proved difficult. And, once I found those numbers, they created more puzzles than they explained. Thus, the central focus of my research became the far greater and more important challenge of conceptualizing and measuring the historical significance of race in American juvenile justice.

In my initial search for statistics, I had barely considered the theoretical and methodological aspects of graphically depicting racial history. The received wisdom on framing race and racial inequality indicated that to capture the salience of race I would need to chart over time the onset and increase of "disproportionate minority confinement" (DMC) in juvenile institutions and, perhaps, in adult jails and prisons. Disproportionate minority youth contact was fundamental to the race problem, and the conception of racism generally highlighted the significance of race to juvenile justice processes and outcomes. The study of "race effects" in juvenile justice thus had to assess whether youth racial status mattered in sanctioning.

After determining the beginning of the DMC problem, I intended to assess the statistical significance of youth racial and ethnic status for sanctioning outcomes through a standard cross-sectional study of government data. Using this slice of time in contemporary juvenile justice, I would examine race in relation to "structured decisionmaking (SDM) tools." Typically using paper-and-pencil forms to generate case assessments and classifications, juvenile justice officials have often used this device to make sanctioning decisions. Did this actually reduce racial disparities in sanctioning, as proponents maintained? The instruments were believed to regulate individual discretion, including racial bias, thus making juvenile justice systems fairer. Did they really increase racial justice? The answer, I assumed, would be revealed in the insignificance of youth racial status to outcomes in more structured or regulated courts. In the course of writing this book, however, I reconsidered whether race relations in juvenile justice are primarily a matter of youth outcomes, whether institutional racism is rooted in unregulated decisionmaker bias, and whether racial justice hinges on the irrelevance of race to justice processes. Actual history shed an entirely new light on these notions as well as on the problem of DMC, on the advent of SDM, and on much of the way in which we understand past and present racial politics of juvenile social control.

At first the near absence of historical background in the race and juvenile justice research struck me as an oddity and an opportunity. The extant literature on race was substantial, but it barely delved into history. Most empirical studies read as though American juvenile justice was suddenly overcome with race problems in the final quarter of the twentieth century. Aside from the black popular and academic presses, few studies were published within, or focused on, the period before 1970. These trends probably resulted from federal and state policies on DMC, whose funding streams created a flood of research focused on this relatively narrow topic and recent time frame.

Even more surprising was the limited analysis of race in the rich historical literature on the institutional development of juvenile justice. Racial and ethnic status and power relations are rarely subjects of sustained scrutiny in this series of historical studies of white American and immigrant European youth and community experiences. Beyond the absence of a racial politics of whiteness, the histories give little account of nonwhite youths and communities, who also had stakes in the emergence of American juvenile justice. The omission of race in historical work on juvenile justice mirrors the exclusion of nonwhites in the earliest practices of juvenile justice. White adults controlled juvenile justice systems, and those systems were typically reserved for white youths, denying nonwhite youths and adults equal recognition, opportunity, and influence. From the founding of houses of refuge in the early nineteenth century until a decade beyond the *Brown v. Board of Education* (1956) ruling, American juvenile justice routinely prioritized rehabilitative intervention in the lives of white children and youths. This "manufactory of citizens," as Theodore Roosevelt once described enlightened juvenile justice, was organized to reproduce a white democracy.[2] The white-dominated parental state engaged for generations in racially selective citizen- and state-building initiatives through juvenile justice policy and practice. By failing to subject "separate and unequal" juvenile justice to close or critical scrutiny, research has historically ignored, mentioned superficially, or assisted in this civic arrangement.

The current costs of this historical oversight mean that today's research, policies, and popular efforts to assess the salience of race and remedy racial inequality are disconnected from an important body of information. History offers distinct insight into the phenomenon of *race effects*, a term researchers use in data analysis to characterize the statistical significance of race variables (e.g., the race of the accused or victim). It reveals dimensions and mechanisms of race relations, including how racial ideology, politics, and structures took shape and changed over time in this institutional context. In short, it tells us how race has mattered in juvenile social control and how these influences relate to the question of inequality. Without history, we lose perspective on the racial structure of juvenile justice, the nature of racial inequality, and the meaning of racial justice.

My search through historical archives eventually resulted in a graph on the background of DMC. Figure 0.1 shows the percentages of white and nonwhite among youths committed to public and private juvenile reformatory institutions in selected years between 1890 and 2000. Below these two lines is one that shows the proportion of nonwhites in the general U.S. population during the same period, providing a basis for roughly gauging the extent of youth DMC. The area between the two measures of nonwhite population shows a gradual, somewhat linear increase in youth DMC over the past century, with escalations surrounding war years, including the 1960s and 1970s. The period since 1980 reflects the general onset of racialized mass incarceration in the United States, indicating a sharp rise in the relative representation of nonwhite youths in juvenile institutions toward the end of the twentieth century.

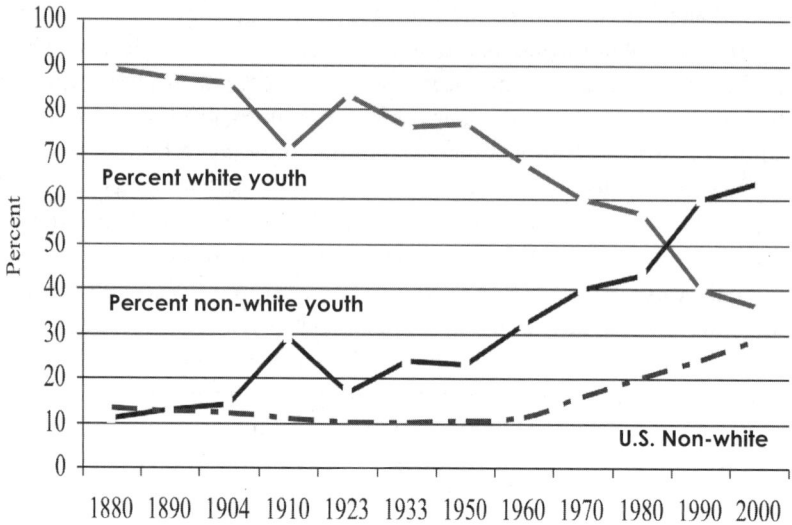

0.1. Whites and nonwhites among male youths committed to juvenile correctional institutions and within the U.S. population, 1880–2000 (in percentages).

This approach has conventionally been used to assess the extent of racial inequality in juvenile justice, that is, as a problem of disproportion requiring a remedy of redistribution. The goal of current race-related juvenile justice policy is to achieve greater proportionality in sanctioning.[3] However, as I detail throughout this book, this historical depiction obscures the racial politics of juvenile justice more than it clarifies its characteristics and significance.

The color line during the first half of the twentieth century is deceptively flat, creating a mirage of relative equality indicated by racially proportionate commitment. Instead, the period is defined by tremendous racial conflict and inequality, including overt racial oppression and domination in the administration of juvenile justice. Racially proportional representation in juvenile institutions was never greater than during the Progressive Era (1890–1920), when Jim Crow juvenile justice was born and black civic leaders first declared war on these systems of separate and unequal juvenile social control. Originally, low rates of black youth confinement were rooted in this racial regime of Jim Crow segregation and its denial of black youth and community access to liberal rehabilitative ideals.

As a gauge of the racial politics of juvenile justice, historically and today, proportionality is limited and misleading. It misrepresents the problem of discrimination against youths, and its depiction of race relations offers no account of adult or community ties to juvenile justice systems, including the question of nonwhite representation and authority in the administration of juvenile justice. Racial group power relations have been key to the historical denial of nonwhite youth and community interests and were the primary concern in the struggle against Jim Crow juvenile justice. In my view, questions of racial group recognition in juvenile justice processes have always been more important than racial distributions of outcomes and still remain so.

Contemporary research and policy have sought to explain the dramatic and disproportionate quantitative increase of black and other nonwhite youths in juvenile and adult detention, jails, and prisons in the post–civil rights period, especially since 1980. I became consumed with the background to these developments, including the relative absence of black youths from early juvenile institutions as well as the question of how black adults experienced and shaped the development of American juvenile justice. How did enslaved and free black youths and communities relate to the nascent nineteenth-century stages of juvenile justice reform? How did black community access to juvenile justice resources and authority change following Emancipation, during subsequent periods of black reconstruction, white redemption, and Progressive Era reform? How did the Great Migration, de jure segregation in the South, and de facto segregation elsewhere shape the history of juvenile justice and racial politics of social control? Finally, how did black communities challenge and alter these racial structures, and what are the legacies or lessons of this racial history today? These basic questions emerged as my original research agenda faded and the present historical study took shape.

This book synthesizes my years spent pondering these questions, collecting relevant research material, and analyzing the complex racial history of American juvenile justice. It details the sociohistorical origins and organization of Jim Crow juvenile justice as well as the social movement by generations of black Americans to replace the white supremacist parental state with an idealized racial structure of democratic social control. The anticipated racially democratic juvenile justice system was thought to provide for equal black youth opportunity and black adult representation or authority in the administration of liberal rehabilitative ideals, enlisting the supposed manufactory of citizens in the production of a racially inclusive liberal democracy. I argue that this racial history of juvenile justice helps fill the research gaps in the historical literature and challenges much of what has been established as general institutional history. Above all, it suggests the need for an innovative conceptualization and measurement of race effects in juvenile justice today, including deemphasis of the ideal of distributive racial justice and greater attention to the deliberative interests in democratic social control at the center of the black child-saving movement.

The Black Child-Savers

Among the first places I looked for racial history was in the sociologist Anthony Platt's *The Child-Savers: The Invention of Delinquency* (1969), a classic study of Progressive Era juvenile justice reform. Having read his book in college and been intrigued by its discussion of race, I thought that it might provide some figures or leads. Indeed, its appendix contains a brief and incidental but unique and compelling study of race in early American juvenile justice. The essay essentially documents the denial of black youth claims to the diminished child-criminal culpability standards of common law—the legal foundation of early American juvenile justice. Platt seeks to illustrate that children and youths were treated more leniently under common law, long before the juvenile court movement, such that this was not the main cultural or institutional significance of juvenile court reform. Yet he notes that this historical protection of youths through law appears to have been reserved for white youths. Unfortunately, however, race is overlooked in the remainder of his study and in the many others that it inspired, so we learn little about the racial identities, ideologies, and power relations of white and nonwhite youths and communities whose worlds were divided and subsequently clashed during the Progressive Era emergence of the juvenile court and Jim Crow juvenile justice.[4]

My book provides another revisionist social history of the development of juvenile justice. It thus reexamines the child-saving movement, a social movement that established various systems of juvenile social control, including juvenile justice. At the center of this analysis is the black American experience. Existing studies typically foreground Progressive Era white elites in the urban North and Midwest as well as the ordeals of white American and European youths. In contrast, I examine the distress and agency of poor, working-class, and middle-class black children, women, and men to understand the significance of race in American juvenile justice, historically and today. Although this approach has limitations—a real need does exist for a historical perspective on other nonwhite group experiences (and race studies of the white experience)—a study of this scope, with the required comparative framework, was not feasible.[5] Yet there is good reason to focus on the black experience. Since the liberal enlightenment of juvenile justice overlaps with the final half century of chattel slavery and the subsequent periods of

Emancipation, Reconstruction, and white supremacist redemption, focusing on the black experience in this evolving context of social control offers a unique view into how the historical development of juvenile justice aligned with the twentieth-century meaning of race in American liberal democracy.

This book has theoretical and methodological characteristics in common with Anthony Platt's original work. *The Child Savers* challenged the standard romantic reading of Progressive Era reforms, including the establishment of juvenile justice, where power inequalities, competing group interests, and ordeals of oppression and domination were glossed over in accounts of liberal enlightenment. *The Child Savers* and other critical revisionist accounts of Progressive Era juvenile justice reform helped uncover the class and gender politics surrounding this institutional history, deepening our understanding of how societal power relations have shaped and been shaped by these systems of social control. My critical analysis of social control examines the parental state and the juvenile justice system as components of a contested and dynamically racialized social system in which racial, class, and gender identities and power relations constantly shape group opportunity, influence, benefits, and burdens. Like *The Child Savers*, this book draws on biographical details and people's experiences in specific places to assemble a sense of their social status and existence as well as to understand how this articulates with the evolving racial structure of American juvenile justice.

Metaphorically, a quilt best represents the racial history of juvenile justice. As such, my research method seeks to identify and piece together important panels of this story about race in America. I pursued William Sewell's notion of an "evenemential," or eventful, method of historical sociology to contextualize social change. In this case, it is the rise and fall of Jim Crow juvenile justice, in relation to the historically dynamic interplay of structure, culture, and agency. The method stresses the "path dependent, causally heterogeneous, and contingent nature" of major sociohistorical events and places the question of how social structures are created and re-created by social action at the center of the research agenda. An eventful racial history of juvenile justice would focus primarily on the social action of black Americans. Of particular concern is the development, evolution, and impact of the black child-saving movement, a decades-long effort to restructure the racial politics of American juvenile justice. The movement began in what was the Progressive Era but also the Black Nadir—the lowest point in black social status and well-being since Emancipation. It lasted until at least the 1960s, with remnants still evident today.

Various dimensions, such as movement duration, regional concentration, strategies, and resources, distinguish the black child-savers from their more studied white counterparts. As Jim Crow juvenile justice became entrenched between 1890 and 1950, the black child-saving movement reorganized and pressed beyond the Progressive Era into the civil rights period. The movement began in the rural South, where most black Americans lived before World War II, and gradually spread, growing strongest in the cities of the North and West. Particularly noteworthy is how the black child-saving movement, as well as its influence, was shaped by historical forces unique to the black world, including the Great Migration, racial uplift ideology, the standpoint of the "New Negro," organized movements for civil rights, and the postintegration period.

The black child-savers' ability to reconfigure race relations in juvenile justice was always extremely limited. Whereas white child-savers typically enjoyed access to white government officials, industrial leaders, and other power brokers essential to advancing their civic initiatives, the black child-savers proceeded from a subordinate social position and were engaged in a conflict movement, a contentious struggle against existing racial power relations. The black child-savers operated on the margins of civil society, and their collective efficacy was constrained by the realities of American apartheid, which left its imprint on movement strategies and resources. They relied almost exclusively on black community resources (such as volunteerism and donations) and on court challenges and protests to broker typically modest reforms. The unheralded black child-savers tell an inspiring American story about the often stark but unstable and penetrable boundaries of race, citizenship, and democracy. Although they did redefine the racial politics of juvenile justice, their movement generally failed to achieve its goal of institutionalizing racial justice in the administration of liberal rehabilitative ideals.

I owe my initial discovery of the black child-saving movement to Professor Vernetta Young of Howard University. During my preliminary search for historical information, among the few published articles on the racial history of juvenile justice were two by Professor Young. Her studies revealed the persistence of an earlier pattern of white youth privilege, which Platt had uncovered. Young documented the establishment of segregated juvenile reformatory institutions, with states routinely prioritizing the creation of white reformatories, or manufactories of white citizens, while refusing to provide equivalent services, if any at all, for black youths.

Discrimination against black youths in early American juvenile justice is not surprising, but the patterns and mechanisms of this stratification are revealing as indicators of the meaning of race. Young's articles outline the oppositional roles of black women in the establishment of early reformatories in response to black exclusion from white-only institutions. If juvenile reformatories existed for black youths, they were typically created and maintained by black adults. This illustrates the complexity of race effects when considering the objectification and agency of racial actors. I was familiar with race research that framed nonwhites as passive subjects—those suffering from race effects resulting in discriminatory sanctioning—yet these articles revealed a more complex interplay of race, structure, and agency, including potentially *progressive* dimensions of racialized social control.

Evidence of black community involvement in early juvenile justice reform intrigued me, so I contacted Professor Young. She generously agreed to meet with me to discuss my historical research interests and the obstacles to finding information. We met in her office, and she handed me a file containing a dozen or so photocopies of pamphlets dating to the early twentieth century, along with essays and other practical writings by members of black women's clubs. These clubs were vital to the collective efficacy of black communities in many pursuits, such as elder and child care, education reform, recreation, and all varieties of activism. The authors were affiliated with the National Association of Colored Women's Clubs and local Southern clubs with intriguing names ranging from the ornate Les Fiddelles Filles (The faithful sisters) of Savannah, Georgia, to the more practical Ten Times One Is Ten Club of Montgomery, Alabama, which emphasized the power in numbers. The writings concerned the crisis of Jim Crow juvenile justice. They placed black civic leaders at the scene of Progressive Era juvenile justice reform and shared their voices of opposition at the founding of the Jim Crow juvenile justice system.

After this exchange, my central research objective was to understand the content and significance of this voice and, more generally, to examine the racial politics of recognition in American juvenile justice. I spent almost a decade amassing material to accompany the voices of these women leaders. Specifically, I sought sources that offered an expansive view of the role of black civil society in the emergence of juvenile justice as well as the broader structural and cultural context of that civic engagement. My larger sample details the ideologies and resources of black Americans who organized against Jim Crow juvenile justice and for alternative racial structures of juvenile social control. From a wide array of primary and secondary source material, I gained a sense of these interventions, the contexts in which they emerged and evolved, and their social and institutional impacts. These interventions clashed, mixed, and meshed with dominant group ideologies and resources to define the negotiated racial history of American juvenile justice.

This negotiation involves a protracted struggle over the racial politics of the parental state. It constitutes a series of opposing racial projects that sought to define and redefine the meaning of race in juvenile justice and, ultimately, in American society. Two ideas of black childhood are at war in the racial projects of Jim Crow juvenile justice and the black child-saving movement. The dominant view caricatures black youths as an incorrigible, undeserving, and expendable breed of human clay, while the oppositional view frames the racialized refusal to extend rehabilitative ideals and resources as a denial of equal protection and a form of structural violence that threatens democratic freedoms. Jim Crow juvenile justice reserved institutional opportunity and influence for white youths and communities, while the black child-savers aimed to racially democratize youth access to rehabilitative ideals and community control of institutional resources. Jim Crow juvenile justice was organized to maintain white democracy and second-class black citizenship, while the black child-saving movement imagined an alternative structure of juvenile justice that could institutionalize progress toward a new multiracial and ethnic democracy. These vital interests were at stake in this nearly century-long struggle for and against racially democratic control, and they remain with us today.

Organization and Argument of the Book

Organized in two parts, this book will offer an account of this historical clash of racial projects. Part 1 covers the sociohistorical origins and organization (i.e., mechanisms) of Jim Crow juvenile justice, while part 2 examines the development, evolution, and impact of the black child-saving movement.

Chapter 1 examines the background of the juvenile rehabilitative ideal and its roots in American liberal-democratic idealism. Mainstream concerns with shaping and molding wayward, neglected, and criminal youths were explicitly linked to unease over the well-being of civil society and the fate of liberal democracy. This setting is vital to understanding why juvenile justice became an early and enduring feature in the struggle over the relation between race and American democracy.

The next three chapters illustrate how imbalanced racial group power relations, white supremacist ideology, and related institutional structures (i.e., law) dictated the administration of liberal rehabilitative ideals. A two-pronged denial of black humanity and democratic standing negated black youth and community claims to rehabilitative ideals. Black youths were rendered unsalvageable and undeserving of citizen-building ambition, while black adults were disempowered in the deliberations of a white-dominated parental state. Chapter 2 examines these developments in the context of nineteenth-century innovations, such as the use of common law in youth sanctioning and the establishment of houses of refuge. This illustrates how white racial group prerogatives and privileges shaped the administration of these earliest institutional reforms. Chapters 3 and 4 consider how black Americans experienced the invention and diffusion of the juvenile court during the Progressive Era and Jim Crow racial oppression and domination in juvenile justice during subsequent decades, with an emphasis on the South and urban North.

Because existing histories of juvenile justice fail to account for nonwhite youth experiences, their conclusions are compromised. They feature the severe mistreatment of predominately poor, white American and immigrant European youths who were subject to early juvenile court interventions and placement in reformatories, all under the banner of rehabilitative ideals. In contrast, black youths experienced ongoing commitment to adult prisons, the convict-lease system, prolonged periods in detention, and higher rates of corporal punishment and execution. Given this perspective, white youths were relatively privileged. Their hardships pale in comparison with the treatment of black youths, buffered as they were by liberal ambitions for juvenile justice reform and the related resources of emerging juvenile court communities. Above all, the contrast signals the partial mainstream commitment during the first half of the twentieth century to white citizens and state building through the administration of rehabilitative ideals.

In the second part of the book, attention shifts to black agency and its influence on the racial history of American juvenile justice. Here, I examine black opposition to Jim Crow juvenile justice systems through waves of social action by the black child-saving movement. The movement's phases are distinguished by historical period as well as by variations in black social status, oppositional politics, and social movement resources. Chapter 5 covers the first wave of reform, which commenced in the late nineteenth century and peaked in the 1920s. This vanguard effort was led by underresourced but well-networked black women's benevolent associations, which generally organized under the banner of racial uplift. This initial phase of intervention brought modest—indeed, cautious—self-help efforts to bear on the crisis of Jim Crow juvenile justice, through local remedies scattered across a vast and primarily southern landscape.

The modesty of the first wave partly reflected the relatively moderate ideology of racial uplift, but the economic and political inequality of the period was even more decisive. This included the risks taken in movement activity and its constrained capacity for introducing major changes in

American culture, law, and politics. Still, black civic leaders in the period pooled meager resources to enhance black collective efficacy in juvenile social control, developing more inclusionary institutions for black court-involved youths, and generating black oppositional consciousness toward Jim Crow juvenile justice.[7] For the movement, it was a capacity-building phase rather than a period of structural change.

In chapter 6, I examine the evolving oppositional politics, expanding resources, and impact of the second wave of black child-saving initiatives, which peaked between 1930 and 1954. As the black freedom movement began to take shape in the early twentieth century, emboldened black civic leaders and their allies shifted attention from modest self-help initiatives to pressure group politics. Beyond seeking to ameliorate the harms of racial inequality in juvenile justice, this advanced phase of black child-saving sought to secure equal opportunity for youth and community influence through the formal integration of American juvenile justice.

As part of the sociohistorical context for the second wave, black migration to American cities expanded the networks and resources of black child-savers. Local black women leaders with limited political and economic resources had primarily led the earlier wave in the South. The second wave, however, introduced a more diverse array of black operatives, many with formal training in law, social science, and social welfare. These *race relations experts*, as professional black activists were described, used their professional training, positions, and networks to document and combat the inner workings of Jim Crow juvenile justice systems.

In my view, the second wave of reform established a more formidable black surrogate parental state, a semiformal structure of juvenile social control organized to serve developmental interests of black youths and to represent black community interests. This apparatus was nationally organized in some ways, but its strength was greatest in urban locales with substantial black economic and political influence and high levels of civic engagement. By leveraging the power of the growing civil rights establishment and threatening more radical black liberation agendas, the second wave eventually negotiated the formal demise of Jim Crow juvenile justice, ushering in the modern era of liberal integration.

In the final chapter and the conclusion, I show that the black child-saving movement played a remarkable, though paradoxical, role in reshaping the racial politics of contemporary American juvenile justice by rearranging— if not eradicating—racial oppression and domination in juvenile social control. The movement aspired, not to make race irrelevant to juvenile justice administration, but rather to alter the "racial contract" by making the administration of rehabilitative ideals more responsive and accountable to diverse constituencies. A strategy of integration was intended to reengineer the racial politics of juvenile justice, by incorporating black youths and adult professionals into a representative system of racially democratic control. Integration was a practical way to mainstream the black child-saving initiative, that is, to institutionalize racial justice in the administration of rehabilitative ideals by including black youths and adults in juvenile justice systems.

Chapter 7 examines the changing racial politics of juvenile justice in the postintegration period (1954–70) to assess whether this agenda was realized. I compare and contrast developments in the American South, where opposition to racial integration still raged, with the unique black urban metropolis of Harlem, where black child-saving attained its most robust expression, to gauge the variable impact of court-ordered integration. In the 1950s and 1960s, sporadic signs appeared of increasing liberal experimentation with racialized social control, especially where earlier progress in establishing equal protection and representation enabled the development of a more cooperative, multiracial parental state. In New York City, for example, influential black civic leaders formulated and partly developed innovative interventions into the growing problems of delinquency. They also introduced laws and policies to protect against racial discrimination in the administration of rehabilitative ideals. Even in Harlem, of course, integration was met with persistent, though subtle, opposition. In areas of greater black marginalization, such as the battleground South, the white parental state openly continued to deny the interests of black youths and communities.

Chapter 7 shows that, despite important signs of progress early in the civil rights era, integrated juvenile justice systems ultimately showed strain and buckled under the weight of somewhat unreasonable expectations that they would institutionalize racial justice. Black child-savers envisioned integrated authorities as race relations experts who would enlighten a new, multiracial, liberal parental state. However, amid an increasingly serious juvenile crime problem and continued discrimination, formal integration appears instead to have hastened a decline of black collective identification and action around issues of juvenile crime and justice. This erosion of black collective efficacy alienated black youths and authorities in integrated juvenile justice systems, limiting the political and practical capacities to reorganize juvenile justice along new racial lines. By the late 1970s, it was clear that formal integration was, by itself, incapable of articulating or advancing black community interests in citizen-building initiatives. Ultimately, resistance to liberal integration and declining collective efficacy isolated black youths and adult authorities in crumbling juvenile justice systems and made black communities vulnerable to a shift after the 1970s away from traditional rehabilitative ideals and toward a new "accountability-based" agenda of juvenile social control.

The conclusion contains an account of this paradoxical and tragic reformulation of racial oppression and domination in the post–civil rights period. Formal integration reconfigured black youth opportunity and community influence in American juvenile justice, but it failed to institutionalize racially democratic control. Instead, subsequent cultural and institutional changes related to a more general late-twentieth-century retraction of the liberal welfare state drained the progressive utility of integration, reducing black youth and community incorporation to more symbolic forms of inclusion.

In contemporary juvenile justice, the "accountability movement" reconfigured the social contractual terms of juvenile justice and the organization of decisionmaking in juvenile justice in ways that undermined the potential for racially democratic control. New notions of "deserving" and "undeserving" delinquents limited presumptive rights to rehabilitation. In this formally race-neutral scheme, "normal" or malleable and less culpable delinquents are distinct from criminally responsible "serious" delinquents, who are not entitled to welfare. Contemporary research indicates that race predicts youth selection into one or the other status group, with nonwhite and particularly black youths systematically classified as undeserving, serious delinquents.[8] By limiting presumptive rights to rehabilitation to the subtly racialized subcategory of normal delinquents, the formally integrated parental state prevents nonwhite youths from accessing traditional citizen-building ideals.

The accountability movement also diminished the influence of black workers and constituencies by increasing national and federal influence over juvenile justice policy and practice. This growing federal role empowered influential national citizen groups and imposed policies on the states. The result was a diminished role for more marginal black constituencies and newly integrated black authorities in the governance of juvenile social control. Juvenile courts, historically dominated by whites, enjoyed wide discretion to "individualize justice," aiding discrimination. In the second half of the twentieth century, however, the imposition of federal and state priorities and procedures of accountability-based juvenile justice curtailed this authority.

Black child-savers expected formally integrated authorities of the multiracial parental state to racially enlighten citizen-building initiatives. Instead, they were bound by new limits and distributions of discretion. SDM technologies curtailed the substantive importance of diversity among arbiters of juvenile justice. Greatly enhanced prosecutorial authority and punitive juvenile laws, such as severe, mandatory sanctioning of serious delinquents, also diminished the ability of black authorities to shape juvenile court decisions and outcomes. These and other changes illustrate how the punitive reconstruction of juvenile justice eviscerated the resources available to black youths through child and social welfare while reorganizing power relations. The real value of black representation among authorities in the post–civil rights period diminished accordingly.

The quilted racial history of American juvenile justice remains only partially understood. My book examines the rise and fall of Jim Crow juvenile justice through a study of its contested cultural and institutional threads. There remains a need for historical analysis of these and other dimensions of racialized juvenile social control. For, if racial identification and stratification are to be reconciled with democratic principles of justice, we must understand how the ideas and practices of justice become intertwined with racial ideologies and structures and, ultimately, produced, reinforced, and at times eradicated racialized democratic exclusion. History is useful to this task. It illustrates how earlier race problems persist today and expands, contextualizes, and challenges our conceptualization of racial justice in an evolving domain of race relations. How was Jim Crow juvenile justice organized, how did the black child-saving movement evolve, and why does inequality persist in the promised land of integration? The answers provide a perspective on what has been achieved, lost, or not yet realized in a century of struggle toward an elusive racial democracy.

This book does not aim to solve a quintessential American dilemma; rather, it helps map the relevant mechanisms of race-linked democratic exclusion. Its primary contribution, I hope, is that it reveals that juvenile justice is a negotiated racial structure. In this actively shaped and contested racialized social system, color lines excluded black youths and communities in systems of social control but also generated progressive opposition and advanced more democratic relations. By examining this dialectic of racial oppression, domination, and antiracist resistance, the book offers a more complex and comprehensive view of how race effects have formed and functioned to diminish and affirm the democratic standing of black youths and communities in this institutional context.

Finally, this book examines how race relations are shaped by the agency of dominant and nondominant racial groups. It situates black Americans as subjects and agents within racial structures of juvenile justice. Moreover, it helps transcend earlier revisionist histories of juvenile justice, in which race is generally ignored. It also challenges the dominant notion of racial justice in contemporary juvenile justice research and policy. In particular, it suggests the limits of the predominant distributive approach to measuring and advancing equality and the need for greater attention to the deliberative dimensions of racial justice, which revolve around cultural recognition in the governance of social control. These are the central mechanisms underpinning the unjust distributional outcomes of Jim Crow juvenile justice, the progressive influence of black child-savers, and the paradox of persistent oppression and domination in the post–civil rights period. Indeed, racial justice has never hinged on proportional distributions of outcomes and will likely always depend on the balance of racial group recognition in ideally democratic institutions of social control.

PART ONE

The Origins and Organization of Jim Crow Juvenile Justice

ONE

Citizen Delinquent:
Race, Liberal Democracy,
and the Rehabilitative Ideal

By the eighteenth century, Western liberal societies commonly regarded children and adolescents as uniquely malleable human beings whose individual developmental potential held a distinct significance for societal fates.[1] Mainstream civic leaders generally believed that children, unlike adults, possessed the capacity to be trained or tailored to fit social norms and expectations. Child development thus required shaping and molding a normal, productive, and mature citizen before the rigidity of adulthood set in. Owing to the cultural and political link between child development and social welfare, juvenile social control became a concern for various, often competing constituencies interested in shaping the nation. That link was central to the republican idealism of early American juvenile justice, the development of Jim Crow juvenile justice, and the nearly century-long struggle to advance racial democracy within and *through* juvenile social control. This chapter surveys how the juvenile delinquent came to be understood as an "embryonic citizen," whose fate was, perhaps, forever linked with the racial politics of American democratic ideals, movements, and institutions.

The Child, the Delinquent, and the State

The origins and significance of childhood as a life-course distinction in Western societies has been the subject of great interest and debate.[2] Since at least the eighteenth century, cultural and legal concepts of childhood have been used to regulate social and political relations. The premise was that child development was in the interest of social welfare and, thus, a responsibility of the family and the parental state.

Early historiographies of childhood in Western European societies emphasize how the cultural and political distinction of the child evolved. Modern conceptions of childhood, they contend, first emerged in the sixteenth century. Before that, children were considered small people and ignored in developmental terms. In the West, only with the decline in infant mortality, the rise of Christianity, increased literacy, and industrialization and urbanization did children begin to be distinguished developmentally. With children and adolescents viewed as distinctly malleable beings, their development into adulthood had great cultural, economic, and political consequences. As the focus of increased concern, children's socialization experiences became more regulated.[3]

Among the earliest and most influential evolutionary studies was *Centuries of Childhood*. In it, the French sociologist Philippe Ariès claims that modern society has progressed "from ignorance of childhood" through the Middle Ages "to the centering of the family around the child in the nineteenth century." Examining children and families in the iconography of French art, architecture, religion, education, and other fields, Ariès maintains that modern conceptions of family life first surface in the sixteenth century and are common by the seventeenth.[4] He and others explain the eventual recognition of childhood as a critical distinction in human development and civil status via demographic and social-organizational developments. Up to the Middle Ages, they maintain, high rates of infant mortality discouraged parents from becoming emotionally attached to offspring; these temporary sources of pleasure and joy were worthy of little sentimental and developmental investment. By the seventeenth century, as rates of infant and overall mortality continued to decline in the West, children were recognized as "potential adults" and beings who might come of age to participate in familial and social affairs. Given this possibility, children represented the future of the familial and societal unit. Parents and religious and secular civic leaders thus took increased interest in ensuring that these malleable beings would "be shaped and molded and formed into righteous, law-abiding, [and] God-fearing adults."[5]

Industrialization and urbanization also changed family dynamics and the status differentiation of children. By the eighteenth century, many teenagers were considered adults. In their primarily rural milieu, they often lived independently of their parents, performed similar labor, and led new families with children of their own. Previously, low levels of education and similar capacities to perform agricultural labor contributed to a lack of distinction between young and old; lack of contact with other people's children in rural environments limited concern about their control. Yet growing literacy rates provided a new basis for age-related developmental and status differentiation. Industrialization, urbanization, and the emerging market economy moved work outside the home, increased competition for labor and relevant skills, and brought young and old into contact and conflict in cities. Free young people grew more dependent on parents and for longer periods, becoming a greater concern in urban areas as the decline of informal controls seemed to increase the threat of dislocated youths. Adolescence was seen as an advanced stage of childhood, the final bridge to adulthood where the possibility for "normalization" through education and other interventions was diminishing and urgent. Adulthood lurked ominously as a point where the child-adolescent "could no longer be changed and would become set in [his or her] ways."[6]

More recent histories challenge aspects of the evolutionary account of childhood; they do see a growing urgency to regulate child development by the end of the eighteenth century. Relying on more direct sources of parent and adult orientations toward children, such as diaries, biographies, and institutional records, these critics demonstrate that some of the allegedly modern conceptions of childhood existed in the Middle Ages and that children were not regularly objectified and brutalized before the modern era. The evidence suggests that parents have for all known time identified and loved their children, in ways that are more consistent with than distinct from modern conceptions but that defy generalization within and across societal contexts.[7]

Critics of the evolutionary view acknowledge changes in the cultural and political conceptions of childhood and related child-welfare practices by the eighteenth century. Such changes are crucial for understanding the general and racial politics of emerging juvenile justice systems. The historian Linda Pollock observes, for example, an "increased emphasis on the abstract nature of childhood and parental care from the seventeenth century onwards." Beyond documenting events of misbehavior and punishments in response, she finds that parents' diaries are increasingly consumed with general "methods of discipline" and the "duties of parents to children" and, ultimately, society. By the eighteenth century, parents were increasingly concerned with the civic utility of child discipline and their accountability for "'training' a child in order to ensure that he or she absorbed the correct values and beliefs and would grow into a model citizen." Faced with this blended concept of child and social welfare, she found eighteenth-century mothers and fathers increasingly "approaching parenthood with apprehension and trepidation, worrying whether their modes of child care were correct, and whether they were sufficiently competent to rear their children."[8]

Despite overstating the novelty and generalizable quality of eighteenth- and nineteenth-century sociolegal conventions related to families and children in Europe, Ariès's sociological and political insights help account for the development and application of child-welfare reform strategies. The key novelty of the seventeenth and eighteenth centuries, he suggests, is not the formal appreciation of childhood as a stage of human development, but the cultural and institutional significance of the child relative to parents, families, and society. In particular, cultural conceptions of children as clay-like souls, the unsettled futures of family and society, and adult sensitivity to civic responsibility in raising children moved eighteenth- and nineteenth-century parents, and, in time, the parental state, to become more deliberately and coercively engaged with issues of child-welfare and juvenile social control.

By connecting the rise of modern society and the growing significance of the "family unit" and the "child" as status groups, Ariès uncovers the tightening of juvenile social control, a "contradiction in denying children their freedom, in the name of their own protection and moral education," as Corsaro puts it.[9] To an unprecedented extent, Ariès claims, a symbolic and constructive unity emerged in the idealized family. Between the medieval period and the seventeenth century, he argues, the child returned to the home, rather than being entrusted to apprenticeship relations, giving the seventeenth-century family its principal characteristic: the child "became an indispensable element of everyday life, and his parents worried about his education, his career, his future."[10]

By the eighteenth century, then, the child's importance grew in private families and public policy. Child welfare and discipline increasingly dominated concerns over success, not merely for individual children (or embryonic citizens), but for their familial and communal attachments. Spreading literacy, growing pressures of conformity and obedience, and the increasing presence of the state in regulating family life raised concerns with the civic utility of child discipline. This broadening of parental responsibility to ensure the proper socialization of children reflects Ariès's notion of the growing significance of the private sphere in regulating social and political relations. "The modern family," Ariès explained, "cuts itself off from the world and opposes to society the isolated group of parents and children." In what clearly applies only to free adults and family units and especially to the more privileged among them, he continues: "All the energy of the group is expended on helping the children rise in the world, individually and without any collective ambition: the children rather than the family."[11] The founding justification for modern juvenile justice, and the logic of reform efforts since, has been that, if the more autonomous and apparently vital conjugal family failed in this child-socialization role, another regulatory apparatus, such as the parental state, would be needed to steer troubled youths into paths of self-discipline and social integration.

The Evil of Juvenile Delinquency

Changing cultural and political perspectives on childhood were not alone in the nineteenth-century development of novel concepts and systems of juvenile social control. Also critical were concerns about dependency and crime among young people and the development of a specific legal framework giving the state the regulatory authority to seek the normalization of child and adolescent attitudes and behaviors, when conjugal families could not. During the eighteenth and nineteenth centuries, social changes including massive waves of European immigration, the rise of a market economy, the perceived inadequacy of informal controls in growing cities, and ideals of participatory democracy stoked the eagerness of societal elites to establish new laws and institutions to regulate child development.

Deviance has existed as long as social norms have, but the popularization of the concept of juvenile delinquency in Western societies can be traced to the late eighteenth century and the early nineteenth, when the United States and older Western European nations were transitioning from rural, agricultural societies to rising industrial powers.[12] The Industrial Revolution and rapid urbanization inspired great excitement and fear; the new metropolis represented both a buffet of opportunity and adventure and a "place [where] scarcity, disease, neglect, ignorance, and dangerous influences" seemed equally abundant.[13]

Growing cities provided especially fertile ground for the rise of juvenile crime as a social problem and subject of popular and official concern. Rural family cohesion and work routines facilitated supervision of children and adolescents, but the Industrial Revolution disrupted family-centered controls. Urban labor markets distanced parents from idle children for longer periods of time, rendering older mechanisms of informal juvenile social control less effective. Population growth and change through urban internal migration and immigration resulted in larger proportions of juveniles in urban populations and increased community disorganization owing to greater crowding and unfamiliarity in neighborhoods. Urbanization also brought potentially delinquent youths into proximity with potential victims and agents of control. This pattern was of tremendous significance to juvenile justice in the twentieth-century black American experience as the

Great Migration brought large numbers of black families to early, primarily urban, juvenile court communities. Well before then, however, movable goods and new relationships of ownership proliferated under industrialization and market capitalism, increasing the possibility of property crime and appeals for intervention. Manufacturers and merchants sought protection from theft through increased surveillance and the formal sanctioning of offenders, many of whom were youths.[14]

In the industrializing West, actual and perceived increases in juvenile crime and deviance drew a steady stream of concern in the first decades of the nineteenth century, the problem usually being attributed to a mix of social disorganization and the pathology of individuals and families in new urban centers. In 1816, for example, the *First Survey of Juvenile Delinquency in London* announced the discovery of "some thousands of boys under seventeen years of age in the metropolis who are daily engaged in the commission of crime." The study's authors blamed this growing "catalogue of criminals" on the neglectful conduct of parents, lack of education, lack of suitable employment, lack of religious observance, and "habits of gambling in the public streets." The secondary sources of this "evil of Juvenile Delinquency" were said to include the "severity of the [criminal] code," the "defective state of the police," and the "existing system of prison discipline," all of which either ignored or worsened the problem of delinquency. In *Further Description of Juvenile Delinquency in London*, a follow-up study conducted two years later, the authors still found it "painful to reflect that the remedy provided by the law should be one great cause of the evil"; they resolved that, for the youngest offenders at least, "absolute impunity would have produced less vice than confinement in almost any of the gaols in the Metropolis."[15] These critics were arguing, not that the state and concerned citizens should do nothing about juvenile delinquency, but rather that it was a novel problem requiring its own solution.

Much of delinquency's novelty was attributed to the foreign element alleged to be common among young offenders. Similar to today's rhetoric, a complex mix of genuine concern for public safety and child welfare, sensationalism, elitism, and xenophobia shaded portrayals of juvenile delinquents and appeals for their control across emerging industrial centers. In 1853, Charles L. Brace, the founder of New York's Children's Aid Society, characterized delinquents in that city as "mainly American-born, but the children of Irish and German immigrants . . . as ignorant as London flashmen [and] far more brutal than the peasantry from which they descend." Rivaling the spectacular "superpredator" rhetoric of over a century later, Brace warned that menaces then were "ready for any offense or crime, however degraded or bloody," and that, without normalizing influences of juvenile social control, "we should see an explosion from this class which might leave [the cities] in ashes and blood."[16]

Enter the Parental State

Juvenile delinquency was believed to grow from the social disorganization of city life and to threaten the life and prosperity of emerging societies. This inspired government and private entities to invest heavily in its control. The differentiation of juvenile and adult offenders in criminal law and punishment is evident "as far back as written records go," but growing recognition of childhood and adolescents as opportune moments for "Americanization," combined with the apparent threat to nineteenth-century ambitions of juvenile offenders, lent inspiration, urgency, and direction to the establishment of modern juvenile justice.[17]

The concept and authority of the parental state provided a cultural and legal framework for regulating the seemingly interdependent social problems of child neglect, misbehavior, and crime. Rooted in the doctrine of in loco parentis, the framework defined the state as the surrogate parent of the nation. The state as the central regulatory authority in the affairs of the child and the family was authorized to intervene as an incubator, whenever either one failed, to promote the successful growth and delivery of embryonic citizens to the body politic.

This legal framework originates in the concept of *parens patriae*, a Latin term first applied in sixteenth-century England to define the role of the state in the lives of children whose deceased parents bequeathed an estate. Holding that, in its capacity as "parent of the country," government assumes the role of natural parents should they become incapacitated, the doctrine initially rationalized the use of a special Chancery Court to manage an estate until its heir reached the age of majority. The doctrine was later applied in *Wellesley v. Wellesley* (1827), where the children of an English duke were removed from his custody following allegations that he was unfit.[18]

Parens patriae was first applied in the United States in the case of *Ex Parte Crouse* (1839), in which the Pennsylvania Supreme Court defended the constitutionality of holding in the Philadelphia House of Refuge a child who had not been duly convicted of any crime. The child in this case, twelve-year-old Mary Crouse, was referred to the court on the complaint of her mother, who submitted that Mary was "a poor person" (whether in financial or moral terms is unclear) in need of court intervention. The court determined that the girl was a pauper and committed her to the Philadelphia refuge. The plaintiff in *Ex Parte Crouse*, Mary's father, argued that the state could not lawfully punish his daughter without a criminal conviction as this denied due process and that she should be released to his custody. The court disagreed, holding: "The object of the [refuge] is reformation, by training its inmates to industry; by imbuing their minds with principles of morality and religion; by furnishing them with means to earn a living; and, above all, by separating them from the corrupting influence of improper associates. To this end, may not the natural parents, when unequal to the task of education, or unworthy of it, be superseded by the *parens patria*, or common guardian of the community?" Through placement in the house of refuge, the court continued, "the infant [was] snatched from a course which must have ended in confirmed depravity; and not only is the restraint of her person lawful, but it would be an act of extreme cruelty to release her from it."[19]

The doctrine of *parens patria* furnished a durably vague justification for the modern juvenile justice system, gradually fortified by an array of child-welfare legislation, institutional developments, and appeals to public sentiment. The doctrine was celebrated as an enlightened moral and legal foundation for the authority of the parental state, at least through the 1950s. "With the constructive laws we built the architecture of the state around its best asset, childhood," a leading U.S. judge and champion of juvenile justice reform recalled a century after *Crouse*. "And for these items of legislation and constructive work I have no apology to make." The constitutionality of *parens patria* did face challenges, with occasional success, but the doctrine provided broad authority for the state to assume custody of children deemed wayward and delinquent, on the pretense of individual and societal salvation.[20]

Citizen building was common to nineteenth-century child-welfare endeavors in the United States, such as the development of compulsory public education, and is vital to understanding both the general and the racial history of American juvenile justice. As in the case of public education, white supremacist notions of human potential and civic utility framed both white youth privilege and black youth oppression in early American juvenile justice, inspiring protracted struggles for racial equality in juvenile social control. While the development of juvenile justice reflected general interests in regulating child development, enlightened ideals of rationalization and humanity in criminal law and punishment, and the positivist pursuit of a perfectible "science of man," all these became inflected with the race, class, and gender politics of a contentious liberal democracy.

Nineteenth-century efforts to regulate the socialization of wayward and delinquent youths through the authority of the parental state came on the heels of American independence and the founding of the new Republic. "Successful defiance of the most powerful imperial nation of Europe, followed by the creation of a large and independent republic," the historian Robert Bremner writes, "confirmed the view that a remarkable experiment in human improvement was occurring in the New World."[21] The experiment required fashioning normal civic actors and norms of civil society from the fabric of a rapidly growing population marked by heterogeneity, poverty, and deviance. In the new Republic, with citizens theoretically called to participate in self-government, the heterogeneity and apparent wretchedness of the civil polity led many elites to loath and limit participatory democracy and inspired liberal reformers to pursue its regulation through elaborate citizen-building initiatives.

This largely motivated the common school movement between 1820 and 1865. Its advocates called for schools to prepare a capable citizenry; its opponents questioned the practicality and justification of public expenditure on a mass citizen-building enterprise. In 1820, the Massachusetts Constitutional Convention delegate Daniel Webster advocated free schools as "a wise and liberal system of police, by which property, and life, and the peace of society are secured."[22] Concerned with a massive influx of non-English immigrants, the president of Middlebury College warned in 1850: "The multitude of emigrants from the old world, interfused among our population, is rapidly changing the identity of American character." "Shall these adopted citizens become a part of the body politic, and firm supporters of liberal institutions," he asked, "or will they prove to our republic what the Goths and Huns were to the Roman Empire?" His answer rested with public education. Teachers would "act the part of master-builders," educating outsiders in the ways of American democracy while also preparing the "[white] native population" to receive and coexist with the newcomers. The project of public education thus was to "engraft" the growing multitude "upon the republican stock, and to qualify them for the duties of free and enlightened citizens."[23]

Liberal educational ambitions faced great skepticism and opposition, inevitably forcing compromises on the path from abstract ideals to institutionalization and practice. Aside from shuddering at the shared expense, likening the investment to socialism, opponents questioned the practicality of public education. Finding "as much cant on the subject of education as on that of religion," a South Carolinian challenged that there is "no necessary connection between learning and freedom . . . [for] liberty is an instinct, not a principle."[24] Critics insisted that the public would remain uneven in knowledge, ignorance, and capacity for self-government, regardless of "the wild projects which may be tried." They warned that "compulsory equalizations" are more likely to "pull down what is above" than to elevate classes below and that, if there were to be public education, it should be organized according to projections of social status.[25]

Southern opposition was particularly candid on the point of "teaching to position." One prominent Virginian reasoned that, since "half of the people of the South, or nearly so, are blacks, we have only to educate the other half." His fanciful model of citizen building would "educate all Southern whites, employ them as free men should be employed, and let Negroes be strictly tied down to such callings as are unbecoming to white men," which would somehow lead to "peace [being] established between blacks and whites."[26] The racial history of public education in the United States clearly illustrates an effort to institutionalize this ideal through the enlistment of common schools in selective white citizen- and state-building initiatives. As we shall see, a similar racial project defines the contentious racial history of American juvenile justice.[27]

The Enlightenment of Criminal and Juvenile Justice

Penal philosophy and reform provided a related eighteenth- and nineteenth-century context for experimentation in human improvement, setting another precedent for the development of American juvenile justice. Most prominently in the Italian philosopher Cesare Beccaria's *Of Crimes and Punishment* (1764), Enlightenment philosophies of criminal law and penology advanced a utilitarian view of the relations between crime, punishment, and the well-ordered society. Influenced by other Enlightenment philosophers, including Hutcheson, Hume, and Montesquieu, and by interest in the "science of man," Beccaria advocated rationality (especially proportionality) in criminal law and the "enlightened state administration" of criminal social control. Law was cast as a tool by which the civil polity could be established and maintained, encouraging "independent and isolated men, tired of living in a constant state of war and of enjoying a freedom made useless by the uncertainly of keeping it, [to] unite in society."[28] By 1800, *Of Crimes and Punishment* had been printed in at least twenty-three Italian-language editions, fourteen French editions, and eleven English editions (three in the United States). The English jurists and philosophers William Blackstone and Jeremy Bentham and the colonial American revolutionaries Thomas

Jefferson and John Adams are among those known to have consulted this work and contributed to the development and application of its utilitarian penal philosophy.

This application was most tangibly expressed in the rise of the modern prison, or what European reformers defined as the *penitentiary*.[29] David Rothman and other historians of criminal punishment attribute the emergence of incarceration as a dominant strategy of social control to its practical flexibility in administering proportionate sanctions as well as its symbolic value to deterrence, considerations that were fundamental to the Enlightenment ideals of criminal justice. Enlightenment philosophy was insufficient to ensure this dramatic and costly shift to reliance on the prison. The reforms ultimately had to be sold to the public and embraced by government officials.[30]

The expansion of a bureaucratic apparatus of crime control was especially critical to the adoption and continued development of "rational" strategies of criminal justice. As the sociologist David Garland has stressed, this expanding state bureaucracy, and its monopoly on formal criminal social control, facilitated focused debate, specification, and eventual institutionalization of apparently humanitarian and liberal democratic ideals in criminal justice. These bureaucracies formed new social networks of government agencies, authorities, and specialists engaged in and defending the "people-processing" work of criminal punishment, deterrence, and rehabilitation. These arbiters of justice varied in their roles, authorities, skills, and ideals, but "all of them, as professional penal agents," Garland argues, "tend[ed] to present themselves in a positive, utilitarian way, as offering a particular service, or carrying out a useful social task."[31] At professional gatherings, in publications, and through informal correspondence, leading American agents of crime control set out grand visions for modern criminal justice and what would simply be called *corrections*, impressing on other typically white, male, educated colleagues, near and far, the possibility and necessity of a more enlightened approach.

By the 1830s, imprisonment was becoming a more common mode of punishment in the United States as prison "facilities proliferated, the [penal] literature thrived, and visitors traveled vast distances to view American prisons in action." The modern prison and its rationale of deterrence and rehabilitation came to be seen as "monumental leaps forward in the rational and humane treatment of criminals."[32]

By the late nineteenth century, agents of criminal control commonly claimed an ability and a commitment to reinvent offenders' souls, and, thus, their social position, through processes of normalization. By dislodging deviant impulses within the criminal and isolating criminogenic influences outside, the state would, allegedly, prepare deviant civic actors to lead more normal, moral, independent, and productive lives. As the social scientists Jeff Manza and Chris Uggen note: "Once reform of individuals became the orienting goal of 'corrections' . . . the sharp line between offender and citizen began to erode," at least in the ideal sense.[33] It is in this vein that Zebulon Brockway, the superintendent of Elmira Prison, presented the 1870 National Congress on Penitentiary and Reformatory Discipline with specific techniques for preparing offenders for "restoration to citizenship." The strategies used libraries, recreation, and elementary and vocational education within the prison to build an offender's "personal fitness for future liberty."[34] Though rehabilitative ideals were neither universally embraced nor necessarily reflected in the administration of Elmira and other penal institutions of that era or since, their circulation established utilitarian interests in the potential citizen and the state-building capacity of criminal social control and, thus, a new link between the administration of justice and the pursuit of American dreams.

Citizen Delinquent: Democratic Ambitions of Early American Juvenile Justice

Republican utilitarianism resonated with child-welfare reformers, encouraging their conceptualization of juvenile justice as a citizen-building institution in the late nineteenth century and the twentieth. Having been defined either as a future criminal and dependent or a responsible and productive civic actor, the uniquely malleable delinquent made a prime target for utilitarian intervention. Early-nineteenth-century discourse on juvenile social control most explicitly emphasized principles of moral and practical education. However, as in the public school movement, notions of child welfare and citizen and state building were strongly linked to these concerns. The civic implications of juvenile justice often were simply assumed rather than explained, as when founders of a new reform school for girls near Boston promised in 1855 that the "beneficial operation" of their allegedly benevolent institution would return "a manifold recompense, purifying in its nature, into the bosom of society."[35]

Application of Enlightenment ideals to juvenile social control was not limited to the rhetoric of penal agents but was apparent in the formal programming of the earliest institutions. For example, the Boston House of Reformation (established in 1826) maintained a disciplinary system that intentionally communicated rights and responsibilities of citizenship.

Beaumont and Tocqueville were moved by how "the young prisoners . . . are treated as if they were men and members of a free society." They were especially impressed by the extent to which young inmates in South Boston, apparently more so than in other refuges they visited, were engaged in self-government through such activities as self-reporting moral and immoral conduct, forming juries to resolve discrepancies in determining and sanctioning bad behavior, and electing officers and monitors among peers. Given their specific interest in the shape of American democracy, the visitors noted (in likely exaggerated detail) how inmates' good behavior determined their democratic standing: "They alone participate in the elections, and are alone eligible [for election]; the vote of those in the first [good] class, counts for two—a kind of double vote, of which the others cannot be jealous, because it depends upon themselves alone to obtain the same privilege. With the good are deposited the most important keys of the house; they go out freely, and have the right to leave their place . . . without needing a peculiar permission; they are believed on their word, on all occasions; and their birthday is celebrated."[36]

The democratic ambitions of juvenile social control were also apparent in reform efforts outside the United States. Aiming to focus attention on the modernization of juvenile justice elsewhere and to encourage passage of legislation in England, the influential reformer Mary Carpenter complained in the early 1850s: "The mass of society are better acquainted with the actual condition of remote savage nations, than with the real life and the spring of action of [delinquent] children." She wrote *Reformatory Schools for the Children of the Perishing and Dangerous Classes and for Juvenile Offenders* (1851) and *Juvenile Delinquents: Their Condition and Treatment* (1853), hoping that amelioration of public ignorance might "stimulate some work in this sacred cause—sacred, for it is the work of the redeemer, 'to seek and save them that are lost.'" Citing examples from the United States, France, and England, where "the state entrusts delinquent children to those who with Christian devotion will take on themselves the parental charge of them," she assured readers that "children, even after numerous convictions, [can] be made good and useful citizens."[37]

By the late nineteenth century, the apparent link between enlightened juvenile social control and the fates of nation-states had become explicit in juvenile justice rhetoric and reform. For example, the running head atop each page of *Childhood's Appeal*, a newsletter published by the Massachusetts Society for the Prevention of Cruelty to Children in the 1880s, was the reminder that "The Child of To-Day Is the Citizen of Tomorrow," a solemn appeal for investment in the well-being of the child and, thus, the prospects of the nation.[38] At George Junior Republic, "a rural haven for delinquent, dependent, and immigrant youth" founded in Freeville, New York, in 1895 and later franchised nationwide, a citizen-building motif dominated the organizational model. Committals to the republic—boys and girls between the ages of sixteen and twenty-one—were called *citizens* rather than *inmates*, and their duties included the production of the *Junior Citizen* newsletter.[39] While touring the Freeville Republic in 1911, former New York Police commissioner and later U.S. president Theodore Roosevelt marveled at this "laboratory experiment in democracy" and was especially appreciative of the equality among "citizens," whether native or immigrant, dependent or delinquent. This egalitarian "manufactory of citizens" would seemingly yield "[delinquents] about as apt [as dependents] to turn out to be a first-class citizen," Roosevelt speculated, "not merely of the Junior Republic . . . but of the larger republic, the republic of the American Nation, when he graduates into it [*sic*]."[40]

Such liberal ambition hardly diminished with the turn of the twentieth century, as continued immigration, industrialization, and urbanization only increased the apparent scale of juvenile crime and delinquency and the urgency to regulate the body politic through enlightened juvenile social control. Alongside and within goals of diverting children from the worlds of adult offenders and institutions and affecting their rehabilitation, the juvenile court model embraced civic ideals of utilitarian social control, including the notion that American juvenile justice should function, in Roosevelt's term, as a "manufactory of citizens."[41] According to the judge of the nation's first juvenile court in Chicago, the role of the parental state was "to take [the delinquent] in charge, not so much to punish as to reform, not to degrade but to uplift, not to crush but to develop, [and not to] make him a criminal but a worthy citizen." At the founding of Kansas City's juvenile court a decade later (1919), its judge heralded a new "age of citizen building," a triumph of enlightened social control where troubled children were regarded as "indispensable in the battle for the nation's destiny."[42]

The same civic ambition would pour forth in proclamations of juvenile justice reformers and practitioners throughout the first half of the twentieth century. Amid growing midcentury skepticism toward the founding principles of American juvenile justice, the venerated "dean of American jurisprudence," Roscoe Pound, described the challenge of the increasingly embattled juvenile court and the responsibility of the parental state as intervening in a "family which . . . is bringing or threatening to bring up delinquent instead of upright citizens contributing to the productive work of the people."[43] Decades later, well beyond the halcyon days of the rehabilitative

ideal, and amid a search for new philosophical and institutional foundations of American juvenile justice, the idea of citizen building continued
to color liberal reform. In 1987, a group of scholars and practitioners assembled by the recently established federal Office of Juvenile Justice and
Delinquency Prevention and Harvard's Kennedy School of Government was
asked to address the topic of the future of juvenile justice. They arrived at
a vision from the past, putting together a three-volume study entitled *From
Children to Citizens*,[44] and assigning late-twentieth-century juvenile justice
the "work of transforming dependent children into resourceful citizens."[45]

Limits of the American Dream: Race, Recognition, and the Rehabilitative Ideal

As the legal historian David S. Tanenhaus notes, American juvenile justice
was from its earliest days imagined and organized as a project in "Americanization."[46] Defining youths as clay-like souls capable of resocialization and
requiring intervention for realization of their civic potential, nineteenth-
century conceptions of childhood provided Progressive Era reformers with
a cultural and legal rationale for modernizing juvenile justice. Given rapid
population growth through immigration, fear of ethnic heterogeneity, and
the idealism of liberal democracy, framing delinquents as potential citizens
capable of redemption by the parental state secured reformers' beliefs and
their ability to persuade others to invest in the welfare of dependent and
delinquent youths. The historian Andy Ashby observes that juvenile justice
advocates and practitioners succeeded in defining wayward youths as "embryonic citizens who represented the cutting edge of the future. Insofar as
society neglected them they became symbols—lonely, ragged, unloved—of
the limits of the American dream."[47]

Yet there have always been limits to the American dream, or, rather,
selective investments in its pursuit. The juvenile justice agenda of Americanization has, thus, been a long-standing "racial project," with power hold-
ers and challengers vying to define its agenda according to idealized racial
and ethnic group relations.[48] Americans of all sorts have held and pursued
dreams of opportunity and mobility, yet the ability to institutionalize group
interests has been constrained by politics of difference and inequality in
power. These boundaries of recognition, their opposition and change over
time, frame the contentious racial history of American juvenile justice. The
remainder of this chapter considers how white supremacist politics distorted
the idea of black childhood and undermined black youth and community
claims to emerging citizen-building ambition and authority.

Existing research on the history of American juvenile justice tends to generalize from the experiences of white American and European immigrant group.[49] It pays limited attention to how status distinctions besides age, and particularly race and ethnicity, have contributed to variation in the notion of childhood and experiences of juvenile social control. Stratification is evident in the racial boundaries of dominant child-welfare ideals and institutions as well as in the rhetoric and reform efforts of nondominant racial groups, who have fought for racially inclusive systems of juvenile social control.

Neglect of the racial politics of juvenile social control is partially rooted historically in racialized exclusion, which limited the involvement of non-white youths and communities in the early history of juvenile justice. The overlap between the nineteenth-century development of juvenile justice and the institution of chattel slavery has especially confounded historical researchers, several of whom suggest that enslavement essentially removed black Americans from the scene of early juvenile justice reform. These treatments gloss over the complexity and variety of the black antebellum experience, including the ways in which free and enslaved youths experienced juvenile social control and what these and other patterns suggest about the relation between race, the idea of childhood, and liberal rehabilitative ideals.

This oversight compromises an understanding of particular group experiences and general interpretations of how ideas of childhood influenced liberal juvenile justice reform. For example, to illustrate the basic idea of childhood, a popular historical study of juvenile justice briefly reflects on the racial epithet *boy* as used to reference a black male adult. Yet the author misinterprets this relation between race and age classification and, thus, how liberal notions of child and social welfare became linked with racial politics of liberal democracy. He notes how "the common practice of calling [the enslaved] 'boy' or 'girl,' no matter what their age," departs from the usual use of these terms. "While it is obvious that slaves aged like everyone else," he continues, "slaveholders generally did not distinguish among slaves on that basis [since] the slaveholder had 'no idea of childhood' when it came to slaves." Such failure to distinguish between adults and children was commonplace in the era preceding the sociolegal construction of childhood, he explains, but "simply held on longer with slaveholders than with other groups."[50] With this simplification of racialized age distinctions and a passing glance at the race question, the study moves on to discuss how juvenile justice systems have cyclically responded to white American and European immigrant children and youths in the United States, while nonwhites disappear.

A more accurate understanding of the idea of childhood among slave-holders and its relevance to American juvenile justice requires closer attention to race-linked age distinctions. Studies illustrate that ideas of childhood existed among antebellum slave owners and were applied to the enslaved. Notions of black childhood were, thus, not absent, but distorted; intentional distortions reflect vested interests in white power structures, including chattel slavery. In her study of childhood among the enslaved, for example, King illustrates that slaveholders were keenly aware of the profit value that black children represented and treated their adult and juvenile chattel accordingly. Slaveholders commonly viewed enslaved children as young commodities that, if properly controlled and nurtured, would yield more docile and productive pools of adult labor.[51] The legal system also recognized black children and supported the notion that they were beings meant to be raised to bear burdens, much like farm animals. Thus, in an estate settlement from 1809 that addressed the custody of two black children whose parents were enslaved, a South Carolina court held: "The young of slaves . . . as objects of property, stand on the same footing as other animals, which are assets to be administered by the representative of the deceased [slave] owner."[52]

Norms of raising enslaved children varied by social context, but slave owners generally preferred an age-graded approach beginning with a protective phase, which was expected to facilitate the gradual socialization of individual slaves and efficiency in developing and maintaining a productive slave population. The strategy was consistent with the idea of regulating child development in the interests of social welfare, except that the welfare of black youths and communities was deemphasized in the arrangement. Describing the logic in his own long-term investment in young slaves, Thomas Jefferson noted: "A child raised every 2 years is of more profit than the crop of the best laboring man."[53] Interest in black children's physical maturation may have given their formative years "a semblance of childhood," the historian Eugene Genovese writes, providing "the time to grow physically and to parry the most brutal features of their bondage through games [and] within limits . . . to feel and enjoy life." Idle moments were filled with children amusing and raising each other.[54] In this spirit of good business, the daily records from 1841 of an Alabama cotton plantation note when it was "too cold for the children to pick." To avoid property damage to future breeders of chattel, the exemption applied to enslaved girls but not to enslaved boys.[55]

Recognition of the line between childhood and adulthood among blacks was apparent in the division of plantation labor. Children were assigned specific work tasks, mostly as assistants and apprentices to their owning family and other slaves, and tasks became more physically demanding as adulthood approached. Age-specific work expectations were very detailed in some cases. On his plantation, Thomas Jefferson ordered: "Children till 10 years old . . . serve as nurses, from 10 to 16 the boys make nails, the girls spin. [A]t age 16 [boys and girls] go into the grounds or learn trades." On many plantations, the enslaved were classified as quarter, half, and full "hands," depending on the amount and quality of labor they could provide, and owners considered slaves to be adults when they became full hands at sixteen or younger. For girls, full-hand status was often obtained once they were capable of reproduction. Many enslaved children were at first eager to work, but, since work defined their maturity and status and, in some cases, the food and other resources allotted to slave families, this enthusiasm was inevitably quelled by brutal realities of forced labor. "Once they went to the fields they experienced the full misery of their condition," Genovese writes, "and the abrupt shift must have been traumatic despite the painstaking effort of so many masters to break them in to hard labor slowly."[56]

The characterization of adult black women and men as children, which Bernard attributed to slave owner's *lack* of an idea of childhood among the enslaved, actually signaled the *distinctiveness* of dominant ideas of black childhood among white elites and, more generally, in the dominant culture.[57] As we shall see, slave owners and their many contemporaries lacked a willingness to recognize the full humanity and social standing of black children *and* adults, but not an appreciation of black childhood as a stage of human development. This distinction is critical to understanding the lives of black children and families, both in the context of slavery and in the overlapping social history of American juvenile justice, where the fates of black civil society became linked to the politics of white supremacy.

In the view of the dominant group, the antebellum black child was never expected to become an economically independent or politically equal participant in American civil society but was instead a profitable beast of burden, raised to accommodate to a subordinate caste status within the racial order. As such, slave owners and their white contemporaries differentiated enslaved children and adults in developmental terms, mainly along physical lines focused on productive capacity (i.e., labor and reproduction). Antebellum black children and adults were not commonly distinguished among by whites on moral, intellectual, or political bases, however, and it was ideologically important to downplay such differences between enslaved children and adults, given the caste status that they were to endure.

To rationalize the contradictions of their bondage and subjugation in the land of freedom and democracy, black Americans were characterized as developmentally stagnant, as an odd subspecies who from birth to death remained morally and intellectually childlike. In this ideological context, a former slave owner remembered her chattel after the Civil War as "so many children to be clothed & nursed & fed & constantly looked after," even though her slaves were largely adults, likely constantly serving her.[58] Discounting the possibility and importance of black maturation reinforced white supremacist ideology and white domination by rationalizing subjugation and actively denying the bases of black self-realization. These elaborate mechanisms of oppression and domination, evident in the denial of power over decisions affecting families and in deprivations of education, health, and spirituality, helped institutionalize the ordeal of racial subjugation during slavery and beyond.[59]

The racial oppression and domination that enslaved children and families experienced was a dialectic of exclusion, or a mechanism of simultaneously rationalizing and reproducing black marginalization in American civil society. The shattering of black families, recounted in numerous slave narratives as a most traumatic event for parents and children alike, weakened the social positions of the nineteenth-century black children and adults and their collective prospects for social mobility. In *Democracy in America* (1835 and 1840), Tocqueville offers evidence of the group's profound marginalization by observing with typical overstatement: "The Negro has no family; woman is merely the temporary companion of his pleasures, and his children are on an equality with himself from the moment of their birth." Although black families resisted complete disruption, the institution of chattel slavery undermined black kinship ties and the ability of black family units to function as what the sociologist Philippe Ariès described as vital modern facilitators of democratic participation and generational mobility.[60]

Several critics of American democracy comment on this pernicious dialectic of racial exclusion. Tocqueville, for example, concludes: "To induce the whites to abandon the opinion they have conceived of the moral and intellectual inferiority of their former slaves, the Negroes must change; but as long as this opinion persists, they cannot change." And, in one of his first antislavery speeches, Frederick Douglass provided an angrier critique, protesting to a largely white audience: "You degrade us, and then ask why we are degraded—you shut our mouths, and then ask why we don't speak— you close your colleges and seminaries against us, and then ask why we don't know more."[61] The race-linked refutation of developmental capacity and denial of developmental opportunity, so evident in the history of chattel slavery, would also define the peculiar institution of Jim Crow juvenile justice.

Ideological and Political Foundations of Racialized Exclusion

The enlightenment of American juvenile justice peaked in the period encompassing the struggle for emancipation, Reconstruction, and Progressive Era reform (1850–1920), the period in which Jim Crow ideologies and policies were intensely crafted and established. At this intersection of progressive and reactionary reform, black youth and adult stakeholders in their welfare were culturally and politically constructed as inferior and undeserving subjects of the white-dominated parental state, with no rights to equal protection or influence in juvenile social control.[62] As we shall see, this denial of black humanity and civil status marginalized black interests in citizen-building ambitions and authority, enlisting the white supremacist parental state in the continued underdevelopment of black civil society for generations.

Rarely did leading juvenile justice reformers, practitioners, and officials explicitly entertain the "Negro question" in their reflections and plans. As with most histories of American juvenile justice, black youths and communities are often simply absent from official and popular reflections on the development of juvenile justice. Race was hardly irrelevant or ignored, however, in these developments. In contrast to an explicit fixation on normalizing white citizens deemed delinquent and, thus, advancing white democracy through juvenile justice reform, the question of how black children, adolescents, and adults would relate to the enlightened ideals of juvenile justice was carried on at broader ideological and institutional levels—in art and science, political cartoons, and law and public policy. These discourses framed dominant group orientations toward black youth and community claims to liberal juvenile social control, generally defining them as so far beyond the pale of enlightened agendas as to be undeserving of specific attention.

Two aspects of this racial discourse and associated law, policy, and practice were especially relevant to the marginalization of black youth and community interests in citizen-building initiatives. First, the notion of the relative developmental incapacity of black people, or the denial of black humanity itself, undermined black youth and community access to citizen-building ideals. Second, and most important, continued identification of the United States as a "white democracy" and opposition to the civic integration of newly freed black Americans (i.e., as voters, jurors, government authorities, etc.) negated black influence over citizen-building initiatives, securing the moral and political authority of a white supremacist parental state.

Hard Clay: The Allegation of Inhumanity

Long before juvenile courts and justice systems came to fruition in the late nineteenth century, black children were culturally constructed as a perennial "lost cause," racially marked by a chorus of dominant lay, religious, legal, and academic voices as embryonic beings lacking the physical, moral, and intellectual capacity on which normalization would depend. In the antebellum period, such rhetoric defended moral contradictions of slavery and interests in exploitation, and, in the post-Emancipation period, it rationalized the broadest refusals of civil rights, including denials of equal protection and representation in juvenile justice administration.

In the years surrounding the landmark ruling in *Ex Parte Crouse* (1838), for example, which extended broad parental state authority over juvenile dependents and delinquents in the interests of child development and social welfare, *Democracy in America* drew a color line through the humanity of society itself. "If we reason from what passes in the world," Tocqueville explained, "we should almost say that the European is to the other races of mankind what man himself is to the lower animals." The Frenchman strained to find any "common features of humanity in this stranger whom slavery has brought among us." "His physiognomy is to our eyes hideous, his understanding weak, his tastes low," he wrote, "and we are almost inclined to look upon him as a being intermediate between man and the brutes."[63]

By the mid-nineteenth century, the alleged physical, moral, and intellectual inferiority of black people was considered by some to be so great that it defied overstatement and hardly required mention. An especially ferocious defender of white supremacist politics, Hinton Helper, for example, maintained that it was "impossible for clean-natured and clean-sighted white men ever to disdain the Negro in a manner at all commensurate with his manifold and measureless demerits." Helper nevertheless dedicated his life's work to conveying an appropriate degree of contempt. In *The Negroes in Negroland, the Negroes in America, and Negroes Generally* (1868), Helper amassed a compendium of quotations on various topics related to the abomination of blackness, liberally combining expressions of leading white men in politics, law, and science. One gets enough sense of the work from its vivid chapter titles, organized by alleged dimensions of black depravity. There is the introductory "Cannibalism in Negroland," a chapter on "Theft, as a Fine Art, among the Africans," one on "Natural, Repulsive, and Irreconcilable Points of Difference, Physical, Mental, and Moral, between the Whites and the Blacks," and toward the end, naturally, a chapter on the "Gradual Decrease, and Probable Extinction of the Negro."[64]

This final point, the alleged natural retardation of the black life course, offers a good example of how white supremacist denials of black humanity and developmental potential undermined black youth and community claims to rehabilitative ideals and resources. If black people ceased to develop beyond a particular age, what sense would it make to provide them with developmental opportunity? The argument was often packaged in racial attributions of black health disparity, such as disease and mortality rates, and claims regarding the limited potential of black intellectual growth. For example, the Scottish lawyer and natural scientist Charles Lyell helped popularize the notion of black developmental incapacity in travel writings from the United States and abroad. In an 1849 follow-up to his popular *Travels in America* (1845), Lyell observed with feigned precision that the brain of a black child simply stopped developing with the onset of adolescence. "Up to the age of fourteen," he wrote, "the black children advance as fast as the white, but after that age, unless there be an admixture of white blood, it becomes, in most instances, extremely difficult to carry them forward."[65] An English traveler to Philadelphia and New York repeated this myth of black developmental stagnation a decade later in a dispatch of his findings from a casual "study of the Negro waiters," where he observes: "The first thing about them that strikes you is the apathetic infantine feeblemindedness of the 'coloured persons' lately called niggers. . . . At present I am quite of the opinion of the wise man who discovered that coloured persons are born and grow in exactly the same way as uncoloured persons up to the age of thirteen; and that they then cease to develop their skulls and their intelligence. All the waiters in this hotel appear to be just about the age of thirteen. There are two who in wisdom are nearly twelve; and one grey-headed old fellow who is just over fourteen."[66] Helper did his part to buttress this notion of black intellectual and, thus, moral and political depravity. As Wesley writes, his compilation reinforced an impression that "the Negro's mind ceased to expand after the age of fourteen" and that "he had neither invention, nor judgment, nor imagination, nor talents for the same."[67]

White supremacist ideology was propagated by all sorts of women and men, some of whom, such as Hinton Helper, were in their own time on the radical fringe, but many of whom were quite influential in the social mainstream.[68] As Lee Baker illustrates in his intellectual history of anthropology, American scientists were key to popularizing the concept of race as a biological distinction in the years leading up to the Civil War. These figures were consumed with proving the inferiority of black people and disguised their subjugation behind postures of scientific objectivity. Such scientific racialism was advanced considerably by the investigations and other influence of the Philadelphia physician Samuel Morton, a celebrated collector of human skulls, by his student Josiah Nott of Alabama, and by the Harvard naturalist Louis Agassiz. These men were not professional scholars, but each helped train the generation of anthropologists, physicians, museum curators, and researchers that, as Baker puts it, "establish[ed] the so-called scientific fact of negro inferiority." Through works such as Nott's quantitative compendium *Types of Mankind* (1854) and the 1896 English translation of Joseph de Gobineau's *Essay on the Inequality of the Human Races* (1853), science provided sturdier foundations for a white supremacist moral universe and associated political system.[69]

As the nineteenth century progressed and the weight of the Negro question grew, the ideologies of white supremacy and black inferiority evolved into conventional wisdom. Its ideological scaffolding was supplied by some of the most respected authorities in the humanities, the sciences, politics, and law, plus an endless column of cranks. In 1854, against the growing rumble of abolitionism (which he optimistically reduced to "harmless humbug, confined to a handful of fanatics"), the lay sociologist and champion of slavery George Fitzhugh proclaimed matter-of-factly: "The theory of the Types of Mankind cuts off the negro from human brotherhood, and justifies the brutal and miserly in treating him as a vicious brute." Straining to ground similar racial politics in the authority of empiricism, the English historian and explorer William Winwood Reade pronounced in 1863 that he could not "struggle against these sacred facts of science . . . [where] it has been proved by measurements, by microscopes, by analyses, that the typical negro is something between a child, a dotard, and a beast."[70]

White supremacist ideology essentially negated the claims of black youths to enlightened social control by defining them as a strange species of rigid or inflexible human clay, a categorically incorrigible group, more suited to neglect and exploitation than to attempts at normalization and civic integration. Refracted widely through American popular writing and art, and cemented through authorities of science and law, such denials of black humanity would help justify ubiquitous assaults on black human and civil rights, including denials of black child- and social-welfare interests in enlightened juvenile social control.

The Denial of Democratic Standing

The denial of black youth and community claims to equal recognition in the context of the parental state had an explicitly political basis. Assaults on black moral, intellectual, and physical capacity, as well as claims of immutable black degeneracy, framed black Americans as incapable of understanding and satisfying obligations of citizenship and, therefore, as undeserving of its full rights and freedoms. The denial of black humanity in decades surrounding the Civil War largely had to do with the defense of what Joel Olson terms *white democracy*, a cross-class alliance among whites to preserve the Republic as a white nation.[71]

The late-nineteenth- and early-twentieth-century modernization of juvenile justice broadly and often violently endorsed this overt racial contract, reserving full moral and political consideration for white and potentially white citizens and providing a bevy of means of preserving white privilege through state and nonstate structures.[72] As such, the early development and operation of the juvenile court and reformatory institutions did not require specification of the racial dimensions of their citizen-building ambitions, especially since the federal government denied black citizens claims to equal protection and representation under the law. In the decade following the establishment of the first houses of refuge, and seven years before the landmark *Ex Parte Crouse* ruling, for example, the then attorney general Roger Taney defended the imprisonment of free black seamen while their ships anchored in South Carolina. "The African race in the [United States] even when free are everywhere a degraded class, and exercise no political influence," he observed. "Privileges they are allowed to enjoy, are accorded them as a matter of kindness and benevolence rather than of right." Although local cultures might vary, the Constitution did not extend rights of citizenship to black Americans, Taney ruled, for blacks "were evidently not supposed to be included by the term citizens."[73]

The argument foreshadowed the infamous U.S. Supreme Court decision twenty-five years later when the then chief justice Roger Taney once again denied black citizenship in *Dred Scott v. Sanford* (1857), a ruling that defined the parameters of American racial democracy for much of the ensuing century.[74] Taney ruled here that black Americans had long been "regarded as beings of an inferior order, and altogether unfit to associate with the white race, either in social or political relations; and so far inferior, that they had no rights which the white man was bound to respect." The judgment held that blacks were "not intended to be included, and formed no part of the people who framed and adopted the [U.S.] Declaration of Independence and the Constitution."[75] Establishing race as a key determinant of democratic standing, the ruling pushed blacks—free and slave, law-abiding and delinquent—"outside the nation's universe of obligation," as the historian Eric Foner has written, excluding them from the subjects of the state to whom "obligations are owed, to whom rules apply, and whose injuries call for [amends]."[76]

The abolition of slavery was logically seen as essential to establishing black human and civil rights, but the abolitionist movement itself conveyed the depth of opposition to black civic integration. For example, many who supported or were resigned to the end of slavery advocated what Thomas Jefferson described as a "second emancipation," freeing whites of the threat of association with newly freed blacks, and maintaining the integrity of white democracy. This ideal inspired widespread calls, including that of President Lincoln, for the recolonization of Africa by black Americans. Meeting with a "deputation of negroes" in 1862, Lincoln sought to win their support for a strategy of colonization rather than civic integration. "Why should not the people of your race be colonized, Why should they not leave this country?" he asked. "You and we are a different race . . . this physical difference is a great disadvantage to us both," he offered. "Your race suffers greatly, many of them by living with us, while ours suffers from your presence. . . . If this is admitted, it shows a reason why we should be separated."[77] In essence, while Emancipation and Reconstruction represented important moments in the renegotiation of the racial contract, white civic leaders desperate to keep white democracy intact commonly resisted the prospect of civic integration.

Not surprisingly, such widespread and impassioned commitments to maintaining racialized democratic exclusion found normative expression in the organization and decisionmaking of the emergent parental state. The persistence of democratic exclusion would affect black youths and adults alike, the former in terms of their diminished access to citizen-building ideals and initiatives, and the latter in terms of their lack of authority or influence in the deliberations of the parental state. Thus, when challenged to find family and work placements for black dependents and delinquents, white officials of the Philadelphia House of Refuge did not consult the interests of these youths, their families, or their communities in rehabilitation and community reintegration; instead, they pursued their emigration. Rather than work to "Americanize" these black children and youths, facilitating their self-improvement and contribution to the community, the refuge sought to devise a "placing-out" program that would ship these mainly Philadelphia-based youths to the distant shores of Africa, never again to return.[78]

The Civic Alienation of Black Delinquents: Summary and Conclusion

The nineteenth century features contradictory progressive and repressive efforts either to advance the enlightenment of a young liberal democracy or to deepen the ordeal of racial tyranny. These patterns collide historically in the peculiar idea of black childhood and the distortion of mainstream child-welfare endeavors concerning black children and communities. The simultaneous liberalization and restriction of American democracy mirrored the prevailing organization and ambition of a galvanized white democratic polity and a republic in which dominion was limited to those deemed worthy of its rights and responsibilities. Critics of the common school plan, defenders of slavery, white supremacist abolitionists, advocates of colonization, and early architects of American juvenile justice shared the ideal of a white capitalist democracy, a New World where citizenship and freedom attached to race more than labor, sex, or age and where whiteness, or potential whiteness, ensured greater access to the fulfillment of human potential and democratic recognition.[79]

Two streams of white supremacist discourse on black humanity and civil rights combined to shape a dominant, civically exclusionary response to black childhood and black collective interests in democratic social control: a normative assertion of black inferiority and a denial of black democratic standing. Black children in white-dominated civil society experienced this denial of black humanity and civil rights, which distorted utilitarian notions of juvenile justice by reconstructing black children as inferior human clay, devoid of the developmental capacity and civil standing presupposed by citizen-building ideals.

By branding black children as the progeny of an inferior and marginal constituency, white supremacist ideology imposed a dominant racial logic on child-welfare ideals and institutions, rationalizing outright refusals and limited institutional investments in black citizen-building initiatives. In a period consumed with the classification and hierarchical ordering of the natural and social world, black children were normatively constructed by white civic leaders and pundits as unsalvageable human beings, the progeny of the most pathological and alien body within the American polity, with little current or future claim to full citizenship.

The definition of America as a white democracy rendered the democratic freedoms of white Americans primary, inalienable, and dependent on denying black freedom dreams. Foundational elements of the white supremacist parental state predated American independence, but its ideological and institutional scaffolding grew rapidly with the establishment of the Republic, the waning decades of racial slavery, and the so-called enlightenment of the juvenile justice system. In this formative context of concern with the child, the evil of delinquency, and the civic significance of juvenile social control, a more overt variant of white supremacist ideology constructed blacks as a biologically and politically distinct subspecies whose moral, intellectual, and physical depravity was considered immutable and just cause for civic exclusion. This racial caricature, which grew amid fears of abolition and resistance to Reconstruction, undermined black interests in equality and rationalized continued denials of social and economic opportunity in relation to education, labor, politics, and other group interests.[80]

Race-based distinction was, thus, sewn into the original fabric of twentieth-century juvenile justice systems, its seam being defined by the stark, if unstable, divide between progressive child-welfare ideals and evolving structures of American apartheid. Yet the denial of democratic freedom through racial oppression and domination in juvenile justice has always been contested. Nineteenth- and early-twentieth-century black leaders and their allies saw the struggle for racial justice as an investment in a better future, one that would largely be revealed in the life chances and trajectories of black children and youths. Notwithstanding dominant group dismissals of their developmental capacity and civil rights, black civic leaders came to define the salvation of their own embryonic citizens and the racial democratization of the parental state as indispensable to black freedom. Consequently, the liberal politics of the emergent parental state mixed and meshed with the racial project of white supremacy but also collided with black oppositional agendas, making American juvenile justice a contentious twentieth-century stage in the struggle for freedom.

TWO

No Refuge under the Law: Racialized Foundations of Juvenile Justice Reform

Enlightened legal and institutional innovations in juvenile justice did not mitigate the scornful neglect and distinctly harsh penalties experienced by young blacks accused of breaking the law during the nineteenth century. In the South, black juveniles were executed, despite their slave status, and died in droves during post-Emancipation confinement in prison labor schemes. In the North, the "many boys of colour" among the inmates in a Boston reformatory caught the eye of the visiting Charles Dickens, yet their songs "in praise of liberty" struck an ironic chord.[1] Little valued as potential apprentices, black boys and girls in northern reformatories experienced prolonged stays in confinement, compared with those of white youths, and their prospects remained constrained by limits on educational and labor market opportunity. This chapter examines the nineteenth-century foundations of Jim Crow juvenile justice, including the racialized applications of common law protections, the racial politics of houses of refuge, and the often horrific ordeals of black youths in the antebellum South. Throughout the United States, these racialized denials of protection under the law and of democratic participation undermined black youth and community claims to opportunity or representation in the emerging juvenile justice system. Ultimately, this new institution of racialized social control, the white-dominated parental state, was organized to underdevelop black citizens deemed delinquent and black civil society generally and, thus, to maintain the boundaries of a white democracy. For that reason, turn-of-the-century black civic leaders organized to improve the life chances of black youths, and prospects for racial equality in American democracy, through juvenile justice reform.

Outside the Commons of Law

American juvenile justice originates in English common law, a body of law dating to 1189, and was introduced into the New World through empire.[2] English law defined the *youthful offender* through an age-based interpretation of criminal responsibility. The law required that "guilty knowledge" be proved when culpability was unclear on the basis of age: "Children under the age of seven were presumed incapable of committing a crime [but] on the attainment of fourteen years of age, the criminal actions of infants [were] subject to the same modes of construction as those of the rest of society." Common law presumed that children between the ages of seven and fourteen were "destitute of criminal design" and required the state to prove that accused youths in this age range were "clearly and unambiguously" conscious of wrongdoing. Court actors found other ways to practice age-graded criminal law, such as bringing diminished charges against children, refusing to prosecute cases, refusing to convict in cases where a severe sentence was possible, and refusing to carry out sentences against children. Common law generically defined the *offender* as a social and legal type conditional on age, yet other categories of difference—such as race, gender, and class—worked alongside age to determine the criminal responsibility of youths and to further specify the commons of law.[3]

The racialization of early common law principles of juvenile social control is illustrated through the age-based criminal responsibility standard in nineteenth-century cases involving black children and adolescents. In his classic *The Child Savers*, the sociologist Anthony Platt provides fourteen sample cases involving serious juvenile offenses. Occurring between 1806 and 1882, these cases emerged decades before the birth of the juvenile court, and their resolution indicates whether and how common law considerations of age-graded culpability diminished the criminal responsibility of these youths and the eventual court sanctions. They provide insight into the racialization of juvenile social control in the nascent stages of American juvenile justice.

Spanning nearly eight decades and as many states, these fourteen criminal cases all involved juveniles. Considering that there were far fewer executions of juvenile than adult offenders between 1806 and 1882, these juvenile sanctions are very telling indicators. Before the twentieth century, comparatively few cases of serious juvenile crime arose; of those, many were not brought to the attention of authorities or formally charged. Cases with very young offenders involving very serious crime rarely appeared before the courts; here, eight of the fourteen accused were charged with murder and the remainder with arson or theft.[4]

There is little indication that the nature of the criminal act explains the severity of eventual sanctions in these cases. Most of the offenders were never punished, despite evidence of their involvement in the alleged acts. Ten of the fourteen young defendants were found not guilty. Four of these were acquittals won on appeal, where the defense showed that the offender did not possess guilty knowledge or the prosecution had not proved otherwise. Procedural matters related to the youth's presumed criminal incapacity under the law, rather than the factual aspects of the case, apparently were also the basis of the other acquittals. Thus, in this sample of cases, common law questions of guilty knowledge were normally considered, indicating that, as Platt stresses, decades before the invention of the juvenile court, young offenders were differentiated from adults in justice administration.[5]

Four of the fourteen young defendants were found guilty, but only two were punished. One of the ten acquittals and both cases ending in formal sanctions involved young black defendants. Among the latter, James "Little Jim" Guild, age twelve, and ten-year-old Godfrey were enslaved when the offense occurred. Each was convicted of murder, sentenced to death, and executed following unsuccessful appeals in New Jersey (1828) and Alabama (1858), respectively. A closer look at these two cases offers insight into how race shaped the common law sanctioning of black children in the period, especially in serious cases involving white victims.

The courts did consider common law criminal responsibility in these trials. In Godfrey's trial in a Mobile, Alabama, city court, jurors were instructed of his presumed criminal incapacity. Several witnesses explicitly testified that he was intelligent for his young age, apparently to show his possession of guilty knowledge. Godfrey was found guilty of killing a younger boy with a hatchet in what the state characterized as a calculated act of revenge for breaking Godfrey's cherished kite. The presiding judge accepted the jury's guilty verdict but reserved sentencing for the appeals court in light of the capacity question.[6] Guild's conviction was similarly passed on to the appeals court for sentencing, apparently in anticipation of scrutiny of the capacity question. This appeal process was common, but it was unusual for both youths to be held criminally responsible following the appeals and for both to be sentenced to death and executed at such young ages.

The parental state's unique willingness to criminally convict and execute these black embryonic citizens provides insight into the nascent stages of racialized juvenile justice. In these cases, but in no others in this sample, the jurors, trial judges, and appellate courts concluded that children should be severely punished, notwithstanding common law questions of criminal capacity, or noted court community practices of refusing to criminally charge, convict, or actually carry out sentences in cases involving young white offenders. Race and its associated human and civil status distinctions were surely factors in this outcome. As Platt writes, while "criminal law recognized that children under fourteen years old were not to be held as responsible for their actions as adults," "black children apparently were not granted the same immunities as white children and it seems unlikely that Guild and Godfrey would have been executed if they had been white."[7]

Beyond discrimination against black youths in early contexts of criminal and juvenile justice, how did race order social relations in these common law cases? Equal protection, offender-victim relationships, and racial group power relations are elemental considerations. Race is in these cases partly tied to the paradox of their formal prosecution. It was somewhat unusual for enslaved youthful offenders to be formally sanctioned by the state, rather than subjected to plantation or popular justice.[8] In the distorted relations of the antebellum period, formal court processing and execution of these young offenders might be seen as a progressive justice system response to black youth crime or a gesture of equal protection. After all, according to the *Dred Scott* (1858) decision, the infamous U.S. Supreme Court ruling handed down the same year as Godfrey's sentence and three decades after Guild's, black delinquents had never been and were not then citizens with rights to equal protection under the law. Although both boys received trials and appeals, they were not, however, accorded the legal protections commonly granted to white youths responsible for similarly serious crimes.

Denial of equal protection was another dimension of racialization in cases involving black perpetrators and white victims, with executions stemming largely from the racial gravity of the offense. In one case, Godfrey was convicted of killing "the son of a white property owner," and "Little Jim" Guild's victim may also have been white.[9] The economic investment enslaved children represented to owners would seem to compel them to press for leniency. However, the seriousness of their offenses, their youthfulness and consequent status as less productive laborers, and the possibility that Guild was a ward of the state may account for their formal prosecution and punishment.[10] Moreover, the likelihood of strong mob pressure for executions in these cases, as is evident in accounts of the hundreds of cases of black youth lynching and execution, made the offenders' deaths a near certainty. A common law legal process resulting in death is neither surprising nor very distinct from extralegal lynching, considering the common racial politics of criminal punishment (i.e., heightened penalties for black offenders of white victims) and the fact that whites dominated sanctioning processes.[11]

A third and essential aspect of the Guild and Godfrey cases is the political dimension of the race relationship between (black) offender and (white) victim in juvenile and criminal social control. There is nothing inevitable about this well-documented relationship.[12] Differential valuation of victims reflects normative relations and power dynamics within justice processes, including patterns of group representation within these deliberative milieus. Relatively greater valuation of white victims, and scorn for black offenders who victimize whites, is an artifact of the differential recognition and influence that white Americans have enjoyed in justice administration. Had Guild, Godfrey, or any of their white counterparts been guilty of murdering black youths, they probably would not have been convicted or executed—at least if jurors and court officials were nonblack or otherwise relatively indifferent to black victimization. Participation and recognition in justice processes contextualizes and, perhaps, supersedes the significance of offender race, or the fact of interracial violence, in explaining these uncommon nineteenth-century cases of juvenile execution. A central theme of this book is the issue of racial group recognition within the authority of the parental state since it defines the racial history of American juvenile justice and remains significant today.

Focusing on how race mattered in this small sample of nineteenth-century cases facilitates a more sociological understanding of racialized juvenile social control. In this common law context, relying on popular judgment and, thus, reasoned deliberation, the issue of racial and ethnic group representation in the normative commons was vital to racial justice. If the interests of victims, the criminally accused, and the arbiters of justice are not held to be in common, there is little possibility of justice where marginal or excluded groups are concerned. The fates of Guild and Godfrey reflect the positioning of black youths and communities *outside* the legal conventions and communities from which modern juvenile justice emerged.

The carnivalesque and macabre scene of Guild's execution dramatically conveyed the foundational significance of race to American juvenile justice. Executions have often been popular spectacles, and thousands came to see "Little Jim" hang. To accommodate the crowd, the gallows were set up in a large field outside town, away from their usual place. Guild's final moments took a harrowing and bizarre turn when, with the noose around his neck, he made a last-ditch appeal to live. Before the trapdoor swung open, he shook off the hood and balanced on the edge of the hangman's drop. The sheriff rushed up the stairs and pushed him to his death.[13] In this dramatic instance, popular white violence, previously masked symbolically through court trials, appeals, and common law death sentences, lost all pretense.

Houses of White Refuge

Race also accounted for the differential experiences of black youths in nineteenth-century juvenile reformatory institutions. The earliest reformatory institution devised for the purpose of addressing juvenile dependency and delinquency was the house of refuge, first introduced in the Northeast seacoast cities of New York (1825), Boston (1826), and Philadelphia (1828). The refuge did not immediately spread to other urban areas, as many local and state governments favored "multifunction orphan asylums," but increased institutional specialization brought houses of refuge and related institutions to other northern and midwestern cities, including Rochester, Cincinnati, Providence, Pittsburgh, Chicago, and St. Louis, in the 1840s and 1850s.[14]

Houses of refuge formally stressed practical training, discipline, and moral guidance. Children were removed from adult institutions and almshouses to avoid deleterious influences from adults and make possible the interventions necessary to assuming moral and productive lives. In the New York House of Refuge, considered by American and European leaders to be a model institution, boys generally worked eight-hour days under the supervision of contractors in manufactures, while girls were assigned domestic chores in the institution. Both spent another four hours in schools that offered "mental and moral instruction," with Sundays devoted to religion. This was meant to prepare the children for indenture, in the short term, where practical skills, discipline, and submission to authority were expected. Ultimately, the refuge was meant to Americanize wayward youths, many of whom were born of immigrant parents, or the recent immigrants themselves, who were deemed presently unfit for integration in American civil society.[15]

Early northern refuges and similar reformatories were typically first open exclusively to whites and often only to males. White girls were soon admitted, in part "for reasons of economy," as administrators sought to avoid contracting labor by pressing girls into "housekeeping chores such as sewing, ironing, washing, mending, and cooking."[16] Such arrangements were initially deemed less suitable for black children. Their rehabilitative potential was doubted, and the specter of racial commingling was haunting. The superintendent of the Philadelphia House of Refuge, for example, justified the exclusion of black children with the logic that it served a white rehabilitative purpose, explaining: "It would be degrading to the white children to associate them with beings given up to public scorn."[17]

In the earliest phases of the emergent house of refuge model, "black delinquents were handled by [northern] society in the most convenient way possible—by callously placing them in existing institutions rather than constructing institutions specifically designed to rehabilitate them." This often translated into incarcerating black youths in adult almshouses, workhouses, jails, and prisons.[18] By the mid-1830s, however, houses of refuge were opened to black children in some northern cities. For example, Charles Dickens noted, as we have seen, "many boys of colour" among inmates he met on a visit to the Boston House of Reformation around 1842, recalling them offering "a chorus in praise of Liberty: an odd, and, one would think, rather aggravating, theme for prisoners."[19]

The New York House of Refuge, a publicly subsidized institution, was the first to admit black dependent and delinquent youths. In 1835, a decade after opening as an essentially white institution, the refuge established within itself a "colored section." The board of managers was concerned about the "unprovided state of the delinquent coloured children" and about black urban crime and delinquency stemming in part, it felt, from "the broad line of separation between the whites and the blacks, being so strikingly drawn, as often to deprive the latter of many employments which are open to the whites." New York's antebellum black population had increased owing to what refuge officials quaintly characterized as "the policy of several of the Southern States which forbids the free blacks from continuing to reside among them." New York City prisons and almshouses consequently grew more crowded with "this description of persons." As in Philadelphia, New York refuge officials feared that admitting black youths to the existing refuge would be "injurious to our institution," so the board appealed to the legislature and public for assistance in establishing a separate black refuge. A refuge for black youths opened in 1835 with the support of state government and the Manumission Society of New York.[20]

Abolitionists in Philadelphia were instrumental in securing a modicum of access for black youths to enlightened juvenile social control. In 1847, the Pennsylvania Society for Promoting the Abolition of Slavery—a Quaker organization—issued a pamphlet critiquing assertions recently published in *An Appeal to the Public on Behalf of a House of Refuge for Colored Juvenile Delinquents* (1846) that black juvenile delinquency was an inevitable consequence of black moral depravity. The need for a black refuge was not at issue, but the society condemned the *Appeal*, calling it a "partial and disjointed"

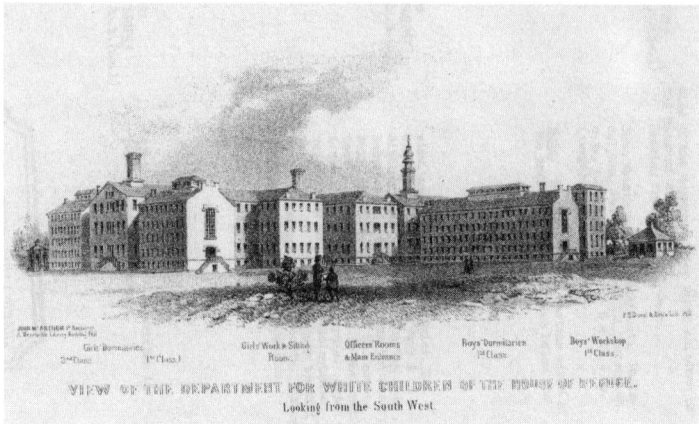

Girls' Dormitories   Girls' Work & Sitting   Officers Rooms   Boys' Dormitories   Boys' Workshop
2nd Class   1st Class   Room   & Main Entrance   1st Class   1st Class

VIEW OF THE DEPARTMENT FOR WHITE CHILDREN OF THE HOUSE OF REFUGE.
Looking from the South West.

2.1. View of the white section of the Philadelphia
House of Refuge, ca. 1858. *Thirtieth Annual Report of the
Philadelphia House of Refuge* (Philadelphia: Ashmead, 1858).
Courtesy the Boston Athenaeum.

proposal that reinforced the ideology of "the slaveholder and his apologist"
as to the "inferiority and worthlessness" of black people. The society reexamined the crime data said to substantiate a finding of black moral depravity and drew alternative conclusions. Instead of "affording evidence of the
alarming moral destitution of our colored population," it wrote, the data
"only serve to show the gross prejudice and injustice of committing magis-
trates towards this people." A reformatory for black children, it argued, must
be defended by "dictates of benevolence, . . . law, and sound policy," rather
than white racism. A house of refuge for black children opened in 1849.[21]

Racial disparities persisted within houses of refuge, although the houses
may have alleviated some of the miseries characteristic of black experiences
in early juvenile justice, especially in the South. Residential segregation was
typical, but stratification by race was apparent in the quality of facilities and
programming. Portraits of the white and colored "departments" included
in the *Thirtieth Annual Report of the Philadelphia House of Refuge* (1858) illustrate these differential investments in the civic futures of white and black
youths and communities.[22] The "department for white children" (fig. 2.1) is
presented as an ambitious and welcoming structure. Its sprawling grounds
are well maintained, open except for the footprint of more than a half
dozen buildings. There are dormitories for boys and girls (classified by age

Girls' Dormitories   Girls' Dining and   Super'ts Rooms   Boys' Dormitories.   Boys' School
                      Sewing Room   & Main Entrance   Rooms

VIEW OF THE DEPARTMENT FOR COLORED CHILDREN OF THE HOUSE OF REFUGE.
Looking from the North West.

2.2. View of the "colored" section of the Philadelphia
House of Refuge, ca. 1858. *Thirtieth Annual Report of the
Philadelphia House of Refuge* (Ashmead: Ashmead, 1858).
Courtesy the Boston Athenaeum.

and behavior), workshops for each gender, a sitting room, an administrative
building, what appears to be a church, and other buildings, the design and
purpose of all showing attention to architectural design, quality materials,
and diversity in programming. The artistic rendering also suggests that the
grounds had an open, community feel, all of which is less apparent in the
contrasting sketch of the "department for colored children."

The view of the department for colored children (fig. 2.2), appearing
in the same *Report*, depicts a more modest and exclusionary approach to
juvenile social control. Its minimalist arrangement includes a dormitory
and administrative and school buildings. These structures—presumably
smaller, given population differences—seem uninspired, with relatively
simple designs and minimal landscaping. The wall is this department's
most prominent feature. Considering that the development of the black
refuge was delayed owing to fear that it would degrade white inmates, its
wall was likely intended to shield the fragile gaze of white inmates as much
as to secure the perimeter. Another indication of this department's inferior
status was that the customarily white officers in charge "were usually paid
less than those who watched over white miscreants."[23]

Given the general absence of child-welfare services for black dependents and delinquents in Philadelphia and elsewhere, contemporaries may

not have been concerned about the inferior design and management of the black section. Space in the Philadelphia Colored Refuge was in great demand from its opening in 1849. In its first year, ninety-three children were committed to it, despite projections of sixty inmates per year. In 1851, barring youths over sixteen (except in "peculiar circumstances") reduced the eligible population; in 1853, the age limit became fourteen. By 1853, the refuge's fourth year, fund-raising and construction were under way for facilities to accommodate an additional 125 black children, likely resulting in the structure pictured in figure 2.2.[24]

Institutionalized Inequality

Race profoundly defined nineteenth-century opportunity structures—in education, labor, politics, etc.—and this societal stratification was institutionalized within white and black houses of refuge. As in public education's concern to teach to position, racially segregated and segmented labor markets were recognized and reinforced in the management of houses of refuge. At the opening ceremony for Philadelphia's department for colored children, the secretary of the Society for Alleviating the Miseries of Public Prisons clarified the bounds of its liberal rehabilitative ideal. "Let us not be misunderstood," he declared, "our object is not to make poets, statesmen, philosophers, or men of letters, but to prepare those placed under our care, by proper education, to discharge faithfully the duties incident to the station in life where it shall please God to place them." Such nineteenth-century references to God's will, when white race leaders were concerned, typically rationalized racial subjugation.[25]

"Proper education" in Philadelphia's black refuge meant preparing black youths for roles as servants in a presumably continuingly white-dominated culture, economy, and polity. Thus, in Philadelphia's white and black refuges, distinct balances were "struck between labor and education, the crucial elements of reformatory programs. While white boys were trained as farmers and skilled artisans and provided with academic instruction, blacks were prepared for manual labor and discouraged from pursuing academic education."[26] The Philadelphia refuge's physical environment suggests a racialized division of labor and education. The white section features a "girl's work and sitting room" and a large "boy's workshop," while the colored section shows a large "girl's dining and sewing room," likely preparing the black girls as cooks, maids, and seamstresses. Black boys were mostly likely engaged in manual work on the institution's grounds since the "boy's school rooms" constituted the smallest building on the grounds.[27] In the New York refuge, an English traveler reported in the 1830s, black youths received their training in "African Schools," which offered rudimentary English education and singing lessons, while the white departments taught "reading, writing, arithmetic, history, geography, and other 'advanced studies.'"[28]

Racial stratification of apprenticeships disadvantaged black youths and communities since those apprenticeships were central to the rehabilitation and social reintegration strategy of the early refuge model. The apprenticeship or "placing-out" system involved discharging inmates to local businesses or rural families outside the cities where most lived. Envisioned by a leading advocate as a means of "draining the city" of poor and delinquent children, placing out to rural families was especially valued for providing a domesticating experience, vocational training, and discipline, all of which civic and business leaders considered key to transforming urban juvenile paupers and delinquents into responsible and productive citizens.[29]

Racial stratification inside and outside houses of refuge limited apprenticeship opportunities for black youths, prolonging their periods of confinement, and limiting their prospects on release.[30] Foreshadowing the contribution of limited placement (i.e., institutional and foster care) options to the confinement of black youths in the twentieth century, black children and youths remained in houses of refuge for longer terms than their white counterparts, in part for lack of placements. The superintendent of the Western House of Refuge in rural New York complained of the difficulty of placing out black boys since it was "hard to find anybody who wants them." Often the only option, Alexander Pisciotta reports, "was to apprentice black boys to sea captains," the one placement willing to take them, and the "least desirable form of release."[31]

Black girls did not fare much better in the apprenticeship programs of northern refuges. A few found welcoming apprenticeships, such as the child sent to fill a New York judge's request for a black girl to serve his family. In their correspondence with New York refuge managers, potential hosts looking for girl domestics commonly specified, "No colored girl please."[32] The preference was for healthy, young, white children, and, according to a placing-out excursion to Michigan in 1856, "the call [was] mostly for girls from nine to twelve."[33] Good looks mattered, too. The assistant superintendent of New York's refuge noted how "physical defects in children otherwise well qualified and desirable, become a bar to their obtaining good places," sympathizing with a pockmarked child of unknown race, too "ugly-looking" to place.[34]

If healthy, young, attractive white girls were ideal apprentices, black girls and boys faced a long wait to be released into work and home placements.

Indeed, in the 1850s, 20 percent of black children, compared to only 4 percent of white, stayed in the Philadelphia refuge for two or more years. By
the 1880s, the average refuge stay for black youths was, according to the
historian Priscilla Clement, almost three years, compared to seventeen
months for whites, a difference largely resulting from disparate apprenticeship opportunities. The ordeal apparently sapped whatever enthusiasm
black youths might have had at the outset of their admission to the refuge.
"White pupils could be assured [that,] if they worked hard at learning to
read, to write, and to cipher, . . . such skills might help them secure a . . .
job upon release," Clement writes. But, she continues, "it was difficult to
convince black students to study" in preparation for a fixed and diminishing
pool of servile labor. As the Civil War approached, opportunities became
even scarcer, and a second, larger wave of European emigration brought an
"influx of immigrants [willing] to fill menial jobs," diminishing the labor
market prospects of black youths exiting the northern refuges.[35]

Refuge managers were not entirely indifferent to the fates of their black
charges. Concerned Philadelphia officials sought to develop effective services for black children but were constrained by their own attitudes about
their limited humanity and marginal civil status. Given the difficulty of
apprenticing black youths and the relatively high death rates in the black
section, white managers of the Philadelphia refuge considered relocating
the colored refuge to a warmer, rural area, presumably one more befitting
children of an "African constitution." Officials attributed black children's
higher mortality to "the law of climate," "results of intermixture of race,"
and an alleged general susceptibility of blacks to death and disease, all of
which traced to contemporary white supremacist conjecture and pseudoscience.[36]

Officials surely conceived their relocation efforts as benevolent and pragmatic, but their strategies betrayed a lack of commitment to the civic reintegration of black American youths. "Experience has proved that a climate, so
far north as Pennsylvania, is unfavorable to the African constitution," the
managers explained when contemplating a western, rural region of Pennsylvania as the new site for the colored section. They also considered sending
its mainly Philadelphia-based youths to Africa. Consistent with colonization plans of abolitionists and others either committed or resigned to the
boundaries of white democracy, refuge managers imagined a one-way transnational apprenticeship system tailored less to black citizen building than
to permanent civic exclusion. Placement would begin in local, rural homes,
where black youths would be trained "in agriculture and horticulture, [and]
prepared for Emigration to Liberia." Similar to most colonization schemes,

their plan never came to fruition; the black and white refuges were, ulti-mately (in 1892), moved from Philadelphia to the rural Glen Mills Farm, where racial segregation continued.[37]

Managers of the New York refuge downplayed the politics of difference within and outside their institution and seem to have entertained illusions regarding race and opportunity in America. In a form letter, refuge officials sought to reassure departing apprentices of the possibility of civic integra-tion. They were exhorted: "Do not be discouraged by what has happened from striving to raise yourself to a respectable station in the world [i.e., by confinement in the institution]. If your life be hereafter exemplary, the errors of your infancy will be forgiven or forgotten. In our happy coun-try, every honest man may claim the rewards he merits. Many of our most distinguished citizens have been the makers of their own fortunes, and in their childhood were as poor and unprotected as you have been."[38] Black youths and adults may have been skeptical, given their longer periods of confinement, the absurd reference to a meritorious "happy country," and the notion that the refuge equally prepared unprotected youths to strive from poverty toward full citizenship, fortune, and distinction.

Differences in early common law rulings and northern houses of ref-uge reveal limited access for black youths and their communities and how early juvenile justice systems reflected and reinforced the racial stratification of the larger society. This dialectic of exclusion—a simultaneous denial of equal developmental potential and equal developmental opportunity—de-fined the racial politics of American juvenile justice from its onset and for generations thereafter. Injustices of the urban North were overshadowed by the more common and often violent ordeals of racial oppression and domi-nation in the nineteenth-century American South. The experiences of black youths in northern refuges were relatively uncommon historical events, as black families rarely lived within the jurisdictions of these early institu-tions.[39] Though the unequal protections, developmental expectations, and opportunities encountered in northern refuges are an important element of the early racial politics of the parental state, the mainstream black experi-ence lies elsewhere. The more common and dreadful ordeals suffered by young black offenders took place in the rural and urban South.[40]

Southern Juvenile Justice in the Antebellum and Postbellum Periods

Black antebellum experiences of southern juvenile justice varied, but it was generally a more malign and violent form of exclusion. Many southern black youths charged with crime in the period were formally convicted, incarcerated, and sometimes executed. Owing to the distorting influence of chattel slavery, they rarely confronted the emerging practice of juvenile justice. Southern governments were generally slow to embrace juvenile justice reforms and were especially disinclined to recognize black youths or community interests in citizen-building initiatives, during or after slavery.

Of the few juvenile reformatory institutions in the nineteenth-century South, none served black youths before the Civil War. By the end of the 1860s, houses of refuge and similar reformatories existed in at least seventeen northern, midwestern, and western states. In the South, only Louisiana, Maryland, and Kentucky had established juvenile reformatories by 1868.[41] In 1822, Louisiana's legislature appointed a former New York City mayor to revise its penal code, making it the first to show an interest in child-welfare-related penal reform. The laws called for a reformatory modeled on northern houses of refuge, but the legislature failed to adopt the code. In 1847, New Orleans opened the first house of refuge in the South. A prison that "did little more than separate children from older offenders," the New Orleans House of Refuge limited access to white boys. Maryland was the only other southern state to establish a juvenile reformatory before the Civil War. When the Baltimore House of Refuge opened in 1855, it was also limited to white boys. A decade later, a separate reformatory for white girls opened in Maryland. In 1873, a half century following the establishment of the first juvenile justice institution in the nation, Maryland became the first and only southern state with a reformatory serving black youths.[42]

Much of the extant research on black youths and families in the South before and immediately after abolition asserts that they were excluded from the early history of American juvenile justice. Several authors hastily dispatch with race in this history by burying the experience in slavery. "White southerners," one author explains, "counted on slavery to control all blacks, young and old," leaving free blacks and nonwhite adults out of the assessment of southern juvenile justice.[43] A major national study of juvenile delinquency and juvenile justice reform from 1825 to 1940 similarly asserts that "plantation discipline took care of the disobedient Negro child" and that "few if any southerners dreamed of considering him as a juvenile delinquent in need of special care."[44] The claims overlook black children who lived in degrees of freedom and the fact that black Americans sometimes constituted the numerical majority of *dreamers* in the South for over one hundred years. Growing obsessed with the special care of black delinquents, the "freedom dreams" of these erstwhile black Americans significantly shaped the development of American juvenile justice.[45]

The Status Offense of Freedom

The institution of slavery did overshadow sociolegal responses to black crime and delinquency in the antebellum period and even later, but this hardly accounts entirely or directly for race-based distinctions in juvenile justice up to the 1860s. More fundamental was the fact that, "when the children of free and slave Negroes encountered the law, their interests were regularly subordinated to those of someone else."[46] Not slavery but the profound power inequality and near absolute denial of black human and civil rights allowed the antebellum parental state to alternately neglect and operate as a hostile force toward enslaved and ostensibly free black youth and community interests.

Racial group power inequalities made free or enslaved status less meaningful than it would seem. The ordeals of free black families and children illustrate this. In the white-dominated parental state, systems of juvenile social control sought to limit and counter the contradiction of black freedom in the context of a white democracy. Well before Emancipation, several southern states formulated policies meant to press ostensibly free black children and adults into forced labor and other forms of subjugation. The strategy amounted to state-sanctioned kidnapping. A statute passed by the General Assembly of Maryland in 1808 "empowered judges of the orphans court to direct sheriffs or constables to bring before them the child or children of 'lazy, indolent, and worthless free Negroes,' and authorized the judges to bind these children out as apprentices." A statutory revision in 1825 eliminated a requirement that apprentices be provided education.[47]

Legislation passed in Maryland in 1829 stipulated that free blacks were subject to banishment or enslavement on release from the penitentiary. As the sociologist Vernetta Young writes, the laws collectively "ensured the maintenance of an unskilled labor force by denying free black children access to educational opportunities and binding them out to lowly occupations."[48] Justice systems were enlisted to reduce or remove status distinctions between formally free black children and their enslaved counterparts. This was a collective punishment since limiting the capacity for free black populations to pursue economic, political, and other group interests undermined social progress and generational mobility.

As the earliest expressions of enlightened criminal and juvenile justice took root in northern and midwestern cities, southern states and locales held firm to more familiar methods of social control, especially where black Americans were concerned. Nearly every southern state had established a modern prison by 1850, but these prisons were not as large or program-matically ambitious as northern versions. Skeptical of rehabilitative ideals, the planter aristocracy was generally "prone to see northern penology as an impractical scheme for the amelioration of the world" and particularly dis-inclined toward reform in the handling of black offenders, whose condition most whites regarded to be immune to improvement.[49]

Southern skepticism toward enlightened penology affected white and black youths in different ways. The South was slow to embrace calls for modern juvenile institutions—such as refuges, reformatories, and, later, specialized juvenile courts. Instead, it depended on an array of informal and formal systems of control to regulate the behavior of deviant youths. Before the Civil War, white southerners were apparently more tolerant of delinquency among white youths, resisting the creation of reformatory institutions until the end of the nineteenth century. In rural areas, it was uncommon for what northerner's labeled *delinquency* to attract official action. In the unlikely event of state intervention, offenders were often pardoned if considered to have respectable families. White youths who were not par-doned might face imprisonment or, more likely, a forced apprenticeship.[50]

Similarly, during the antebellum period and for some time afterward, the South looked to available penal institutions and old techniques to con-trol deviant black youths, including disciplinary regimes of chattel slavery, court-ordered apprenticeships, jails, prisons, and the whip. Before the Civil War, this was simply practical. Mass reliance on formal criminal prosecu-tion and institutionalization to control black adult and young offenders would have undermined the exploitation of slave labor and required pub-lic expenditures.[51] Instead, as Adamson observes: "For a fee, masters could send disobedient bondsmen to municipal jails for a whipping . . . [but] penal custody was not suitable. . . . Southern states were more likely . . . to rely on extra-legal and informal . . . authority; vigilantism instead of profes-sional police forces, dueling as an alternative for litigation, [and] the lash and the noose as much cheaper expedients than regular prison discipline."[52] Throughout the nineteenth century, a "penchant for business rather than institutional solutions for crime" distinguished justice systems in the South from those in the North and West.[53] This slowed the adoption of modern juvenile justice in the antebellum South and distinguished racialized juvenile social control in the region well into the twentieth century.

A New Lease on Bondage: Post-Emancipation Ordeals
of Racialized Social Control

The loss of the Civil War and the abolition of slavery in 1863 spawned widespread reform in southern criminal and juvenile social control, yet old practices died hard. The most pervasive penal reforms in the region were geared toward preserving the status quo, including white social, economic, and political interests threatened by black freedom. In Maryland and other states, legal frameworks had already been devised to limit black freedom, and, just before slavery was abolished in 1864, "tenacious slaveholders speedily took advantage of [the] old provision in the 'Black Code' that negro slave children could be bound out for terms of apprenticeship without the consent of their parents." White elites threatened with rising labor costs counted on "the more or less open connivance of white court officials" in their defiance of looming black constitutional protections.[54]

Against the pleadings of black parents soon to come into possession of civil rights, white owners used their exclusive influence in Maryland courts to arrange for enslaved children to become their apprentices until the age of legal majority (sixteen years), extending de facto bondage well into the post-Emancipation period. No data exist on the number of black children and youths affected, but the historian Eric Foner suggests that thousands were bound out for uncompensated labor. Courts in some areas also abused juvenile apprenticeship laws to control blacks who were not minors, such as an alleged orphan apprenticed to a turpentine mill while he was himself supporting a wife and child.[55]

Such maneuvers foreshadowed a dominant pattern in post-Emancipation strategies of racialized social control, namely, leveraging nearly exclusive white influence in legislatures, courts, and law enforcement to continue to subjugate ostensibly free black men, women, and children, especially through criminalization. With the demise of chattel slavery and its coinciding social order, the white-dominated state became an increasingly central and direct obstacle to substantive black freedom in the South, especially through its capacity to define and control behavior defined as criminal.

In the decades following Emancipation, an array of racially targeted but sufficiently vague criminal statutes combined with new penal systems, such as the convict-lease system, to facilitate a rediscovery of "black gold." Sharp fiscal crisis, declines in the availability of cheap labor, trampled infrastructure, and vehement white supremacism in the postbellum period were critical to these post-Emancipation systems of black subjugation, yet none alone could ensure their success. Legitimizing repression after Emancipation made it necessary to duly convict blacks, making the criminalization of black people and the administration of criminal justice vital mechanisms of oppression and domination in the waning decades of the nineteenth century. After showing comparatively little interest in formal systems of criminal social control, the region now found in criminal justice new ways to mirror the institution of slavery, to re-create and control exploitable black labor, and to limit black power and influence. Profit motives and deeper social and political dimensions prompted an emerging southern strategy of racialized criminal justice. As the historian Mary Curtin observes in her study of black prisoners in Alabama from 1865 to 1900, "after Emancipation the courtroom became an ideal place to exact racial retribution" and the whole apparatus of criminal social control became "a subterfuge for political revenge."[56]

By manipulating legislatures, police powers, and the authority to sentence and imprison, the white-dominated court communities of the post-Emancipation period became powerful arms of white racial tyranny and opposition to black freedom. That southern criminal and juvenile justice systems were enlisted to perpetuate black subjugation is not surprising since the strategy was essentially scripted in the amended U.S. Constitution. Article 1 of the Thirteenth Amendment, which defined this new freedom, did not declare slavery illegal, but it did specify: "Neither slavery nor involuntary servitude *except as punishment for a crime* whereof the party shall have been *duly convicted*, shall exist in the United States."[57]

The amendment's cavernous loopholes—especially the meanings of crime and legitimate conviction—were exploited by those who wished to reinstate the "peculiar institution," or something similar in form and function, through the enactment of Black Codes. Across the South following Emancipation, Black Codes proliferated. These laws were specifically devised to control black populations by criminalizing the most mundane behaviors and movements of free men, women, and children. The Freedmen's Bureau and black elected officials in Reconstruction Era state and federal government briefly managed to remove or weaken these white supremacist laws and crime control practices. "With the levers of local office in their grasp," Hahn writes, "black Republicans, with the support of some of their white allies, moved to adjust the balances of power and shift important resources toward their communities."[58]

The Freedmen's Bureau was established in 1865 through a bill that created an office for handling matters pertaining to refugees, freedmen, and land in the postwar South. It sought to protect the civil liberties and substantive freedoms of black Americans. Among the bureau's massive tasks was its duty to protect the black man "against violence and outrage, to protect him from any permanent, temporary, or partial system of slavery, to defend his right to hold property, to secure the enforcement of his contracts, to see that he had a fair trial, that his testimony was received in court, and that his family relations were respected."[59] Indeed, bureau agents enforcing Reconstruction acts of 1867 freed hundreds of black children of former slaves who had been illegally apprenticed to their parents' former owners. In just three counties of Maryland and Virginia, 255 black children were freed in a single year, and other southern states, including Alabama and Kentucky, took similar action.[60]

The "unfinished revolution" of federal Reconstruction and the brief tenure of the Freedmen's Bureau, black representation in government, and an unprecedented experiment in racially democratic social control ended in 1877 with the compromise over the contested presidential election of 1876. Institutions of law and justice administration fell back into the hands of exclusively white legislatures, police, courts, and juries. Dramatic power imbalances followed reenactments of Black Codes and other means of subjugating black men, women, and children through racialized criminal and juvenile social control.[61]

Black Codes were effective legal mechanism for stripping away newly won freedoms because they were so vague that virtually anything could be constructed as a crime. In some states, vagrants were defined as persons who were idle, were disorderly, or misspent earnings, a net that could ensnare most of the population. To comply with the Civil Rights Act (1875), the language of vagrancy law was often race neutral, but it was understood that "the vagrant contemplated was the plantation negro," as an Alabama planter and Democratic Party operative put it.[62]

Southern legislators were often clear about the racial politics behind their support of the Black Codes. In 1876, for example, the Mississippi legislature passed a crime bill known as the "Pig Law," defining theft of farm animals or any property worth at least ten dollars as grand larceny, a crime punishable by up to five years in prison. The desperation and hunger associated with poverty and disenfranchisement assured that the measure would disproportionately affect blacks; one legislator apparently attributed the subsequent rise in the prison population to "the affinity of our Brother in Black for fresh pork." Convict-leasing interests, who supported this bill, saw Mississippi's convict population swell from 272 in 1874 to 1,072 in the first year after the law took effect. This new convict labor population included many black children and youths.[63] The population confined in Mississippi prisons did not increase as dramatically and declined and leveled off after 1877. The increase was due in part to an 1875 law that permitted convict subleasing and that was enacted over "the opposition of the declining number of black legislators" to using convicts on plantations. The swelling ranks of convicts were sent straight to the fields and work camps. Here and in other southern states, Black Codes and convict leasing combined to "make forced labor more easily available to leading planters" and to otherwise restore powers and privileges that the white economic and political elites stood to lose in the racialized social system of the post-Emancipation period.[64]

Legislative changes that expanded discretionary power in sentencing also helped secure the foundation of this new but familiar system of racialized social control. Unlike antebellum court actors, decisionmakers could now impose a broader range of sanctions for specific offenses and, with Emancipation, had greater incentives to do so. Sentencing options for "vagrancy, rape, arson, and burglary—crimes whites considered peculiarly 'black'—widened considerably in the first years after the [Civil War]," and courts were expressly authorized to use corporal punishment against black offenders.[65] Court actors could punish by fine, forced labor, or imprisonment, but a fine alone often ensured the imprisonment of impoverished free men, women, and children, who, lacking means of payment, quickly fell into default and violation of court orders.

By the 1880s, American criminal justice had become "a dragnet for the negro." Black youths and adults swelled the ranks of convicts and ensured that crime and punishment would become key twentieth-century elements in an ongoing struggle for freedom.[66] White-dominated legislatures introduced new laws and criminal justice policies throughout the South, and white-dominated police and court organizations produced a massive new supply of black bondsmen and -women, including boys and girls, through lengthy sentences. As in Mississippi, duly convicted black Americans were pressed into a uniquely racialized and violent placing-out system devised in the post-Emancipation period, the convict lease.

Placing Out in the New South: Black Youths in the Convict Lease

Convict lease refers to various uses of prison labor by public and private interests. Varying widely across time and place, leasing arrangements were experimented with by several northern and southern states before the Civil War. Typically, prison labor was contracted to private interests that employed inmates within a prison, under the supervision of a warden and guards. In 1825, Kentucky transferred its penal system to private operators. In 1846, "wanting to wash their hands of the whole convict problem," the

Alabama legislature leased its whole debt-ridden penitentiary—physical plant, staff, and inmates—to a businessman for six years. These were exceptional pre–Civil War cases, where lessees gained full control of penitentiaries or autonomy in using inmates, but they anticipated arrangements to come.[67]

Post–Civil War southern convict-leasing schemes assigned greater responsibility for the supervision, provision, and discipline of leased prisoners to private interests, partly out of necessity. The Civil War, staged primarily in Confederate territory, decimated the South's infrastructure and productive capacity. Southern prisons were often used to manufacture and store ammunition and other war materials, making them targets of Union armies. In Tennessee, "prisons, railroads, factories, and much of the land itself was almost totally destroyed" in the war. The situation differed little elsewhere. "With the exception of the Texas penitentiary," one historian reports, "every southern prison was extensively damaged during the Civil War." Incapable of financing repairs or new prisons, and needing revenue, state and local governments found privatization of imprisonment through leasing arrangements an attractive option, economically and otherwise.[68]

The "New South" found substantive and symbolic remedies in novel systems of racialized social control. Black Codes and the convict lease helped appease white populist sentiments while disenfranchising blacks, stabilizing a white power structure threatened by Emancipation and Reconstruction.[69] New leasing arrangements also benefited entrepreneurs, offering "a system of forced labor in an age of Emancipation" and leverage against organized labor.[70] Entrepreneurs used leased convicts for tasks that free labor avoided, including work in coal and iron mines, sawmills, and turpentine camps, railroad and levee construction, and the clearance of "treacherous, malaria-infested swamplands." This claimed many prisoners' lives, outraged civic leaders, and reduced the bargaining power of free labor.[71]

The gradual encroachment of the child-saving movement in the South did not spare black children and youths from the brutal ordeals of the lease systems (see fig. 2.3). In 1868, nearly 70 percent of the inmate population of the Louisiana penitentiary was black, and "of the 222 convicts . . . 116 were under the age of twenty five, 73 . . . in the twenty-to-twenty-five year age group, 40 between the ages of fifteen and twenty, and 3 between ten and fifteen." A Savannah, Georgia, newspaper reported in 1893 that its local penitentiary held "80 [inmates] below the age of fifteen, 40 below the age of fourteen, 27 below the age thirteen, 15 below the age of twelve, 2 below the age of eleven, and one who is only ten years old." In North Carolina, relatively comprehensive data show that the proportion of prison inmates

2.3. "Juvenile convicts at work in the fields," ca. 1903. Library of Congress, Prints and Photographs Division, Detroit Publishing Company Collection (reproduction number LC-D4-10865).

under the age of sixteen ranged from 1 to 9 percent between 1883 and 1918 and that black Americans consistently made up more than half of these child convicts.[72] Among the black juveniles in Mississippi's convict pool were Robert Day, a twelve-year-old given a life sentence in 1872 for murder, and thirteen-year-old James Harrington, sentenced in the 1870s to ten years for burglary and "intent to rape." There was also six-year-old Mary Gay, sentenced in 1881 to thirty days in prison and court costs for stealing a hat.[73]

The criminalization of these black children and youths led to suffering and injustice far worse than labor exploitation or denials of due process, and many experienced firsthand why the ordeal has been called "worse than slavery."[74] Coupled with a disregard for black humanity and civil rights, the economic principles of convict leasing reduced black convicts to a form of chattel less valued than the enslaved laborers they replaced. Brutal mistreatment, terrible working conditions, and high death rates resulted. Lessees paid little for convict labor. Immediately after the war, the cost to a firm controlled by the Alabama and Chattanooga Railroad for a six-year lease of 374 convicts was $5.00. In 1876, the monthly fee for a four-year lease in Mississippi was $1.10 per convict, "with the first 140 convicts free."[75] Prices fluctuated by state and with each arrangement, but convict labor was almost always a great bargain. Even the priciest convict labor, such as the "first-class" convicts Alabama leased for $222 per year in 1888, was less than half the cost of comparable free labor.[76]

Unlike slave owners, lessees did not have to invest heavily in the maintenance of workers to realize the value of their investment. Lessees did not pay for the subsistence and reproduction of entire communities (e.g., food, clothing, and shelter for enslaved communities of children, adults, and the elderly); instead, they invested minimally in the subsistence of individual, productive workers. Those unlikely to produce were refused, and those proving unproductive could be returned to the state, or worse. A South Carolina warden acknowledged this in 1880 when he suggested that mortality rates among prisoners in his state would have been far lower "if convicts were property having a value to preserve."[77] Three years later, a lessee made it even plainer: "Before the war we owned the Negroes. . . . [I]f a man had a good nigger he could afford to take care of him; if he was sick, get a doctor. He might even put gold plugs in his teeth. But these convicts; we don't own 'em. One dies, get another."[78]

The state offered a seemingly endless supply of convict labor, contributing to the brutality of the system. In most southern states after the Civil War, the number of black inmates grew, and the convict-lease industry was deregulated to facilitate its expansion, such as by allowing subleasing. Low costs, large supplies, and weak regulation made convict bodies expendable, virtually assuring their exposure to deadly conditions. Many would succumb. Forty-one percent of Alabama's convicts died in 1870; 25 percent of prisoners in Arkansas died in 1881; 15 percent of Tennessee's convicts died in 1884; and, between 1880 and 1885, Mississippi's convict mortality rate hovered around 11 percent. At specific work sites, death rates exceeded 50 percent. In a Mississippi railroad construction project, "forty-five of the seventy-two convicts [63 percent] did not return." According to the historian Leon Litwack: "Southern states had an average death rate among prisoners nearly three times the rate in northern states." And this omits the scores of "broken-down men, [women, and children] who," no longer useful to the lessee or state, "obtained pardons and went home to die."[79]

Many who did not die in confinement likely wished that they had. Theophile Chevalier, a black prisoner in Louisiana, was forced to work barefoot in the winter of 1884. Overcome with frostbite and gangrene, the indifference of the lessee allowed one foot to "rott [sic] off" while the other was amputated with a pocketknife. A New Orleans newspaper editor and critic of the lease system suggested that it would be more humane "to impose the death sentence immediately upon anyone sentenced to a term with the lessee in excess of six years . . . because the average convict lived no longer . . . anyway." Most vulnerable were young convicts. Subject to the predations of older convicts, including rampant sexual violence, their minds and bodies were likely no match for the lease ordeal. In the 1890s, Georgia pardoned a black American named Wade Hampton who at time of conviction for burglary was a child and lost a leg after confinement.[80]

Saving the Race: A Rising Tide of Opposition

Exploitation of black youths in southern convict-lease and work gangs moved late-nineteenth-century black civic leaders to embark on the black child-saving movement, an effort to transform racial group status and power relations in American juvenile justice. The movement's primarily women leaders witnessed firsthand the racialized assault of southern injustice in the post-Emancipation period. They grew increasingly concerned about its impact on the bodies and souls of black children and, by extension, about the collective future of black families and communities. Thus, they resolved to take action on behalf of the immortal youth.

At the first national meeting in 1899 of the National Association of Colored Women's Clubs (NACW, founded 1896), an Atlanta club representative presented the paper "The Convict Lease System as It Affects Child Nature." It made a profound impression on the over one hundred delegates representing forty-six clubs from sixteen states.[81] Underscoring the message a year later, M. Louise Jenkins, a prominent Alabama club member, published a rallying essay entitled "Do We Need Reformatories?" in the NACW's *National Notes*. Addressed to other black women leaders in Alabama, her essay reflected on how her regular encounters with convict work gangs revealed an urgent need for race-related juvenile justice reform. "One of the most important questions that confronts us, at the close of the century," she wrote, "is what to do with our boys and girls that have reached the age of ten, twelve and fourteen years, and who show a predisposition toward crime. It is a fact that our streets are filled with little criminals of this age . . . going from bad to worse, till detected in some crime, they are sentenced to hard work on the streets or sent to the coal mines." Protesting that this "makes them no better," she explained:

> There they associate with hardened, vicious criminals, who delight in filling the ears of the young with immoral teachings. I saw a case of that kind this morning, just in front of my door, where a gang of prisoners were at work. Among them were several boys, the youngest about ten years of age. This lit-

tle fellow, as dirty as he could be, with the regulation prison stripes on, was carrying water for the others. Between his lips was a cigarette, which he evidently enjoyed, and occasionally passed to some of the men, who would take a whiff or two at it. A visit to the prisons and a careful study of them, would [illustrate] that the methods now in vogue for punishing criminal youth are very faulty, indeed.[82]

Jenkins sought a reformatory solution to the problem of black juvenile crime, an enlightened institution that might yield "healthful citizens." She educated fellow clubwomen about the rehabilitative potential of modern juvenile reformatories, anticipating that the term *reformatory* would merely call to mind "iron bars and high prison walls." "To the contrary," she explained, "every means is now taken to make these places as home-like as possible. . . . [A]t these institutions [the inmates] establish a new foundation for useful, virtuous lives." Ironically, Jenkins's model was the Philadelphia House of Refuge in Glen Mills, which had explored shipping black youths to Liberia. "[It] is said by an eye-witness to be a most beautiful place—more like a summer resort than a reformatory," she wrote. "We certainly do not, nor can we, expect such an institution [as grand] as that at Glen Mills; at least for a long time," she reasoned, "but we can make a beginning, and now is the time to do it."[83]

As a further inducement, Jenkins noted that plans for a juvenile reformatory were already afoot in Alabama, but one exclusively for white youths. White women leaders had obtained "a charter for the establishment of a boy's reformatory, to be situated near Birmingham." This included a donation of public land and a three-thousand-dollar appropriation for buildings and operations during the last legislative session. She protested that there was "no provision whatever being made for colored boys." "If such institutions are needed for white boys, who have had hundreds of years of culture behind them," Jenkins asked, "how much more do we need them for our boys?"[84]

Though the early racial history of juvenile justice is defined by profound power inequalities and ongoing patterns of racial injustice, the white-dominated parental state was a contested and dynamic racial structure. Differential legal and institutional treatment of enslaved and nominally free black youths was met by the strivings of black adults who were outraged by early signs of Jim Crow juvenile justice. Reform efforts by nineteenth-century black leaders were motivated by a sense of "linked fate," a notion of correlated individual and group interests. Prior histories attribute juvenile justice reform to interests favoring the imposition of coercive controls or middle-class mores on poor and otherwise marginal populations. However, reformers reveal a responsive, ameliorative, and liberal-democratic interest in juvenile justice reform.[85] For black civic leaders in the American South, juvenile justice reform was a forward-looking venture in black community reparation and freedom. "When we think of the number of boys and girls wearing prison stripes and realize that the boys and girls of to-day will comprise the next generation," Louise Jenkins wrote, "it makes us shudder." "It behooves us as colored women of the South," she declared, "to wake up from the lethargy which has so long bound us to work more in unity and to devise some remedy for this growing evil." Her concern with black youth crime and vice referred, not simply to the evil of delinquency, but to what Alexander Pisciotta has described as the "racist and sexist" parental state.[86] A 1908 follow-up to Jenkins's early appeal described the fledgling movement for race-related juvenile justice reform as a struggle to "save black children from the slavery of an iniquitous justice system."[87]

The earliest black child-savers were greatly concerned with eventually enhancing the progress of black America through equal protection of black youths in relation to rehabilitative ideals. Reforms sought to ensure that black and white youths would enjoy the same development considerations before the courts and equal access to child- and social-welfare approaches of enlightened juvenile justice. Everything depended on the empowerment and equal recognition of black adults and communities in the administration of juvenile justice. These institutional changes were generations away when the earliest signs of black American outrage at separate and unequal juvenile justice surfaced at the close of the nineteenth century. Meanwhile, black children and youths coming of age in the South enjoyed little refuge under the law. Their status as second-class citizens and members of a marginal political constituency was matched by limited access to citizen-building ideals and institutions until the middle of the twentieth century.

No Refuge under the Law: Summary and Conclusion

During the initial development of the American juvenile justice system, the dominant racial ideology framed black childhood as a fixed, inferior moral, intellectual, and political condition, alien to the human family and democratic polity. This ideology of white supremacy rationalized denials of black youth and community interests in rehabilitative ideals and resources. Political and economic exclusion further ensured that black youths and communities would be denied equal access to the allegedly enlightened, citizen-building agenda of the emergent parental state. Instead, this liberal agenda of American juvenile justice became aligned with a goal of maintaining the boundaries of a white democracy, from its founding in the nineteenth century through the Jim Crow period.

Prior historical juvenile justice research has stressed the disadvantage and mistreatment poor white and European immigrant youths faced at the hands of Progressive Era reformers. Yet a comparative perspective on black youth and community experiences alters this common perception that poor white and European immigrant youths and families were subject to oppression under the guise of rehabilitative ideals. However unfortunate their disproportionate encounters with early juvenile institutions proved to be, their access reflected racial privileges in an unyielding white democracy. As David McLeod writes, white youths and communities were beneficiaries, if not signatories, of a racist bargain in progressive reform. "If rural whites accepted reform," the deal went, "black children would get nothing." "North or South, the basic pattern was that upper-middle-class, native stock, urban whites would try to reform poorer whites," with the aim of their incorporation into the economy and body politic. This "cross-class alliance" in American white democracy gave native whites and potentially white European immigrants priority access to the Americanizing ambitions and resources of juvenile justice reform.[88]

Racially selective investment of early American juvenile justice in white citizen- and state-building initiatives is evident in early common law cases as well as in the development of refuges and reformatories. Although ordeals in the urban North were less violent and explicitly exploitative, they similarly reveal the prioritization of white youth and community interests in liberal strategies of social control. For example, North and South, reformatories for white children came first, and programs and resources privileged white youths. In northern houses of refuge, even when white administrators proclaimed rehabilitative ideals and admitted black youths, their institutions and reform strategies revealed deep investments in white supremacist ideology and racial caste relations.

Most black Americans lived in the South well into the twentieth century, where disregard for black embryonic citizens was more violent and explicit. In the post-Reconstruction period, southern criminal social control by slaveholders and their overseers was supplanted by the criminalization of the black population to assure ongoing social, economic, and political control. The criminal justice systems of the South were filled with black Americans, young and old, and populations of local jails and state prisons grew "darker by the year."[89] Louisiana prison officials even asked legislators to investigate why so many black Americans had been sent for long terms of incarceration "upon the most trivial charges," wondering whether beneath this trend lurked "the low, mean motive of depriving them of the right of citizenship."[90] That such a motive inspired penal reform in the postbellum South was obvious to others witnessing "the whole criminal system [being] used as a method of keeping Negroes at work and intimidating them."[91]

The gradual development of a separate and unequal juvenile justice system in the South reveals the persistence and diffusion of this agenda. Black youths remained subject to institutionalization with adults far longer than was the case for whites, largely as a result of refusals to invest in black child and social welfare. Even when planned and approved, state-sponsored reformatories for black children were delayed for decades.

Baltimore's House of Reformation for Colored Children opened in 1873, nearly fifty years after the first house of refuge appeared in the United States, and was the first in the South to serve black youths.[92] Founded ten years after Emancipation and in the midst of Reconstruction, it was clearly designed with these cataclysmic events in mind. Absent slavery, and with forced apprenticeships and other Black Codes having come under greater scrutiny following the 1866 Civil Rights Act, Maryland had few options for controlling black youths.[93] Many were confined in adult prisons and jails, but unsatisfied authorities hoped to more purposefully prepare black youths for post-Emancipation roles. "There is no probability that the colored race will be removed from among us," Baltimore officials conceded in 1868; "interest, therefore, as well as humanity would dictate all that can be done to elevate them should be done."[94]

The board of managers envisioned uplift as providing for "the need for agricultural labor through the state, as well as the great want of competent house servants." The managers believed that black youths under their control were not capable of much more and bemoaned training those "whose natural inclination toward mental improvement" is "not in our favor." The house of reformation resolved to instruct black boys in only the fine points of manual labor, including "how to handle the hoe, shovel and spade; to manage horses, mules and cattle, to plow, to sow, and to reap." Black girls would "learn to scrub, wash, and iron, to bake and cook; [and] to wait upon the family."[95] It thus sought to transform the raw material of black delinquents into a class of servants and laborers to serve whites. As a political consideration, managers expected black youths thus disciplined to accept their caste status and eschew efforts to obtain equality in the New South through the "mischievous" use of new rights. An 1881 report proposed that black youths' future "value both as citizens and laborers will depend largely upon their intelligence, their good habits as citizens, and their early industrial training and discipline." "The more cultivated the intellects of these people become," the board wrote, "the less will vicious excitements be necessary to them, and the less will their political rights be instruments of mischief."[96]

These institutional strategies reflect a rehabilitative ideal tailored more to white interests than the advance of black freedom. The training black and white youths encountered in comparable institutions was similar in some ways and preferable to adult penal systems, at least in terms of basic survival.[97] The Baltimore plan was also somewhat consistent with the Hampton-Tuskegee model for industrial education, which, as we shall see, enjoyed support among some black leaders, including early juvenile justice reformers. Yet black leaders specifically opposed the industrial model when it was limited to training for menial labor and lacked black administrative influence. W. E. B. DuBois clarified black opposition to industrial education by noting that such narrow approaches as evident in the Baltimore reformatory were distrusted because they "perpetuate the American Negro as a docile peasant and peon, without political rights or social standing, working for little wage, and heaping up dividends to be doled out in future charity to his children."[98]

After the Civil War, institutions for black juvenile delinquents began to proliferate, their designs largely dictated by the race, class, and gender politics of white civic leaders. The end of the nineteenth century saw the opening of the Louisville House of Refuge for Colored Children (for boys, 1877), Maryland's Industrial Home for Colored Girls (1882), a house of reformation in Texas that initially admitted black and white boys (1890), two county-run industrial and training schools in Tennessee that accepted white and black boys and girls (1897), and the Negro Reformatory for boys, established in Hampton, Virginia, in 1899.[99] Some southern states established segregated race- and gender-inclusive institutions, such as those in Texas (1890) and Kentucky (1900). Physically separate institutions were the norm, with construction, funding, and programming typically privileging white youths. The 1899 Kentucky legislature designated a farm in Lexington for use as a reformatory for male criminals under sixteen years of age, admitting both black and white youths, yet it was soon deemed unsuitable for a "true reform school." In 1906, a more suitable reformatory was established and restricted to white boys. As early as 1896 in Arkansas, the Populist Party proposed establishing a reform school. Initially, a prison camp for white boys was created, separating them from adult prisoners. In 1905, Arkansas governor Jefferson Davis protested that 115 white boys, 217 black boys, and 20 women (race unspecified) aged seventeen and under had been committed to the penitentiary. Unsatisfied with the legislature's slow progress, Davis pardoned all white boys under eighteen held in Arkansas's prison.[100]

Under the best and worst local circumstances, black youths and communities met an emerging American juvenile justice system that provided little refuge under the law and variously organized to perpetuate black second-class citizenship and white advantage in what remained a white democracy. Tragically, the nineteenth century marks only an opening chapter in a longer-term ordeal of racial oppression and domination in the arms of a white supremacist parental state. These early black youth and community experiences foreshadow the institutional development of separate and unequal juvenile justice through the first half of the twentieth century, beginning with the Progressive Era establishment of Jim Crow juvenile courts.

THREE

Birth of a Juvenile Court

The Progressive Era (1890–1920) is often heralded for scientific innovations and liberal reforms that help define the modern nation. In American juvenile justice, the cultural and institutional crown jewel of this reform impulse was the modern juvenile court. Along with its orbiting network of service agencies and reformatory institutions, the court introduced a more technical and autonomous apparatus of social control, a dramatic and enlightened advance of juvenile justice in the view of many supporters.[1] This chapter examines how Progressive Era black youths and communities experienced the emergence of the juvenile court, an encounter dramatized by mass black migration to urban centers where modern juvenile courts emerged. Just as black Americans were migrating to the urban North in search of opportunity, the earliest juvenile courts were beginning to spread to cities with booming black populations, such as Chicago, Boston, and New York. These court communities could have played an important role in advancing black civic and political integration, offering unprecedented access to citizen-building initiatives to the first generations of immortal youths born into formal freedom. Yet this progressive opportunity was largely lost, even in the urban North, where black youths and communities encountered nuances of "Up South" racial exclusion, a subtler but familiar ordeal of diminished access to white-dominated juvenile justice resources. In the Progressive Era South, Reconstruction gave way to the rise of white supremacist redemption, subjecting black youths and communities to more explicitly neglectful, exploitative, and violent forms of Jim Crow juvenile justice. North and South, growing juvenile court communities embraced the racial project of white citizen and state building, prioritizing white youth opportunity and community interests in their pursuit of rehabilitative ideals. Institutionalization of separate and unequal juvenile justice throughout the United States, not a new multiracial democracy, was the Progressive Era legacy of juvenile justice reform in the African American experience.

A Kind and Just Parent: Juvenile Court Reform's Promise

Advocates of juvenile court reform maintained that adult courts and penal institutions wasted the constructive potential of juvenile social control. They called for a separate, specialized court, procedurally oriented and professionally staffed, to handle social and legal issues unique to children and families. The juvenile court model married the authority of the parental state to professionalism in human services, the goal being to sculpt well-adjusted young adults from the raw material of wayward, dependent, and criminal children. The court was envisioned as a cornerstone of a more diagnostic, individualized, and formalized solution to juvenile crime and dependency, an institutional network in which officials, "through modern science, would discover the root causes of delinquency, and through active intervention, prevent it."[2]

In this model, the court dispatched youths to public and private entities, operators of institutions, and agencies for services or prescribed interventions. The court and its supporting agencies—the state and local networks of control agents and institutions (juvenile court communities)—were to be a more personalized, informal, and rehabilitative system of juvenile social control. Troubled and troubling youths and adolescents were to be connected to programs and individually tailored services that would promote their civic futures. A judge in a Cook County, Illinois, juvenile court declared that the "idea of a separate court to administer justice . . . [had] gone beyond the experimental stage and attracted the attention of the entire world." It functioned "like a kind and just parent ought to treat his children." Evidence of the promise and importance of the modern juvenile court was its steady diffusion. By 1917, at least one juvenile court existed in all but three states, with most located in rapidly growing American cities.[3]

At the turn of the twentieth century, black communities had much to gain from a formal, autonomous juvenile court community. Barely a generation into freedom from the civil death and disability of slavery, the black majority sought to formally consolidate their civil rights and status as citizens. A growing presence in cities, black civic actors looked to the juvenile court as a resource for black families and the community.[4] The promise of a clinical and restorative juvenile court community was intimately related to historical injustices suffered by black children and families. Chattel slavery had explicitly underdeveloped the family unit. For Progressive

Era reformers, the family was the incubator of civic participation, essential for normalization, participation, and group progress in liberal democracy. Massive numbers of these newcomers to American citizenship flowed from the rural South to the growing cities in the Northeast and Midwest. There, an imagined "promised land" and the first juvenile court communities awaited them.[5] The heightened cultural and institutional commitment to an enlightened parental state and the growing concentration of free blacks in urban centers should have improved opportunities for black youths and the influence of black adults in the administration of juvenile justice.

Progressive Era black stakeholders and their allies had little reason to expect that the parental state was a fitting or judicious instrument for building black citizens in a multiracial democracy. Nineteenth-century courts had long exaggerated the criminal culpability of black youths, in contrast to their white counterparts, and imposed sanctions that ignored black youth and community developmental needs and interests. Even in northern houses of refuge and reformatories, the civic ideals underlying the treatment of black youths sought to maintain the status quo and were dictated by white authorities.

More daunting was the deterioration of American race relations during the Progressive Era. Black community access to citizen-building ideals and institutions still hinged on the Negro question—the question of black America's present and future standing in American liberal democracy.[6] Given the Progressive Era response, black Americans had little reason to believe that the juvenile court would intervene as a "kind and just parent."

Progressive Era Racial Politics and Juvenile Court Reform

The final decades of the nineteenth century brought dramatic progress and reversals in black Americans' struggle for human and civil rights, setting the stage for their interest in, and experience of, the juvenile court movement. Legal and legislative developments between 1865 and 1875 marked momentous advances in racial reconciliation and democratic inclusion— declaring slavery unconstitutional, extending rights of equal protection to black Americans, and providing blacks the right to vote. Civil rights acts in 1866 and 1875 further recognized black citizenship and offered protections against discrimination. Federal Reconstruction facilitated unprecedented black representation in state and local government and formally increased opportunities for black Americans in education, employment, and other vital areas.[7]

Formation of black civic associations and other supportive institutions in the late 1800s enhanced the organizational means for defining and advancing black interests, facilitated greater social networking and self-help initiatives, and provided a voice in the public sphere. Black Americans had, thus, come closer to equal opportunity and influence in American civil society, and the Republic was closer than ever to becoming a multiracial democracy. Had these trends continued, the juvenile court could have been an important component of Reconstruction as well as of the political, economic, and social advance of the post-Emancipation generation. Instead, black Americans in the Progressive Era experienced a broad, often violent retreat in Jim Crow juvenile courts.

A consequence of the collapse of Reconstruction was that the progressive potential of the juvenile court for black Americans was undermined. Its legal and policy protections were either short-lived or not enforced. Moreover, a new storm of white racial violence and redemption was gathering, a terror building particularly in the South but with national implications for race relations.[8] In the South, limited but hard-won black gains in civil and political standing nearly vanished by the start of the Progressive Era. From Reconstruction's inception, white opposition had sought to reverse attempts to redefine southern race relations. Since 1866, a wing of the white Democratic Party leadership had led the effort, employing populist rhetoric and a policy platform of redemption. Their campaign featured "white supremacy, low taxes, and the control of black labor." The party promised to reclaim white community control of southern state and local governments, and it delivered over the ensuing decades. As the twentieth century approached and the redeemers rose to power across the South, "everywhere one turned black rights were trampled," leading scholars of U.S. racial history to characterize the period from 1877 to 1901 as the nadir—the lowest point in black social status since Emancipation, barely a notch above enslavement.[9]

Redeemers in former slave states reinstated and expanded Black Codes that Reconstruction governments, which for the first time included significant black representation, had eliminated or curtailed. By 1890, black civil and political rights and representation had diminished, and a reign of racial terror had erupted in the South and beyond. During the Progressive Era, white mob violence, including lynching, peaked. Often it occurred with the consent or collaboration of white law enforcement and legal authorities. Of the more than three thousand black Americans lynched from 1882 to 1947, over one-third were murdered between 1890 and 1900, the decade when the first juvenile courts were established. Between 1890 and 1917, "some two to three black southerners were hanged, burned at the stake, or quietly murdered every week."[10]

Beyond the South, the federal government's withdrawal of its defense of black freedoms aided a national resurgence of white supremacist violence and politics. Legislative, judicial, and executive branches of the federal government, over which southern economic and political elites held great influence, collectively retreated from enforcing and maintaining black constitutional protections by failing to intervene against lynching, oppose segregation, or protect black voting rights. In 1883, immediately before the Progressive Era, Congress repealed the Civil Rights Act of 1875 on the grounds that it violated state sovereignty.

Freed from federal oversight and interference, Progressive Era white leaders quickly disenfranchised black voters to maintain state power and their ability to deny black claims to equal protection and representation. In 1890, the Mississippi Constitutional Convention passed a measure that disqualified black voters. In 1898, the Louisiana legislature enacted its infamous "grandfather clause," which denied voting rights to those whose grandfathers had not voted, meaning nearly every black person in the state.[11] The U.S. Supreme Court legalized the general "separate but equal" doctrine of racial segregation (*Plessy v. Ferguson*, 1896) and the barely veiled methods of black political disfranchisement (*Williams v. Mississippi*, 1898) at the start of the Progressive Era.[12]

Exclusive control over legal and political institutions allowed Progressive Era white constituencies to dictate the shape of democratic institutions, including the earliest public schools and juvenile courts. Access to public education, which civic leaders long recognized as a vital resource for self-realization and informed democratic participation, was a primary target in the racial project of white redemption. Emancipation and federally enforced Reconstruction gave southern black and white youths access to a common school education. Redeemers and their constituents sought to limit these opportunities to white youths alone. An educated black person, they believed, was a likely insurgent, a radical who threatened the desired order of white democracy. Black educational ambition was, thus, criminalized in many slave states and regulated by other means in the post-Emancipation period, including racial terror and institutionalized denials of rehabilitative ideals.

White supremacist ideology, white mobs, and white-dominated court and government authority were powerful mechanisms of resistance to Progressive Era black interests in educational opportunity and political integration,

including youth opportunity and adult influence in juvenile justice administration. Fishing for white votes, southern gubernatorial candidates openly
vowed "not to spend one dollar for nigger education, because education un-
fits the nigger."[13] Elected officials indulged white constituents with various
schemes to keep black children out of schools or provide inferior opportunities. Emboldened white mobs commonly attacked black teachers and
schools.[14] White citizens and officials opposed taxation and other support
for black schools and used their domination of government institutions to
see that "public school funds for black children were diverted to white children." Progressive Era "whites all over the South seized school funds belonging to the disfranchised black citizens, gerrymandered school districts
so as to exclude blacks from certain local tax benefits, and expounded a racist ideology to provide a moral justification of [this] unequal treatment."[15]

Racist ideologies and politics related to education were easily adapted
to penal reform. In 1906, Mississippi governor James Vardaman touted enlightened prison reform and a partial end to the exploitation of prison labor,
claiming to be "more interested in the salvation of men than the hoarding
of gold." Yet his sense of potential moral and mental cultivation and commitment to using state funds for such purposes had race-linked limits:

> A dollar invested in the development of the mind of the white child and
> the cultivation of the mind of the white man and woman, is the best invest-
> ment the State ever made. On the other hand, every dollar invested on negro
> education . . . is an indefensible and unwarranted prodigality of cash. It is a
> crime against the white man who furnishes the dollar and a disadvantage to
> the negro upon whom it is spent. There must be a moral substratum upon
> which to build, or you cannot make a desirable citizen. The negro, as a race,
> is devoid of that element.

The disavowal of a black "moral substratum" subjected formally free black
men, women, and children to all manner of human indignity and social
injustice. Vardaman's insistence that "God Almighty created the negro for
a menial—essentially a servant" defended ongoing exploitation of young
and old black prisoners in Mississippi and the denial of other rights and
welfare resources.[16]

Exclusion of black youths and the black community from juvenile justice
reform was exemplified in a Progressive Era Mississippi legislator's efforts
to gain support for a juvenile reform school mainly serving black children.
He could not overcome the refusal of white taxpayers to invest in black
youths. With black constituents silenced, whites, convinced that "it was no

use trying to reform a Negro," easily defeated the bill.[17] In their 1911 pamphlet *Mississippi's Boy Delinquents*, white leaders of the Juvenile Reformatory Association discussed their policy of denying educational opportunity, political representation, and rehabilitative ideals to black constituents. "We have a Agricultural High School without Negroes; we have a State Normal School without Negroes; we have elections without them," the Association reasoned, "surely we can have a Juvenile Reformatory without them if it is deemed necessary." Mississippi lacked a public reformatory for black youths until the 1940s.[18]

The Progressive Era featured a three-decade-long backlash against black citizens that often turned violent. It was open season on black rights and bodies, and the hunting extended beyond the South. Over two dozen race riots erupted during the 1919 "Red Summer" in northern and southern cities. White mobs attacked black communities to oppose their growing presence, economic competition, and calls for civil rights during the mass exodus from the Jim Crow South. A young J. Edgar Hoover, head of the new Radical Division of the U.S. Department of Justice, investigated the causes of rioting during Red Summer. Black radicalism and subversion, he concluded, not the white community's aggression identified by his federal investigators, had caused the violence.[19]

Black Urban Migration and the Juvenile Court, 1900–1920

Because they were absent in small cities and rural districts, where most Americans still lived, the earliest juvenile courts served only a fraction of the total U.S. population. Just 43 percent of the U.S. population, the Children's Bureau estimated, had access to juvenile courts in 1917 (table 3.1). The nation's largest cities offered full access to courts "specially organized for children," and most residents had access in midsize cities. Access was far more limited in small towns and rural areas, where over half the U.S. population in 1917 lived. In small towns and rural areas, 16 percent of residents had access to juvenile courts.[20]

During the Progressive Era, most blacks lived in the rural South; those who did not were more likely than whites to live where juvenile court reform had been introduced. As table 3.2 illustrates, blacks residing outside the South in 1910 were concentrated in urban areas, more so than whites. In 1910, one-quarter of the black population lived in urban areas; three-quarters of blacks in the North and West were city dwellers, compared to half of whites.[21] Black urban concentration increased with each wave of emigration from the rural South to the city. Black proximity to, and interests

Table 3.1 Percentage of U.S. population served by juvenile courts in 1917 by area

Area (population size)	Proportion of U.S. total population	Proportion served by juvenile court
U.S. total population	100	43
Large cities (100,000+)	25	100
Midsize cities (25,000–100,000)	9	70
Small cities (5,000–25,000)	11	29
Rural and towns (less than 5,000)	55	16

Source: Katharine Lenroot and Emma Lundberg, *Juvenile Courts at Work: A Study of the Organization and Methods of Ten Courts* (Washington, DC: U.S. Department of Labor, Children's Bureau, 1925).

in, juvenile court communities heightened the paradox and conflict inherent in denials of black youth opportunity and adult influence in Jim Crow juvenile justice.

The flagship Chicago Juvenile Court illustrates common aspects of this ordeal of exclusion. In an early study, black youths were significantly represented in the court's caseload. Few black Americans lived in Chicago before the waves of migration around World Wars I and II; in 1903, only 2 percent of Chicago's population was black. That year, the first for which race data are available, about 2 percent of male cases and 6 percent of female cases before the three-year-old Chicago court involved black children. By 1927, black Americans constituted nearly 7 percent of the city's population and black youths 22 percent of the juvenile court caseload. Despite unequal access to rehabilitative court services, the juvenile court movement significantly affected Chicago's rapidly growing black population.[22]

Racial segregation in juvenile court resource allocations influenced outcomes for black dependency and delinquency cases in Chicago and other cities. In a 1927 report, the Chicago juvenile court's chief probation officer called the "difficulty of providing adequate care for the dependent and neglected colored children one of the greatest problems with which the court has to deal. The situation is complicated by a lack of resources in the community comparable with those available for white children in the same circumstances." He explained that "practically no institutions are to be found in the community to which [black] children may be admitted."[23]

Two decades after the Chicago court's creation, a persistent lack of services derailed the rehabilitative ideal for black youths. Without other placement options, officials in Chicago and other cities committed black youths to detention facilities and jail at greater rates and for longer periods than was common for white youths. Contrary to the principle of juvenile justice reform, more black youths were committed to adult prisons. For court-

Table 3.2 Percentage of population residing in urban areas by race and region (1910)

Region	Race	
	Black	White
United States (total)	27.4	48.7
South (total)	21.1	23.2
South Atlantic	22.1	27.0
East South Central	19.2	18.5
West South Central	22.0	22.6
North (Total)	77.4	58.3
New England	91.8	83.2
Middle Atlantic	81.2	70.8
Midwest	76.6	52.3
Plains	67.7	36.6
West (total)	78.6	49.2
Mountain	72.0	36.7
Pacific	83.4	57.0

Source: Bureau of the Census, *Prisoners and Juvenile Delinquents in the United States, 1910* (Washington, DC: Department of Commerce, 1918).

involved black youths, little had changed since the early houses of refuge. A 1913 Hull House study of Chicago's jail populations found that blacks represented less than 3 percent of the city's population but that black boys and men made up 12 percent of the jail population and black girls and women made up nearly one-third of all females in jail. A 1925 Urban League study of detention in New York found that white youths were rarely detained for more than twenty-four hours while black youths commonly spent weeks and months in detention.[24]

When juvenile institutional commitments did come to Chicago's juvenile court, black dependent and delinquent youths of various types and needs were uniformly sent to a state-run institution intended for serious offenders. Juvenile court resources were especially limited for black girls. Barred from private institutions, and accepted only in small numbers at the state-run institution, they remained in detention longest. Thus, dependent black girls had virtually no access to rehabilitative services through Chicago's early juvenile court.[25]

Black Americans settling in other early-twentieth-century cities had similar experiences. White supremacist redemption affected racialized criminal social control, and the Progressive Era witnessed unprecedented mob violence, lynching, and dramatic increases in black criminalization, incarceration, and executions throughout the United States. For black youths, this pattern intensified over the first decades of the twentieth century.[26] Early juvenile court caseloads and commitments suggest that black youths received greater and even disproportionate attention. They entered Progressive Era juvenile courts in large numbers but were denied equal access to the child- and social-welfare networks of juvenile court communities.

Relating Race, Citizenship, and Region to Sanctioning Disparity

The Progressive Era brought increasing rates of black criminalization and confinement as well as continued evidence of sanctioning disparity, including severe punishment of black youths. Shifts in racial group distributions of confined juveniles and adults during the first decade of the twentieth century reveal that black youths and communities were often excluded from mainstream juvenile justice reform. The unique but variable significance of race for equal protection is clear in the different treatment black American and European immigrant delinquents received, in regional variations in juvenile commitments, and in patterns of youth execution following juvenile court reform.

Between 1904 and 1910, the two years for which Progressive Era data on race and incarceration are available, the number of black adults and children in the U.S. incarcerated population increased dramatically (see table 3.3).[27] The increase is especially pronounced for black women and girls. In the 1904 census, black male and female children represented 13 and 15 percent, respectively, of juveniles incarcerated in public institutions nationwide, whether committed to juvenile or adult institutions. By 1910, the proportional representation of black male juveniles in U.S. carceral institutions had doubled to 27.5 percent while that of black girls nearly tripled to 39 percent. Among black incarcerated adults, increases were slightly less, with black women contributing disproportionately to the unprecedented Progressive Era "celling of black bodies."[28]

Prior historical research stresses that poor and foreign-born white youths were a primary target of early child-saving initiatives.[29] Most accounts overlook how this focus disguised the way in which racial privilege was based on a shared white or potentially white racial status, despite distinctions. Nonwhites were racially defined as "subpersons" and regarded as less deserving of access and influence in education, labor, and politics.[30] For liberal rehabilitative ideals, the difference was critical. Under the rubric of *rehabilitation*, white authorities sought to "whiten" European immigrant delinquents (and others) through forced acculturation, discipline, and punishment.

Table 3.3 Group percentages of U.S. incarcerated population by age, race, and gender, 1904 and 1910

Age group and year	White		Black	
	Male	Females	Males	Females
Juveniles:				
1904	87.0	84.5	12.7	15.4
1910	72.2	60.8	27.5	39.1
Adults:				
1904	84.1	78.2	15.3	21.3
1910	79.8	56.8	19.3	42.8

Sources: Bureau of the Census, *Prisoners and Juvenile Delinquents in the United States, 1904* (Washington, DC: Department of Commerce, 1907); Bureau of the Census, *Prisoners and Juvenile Delinquents in the United States, 1910* (Washington, DC: Department of Commerce, 1918).
Note: Juvenile figures include youths committed to adult or juvenile institutions.

European immigrants themselves aspired to whiteness, rightly understanding this status as a valuable form of social capital for upward mobility.[31] Progressive Era white Americans often resisted characterizing European immigrant adults and youths as racially white, with all that implied in terms of sociopolitical inclusion. These outsiders were ridiculed and condemned, with the Irish, for example, caricatured as "niggers turned inside out" to delegitimize their claims to equal opportunity and influence in American society.[32]

Irish and Italian immigrant youths—typically the primary focus of control agents—were thought to be inferior to native whites. They were constructed as marginally superior to nonwhites, however, owing to trace civilizing influences of European ancestry buried beneath ethnic group attachments. Unlike blacks and other nonwhites, European immigrants and their embryonic-citizen children could potentially be reformed into whiteness, a requirement for eventual assimilation into the white body politic.[33] Foreign-born white boys were twice as likely as native ones to be committed to carceral institutions, but in 1910 there was virtually no difference in commitment rates for native and nonnative white girls. This suggests a more general concern with regulating the behavior and development of white girls, reflecting patriarchal interests in enforcing gender norms, and linked to racial politics of Americanizing the stock of potential mothers and wives for future white American families.[34]

Differences in commitment rates between black and white youths and qualitative differences in the nature of institutionalization illustrate how race stratified opportunity in Progressive Era juvenile justice. This was distinct

Table 3.4 Differences in rates of juvenile commitment per 100,000 in the U.S. population, by race, gender, and nativity (1910)

	Coefficients of difference	
Comparison	Boys	Girls
White foreign-born compared to white native (overall)	2.22	1.09
White foreign vs. second-generation native	1.81	1.22
White foreign vs. third-generation native	2.94	1.29
	2.97	4.59
Black compared to white native (overall)		
Black vs. second-generation native	2.42	5.14
Black vs. third-generation native	3.93	5.44
Black compared to white foreign	1.33	4.22

Source: Bureau of the Census, Prisoners and Juvenile Delinquents in the United States, 1910 (Washington, DC: Department of Commerce, 1918).
Note: A value of 1.00 indicates no difference in rate of incarceration, controlling for representation in the population.

from white class and ethnic differences. Black youths came to the attention of Progressive Era courts, as in Chicago, but their sanctioning had a distinct pattern. As table 3.4 shows, in 1910, black juvenile males were nearly three times more likely to be committed to institutions than their native white male counterparts were (and slightly more likely than foreign-born white males). Gender and race interactions feature prominently in the high commitment rate for black girls, who were far more likely to be incarcerated in 1910 than their native and foreign-born white female counterparts were.

Distinct black youth sanctioning appears when disaggregating second- and third-generation white natives.[35] Black males were confined at a rate nearly four times greater than third-generation native white males and approximately three times greater than second-generation native white males. Small differences appear in commitment rates for black and white foreign-born male delinquents, and black girls were over five times more likely than second- and third-generation white girls, and four times more likely than foreign-born white girls, to be institutionalized in 1910. These commitment rate differences are partly related to the greater urban concentration of black and European immigrant youths.

Regional distinctions are also noteworthy. In 1910, black juveniles in the South were confined at rates between three and five times greater than second- and third-generation native whites, respectively, and slightly more frequently than foreign-born whites. These differences pale in comparison with rates outside the South (see table 3.5). In the Midwest (i.e., Ohio, Indiana, Illinois, Michigan, and Wisconsin), for example, black children

Table 3.5 Differences in rates of juvenile commitment per 100,000 in the U.S. population, by race, nativity, and region (1910)

Region	Coefficients of difference		
	Black compared to third-generation white native	Black compared to second-generation white native	Black compared to white foreign-born
New England	7.1	4.4	4.2
Mid-Atlantic	9.6	6.0	4.6
Midwest	13.8	12.8	5.6
Plains	18.2	32.0	10.0
South (Atlantic)	4.4	3.5	1.9
South (East Central)	4.7	4.2	1.3
South (West Central)	3.6	5.0	3.7
Mountain	15.9	10.4	4.2
Pacific	8.0	11.2	6.4

Source: Bureau of the Census, *Prisoners and Juvenile Delinquents in the United States, 1910* (Washington, DC: Department of Commerce, 1918).

and youths were institutionalized at a rate more than ten times greater than second- and third-generation white youths and more than five times greater than foreign-born white youths. In the Mid-Atlantic (New York, New Jersey, and Pennsylvania) and New England (Maine, Massachusetts, Rhode Island, Connecticut, Vermont, and New Hampshire) regions, black youths were committed at rates between five and ten times greater than white youths. In the Mountain and Pacific regions, where black populations were especially small before World War I, black juveniles were committed at rates substantially greater than those for native and foreign-born white children.

The greatest differences in commitment rates occurred in the Plains states (Minnesota, Iowa, Montana, North Dakota, South Dakota, Nebraska, and Kansas), where, in 1910, black children and youths were confined at rates seventeen times greater than second-generation white natives, thirty-two times greater than third-generation white natives, and ten times greater than foreign-born whites. Racial group differences in urban concentrations were also largest in the Plains states, with nearly 70 percent of blacks, and less than 40 percent of whites, living in urban areas that year. In the Midwest and Mountain states, substantial commitment rate differences also correspond to black urban concentrations.

Urbanization and confinement rates for white subpopulations are not broken out in the data. Given patterns of immigrant settlement, foreign-born and second-generation white youths were likely more concentrated in cities. Aside from criminal involvement or court bias, such social-organizational factors increased the likelihood of contact with agents and institutions of juvenile social control. This probably accounts for the comparable commitment rates of black and nonnative white delinquents, who often came to the attention of juvenile justice authorities.

Race-related differences in regional commitments must account for the small number of blacks living outside the South, which inflates their commitment *rate*. Moreover, rigidly enforced racial segregation forced down black institutionalization in the Progressive Era South, exacerbating commitment rate differences between regions. Jim Crow did operate outside the South, but race ordered relations differently by region, in ways that affected criminal justice outcomes. In the South, institutions of social control were less inclined to provide remedial services to blacks, and black subjugation discouraged black families from seeking services from law enforcement and the courts. Many Progressive Era black families moved to centers of juvenile court reform from areas least likely to have specialized courts for black youths. Urban migration thus played an important role in the limited racial integration of juvenile courts and in patterns of institutional commitment and other sanctioning experienced by black youths.

Limits of Early Juvenile Court Contact: Inequality in Institutional Commitments

Black community leaders did not believe that high rates of commitment to juvenile institutions among black youths were disadvantageous. Placements in rehabilitative institutions were coveted for criminal or dependent youths deserving sanctioning, intervention, and support. However, greater black youth exposure to burgeoning juvenile court communities and high rates of juvenile institutionalization generally did not translate into equal black youth and community access to the juvenile court movement's citizen-building ambitions.

Removing criminal and wayward youths from the world of adult courts and prisons was a core objective of the juvenile court movement. Efforts to develop a more diagnostic juvenile court environment and supporting institutional resources (i.e., reformatories) followed this logic. Among the lowest priorities of white-dominated court communities was the development of specialized resources for black dependents and delinquents. Consequently, black youths were extensively committed to adult rather than juvenile institutions in most regions with significant black populations. A decade into the juvenile court movement, nearly three-quarters of committed black

Table 3.6 Percentage of committed youths confined in adult institutions (prisons, jails, and workhouses), by race and region (1910)

Region	Race	
	Black	White
United States (Total)	72.3	35.9
U.S. South (average)	81.8	42.5
South Atlantic	81.6	35.8
East South Central	87.3	41.7
West South Central	76.6	50.1
U.S. North (average)	41.8	32.5
New England	30.0	30.6
Middle Atlantic	47.9	44.3
East North Central	35.9	27.2
West North Central	53.3	27.8
U.S. West (average)	19.8	28.1
Mountain	32.6	34.1
Pacific	6.9	22.0

Source: Bureau of the Census, *Prisoners and Juvenile Delinquents in the United States, 1910* (Washington, DC: Department of Commerce, 1918). Note: Remaining proportions within each racial group were committed to juvenile institutions.

male youths were confined in adult prisons, jails, or workhouses, compared to one-third of all committed white male youths (see table 3.6).[36]

National patterns of black youth commitment to adult institutions largely reflect practices in the South, where most incarcerated black youths were confined during the Progressive Era. In the South, black youths subject to incarceration were almost always confined in adult institutions until the black child-saving movement began to make substantial inroads in the provision of rehabilitative services for black youths around the 1920s. Outside the South, where relatively small black populations were concentrated in urban areas, court-involved black youths were far more likely to be committed to juvenile reformatories, except in the midwestern states, where institutionalized black youths largely remained in adult jails and prisons.

Rates of black youth commitment to institutions vastly exceeded those for native and immigrant white youths in most regions, likely owing to urban concentration and differential rates of court contact. However, comparisons of the types of institutions to which black and white male youths were committed suggest that even marginal white youths enjoyed privileged access to the rehabilitative programs and institutions of juvenile court communities, especially in the South, but also in northern states.[37] The anomaly of black youths in the West being relatively *more likely* than whites to be committed to juvenile rather than adult institutions is likely related to the small number of blacks residing there and the small number of black youths committed to any institution in the West in 1910. However, black youths committed to Progressive Era juvenile institutions nationwide remained subject to segregation and discriminatory treatment.

Differential Involvement in Crime?

The relative seriousness of their offenses is a possible factor in black youths' higher commitment rates and their more severe sanctioning, including commitment to adult prisons. Unfortunately, historical data are inadequate for assessing the relationship of race, offense, and sanctioning. Census data from 1910 do indicate that incarcerated black Americans, regardless of age, were committed for more serious offenses. Blacks represented about 11 percent of the U.S. population in 1910 but constituted 56 percent of "grave homicide" commitments, 49 percent of lesser homicide commitments, 41 percent of assault commitments, and 33 percent of robbery commitments that year.[38]

Since they are not disaggregated by age, national commitment offense data are of little use for interpreting racial group differences in Progressive Era juvenile offending and confinement. Local juvenile offense data do suggest that, although serious juvenile offenders existed during the Progressive Era, relatively few youths were committed to institutions for grave homicide or other serious person or property offenses. Regional differences cannot be isolated in these data, a necessary condition for distinguishing southern justice systems. Yet local data from at least one southern state suggest generally similar patterns of offending among white and black youths. These data do not indicate offense history or other aggravating and mitigating factors, which is necessary for accounting for the relation between offending, varying rates of commitment, and the severity of sanctions.[39]

Progressive Era official statistics based on police and court decisions pose problems because of the political nature of law and law enforcement. This affects interpretations of race-related commitment differences. Legislatures, law enforcement officials, and courts controlled by white authorities were hostile or indifferent to black claims to equal protection. They were prone to overenforcement in cases of black offenders and underprotection in cases of black victims, distorting records of crime and justice processes. In Thorsten Sellin's view, using institutional commitment statistics to interpret criminal behavior assumes that "the proportionate number of arrests, convictions, or commitments to the total number of offenses actually committed is the same in [black and white racial] groups. This assumption is untenable, for there are specific factors which seriously distort the arrest, conviction, and commitment rates for Negroes without affecting these rates for whites in a similar manner. No measurement has as yet been devised for the evaluation of these factors."[40]

The corrective must account for the many cases in which false charges were lodged against blacks for rape and murder, for example, in consensual relations and self-defense and in which white perpetrators of grave homicide by lynching and other means, manslaughter, aggravated assaults, arson, etc. eluded crime and incarceration data because police and the courts overlooked their acts. Unpunished white crime committed during crime-prone youth and young adulthood, including mob violence against blacks, was significant but is of unknown quantity.[41] White children commonly witnessed lynchings and often participated without legal consequences. In 1917, adults compelled a ten-year-old to castrate a black lynching victim in Texas, and adults held up a young boy to throw the rope over the branch of a tree before a 1931 lynching in Maryland. In 1903, the *Chicago Herald* reported that a Wilmington, Delaware, lynching involved a white mob of "300 men and boys," and, in 1900, a mob composed exclusively of white boys unsuccessfully tried to lynch a twelve-year-old black youth in Richmond, Virginia; four of the white boys, all under thirteen years of age, were arrested, but their only punishment for this attack was a fine.[42]

Arrest, prison commitment, and other official data from the period cannot account for differences in the severity of sanctioning or for differential involvement in crime. They do enable comparisons of the charges against and the sanctioning of black and white youths appearing in early juvenile courts. Detailed juvenile offense and sanctioning data from North Carolina illustrate that black and white delinquents entering Progressive Era juvenile justice systems were differentiated, not by offense differences, but by the racial politics of juvenile justice administrations. They highlight the explicit neglect, exploitation, and violence of Jim Crow juvenile justice in the South, which encompassed most black Americans.

Juvenile Court Reform in the Jim Crow South

Liberal penal reforms and the juvenile court movement came late to the South. The court first took root in North Carolina in 1915, but a skeletal statewide system appeared only in 1919, as the Progressive Era was coming to a close. As the Children's Bureau observed, rural areas, including much of

North Carolina, were especially slow to adopt the new courts. Even "specially organized" courts typically failed to live up to the distinction. "Many of the county juvenile court judges were unfamiliar with principles and procedure of juvenile courts," a state investigation concluded, "and in some instances the judges were actually hostile to the juvenile court movement, thinking it was merely a method of 'letting the youthful criminal go free.'"[43]

To philosophical differences were added financial and political impediments to meaningful reform. Reluctance to appropriate state funds to operate separate courts and youth services further delayed and limited the development of North Carolina's juvenile justice system. Formally in place by 1919, the new juvenile court was slow to implement progressive principles and, thus, to supplant older patterns and practices of social control, especially for disenfranchised black youths and communities.[44]

North Carolina's Juvenile Cases and Sanctions

Between 1919 and 1934, North Carolina gradually and selectively embraced the juvenile court movement. These courts reveal much about southern Jim Crow juvenile justice. Data on race and youth outcomes provide a detailed, though distorted, perspective on differences in adjudicating and disposing of black and white delinquency and dependency cases. Only 4 percent of adjudicated delinquents in this period were charged with person offenses. Black delinquents, especially girls, were somewhat more likely than their white counterparts to be determined delinquent for person offenses. Delinquency adjudications for person offenses ranged from 3.8 (1919–29) to 3.1 (1929–34) percent for white males and 5.7 and 5.2 percent for black males. In these periods, 1.1 and 0.5 percent of white girls were adjudicated delinquent for person offenses, compared to 5 and 7.3 percent of black girls. Differences between black and white youths remain clouded by racial discrepancies in official responses to crime, including racial violence.[45]

Second, property and status offenses were most common in male and female delinquency adjudications. Over half of white (52.57 and 58.5 percent) and black (55.1 and 64.3 percent) males were found delinquent for property offenses in the periods 1919–29 and 1929–34, respectively. Girls were sanctioned for property offenses less frequently than boys were, with adjudications more common among black girls (29.4 and 32.3 percent in the two periods) than among white girls (10 and 15.5 percent). Most male and female delinquency adjudications for property offenses involved larceny.[46]

Finally, most girls adjudicated delinquent in North Carolina courts in the period were status offenders, that is, sanctioned for noncriminal acts, such as immorality, truancy, and running away, pertinent only to juveniles. In these periods, status offenses made up 79 and 70 percent of white girls' adjudications and 55 and 47 percent of black girls' delinquency adjudications. Smaller but significant numbers of white (28 and 24.4 percent) and black (25 and 20 percent) boys were sanctioned for status offenses.[47]

Reported involvement in serious crime did not differ significantly for white and black delinquents. Between 1919 and 1934, 12 percent of white males and 9 percent of black males were charged with serious *property* offenses (burglary, arson, breaking and entering); figures for white and black girls were 1 and 2 percent, respectively. In this period, serious *person* offenses (i.e., robbery, murder, manslaughter, rape, and attempted rape) were evenly distributed, constituting about 1 percent of white and black male adjudications and less than 1 percent of white and black female adjudications. Overall, 13 percent of white boys, 11 percent of black boys, 1 percent of white girls, and 1.5 percent of black girls were adjudicated delinquent in North Carolina juvenile courts for serious person or property offenses.[48]

Given the similar severity of white and black offenses, nearly proportional group distributions across categories of court sanctions might be expected. Instead, certain sanctions were reserved mainly for white youths and others for black youths. Though white male and female youths constituted about 55 percent of all delinquency adjudications between 1919 and 1929, they made up over 75 percent of all delinquents placed in juvenile reformatories. Of the approximately 44 percent of delinquents who were black, 80 percent were hired out to private interests. Black youths were also overrepresented among those punished by parents, sentenced to county jail, and sent to the county home, "where dangers of moral contamination [were] almost as great as in the county jail."[49]

Salient details about the mechanisms and implications of racialized social control are buried within official statistics on race and case characteristics in the state. Like 1910 census officials, Sanders and his colleagues noted that North Carolina juvenile crime and commitment data could be read only in relation to the state's race and gender politics of juvenile justice. The "juvenile courts are white courts," the researchers explained, and "the judge of the juvenile court and the chief probation officer in every case is a white official." In "only a few instances are there subordinate Negro probation officers for handling the cases of Negro children." "The judges of the juvenile court are all men," they add, "which might color the attitude of the judges in handling [white and black] boys' cases as compared with girls."[50]

These factors likely influenced all cases, but Jim Crow juvenile justice is distinctly revealed in dependency and status offense cases, in the differential treatment of black girls, and in the oppositional responses of black communities. The juvenile court model promised novel, individualized responses to an array of problems and needs presented by children and their families, including youths who violated criminal laws, status offenders and dependents, and children and youths deemed in need of parental state support to compensate for the failure or death of natural parents or legal guardians.

In North Carolina and other states, white youths enjoyed privileged access to a range of innovative and protective child- and social-welfare services. Between 1919 and 1934, nearly 20 percent of white males and 60 percent of white females coming before North Carolina's juvenile court were dependency or neglect cases, compared to 10 and 30 percent of black male and female cases, respectively. Since black Carolinians in the period had "a higher illegitimacy rate, higher death rate, less stable form of family life, more desertion, etc. than the whites," researchers expected to find comparable, if not greater, group distributions in black delinquency and dependency cases. Just 6 percent of black girls were charged with "sexual immorality" (a status offense) or premature sexual activity, compared to 24 percent of white girls. Researchers looked more closely at the official infrequency of black sexual immorality because the figures were "so much at variance with experiences of white and black social workers in the state" assisting in the North Carolina studies.[51]

The low representation of black youths (especially girls) among status offenders and dependency cases was due to racial oppression and domination in the state's Jim Crow juvenile courts. The black community had resisted, but white court officials, the authors determined, were disinclined to consider the nuances of black juvenile dependency and delinquency cases or to individualize responses to their apparent problems or needs. Much has been made of the gendered oppression of the parental state, such as its efforts to police and control the sexuality of girls and women, but North Carolina's white, male-dominated juvenile court communities were indifferent to the precocious sexuality of black girls and little concerned with their equal protection. "Just as there is a dual standard of morality for boys and girls," Sanders and his colleagues explained, "there is a dual standard of morality for the whites and the Negroes. The juvenile court judges are white officials, and consequently regard a sex offense by a white girl far more seriously than a similar offense by a Negro girl. Many white people, among them court-house officials, hold the view that practically all Negro girls are sexually delinquent, and if a judge of a juvenile court began hearing cases of this sort he would be swamped with work."[52]

Some white state officials shared the pervasive belief that the early sexual activity of black girls protected the more important priority of defending white delinquent daughters, future white families, and white civil society. When interviewing for the position of county superintendent of public welfare in a North Carolina jurisdiction, a white male applicant was asked whether there was significant delinquency where he worked before. He answered: "There was practically none among the white girls [but] of course, there were some white boys who had sex relations with Negro girls." This was "a good thing," he added, "because it protected the white girls."[53]

The predominance of dependency and noncriminal delinquency cases among white girls stemmed from their differential access to services in southern juvenile court communities. Relatively few North Carolina juvenile reformatory institutions served black delinquent or dependent youths before the 1940s. At the time of the studies in question, two orphanages were available to black children in the state. With a capacity of 355 children, they provided the only dependency services to blacks; serving white dependent and neglected children in the state were twenty-eight institutions with a capacity of over 4,500.

This structural inequality distorted North Carolina juvenile court data. Despite being dependency cases, many black dependents were adjudicated delinquent to gain placement in an institution. The court often released black children without processing because judges were disinclined to hear cases when no institution was available for commitment.[54] Finally, black communities refused to subject black youths to the court's denial of equal protection.

Black North Carolinians countered separate and unequal juvenile justice by relying on mutual aid, rather than the court, to provide support for troubled black children and families. "[Since] the Negroes have had such a hard time getting justice in the white man's adult criminal court," Sanders and his colleagues report, "they refused to report their delinquent children to the white man's juvenile court." They continue: "Negroes, [as] a minority group, have developed a persecuted race complex and stand by one another in time of trouble to a far greater degree than the white people. When Negro children are left orphans through the death of their parents, their relatives or even their neighbors gladly take the orphans into their own home. When white children are left orphans the first impulse of the white community, including the white relatives, is to send the children to an asylum." Before the 1940s, the combined racial politics of "the white man's court" and black community resistance to Jim Crow juvenile justice resulted in "the great majority of immoral Negro girls never coming to the juvenile court."[55]

These detailed North Carolina studies remain among the most penetrating examinations of the complex, fluid, and contentious racial politics of American juvenile justice. They reveal how Progressive Era reforms and official data on racial differences in delinquency and dependency were distorted by the patterns of oppression, domination, and resistance characteristic of Jim Crow juvenile justice.[56]

Severe Sanctioning of Black Youths in the Progressive Era South

Jim Crow juvenile justice systems subjected black youths to severe and violent punishments, including executions, whippings, commitment to adult prisons, and continued ordeals of convict-labor exploitation. Records from multiple southern states offer a chilling portrait of this indifference to the well-being of black children and youths in the decades surrounding the juvenile court movement. Over 80 percent of black youths confined in the South were committed to adult penal institutions in 1910; the figure for their white counterparts—who bore a similar but lighter burden during the South's embrace of the juvenile court movement—was 40 percent.

From 1900 to 1950, as the South developed juvenile court communities and institutionalized segregation, the experiences of southern black and white youths in American juvenile justice became increasingly dissimilar and unequal. In 1910, the year Tennessee established its first juvenile court, 83 percent of the juvenile inmates in its adult workhouses and jails were black. Between 1890 and 1915, "the percentage of [state prisoners] under 20 years of age was consistently around one-third," and over 80 percent were black. Despite rhetoric about modernizing Louisiana's juvenile justice around 1900 and the opening of a reformatory in 1910, "six white and nineteen black youths, all between twelve and sixteen years of age, could still be found among the adult offenders" two years later.[57]

In Mississippi, where "white taxpayers refused to 'waste' money on the needs of 'incorrigible' young blacks," the mainly black prison population raised cotton from before sunup until after sundown, in conditions rivaling antebellum plantations. Managers of the Mississippi State Penitentiary at Parchman relied on techniques borrowed from plantation slavery, such as a system of trustees and liberal recourse to "black Annie," a leather strap, three feet long and six inches wide, used to publicly whip inmates and coerce compliance with prison orders. The lash was deemed an especially suitable technology in a prison filled with "the wayward children of former slaves," a Parchman physician explained, providing a familiar means of punishing and intimidating these inmates, thus "keeping them at the labor required of them." Black youths were prominent among Mississippi prisoners in the late nineteenth century and the early twentieth. According to David Oshinsky, "black children [were] a vital part of Mississippi's powerful convict labor machine," such that, by 1880, "at least one convict in four was a black adolescent or child—a percentage that did not diminish over time." Among them was eight-year-old Will Evans, sentenced in 1891 to two years in prison for "grand larceny," specifically, "stealing some change from the counter of a dry goods store."[58]

Between 1918 and 1931 in North Carolina, where approximately 30 percent of all juveniles (residents sixteen years of age and younger) were black, 60 percent of youths sent to state prison in this span were black. Among them were "eight children, all Negro, under fourteen years of age, and hence belonging under the exclusive jurisdiction of the juvenile court [and] committed illegally to the State Prison." They received far lengthier sentences in North Carolina state prisons than their white counterparts did, with 31 percent of black youths, compared to 17 percent of their white counterparts, facing sentences of five years or more. "[Since] there is no difference in the seriousness of offenses of whites as compared with Negro children," Sanders and his colleagues note, "the difference in length of sentences of the two races is due apparently to race prejudice."[59]

A related factor was the interest in exploiting black labor. In the first half of the twentieth century, especially in the South, a prison sentence for a juvenile was severe in relative terms, often translating into extreme violence and exploitation. Well into the twentieth century, black youths remained subject to the brutal convict-lease system and other penal labor arrangements. Most states, including Mississippi (1890), Alabama (1893), Tennessee (1896), South Carolina (1897), Louisiana (1901), and Georgia (1908), legislatively abolished convict leasing around the turn of the century, but the exploitation of prison labor endured in new forms, such as chain gangs, which often included black children and youths.[60]

Progressive Era social reformers and labor unions were influential in the demise of the convict lease, as were opportunistic government officials, who realized the profit value of retaining control of prison labor.[61] "If the State can make money working a private individual's land and giving that private individual half of the products toil," Governor Vardaman of Mississippi reasoned in a 1906 speech to legislators, "I cannot understand why it cannot make more money working its own land and keeping the entire product of the convict's toil." Such arguments crippled a lease system that was overrun with critics, facilitating the rise of the convict work gang as "the prominent penal reform in the early-twentieth-century South."[62]

To rationalize the shift to chain gangs, it was argued that the state had too long shirked responsibility for managing convicts while pilfering the public treasure. They emerged as a novel but familiar blend of racialized populist and exploitative ideals, with explicit links to chattel slavery. Apparently with the Thirteenth Amendment in mind, one reformer argued for replacing the private lease with a state-run system: "The convict is as much the property of the state as the slave before the war was the property of the slave owner." Another advocate reasoned that the state is the convict's real master and, as such, is responsible, not just for his well-being, "but for the productivity of his labor to the end that the community at large may be served." That interest did not include the free black communities from which most prisoners would come, and hoped to return to, following their terms of penal enslavement.[63]

Similarities between convict work gangs, lease systems, and the ordeals of slavery that they replaced are evident in the racial ideology rationalizing their exploitation and violence.[64] In Georgia, where more than 90 percent of convict laborers were black, chain gang work on public roads was commonly defended as "particularly appropriate to southern conditions because blacks were perceived as suited to the heavy unskilled labor it required and . . . the discipline of coerced outdoor labor was perceived as beneficial to [them]." This logic appealed to white southerners, small local governments, and federal officials. A federal engineer argued in 1912 that the chain gang was perfect for the South since the region was dominated by black prisoners "who benefited by outdoor manual labor, and whose moral standard is not lowered" by working in public wearing prison stripes.[65]

This enduring claim that blacks were amoral maintained a dialectic of exclusion. It rationalized chattel slavery and, later, the inhumanity of the lease and the chain gang, the strategic neglect and exploitation of sexually active black girls in North Carolina, the blocking of access to education for black youths and communities, and other Progressive Era denials of citizen-building ideals and resources.

Continued confinement of black youths in adult prisons was not found solely in southern juvenile court communities. Progressive Era black youths in the North and West were more likely to be committed to juvenile institutions, but they also encountered more subtle boundaries of Jim Crow juvenile justice. Black youths in the Plains states were far more concentrated in urban areas and were committed to institutions at higher rates than were white youths in this region. They were far *less* likely than white youths in the region to be sent to reformatories. Indeed, this is the only nonsouthern region where most confined black youths were in adult institutions.

Two decades after juvenile courts were established in Philadelphia and Pittsburgh (in 1903), black youths were still being sent to state prison. Examining juvenile commitments to state prison in the 1920s, Wolcott and Schlossman report: "Blacks constituted approximately 3.3 percent of Pennsylvania's population in 1920 (and 3 percent of males 15 to 19), [but] 30 percent of the mid-teens sent to prison." Elaborating on these disparities, they write: "We might be tempted to guess that blacks were more likely than whites to perpetrate serious crimes that could land them in prison, but this was not the case. In fact, the offense profiles of both racial groups were strikingly similar. . . . Thus, judges may have been quicker to pull the trigger of state prison on young black offenders than on young white offenders. It may have required less severe or persistent crime before judges were ready to impose the harshest penalty in their arsenal—state prison—upon [black youths]."[66] The relative absence of juvenile institutions serving black youths in Philadelphia, Pittsburgh, and other Pennsylvania cities accounts for higher rates of black youth incarceration in adult prisons. Reforms in juvenile justice remained focused on white youths and communities, as elsewhere in the United States.

Beyond the influence of patterns of urbanization and the diffusion of the juvenile court on commitment rate differences among black and white juveniles, other factors more powerfully affected racial differences in Progressive Era case outcomes. Among the institutional ordeals that youths faced were persistent power imbalances in racial groups, race-based commitments to rehabilitative ideals, and selective investments in the institutional resource base of white civil society. Through inadequate resources for black youths, white-dominated governments defined Progressive Era juvenile justice reform as a white citizen-building initiative.

Black communities would wait decades before their youths would enjoy the presumptive right to rehabilitative ideals and resources. Yet many black youths who eluded confinement in adult institutions often found similarly exploitative and violent regimes in juvenile reformatories. The Tennessee State Training and Agricultural School for Colored Boys illustrates the systemic nature of Jim Crow juvenile justice during and after the Progressive Era. The school opened in 1921 and held black and white youths (in separate branches). Following the discovery of timber and mineral resources in the area in 1935, however, it was used exclusively to forcefully extract the cheap labor of black boys. As reported in the early 1940s: "No academic or formal education existed in this institution and work consisted of farming, mining, dairying and work in the dining hall." A minister visiting the "school" in 1944 protested the discipline maintained through "brute force, with a club to support it." To counter the considerable temptation to escape, the school maintained a "neighborhood-watch" system whereby "local farmers could collect $10 and a sack of grain for every escapee brought back to the institution, dead or alive."[67]

Jim Crow Juvenile Justice: Summary and Conclusion

For the historian John Dittmer, "the term Progressive Era has not well served to define the United States during the early twentieth century."[68] Liberal reforms, scientific innovation, professionalism, and other forces behind the invention of the juvenile court stacked up against the high point in black lynchings, poll taxes, racist pseudoscience, and generally exclusive white influence in government, including the parental state. Black America saw the birth of the juvenile court, like the popular film *Birth of a Nation* (1915), as a testament to the resilience and determination of a white democracy, rather than a cultural symbol or institutional resource for impending democratic inclusion.

Development of the juvenile court expressed the liberal democratic idealism coinciding with Emancipation and Reconstruction and could have been a unique institutional asset for racial reconciliation and the generational redistribution of racial group opportunity and influence in American civil society. Had the unfinished revolution of Reconstruction continued beyond the 1890s and through the Progressive Era, the juvenile court may have helped redefine the social position of black America and push the nation toward a new multiracial and ethnic democracy. Instead, the juvenile court represented a progressive opportunity lost, especially for black Americans.

Early juvenile court reforms did not achieve the ideal of a new diagnostic, individualized approach to juvenile social control. The citizen-building agenda of the rehabilitative ideal was neither well executed nor consistently realized. Such reforms were linked to earlier, ongoing commitments to racialized civic exclusion through the moral and political choice to limit liberal experimentation to white and potentially white youths. A remarkable experiment in racial democracy may have flourished had the juvenile court movement genuinely embraced nonwhite youths and communities, extending equal protection and representation in the administration of rehabilitative ideals.

By institutionalizing white supremacist politics and black democratic exclusion, the juvenile court movement played a unique role in the generational maintenance of separate and unequal race relations. Black contemporaries recognized how Jim Crow juvenile justice systems maintained white power and undermined black freedom. They struggled for generations to dismantle its mechanisms of racialized civic exclusion. The next chapter will consider the social organization of Jim Crow juvenile justice, with its characteristic racial oppression and domination, to further contextualize the black child-saving movement.

FOUR

The Social Organization of Jim Crow Justice

Having described general dimensions of racial inequality in American juvenile justice over the nineteenth century and the early twentieth, I focus
in this chapter on the societal mechanisms and implications of Jim Crow
juvenile justice. This sociological interpretation helps account for the formation and endurance of this peculiar institution while also providing
context for the *oppositional* racial project it inspired—the black child-saving
movement—which is the focus of the second part of the book. My basic
argument here is that Jim Crow juvenile justice was a racially oppressive
social system that grew and flourished amid the racial group power imbalance created by denials of black representation. Without reciprocal black
authority, white supremacist notions of child and social welfare situated
black youths, families, and constituencies outside the moral universe of human and civic obligation. An ethic of care concerning black dependents and
delinquents existed but was marginalized in Jim Crow juvenile court communities. As the early Boston, New York, and Chicago juvenile court communities demonstrate, the well-being of black youths was considered, but
it was not a priority of the white-dominated parental state. Black Americans
showed tremendous concern for black youth protection, in the interest of
youth and community welfare, yet white domination of the public sphere
led to monopolization of child-welfare resources and authority. Thus, Jim
Crow juvenile justice was defined by a dynamic of underdevelopment, a systematic attempt to deny black youth (and, therefore, community) development, or self-realization, through the racially selective provision of parental
state resources.[1] In the urban North, this oppression typically manifested
as institutionalized neglect or subtle exploitation, while the oppression of
black youths and communities in the South often took more explicit, violent, and politically expressive forms.

Denial of participatory parity or equal racial group influence in the administration of justice was the most prominent organizational feature.[2] Until the second half of the twentieth century, white adult authority was nearly absolute, with black adults excluded from the deliberative legal and legislative milieus of juvenile justice. Few black authorities worked in juvenile court communities, especially outside marginal service roles, and the wider power structure—which denied voting rights, quality education, and labor market opportunity—severely limited the collective capacity of the black community to express and protect group interests in juvenile justice policy and practice. Early attempts to diversify the legal domain generally occurred under the pretense of maintaining racial hierarchy. Black juvenile probation officers and other service workers were sought as specialists to serve in black communities, but they were underpaid and underresourced and possessed little authority. The most fundamental characteristic was the absence of democratic control since this was the key *mechanism* rather than an outcome of Jim Crow juvenile justice. These relations of racial oppression and domination, which defined Jim Crow juvenile justice systems, became the main target of oppositional movements to transform the racial structure of American juvenile justice.[3]

Loving the White Delinquent: Regional Patterns

Nationwide, domination and oppression were characteristic of Jim Crow juvenile justice during the first half of the twentieth century. These relations were dynamic and variable across time and social context. Most acute and dramatic in the American South, where most blacks lived until World War II, they were also realities in places such as Chicago, New York, and Los Angeles, where black adult influence and youth opportunity were more subtly denied. Contact of black youths with the juvenile courts became more common, but black adults enjoyed little recognition or influence in terms of the authority of the parental state. Before the post-1960 civil rights reforms, black youths were typically denied equal access to rehabilitative court resources.

Black migration patterns and population characteristics are reflected in regional variations in Jim Crow juvenile justice in the American South and urban North (see table 4.1). Until the late 1920s, over eight of ten black Americans lived in the South. In the first wave of the Great Migration (1910–40), over one million southern blacks moved to midwestern and northeastern cities. Far fewer made it to the American West. Several million more seeking equal protection and opportunity joined a second wave of

Table 4.1 Regional concentrations and proportions of the black population in the United States, 1880–1970

Year	Black population (% of U.S.)	Concentration of black population (%)					Year	Black proportion of population (%)			
		South	Northeast	Midwest	West	Total		South	Northeast	Midwest	West
1880	6.581 (13.1)	90.5	3.5	5.9	.2	100	1880	36.0	1.6	2.2	.7
1890	7.470 (11.9)	90.3	3.6	5.8	.4	100	1890	34.0	1.6	1.9	.9
1900	8.834 (11.6)	89.7	4.4	5.6	.3	100	1900	32.3	1.8	1.9	.7
1910	9.828 (10.7)	89.0	4.9	5.5	.5	100	1910	29.8	1.9	1.8	.7
1920	10.463 (9.9)	85.2	6.5	7.6	.8	100	1920	26.9	2.3	2.3	.9
1930	11.891 (9.6)	78.7	9.6	10.6	1.0	100	1930	24.7	3.3	3.3	1.0
1940	12.865 (9.8)	77.0	10.6	11.0	1.3	100	1940	23.8	3.8	3.5	1.2
1950	15.042 (10.0)	68.0	13.4	14.8	3.8	100	1950	21.7	5.1	5.0	2.9
1960	18.860 (10.6)	59.9	16.0	18.3	5.8	100	1960	20.6	6.8	6.7	3.9
1970	22.580 (11.1)	53.0	19.2	20.2	7.5	100	1970	19.1	8.9	8.1	4.9

Source: Campbell Gibson and Kay Jung, *Historical Census Statistics on Population Totals by Race, 1790 to 1990, and by Hispanic Origin, 1970 to 1990, for the United States, Regions, Divisions, and States*, Population Division Working Paper no. 56 (Washington, DC: U.S. Census Bureau, 2002).
Note: Population is given in millions (rounded to tens of thousands).

migration (1940–70) to the urban North and West. Most blacks going west moved to California, settling especially in Los Angeles and San Francisco.[4]

Before 1950, juvenile court communities out west were anomalous given the relative absence of black youths and families. The topic merits study, but, since this book focuses on the South, Northeast, and Midwest, where black Americans were overwhelmingly concentrated, I draw on existing research for the social organization of Jim Crow juvenile justice in the western United States.[5]

Despite the realities of oppression and domination in the West, the region afforded black youths greater access to juvenile justice resources than was common elsewhere.[6] Given the West's smaller black populations, white-dominated juvenile courts were more willing and able to provide reformatory access to black dependents and delinquents. Black populations were less threatening to white social, economic, and political interests. Absent were key elements of white opposition to black child- and social-welfare initiatives elsewhere: black youths could be accommodated without jeopardizing access for white youths and without the need for substantial investments of public funds in separate services.[7] Thus, institutionalized black youths in early western juvenile court communities were as likely to be committed to reformatories as their white counterparts were. In 1910, 78 percent of black youths and 72 percent of white youths were committed to juvenile institutions (fifty-six black youths vs. nearly one thousand white youths).[8]

Black populations in some western jurisdictions voluntarily relied more often on juvenile court services owing to perceived opportunities for relatively equitable treatment and the lack of community-based alternatives, such as the mutual aid North Carolina's black communities developed during the 1920s and 1930s to shield youths from oppressive justice systems. Black parents in Los Angeles, and particularly single mothers, sought assistance from the court in disciplining their children. The interactive nature of systems of social control highlights how structure and agency combine to shape these processes and influences efforts to reorganize the racial structure of American juvenile justice.[9] In the interim, small black populations in the West lacked alternatives besides appealing to the court for support. Compared to white and Latino youths, black youths were less prone to escape from a southern California reform school, and they had smaller support networks to turn to in less entrenched black communities.[10]

In some western jurisdictions, black youths had better access to juvenile institutions, and some parents were inclined to use it. Ongoing white domination of justice administration concerned black leaders in the West, who looked to participatory parity in local, state, and federal government agencies to secure quality employment and to protect black youth and community interests.[11] Mary Odem's study of Progressive Era juvenile justice reform in Los Angeles notes that black "citizens had organized in 1914 and 1921 to demand the instatement of black juvenile probation officers, but the probation office would not alter its hiring practices."[12] White domination of deliberative milieus varied little across regions before the 1940s and 1950s, compared to black youth access to services. The denial of black adult authority was a distinct mechanism common to the development and maintenance of separate and unequal juvenile justice throughout the United States.

Oppression and domination appear most prominent in the Jim Crow juvenile justice systems of western states closer to the Deep South and with larger black populations. Texas modernized its juvenile justice system in 1913. Passage of its Juvenile Delinquency and Neglect Act established the juvenile court.[13] Several years passed before the state provided separate services for youths. Having nowhere to commit delinquent girls until 1916, a prominent Texas judge admitted that, despite the juvenile court legislation, the parental state had been doing "nothing for delinquent girls at all in Texas . . . just [waiting] until they became of age, old enough to be put in the penitentiary."[14]

Reforms in Texas illustrate the broader social-organizational roots of Jim Crow inequality in juvenile justice. Patrick Henry, the president of Wichita Business College, resigned in 1913 to address the lack of a separate juvenile court and justice system in Texas. He ran for the Texas legislature "for the avowed purpose only of passing a juvenile court law." After the juvenile court law passed, a judge encouraged Henry to sponsor a girls' training school bill, which he had already written. The judge and a law professor at University of Texas Law School, which included no black students or faculty and was openly hostile to civil rights, had already "worked out an ideal bill dealing with a training school [for girls]."[15] Thus, a marriage of racialized moral conviction and white domination of the public sphere brought another reformatory for white youths into the Republic.

In 1916, the governor of Texas signed legislation creating the Gainesville State School for Girls, a 161-acre facility just outside a town founded in 1850 on the California Trail. Its "ideal plan" reserved the reformatory for white girls. Although the reformatory was partially supported by public funds, black girls were unwelcome. A decade later, the 1927 Texas legislature established a reformatory for black girls. Since no funds were appropriated, no institution was established.[16] Not until 1947 did Texas establish an

institution open to black girls. The new reformatory was located at a shuttered federal internment camp in a remote area near Brady. The town was in
the middle of the state and over two hundred miles from the nearest black
metropolis in Dallas. Use of the internment camp conveyed an aversion to
the idea of black citizen building and was akin to nineteenth-century plans
at the Philadelphia House of Refuge to send black youths to Liberia and to
frequent juvenile court characterizations of *colored* as a foreign nationality
rather than a category of U.S. citizens. Black delinquents and dependents
remained prisoners of yet unresolved civil wars over the boundaries of
American democracy. Long before they were born, girls confined at Brady
had been defined as the "extravasated blood" of the nation—alien and
expendable—so it would seem appropriate within the racial logic of the
white parental state to commit black youths (and adult workers) to a
disused prison for outsiders.[17]

The Brady State School for Negro Girls was doomed to fail. Led by a black
woman superintendent, as was not uncommon by the 1940s, it struggled
to recruit and retain a qualified staff owing to its low salaries and undesirable location. After barely three years, the school was closed, relocated, and
renamed. It reopened as the Colored Girls Training School in the east Texas
town of Crockett. The site was chosen because over 80 percent of black
Texans lived in segregated communities within one hundred miles in every
direction. Twenty-nine black girls were transferred from Brady to Crockett
in 1950. In 1954, the *Brown v. Board Education* decision threatened to break
up the historically black Crockett School, yet the separate and unequal
institution lasted for more than another decade while desegregation was
contested. In 1966, *colored* was finally dropped from the school's name.[18]

Institutionalized Neglect: Jim Crow Juvenile Justice in the Urban North

Black youths and communities in the urban North encountered less violent
and often more benign forms of neglect at the hands of a white-dominated
parental state during the first half of the twentieth century. White civic leaders, who exclusively controlled the parental state until the mid-twentieth
century, often expressed concern for the well-being of black children and
families. Nonetheless, black community influence remained marginal to
citizen-building efforts and to access to resources. In Chicago's early juvenile court community, black youths remained in detention homes for extended periods. These facilities were intended for short-term confinement
and offered few rehabilitative services. Secular and religious organizations
generally refused to serve nonwhite dependents and delinquents. Black

youths were sent to any institution that would take them, regardless of individualized needs or whether they were dependency or delinquency cases. Outcomes were better than in the South, where racial status was also the primary criterion, but the absence of a service continuum for black youths in northern contexts similarly restricted access to rehabilitative ideals and services.

Indifference was not necessarily the issue. Hull House leader Louise deKoven Bowen, who served as a trustee, the treasurer, and the board president of the Chicago settlement house, wrote in 1913 of the organization's involvement with the city's growing black population. The Hull House–based Juvenile Protective Association of Chicago, of which Bowen was president, studied boys in the county jail. The association was "startled" to find black boys and young men so disproportionately represented. "Although the colored people of Chicago approximate one-fortieth of the entire population," its study reported, "one-eighth of the boys and young men, and nearly one-third of the girls and young women, who had been confined in the jail during the year, were Negroes." The association learned that employment agencies were sending young black women to work as maids in houses of prostitution. Such referrals would never be made for white girls, it complained, given their protected "moral fragility" and the probability of pandering charges.[19]

Neither Hull House nor the Chicago juvenile court intervened to reduce these disparities, probably because black community needs were a low priority. "More than most of their generation," one study concludes, "Hull House residents were troubled by the unequal lot of the Negro, and certainly more than most, they tried to do something about it. But because there were not many Negroes in their neighborhood, because there were so many other problems, and because of the racist attitudes of their day, Hull House residents, in the period before World War I, devoted a rather small amount of time to the situation of black people." The Juvenile Protective Association expressed alarm but left it to black clubwomen to create their own employment referrals, safe homes, and other services for black girls and young women migrating to the city.[20]

Immediately following the founding of the juvenile court in Boston in 1906, court social workers recognized that court services for black children were inadequate. Boston settlement house leaders responded in 1908 by establishing the Robert Gould Shaw House as an auxiliary to the white South End Settlement House. Named for the white commanding officer of the first all-black regiment to enter the Civil War, Shaw House was described by its directors as "unique among Boston's neighborhood houses in that it alone studies, and, to the limits of its power and resources, deals constructively with America's most pressing problem—the race question." Boston's South End was the "most densely populated Negro section," and Shaw House was meant to respond to the discrimination faced by the city's rapidly growing black population. Noting how the "bias of the Whites in settlement clubs and classes acts practically to close settlement opportunity to the Colored people," Shaw House declared itself "dedicated to ideals of fair play and equal opportunity." It gave black families and youths in the South End "first claim" to its services but did not deny access to whites: "The House stands for cooperation, looking to a finer citizenship for both races."[21]

Shaw House's focus on race-related investigations and interventions owes much to the inspirations and experiences of its head social worker, Isabel Eaton. Her father was a Union general who assisted slave "contraband" during the Civil War and later became a southern superintendent of education during Reconstruction. In 1898, the black scholar-activist W. E. B. DuBois closely supervised her master's in social work thesis, from which she prepared the "Special Report on Negro Domestic Service" to accompany DuBois's *The Philadelphia Negro* (1899). Having been introduced to "community-based social work" by Jane Addams and honed her social work experience in Philadelphia and New York City's East Side, Eaton applied her passion for racial justice to the organization and programming of Shaw House in Boston. With DuBois, Addams, and other civic leaders, she was a founder of the NAACP in 1910.[22]

Shaw House offered an array of social clubs, courses in the trades, arts, and etiquette, a Saturday morning kindergarten, and study halls. Given the paucity of services for black youths offered by Boston's juvenile court, Shaw House oversaw black boys put under probation by the juvenile court. The settlement served as a community-based black juvenile probation department in Boston's South End. Of the 170 children enrolled in Shaw House clubs and classes in 1908, only 15 were white. No record exists of the probation caseload or the services probationers received. Shaw House initially featured white leadership but relied on a largely black, volunteer workforce and included black Bostonians in management. Despite overcrowding and inadequate resources, it was a unique early venture to address the needs and interests of black youths and communities. Its holistic approach incorporated education, job training, and public health to facilitate youth and community development. The institution's racial inclusiveness was unique in terms of participatory parity, which contributed to its vision and community impact. Credit for these distinctions goes to the local leaders who developed and supported Shaw House and to the relatively small size of Boston's black population. During the Great Migration, Boston's black population grew five times less than New York City's and eight times less than Chicago's.[23]

New York City's rapidly growing black population struggled to gain recognition in justice administration. In 1925, a team led by Charles S. Johnson, the National Urban League's director of research, conducted a study of racial inequality in New York's juvenile court. It found that black youths were overrepresented in the juvenile court and detention and that black children were in court for less serious offenses than nonblack youths were. Overrepresentation was attributed to inadequate informal social controls, such as social work services and recreational opportunities in black communities. To a lesser extent, black parents relied too heavily on the court, "doubtless due to the lack of intermediary agencies for them."[24] As in Los Angeles and, likely, in most midwestern and northeastern cities, New York City's black parents looked to the court as a resource but found few services that met their growing community's needs.

Of primary concern to the Urban League committee was the overt neglect of black community interests through denial of juvenile court services to black dependents and delinquents. The presiding judge of Manhattan's Children's Court agreed with the Urban League complaint, acknowledging in the introduction to its team's report: "The Children's Court is confronted almost daily with its inability to deal constructively with colored children under sixteen years of age who are in need of custodial care by reason of the scarcity of institutions willing to accept such children." Low rates of institutionalization among black court-involved girls and boys were, not an indication of the lack of black dependency or delinquency cases, but rather "an index to certain institutional inadequacies."[25]

Racial discrimination by New York's juvenile court service providers led to prolonged confinement of black girls and boys in shelters and detention facilities that were intended for short-term custody and offered few developmental services. The Manhattan and Brooklyn Societies for the Prevention of Cruelty to Children, which ran city shelters, complained of the "serious lack of adequate institutional provision, public or private, for colored children, [and] particularly girls." The black population of New York City had increased by some seventy-five thousand between 1915 and 1925. No commensurate increase took place in juvenile court provisions for black youths, "the result [being] that in certain classes of cases, particularly those of girls, where the Children's Court has made commitments and there no vacancies in institutions . . . children are often left in the Society's shelter for longer periods."[26]

According to Urban League calculations, average periods of delay ranged from a few days to several months for black youths. Shelters were meant to give temporary care, and this time was wasted "since they are not being given the sort of training which they need and should get." White children seldom remained in shelters for more than twenty-four hours. "To an extent evidenced by probably no other group in the city," the report concluded, "the Negro finds himself with inadequate facilities in the recreation field and in the field of care of dependent and delinquent children." Black service providers would not fill this void, the committee of mainly black civic leaders concluded, because "unlike certain other racial groups the Negro has not accumulated sufficient wealth as yet to make it possible for him to do much toward meeting the problems of his own people."[27] Another decade passed before black civic leaders, service providers, and their allies in New York City—including the nation's first black woman judge—began to defy this assessment of black collective efficacy.

The Expressive Violence of Southern Jim Crow Juvenile Justice

Jim Crow juvenile justice was unequal in a social, organizational sense. It communicated racial status distinctions and reproduced racial group inequality across generations. This was especially apparent in the South, where often violent denials of self-development for black youths and participatory parity for black adults were most overt and commonplace. The oppression of southern Jim Crow juvenile justice was also more expressive, or intended to convey normative moral and political orientations. For example, when pressed to provide rehabilitative services for black delinquents in 1905, Arkansas governor Jeff Davis proposed that the state build a reform school "where white boys might be taught some useful occupation and the negro boys compelled to work and support the institution while it is being done." "This would prove a blessing," he assured the all-white House of Representatives, "not only to the white boy, but to the negro boy as well."[28] Lacking provisions for black youths in the state, and given the more extreme violence that black youths suffered in adult penal systems, Davis's claim that his exploitative model marked progress was somewhat truthful. Yet the compromise illustrates how oppression and domination were openly endorsed as means of institutionalizing white youth and community advantages within juvenile justice and the larger society.

Whippings, a sanction deeply rooted in American racial history, further illustrate the expressive racial violence characteristic of southern Jim Crow juvenile justice. Researchers in North Carolina deemed whippings "the most unnecessary and brutalizing type of disposition" employed by the juvenile court in the first few decades of the twentieth century. The data suggest that whipping was reserved almost exclusively for black children and youths in North Carolina's courts. One hundred fifty-nine children were punished in this way in 1933 alone, with black children receiving all but twenty-five (over 80 percent) of the beatings.

White officials subscribed to "a widespread feeling among county juvenile court judges that whipping is the most effective way of handling delinquent Negro boys." An official from one of the larger cities admitted that he preferred to send "delinquent Negro boys downstairs with a big police officer and have them flogged." White children were whipped in just seven of North Carolina's one hundred counties between 1919 and 1929, while black children were whipped in twenty-two of them. Girls, especially white girls, were whipped relatively rarely. Fifty black girls, but only three white girls, were officially whipped between 1919 and 1929. No record of the intensity or other qualitative dimensions of these physical punishments exists.[29]

Social control through whippings of black women and men was common during chattel slavery. Following Abolition, North Carolina forbade the whipping of criminal offenders. Reconstruction Era state constitutional amendments from 1868 made corporal punishment of adult criminals illegal, and rulings as recent as 1921 and 1923 held that the restriction also applied to juvenile offenders. Objections to juvenile whippings were based on equal protection arguments and the fact that they ran counter to perception and law regarding the "best interests" of youths, especially as defined by the juvenile court movement. "Whipping of delinquents has no place in our civilization," a North Carolina researcher admonished, since "it is wholly contrary to the spirit of the juvenile court law, which has for its aim the protection of children, and not their punishment." Given over one hundred documented whippings of youths in over twenty counties, the law and the rehabilitative ideal were flouted, particularly in the sanctioning of black youths. Researchers protested that "to whip delinquent Negro boys, but not the white, is racial discrimination of the greatest kind" but overlooked current realities when adding that "to whip girls of either race is a relic of our barbaric past when we branded felons with a red hot iron, and nailed their ears to a pillory."[30]

Well into the twentieth century, juvenile court communities nationwide and especially in the South subjected black youths to far more severe sanctions. Hundreds of black youths were lynched across the South, often with the cooperation of legal officials.[31] Juvenile executions represent the official killing of embryonic citizens. They became more common and limited to black youths as the twentieth century progressed. American juvenile justice has always stressed that age limits the maturity and culpability of a person accused of violating the law. For young offenders, diminished criminal capacity has been held to warrant lenience in sanctioning and optimism about reform through rehabilitative intervention. Executions of black youths and the degree of racial disparity increased after Progressive Era juvenile court communities were established. This illustrates the limitations of liberal principles of juvenile social control when back youths are concerned. Most black youth executions occurred in the South, primarily owing to the disregard of black child and social welfare among the dominant group and the lack of participatory racial parity in the administration of justice.[32]

Between 1900 and 1959, at least 162 persons eighteen years of age or under were executed.[33] Compared to all those subjected to court sanctions during that period, the number is small. However, those executions offer insight into Jim Crow juvenile justice. Patterns of execution by racial group reveal the relation between race, youth execution, and Jim Crow juvenile social control (see table 4.2). Four historical periods related to the general and racial history of American juvenile justice are distinguished: the antebellum period (pre-1865), the period between Emancipation and the establishment of the first juvenile court (1865–99), the period of early juvenile court diffusion (1900–1930), and the period in which juvenile justice reform became nationally established (1931–59).

Several patterns are noteworthy. Youth executions increased significantly following Emancipation and through the first half of the twentieth century. Over one-third of *all* recorded youth executions occurred between 1931 and 1959, when juvenile justice reform was well established. Improved age-data collection over time skews the statistics. Youth executions by race, however, are dramatically uneven in each period and more so over time, notwithstanding the far greater problem of missing age data for black executions.[34]

Nearly 70 percent of all documented youth executions involved blacks. The number and relative proportion of white youth executions declined consistently across historical periods. As Emancipation, Reconstruction, and the juvenile court movement proceeded, the number and group proportion of black youths among those executed increased.[35] The proportion of executed youths who were black rose from 42 percent in the earliest period (through 1865) to 82 percent in the latest (1931–59). Over 70 percent of black youth executions recorded in the Espy data occurred *after* the birth of the juvenile court, contradicting the apparent advance of enlightened juvenile social control.

This paradox illustrates the dynamic racial politics of Jim Crow juvenile

Table 4.2 Race and youth executions by juvenile justice periods

Racial groups	Period Pre-1865	1866–99	1900–1930	1931–59	Total
Black:					
Count	17.0	45.0	65.0	97.0	224.0
% by group	7.6	20.1	29.0	43.3	100.0
% by period	41.5	54.9	72.2	82.2	67.7
White:					
Count	18.0	28.0	21.0	17.0	84.0
% by group	21.4	33.3	25.0	20.2	100.0
% by period	43.9	34.2	23.3	14.4	25.4
Other:					
Count	6.0	9.0	4.0	4.0	23.0
% by group	26.1	39.1	17.4	17.4	100.0
% by period	14.6	11.0	4.4	3.4	6.9
Total:					
Count	41.0	82.0	90.0	118.0	331.0
% by group	100.0	100.0	100.0	100.0	100.0
% by period	13.0	25.0	27.2	35.7	100.0

Source: M. Watt Espy and John Ortiz Smykla, *Executions in the United States, 1608–2002* [computer file] (Ann Arbor, MI: Inter-University Consortium for Political and Social Research, 2004). *Note:* Tabulations include all known executions of youths (persons aged eighteen or under at the time of execution) for which race/ethnicity is also reported (N = 331). Sixty-eight percent of these cases involved black youths. The earliest reported youth execution in these data was in 1642, and the last known one occurred in April 1959. Reported cases of Native American (N = 10), Latino (N = 9), and Asian (N = 4) youth execution are combined in the category "Other." Percentage totals may not equal 100 owing to rounding.

justice. In the Espy data, 24 of the 224 recorded black youth executions occurred outside the South. Georgia accounts for nearly one-fifth of all black youth executions (44), and over 60 percent of these occurred after 1930. In Georgia, of the 47 recorded youth executions, only 3 were not black. Most prominent among killing parental states after Georgia were Virginia (26), Alabama (20), and North Carolina (19). All but one of these executions involved black youths. South Carolina (15), Texas (13), Mississippi (11), Maryland (10), and Louisiana (5) report only nonwhite youth executions, with most occurring after 1930.[36]

The growing frequency and racial disparity of youth executions was related to the intensifying struggle for equal rights. When whites sensed an increased threat, they responded with racial violence. John Dittmer's historical research on the Mississippi civil rights movement shows that racial violence increased in the World War II era owing to growing concerns in the white community over emboldened black militancy and potential civil rights agitation. Black soldiers had called for "Double Victory"—liberty at home and abroad—provoking fears among whites that militarism offered the *means* to genuinely challenge Jim Crow segregation. Experiencing "fear and uncertainty," Dittmer suggests, white Mississippians employed racial violence to defend the status quo. "Lynching had always been the ultimate form of social control," he continues, "and neither youth, old age, nor social class offered protection for Negroes who did not stay in their place."[37] Two of the many victims of white reactionary violence were Charlie Lang and Ernest Green. These boys were fourteen years old when, in October 1942, a passing white motorist spotted them chasing a young white female playmate and reported the "incident" to police. After their arrest on suspicion of attempted assault, a white mob entered the local jail, took the boys, and hung them from a bridge.[38]

The rise of the black freedom movement and the denial of black authority within the parental state made black youths susceptible to the racial vengeance of Jim Crow juvenile justice systems. As white perceptions of racial group power threats became heightened, youthful indiscretions by blacks drew more severe sanctions from a racial state committed to the status quo, for black and white citizens alike. One execution involved fourteen-year-old George Stinney (fig. 4.1). He was accused of murdering a young white girl in South Carolina in 1941. In a grotesque spectacle, South Carolina officials struggled to fit the adult electric chair to Stinney's little body. After several botched attempts, he was finally dead.[39]

The "substitution thesis" attempts to explain the increased executions of black youths during the middle third of the twentieth century. In this notion, "legitimate" state executions replaced extralegal lynching.[40] News accounts of these executions support this thesis, observing the presence of white mobs within the court or otherwise pressuring legal officials, and blurring legal and extralegal distinctions of racial violence in the period.[41]

Despite Espy's data on official offenses behind juvenile executions, legal variables are insufficient explanations for black youth executions. Many involved racial taboos on black self-defense and sexual involvement with whites, activities that invited mob violence and charges of assault, murder, and rape, with the severe sanctions associated with these crimes.[42] A disputed case in 1946 centered on James Lewis and Charles Trudell, ages fifteen and sixteen. An attempted robbery of their employer, a white farmer, ended with all of them dead, the farmer from gunshots allegedly fired by these youths and the youths at the hands of the state. The only evidence was their forced confessions. In a trial that their NAACP federal appeal lawyer,

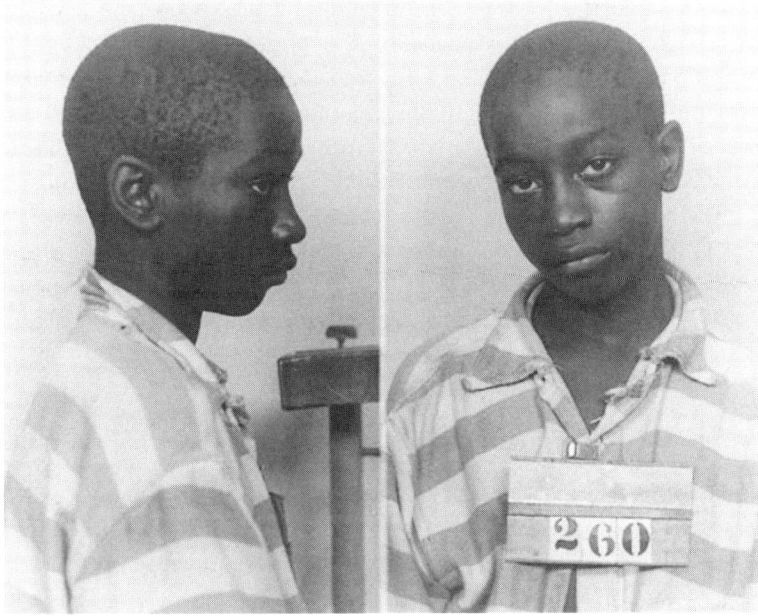

Figure 4.1. George Stinney, electrocuted in 1941 at age fourteen by South Carolina.

Thurgood Marshall, likened to Scottsboro, an all-white jury found Trudell and Lewis guilty. They were sentenced to death and executed in July 1947. A decade before Emmett Till was lynched in Money, Mississippi, the Trudell and Lewis case provoked a global outcry against "juvenile murder" and "white justice" in the United States. Protests came from far and wide, including London's League of Colored People, the West African Student Union, and the government of India. The U.S. embassy in London received over three hundred communications protesting the death sentences, including forty-eight petitions containing hundreds of signatures. Three members of the British House of Commons sent a telegram to President Truman urging him to "protect basic human rights by intervening" to stop the executions.[43] Shunning this opposition, Mississippi's governor and courts, and eventually the U.S. Supreme Court, rejected calls for clemency and to review the capital sentences. This conveyed a resolve to defend white democracy, or, at least, the sovereignty of white supremacist Mississippi.[44]

The *Chicago Defender*'s close coverage of the case presented it as clear proof that the absence of black power in government would continue to facilitate domination and oppression under the law. "Not until Negroes have equal representation in the courts and all law enforcement agencies," the newspaper reported, "can Negroes expect equality."[45] Appeals exhausted, and execution day approaching, Lewis and Trudell's local NAACP lawyer suggested that the boys would be too short to fit in Mississippi's portable electric chair. Several big books would be needed to "raise the boys so that their heads can reach the lethal cap." The writer recommended using the Bible, the U.S. Constitution, the *Age of Reason*, and *The Rise of Democracy* "so that Mississippi can destroy them all at the same time." On the day of the execution, a small crowd of white spectators gathered to celebrate the killing outside the jail. This scene helped blur the distinction between extralegal mob violence and death at the hands of a white-dominated parental state.[46]

The Interaction of Oppression and Domination in Jim Crow Juvenile Justice

Racial domination in Jim Crow juvenile justice is rooted in the late-nineteenth-century collapse of radical Reconstruction and efforts of white redeemers to eliminate black representation in government. By resurrecting laws that criminalized black racial status and poverty and passing legislation that excluded black workers and professionals from legal and law enforcement positions, redeemers subjected blacks to greater control and placed lawmaking, law enforcement, and justice administration under the control of white civil society.[47] This served symbolic and practical purposes. As the historian Leon Litwack explains: "To extinguish the memories of black jurors, judges, police and legislators during Reconstruction was to make clear the undisputed and permanent authority of whites. To impress upon the first generations of freeborn blacks the constraints and discipline once associated with slavery was to remind them constantly of their circumscribed place in southern society. The entire machinery of justice—the lawyers, the judges, the juries, the legal profession, the police—was assigned a pivotal role in enforcing these imperatives . . . underscoring in every possible way the subordination of black men and women of all classes and ages."[48]

A 1909 dispatch from Atlanta University highlighted the practical role of white domination in justice administration. "In the South, especially the lower South," W. E. B. DuBois wrote, "the colored people are almost helpless. They have few or no representatives on the police force; no influence in the police or courts; [and] no control over jail or methods of punishment." "Personal influence may do something," he protested, "but for the most part [blacks] have to sit by and see children punished unintelligently and men and women unjustly."[49]

In 1913, DuBois again protested the lack of black representation in systems of social control. Concerning the leadership of a black orphanage in New York City, he declared it "a great mistake to have a governing board over an institution for colored people on which the Negro race is not represented." "There is no argument of social compatibility, wealth or education," he insisted, "which should for a moment defend such an anomaly and injustice." Lack of black representation on the board affected all race relations in the institution, including the diversity and quality of its teachers and the experiences of white and black youths. "The white teachers do not as a rule love or sympathize with their poor little black charges," DuBois wrote, and the all-white board supported only "submissive Negro teachers," who also did little for black youths.[50] The result was unjust and "unintelligent" treatment of black youths in a white-dominated system that systematically denied the interests of blacks in enlightened citizen-building initiatives and equal democratic participation.

Black child-savers pressed for greater professional representation in a wide range of juvenile justice–related occupations beginning in the 1920s. They made important inroads in the 1930s and 1940s. Not until the 1950s, however, did black Americans gain significant representation among legal and law enforcement authorities. Today, black representation at executive, professional, and administrative levels remains relatively limited. Diversification of justice-related occupations before the civil rights period was concentrated in the urban North and in lower service roles, such as segregated police units, segregated probation departments, and the staffing of black reformatories.[51] Meanwhile, the dearth of black representation among law enforcement officials and court authorities, in local, state, and federal government, and in academic and policy circles made for negligible participation in juvenile justice policymaking, funding decisions, and delinquency prevention and intervention efforts. This was the bureaucratic foundation of Jim Crow juvenile justice.

Even the initial recruitment of black authorities in American juvenile justice and other legal domains often came under a pretense of maintaining racial hierarchy. The first black American police officers were organized to counter slave rebellions, and, in the first half of the twentieth century, black police were usually restricted to policing black communities, with limited police powers, especially over whites. Even when black juvenile probation officers and other service workers were sought as specialists in black communities, they were underpaid and underresourced and had little ability to advance black interests in countering Jim Crow policies and practices.[52]

Early efforts to racially diversify caseworkers in North Carolina illustrate this point. In the 1940s, the State Eugenics Board and State Board of Public

Welfare sought to determine how often state institutions used sterilization procedures and how to increase their use. The agencies commissioned the British psychiatric social worker Moya Woodside as a research assistant at the University of North Carolina to evaluate the state's program of eugenic sterilization. Woodside proposed that increased black representation among social workers would boost access to black communities, where more sterilizations could be performed.

To her credit, Woodside rejected typical white supremacist explanations for the vast differences in life circumstance and life chances dividing white and black America, giving little credence to racist assertions of black inhumanity. Woodside traced black "deviant marital behavior," sexuality, morbidity, juvenile delinquency, and other apparent pathologies of interest to eugenicists to the social and institutional history of southern race relations. "It is not so long since Negroes were white men's slaves," she wrote in 1950, "subject to direction in almost every detail of their lives, and considered . . . inferior beings to whom the ordinary human rights did not apply. Although the plantation system has almost disappeared and Negroes have been accorded a varying measure of education and equality, tradition and custom of former days still influence the behavior of the more ignorant people of the South." The result: "Negroes are not assimilated: they live side by side with whites but in a separate social world of their own." Only a relatively small proportion, she added, have "middle and upper class status, and the mass of the Negro people [are living] under conditions of poverty, neglect, and rural isolation."[53]

For the Eugenics Board and State Board of Public Welfare, the most pressing question regarding segregation was how to extend eugenic sterilization to isolated black communities. The centerpiece of this inquiry was a survey submitted to county departments of public welfare in North Carolina in November 1947. Ninety-five of one hundred surveyed departments replied. This high response rate fed a delusion that the study captured a representative impression of interests and experiences in the state. "No one could be better qualified to speak, since these administrators, both men and women, are representative of the general population, know local problems, and work directly with people," Woodside opined, ignoring the problem that blacks—who made up one-quarter of the state population—were not among the heads of county public-welfare departments.[54]

The survey uncovered evidence that blacks, particularly poor ones, were skeptical of eugenic sterilization. Enlisting black social workers to promote such control measures might overcome the ignorance, fear, and superstition behind the skepticism. The conclusion was odd since the all-black staff running the state's only institution then serving black girls, the State Training School for Negro Girls, had expressed little interest in sterilization and no procedures had been performed there. The school (Dobbs Farms) had been established in 1944. When Woodside visited it in 1947, the black superintendent with whom she met had "little experience with sterilization." She had little interest in pursuing it since the school lacked the authority, funds, or facilities for such measures. "It was agreed," Woodside recalled, "that sterilization could be one resource for wise planning for a girl's welfare in some cases."[55]

Setting aside black community interests, the study recommended training more black social workers to attain higher black sterilization rates. "The employment of more Negro social workers is likely a way in which the acceptance of sterilization could be speeded among lower-class Negro groups," Woodside writes, "since they have better understanding of Negro habits and attitudes and their advice would often command a confidence not always accorded white people." As Woodside realized, in the 1940s, this was an untenable solution, given denials of educational and other opportunities in the Jim Crow South. "At present there is an increasing demand for trained Negro [social] workers, from both public and private agencies which have large Negro caseloads," she noted, "but too few candidates are locally available. In North Carolina, there is at present no school for educating Negroes in social work, and all Negroes interested in such training have to go outside the State from whence they may feel no obligation to return."[56]

Black civic leaders had their own views on the importance of increasing black representation in social work, probation, policing, the courts, and other contexts of authority, eyeing this participatory parity as way to express and protect black community interests in the (re)organization of social control. Young black professionals trained elsewhere would not likely return to the Jim Crow South. Even with credentials, as the Woodside plan suggests, their own professional visions and voice—their agency—had no place. For coming generations of black social workers and other professionals, eradicating poverty and racism and the resulting injuries to black well-being were higher priorities than sterilizing the black poor.

The Social Organization of Jim Crow Juvenile Justice: Summary and Conclusion

The first section of this book has explored the oppression and domination that characterized the racial history of American juvenile justice. Youth advantages and disadvantages were distributed along socially constructed racial lines. The systematic denial of self-realization for black youths and self-determination for black adults distinguishes Jim Crow juvenile justice. For over a century, systematic underdevelopment of black youths was rooted in racial group power inequality and dominant group refusals to acknowledge and cultivate the humanity and welfare of black dependent and delinquent youths. Despite local and regional variations in the social organization of separate and unequal juvenile justice, this pattern was fundamental to the history of American juvenile justice.

The twentieth-century history of Jim Crow juvenile justice illustrates that race effects operated in multiple, interactive ways to define the color lines of juvenile social control. This includes subtle and overt discrimination against racially defined populations, the privileging of other populations, and levels of participatory parity. This theme will be more fully developed by focusing on the contested and dynamic nature of this racial and institutional history and how culture, structure, and agency have combined to (re)shape the racialization of American juvenile justice.

Emerging black community leaders were quick to identify Jim Crow juvenile justice as a unique problem of structural violence targeting youths but also disempowering the whole group.[57] By the 1890s, black civic leaders had begun to express concerns that Jim Crow juvenile justice systems institutionalized social, economic, and political deprivation, broadly or collectively injurious to black community development and social standing. To the extent that liberal juvenile justice could secure the fates of salvageable citizens and define the color of American democracy—a belief held by white and black contemporaries—the white-dominated parental state threatened quests for black freedom and equality. The emerging black freedom movement therefore prioritized juvenile justice reform, aspiring to remake American juvenile justice into a symbol and substantive resource of multiracial democratic inclusion. The struggle began modestly, with marginalized black women and men mobilizing meager resources to create semblances of black juvenile justice systems where there had been none before.

PART TWO

Rewriting the Racial Contract:
The Black Child-Saving Movement

FIVE

Uplifting Black Citizens Delinquent: The Vanguard Movement, 1900–1930

At the turn of the twentieth century, black clubwomen led the first wave of black opposition to Jim Crow juvenile justice. The vanguard movement organized in various states to advance racial equality in juvenile social control. This chapter surveys its logic and organization, including its background, ideology, and the way in which the resources of early reformers shaped and limited their collective efficacy and societal impact. Pragmatic and conservative strategies, extremely limited political capital, and a reliance on private resources moderated their advances. Yet this early effort to "uplift the race" through self-help set the stage for future civil rights challenges and the eventual legal demise of Jim Crow juvenile justice.

Black Youths and Race Work: The Case for Juvenile Justice Reform

Several historical factors combined to establish juvenile justice as an early and enduring stage of the black freedom movement. The close of the nineteenth century brought dramatic reversals in the civil rights and civic prospects of black Americans, particularly in the American South, but also nationwide. This retraction of democratic freedoms, ironically coinciding with Progressive Era reform, did not go uncontested. The ubiquity and gravity of racist assaults in the post-Reconstruction period led black Americans to organize in defense of fleeting citizenship rights. Between the horrors of the Black Nadir and a dying commitment to Reconstruction, Progressive Era black leaders realized that, in the words of the influential and radical journalist T. Thomas Fortune, "we have got to take hold of this problem ourselves." The new "slavery of iniquitous justice systems" was among the primary concerns attracting black resistance through self-determination.[1]

Modern ideas of childhood and child welfare also contributed to black community interest in juvenile justice reform. These cultural notions positioned children as the central focus of the modern family and as progeny of the parental state. Despite the inclination of the white-dominated parental state to deny the malleability of black people and to exploit and neglect black youths, through much of the twentieth century black juvenile justice reformers regarded the equally malleable souls of black children as indispensable to the black family and to black ambitions for equality in a future American society. Local black ideals of racial uplift would, thus, mix and mesh with abstract notions of childhood to make race-related juvenile justice reform a logical and pressing objective.

Finally, early black involvement in these reforms was inspired by progressive dimensions of the child-welfare institution itself, and the promise of a struggle to save youths through the citizen-building machinery of a "kind and just" parental state. In retrospect, the exclusion of black youths from early liberal experiments in juvenile justice had paradoxical benefits, considering the apparent failures and abuses of the juvenile court and its rehabilitative ideal and institutions. Black contemporaries understood this as another refusal of equal opportunity by denying cutting-edge, progressive child-welfare strategies of juvenile social control. At the dawn of the twentieth century, black Americans were eager to realize the still elusive democratic freedoms promised by Emancipation and Reconstruction. Few freedoms were more valued than access to education and equal protection under the law.[2] Juvenile justice claimed to embody both these pivotal concerns as they pertained to troubled children and youths. Equal access to the modern idea and practice of juvenile justice thus signified an avenue to freedom. Black civic leaders therefore grew determined to racially liberalize American juvenile justice or else build their own manufactories of citizens in the interest of freedom.

The struggle to abolish racial discrimination in juvenile justice spans from at least the 1890s through the first half of the twentieth century. Yet the movement may best be understood as multiple waves since organizing strategies, resources, and circumstances varied. This chapter focuses on the stage of the black child-saving movement commencing in the late nineteenth century and peaking by the 1920s. After drawing a general portrait of the early black child-savers, I focus on the black clubwomen who initiated it. I then describe initiatives in the period between 1898 and 1920, especially in the American South, where the early wave of reform efforts was concentrated. Finally, I consider the politics and impact of the early black child-savers and their limited immediate ability to transform race relations of juvenile social control. Ideological factors and especially resource limitations blunted the impact of the earliest interventions. Yet they set in motion a larger and more direct civil rights challenge of Jim Crow juvenile social control that redefined the meaning of American juvenile justice for generations to come.

Black Clubwomen and the Organization of Influence

Concerned black citizens and their allies initiated "race work" in juvenile justice as early as the mid-1880s. The effort involved hundreds, if not thousands, in a black child-saving movement. An 1886 article in the *Cleveland Gazette*, a black newspaper, mentions one of the earliest black child-welfare initiatives specific to criminal justice. It protests the exclusion of black delinquent girls from reformatories operated by the Catholic Church. Ten years later, a little-known local black benevolent association, the Women's Clubs of Atlanta, protested the treatment of black women and girls in Georgia jails, including their ordeals in state chain gangs, and shared their eyewitness accounts in a publicly distributed pamphlet. Invoking new constitutional protections and expectations of civil rights, the group lobbied the governor to address these practices of "cruelty and injustice." The protest's impact was limited in the short run, being contingent on a government response (an investigation was promised). These alarms helped place juvenile justice reform high on the agenda of an emerging regional and national network of black clubwomen's organizations.[3]

Black clubwomen and their local, state, and regional associations remained at the center of black community opposition to Jim Crow juvenile justice throughout the Progressive Era. Mary Church Terrell, Anna Julia Cooper, and Mary Jane Patterson established an early group, the Colored Women's League of Washington, DC, in 1892 as "a united black womanhood to solve the race's problems." The following year, Josephine St. Pierre Ruffin established the Women's Era Club in Boston. Its agenda was identical, and its motto was "Make the World Better."[4]

The Women's Era Club extended longtime efforts by Ruffin and her family to promote social justice through black and integrated reform organizations. It reflected her interest in race and gender issues. Josephine Ruffin was the child of an interracial couple and an intermediary between progressive white and black elites. This made her all too aware of the complex politics of difference. Like Mary Terrell and other leading black clubwomen, Ruffin came from an influential black family, which she helped build. At age fifteen, she married George Lewis Ruffin, the first black graduate of Harvard

Law School. He became the first black judge in the North, Boston's first black city councilor, and a member of the Massachusetts legislature. Among Josephine Ruffin's friends and associates were William Lloyd Garrison, Lucy Stone, Susan B. Anthony, and Booker T. Washington.[5]

Ruffin was a key force in the black women's club movement. She emphasized to peers that black women and communities faced distinct challenges that could not be left for others to address. After her husband's death in 1882, with her daughter she founded and edited *Woman's Era*. The nation's first newspaper to be run by a black woman and to target black women, this illustrated monthly called on black women to organize for suffrage and civil rights. Ruffin's writing and public addresses advised other black women to advance their intersecting group interests. "We need to talk over not only things which are . . . of vital importance to us as women," she urged, "but also things . . . of especial importance as colored women . . . for the sake of our own dignity, the dignity of our race, and future good name of our children." Influential black women were obliged to "stand forth and declare ourselves and principles, to teach an ignorant and suspicious world that our aims and interests are identical with those of all good aspiring women."[6]

As local black women's associations spread, Ruffin and other leaders saw the need for a national organization to coordinate strategy and resources. The first national conference of clubwomen was convened in Boston in 1895, drawing one hundred women, and representing twenty clubs in ten states. Ruffin's opening speech to conferees defended black women's collective action. "We are not drawing the color line," she explained, "we are only coming to the front, willing to join any others in the same work and cordially inviting and welcoming others to join us." Her call for a black woman's organization subtly critiqued the race and gender politics of white women leaders, whose national associations had just voted against recognizing black women's clubs, especially to appease southern affiliates. Their segregation policy would stimulate the development and networking of black women's clubs. Black clubwomen continued to organize locally, regionally, and nationally for their own reasons. They needed to raise and pool private resources and to advance their activist agenda.[7]

The National Federation of Afro-American Women was established at the Boston conference. Its first elected president was Margaret Murray Washington, the wife of the period's most influential black leader, Booker T. Washington. In 1896, the Colored Women's League and the National Federation consolidated to form the National Association of Colored Women's Clubs (NACW). The organization drew on a rapidly growing membership of two hundred clubs by the end of its first year. In 1909, the NACW membership included several hundred local clubs, twenty state federations of black women's clubs, and northern, north central, northwestern, and southern regional federations. By its 1916 national convention, the NACW reported the affiliation of fifteen hundred regional, state, and local black women's clubs. One of these was a Montgomery, Alabama, group called the Ten Times One Is Ten Club, whose name belied the logic of leveraging the power in numbers—if ten times one made ten, ten times fifteen hundred clubs made a small army of fifteen thousand reformers. Viral expansion of black women's clubs provided a critical network for building oppositional consciousness and coordinating and funding civic initiatives in response to a host of social problems.[8]

The specter of Jim Crow juvenile justice was highlighted by representatives of the Women's Clubs of Atlanta at the first annual convention of the NACW in 1897. They and other clubwomen protested racial inequality in criminal justice and especially its harmful impact on black children and youths. Rejecting dominant group denials of black humanity and citizen-building ambitions, these clubwomen were confident about the "great possibilities for good and evil in every child" and declared it their "duty to foster the good and root out the evil." Among the convention's first resolutions was a commitment to support the establishment of juvenile reformatories for black children and youths.[9] Over the ensuing three decades, this effort featured prominently in the work of black women's clubs. Alongside other individual community leaders and civic associations, NACW affiliates struggled to advance black youth and community access to rehabilitative ideals in the face of dominant group opposition and indifference.

Inventions in Black Child-Saving, 1890–1930

A survey of leading southern black child-savers and initiatives provides a more detailed account of who the reformers were, what they aimed to achieve, and how their reforms affected and expanded the color lines of juvenile social control. Reformers intervened on behalf of black dependents and delinquents in various ways. Many black child-savers brought food, clothing, and other resources to black youths and adults in prisons or opened their own homes to black youths otherwise bound for prisons or other ordeals of injustice. This was characteristic of the individual agency and modest political intervention of the early movement. More organized and influential reformers, including black clubwomen, appealed to the state to remove black children from adult institutions, petitioned to establish reformatories for black youths, and operated reformatories of their own. Some were instrumental in establishing juvenile courts and institutions that ostensibly benefited all dependents and delinquents, regardless of race. These reforms sought to advance the interests of black youths and their communities in juvenile social control, but never by diminishing the legitimate rights of others.

The early black child-saving movement relied on a cross section of black civil society, a collective defined by intersecting race, class, and gender differences. This movement was also somewhat popular. Some club leaders—such as Mary Terrell and Josephine Ruffin—were members of a small and influential black elite. Their incomes and educations gave them advantages that other black women lacked. In economic, social, or political terms, their black elite status did not compare favorably with that of their white child-saving counterparts. In a white democracy, black communities had a flatter class structure, and all blacks were marginalized politically. Rank-and-file black clubwomen and others supporting their work were often of more modest means and engaged in race-related juvenile justice reform alongside more common labors.[10]

In Louisiana, the unique and relatively marginal social position of the earliest black child-savers affected their impact. Leading these efforts was Frances Joseph-Gaudet. She was born in a Mississippi log cabin in 1861, but as a child she fled with her mother, uncle, and grandparents to New Orleans after the uncle killed a white overseer suspected of raping his wife. In New Orleans, Gaudet attended college but did not earn a degree because she needed to work instead as a full-time seamstress. She became best known and remembered for her prison reform work.[11]

Like many reformers, Gaudet was especially disturbed by the confinement of black children in adult jails and prisons. She even arranged to take custody of and care for court-involved children within her own home. As a representative of the Negro chapter of New Orleans's Women's Christian Temperance Union, she eventually brought about reforms in child welfare and juvenile justice. She established the city's first kindergarten for black children in 1899 and in 1902 founded the Colored Industrial and Normal School, an orphanage and academic institution built on the industrial model encouraged by Booker T. Washington. She is also credited with leading the drive to establish the first juvenile court in the city. A white supremacist friend was so impressed with her reform prowess that she gushed, in what was intended to be a compliment: "My, you have a fine mind, you ought to be a white woman."[12]

In the face of racial oppression and domination, Gaudet's success in establishing moderate, segregated institutions is characteristic of the challenges and accomplishments of the early wave of reform. The profound social, economic, and political marginalization of black citizens, including black elites, generally overshadowed their initiatives and dimmed their immediate impact. By helping advance opportunities for black youth and community recognition, this vanguard movement initiated important shifts in the racial politics of American juvenile justice. Yet immediate results were limited and did little to disrupt the sociolegal structure of Jim Crow juvenile justice. The advances and constraints of efforts in Alabama, Virginia, Tennessee, and other states are illustrative.

"To Save the Youth We Save the Race": Black Child-Saving in Alabama

In 1904, Judge N. B. Feagin of the police court in Birmingham, Alabama, proposed a novel placement program for black juvenile offenders, stirring considerable interest and activity among black and white Alabamians. This approach to delinquency intervention had existed for decades in the North and South in programs that placed urban youths with rural families. But for a white judge in the South to propose such a plan on behalf of "little Negro delinquents" was unique. Until then, they were generally subject to extremes of neglect or severe sanctioning and ignored by enlightened approaches of juvenile social control. "Until [Judge Feagin] took up the matter," the philanthropic journal *Charities and Commons* reported, "the pickaninny caught stealing an orange was locked in with grown, hardened criminals, as the only reform school admitted none but white youth."[13]

Judge Feagin's sponsorship of a successful juvenile court bill promoted more comprehensive reform. Placing-out efforts had been limited by the number of farm families willing to receive black children and the inclination of judges to impose that sentence. The juvenile court bill promised relief from the common practice of committing black youths to adult prisons, jails, and work gangs. It made it illegal to place children under fourteen years of age in adult correctional facilities, required separate hearings for children, called for the establishment of juvenile detention facilities in each Alabama municipality, and authorized judges to appoint probation officers to manage individual cases.[14]

In theory, the new legislation rigidly differentiated children charged with crimes from adults and focused on protecting the former from the penal apparatus of the state through various rehabilitative practices. The law applied to all children under fourteen years of age, regardless of race, but in practice black community stakeholders soon realized that it applied exclusively to white children, especially in terms of access to reformatory and juvenile probation supervision. Judges had few new options given the state's failure to establish reformatories for black youths. Rural placement spared black youths from incarceration, but their labor was still exploited, and they were denied educational opportunities. Any further benefit black children might reap from Alabama's juvenile justice reform legislation would result from the institution-building efforts of black Alabamians.

Leaders of local and state branches of the new NACW soon accepted the challenge. One local leader recalled decades later that the juvenile justice reform efforts of black clubwomen had begun by 1898, one year after the NACW convention. She recounts that they went

> from house to house in the city of Montgomery, [where they] talked and prayed and planned concerning the problem of the youthful lawbreakers of their race. Their mother-hearts went out to the small boy arrested, not always for crime, but for misdemeanors sufficiently grave to bring him under the ban of the law and to send him to prison or to coal mines. . . . One day they decided that this was a work big enough to enlist the sympathy and aid of their sisters statewide. The matter was brought before the State Federation . . . and was finally adopted as the work of that organization.

After years of planning, "educating public sentiment," and soliciting donations from affiliated clubwomen and others, the federation purchased a plot of land and commenced construction of a reformatory for black delinquents.[15]

The clubwomen raised about $2,000—"a large sum to them," the white philanthropic journal smirked—that was used to purchase twenty-five acres of land and build a six-room cottage to serve as a reformatory for black delinquents. The site was just twelve miles outside Montgomery, making it "easily accessible to the capital . . . [so that] legislators might be induced to visit the institution and so be led to favor a State appropriation for its maintenance." Yet the legislature rejected the federation's appeal that year for an appropriation. More pressing matters awaited, it explained, but it gave $50,000 to an institution for white delinquents in the same session. White residents living near the planned black reformatory site protested its establishment. Despite these and other setbacks and delays, in 1907 the federation opened the Alabama Reform School for Juvenile Negro Lawbreakers using private funds.[16]

The federation hired W. B. Tyrell, a college-educated black man, as the reformatory's superintendent. He had studied for several years in Europe and served as a missionary in Africa. *Charities and Commons*, a white periodical, dismissed Tyrell's work abroad as time wasted "in the wilds of Africa with its long heritage of savagery and Mohammedan superstition." For Tyrell and his directors, leading a black reformatory in the alleged civilization of Jim Crow Alabama was another righteous mission to advance humanity and the interests of the race.[17]

A disciple of Booker T. Washington's, Tyrell reportedly sought "to turn the Negro child into a farmer, to develop a love for nature, to teach scientific agriculture, and to keep him away from the city." In this context, his reforms were profound despite being conservative in some respects and recalling such mainstream strategies of juvenile social control as the apprenticeship or placing-out system. Beyond its mission to rescue black children from the city's criminogenic influences and to offer a moderate program of industrial education, the reformatory was to supplant the neglect, exploitation, and brutality of Jim Crow juvenile justice with an inclusionary, if still racialized, ideal of juvenile social control. The Hampton-Tuskegee model of industrial education was hardly a revolutionary approach to juvenile rehabilitation. Given the reality of racial tyranny, however, black child-savers in Alabama understood this as a modest effort to "save black children from the slavery of an iniquitous justice system."[18]

Dismantling Jim Crow juvenile justice in this way was also pragmatic. It protected black reformers from opposition and reprisals and engendered further support.[19] Judge Feagin was so impressed by their efforts that he expected the state might "soon extend a helping and protecting hand." After the federation leveraged its own modest resources for six more years, aid did reluctantly come. In 1911, the state legislature passed a remarkable act that supported the institution through a per capita maintenance fund, an allotment for plant improvement, and a clause stating that the federation shall, at all times, have representatives on the state board of control.[20]

Alabama's black clubwomen rightly celebrated their achievement, both for its general affirmation of over a dozen years of effort and for the practical inroads made in the state's child-welfare network. "Having done this definite work for boys," the federation president, Cornelia Bowen, proudly reported to the NACW in 1913, "our next effort is to prepare a home for our girls." Rallying black clubwomen everywhere to associate juvenile justice reform with their racial uplift agenda, she declared: "To save the youth we save the race." Likely with this in mind, in 1915 members of the Tuskegee Woman's Club "made thirty visits to the black men and boys in the town jail, taking food and clean clothing on each visit."[21]

"Cared for as Growing Citizens Should [Be]":
Black Child-Saving in Virginia

Expressions of black individual and collective agency are an important, if overlooked, aspect of the history of American juvenile justice. Less organized black civic leaders joined civic organizations, such as black women's clubs, in early-twentieth-century efforts to establish a racially inclusive rehabilitative ideal. Throughout the black child-saving movement, the combination of individual initiative and collective action proved crucial.

In 1909, a black Virginia attorney privately convinced a white judge to suspend the sentence of a black delinquent and grant him custody instead of sending the child to prison. Such appeals and volunteerism were repeated across the South. Informal probation arrangements grew into a small enterprise. Soon, the Virginia lawyer supervised several black children. They stayed with him until a family was found with which to place them. In three years, he had saved nearly 150 black children from time spent in Virginia prisons.[22]

A collaboration of civic leaders called the Negro Reformatory Association of Virginia was one of the earliest black juvenile institution-building efforts in Virginia. With minimal state support, the association established a reformatory for black male delinquents in 1900. Headed by John H. Smyth, a former U.S. ambassador to Liberia, it employed his noted eloquence and network of influence for raising private support. Like the black clubwomen who protested the convict-lease system, Smyth appealed to the Twenty-Fifth National Conference on Charities and Correction. "It would be better to kill the unhappy children of my race," he claimed, "than to wreck their souls by herding them in prisons with common and hardened criminals."[23]

Rooted in the moderate rhetoric of racial uplift, Smyth's appeal sparked support in this influential white audience. A conference attendee encouraged philanthropic assistance of the proposed reformatory by suggesting that Smyth's efforts would "[place] his name beside that of Booker T. Washington as a benefactor of the race." The original name for the new institution, the Virginia Manual Labor School for Negro Boys, Girls and Youths, reflected the Hampton-Tuskegee model of racial progress. It is unclear why the institution did not serve black girls and was soon renamed the Virginia Manual Labor School for Negro Boys.[24]

An association annual report rendered its impact on reformation through racial uplift using a photograph of a black citizen delinquent (fig. 5.1). Beyond documenting past accomplishments, the dramatic image was meant to secure future financial and other support.

Janie Porter Barrett was Virginia's leading advocate for black depen-

NEW COMER   ELIGIBLE FOR PAROLE

Figure 5.1. An apparently uplifted black delinquent (Virginia, ca. 1916). Negro Reformatory Association of Virginia, *Seventeenth Annual Report to the Board of Trustees* (Hanover, VA, 1916), 12.

dents and delinquents. The daughter of a black housekeeper and servant in a wealthy white home, her complexion was light enough to pass as a white woman herself. Relative privileges flowed from Barrett's family stability and social capital, including a quality education and good housing as well as the freedom to operate in public. When she was thirteen, the comforts of that world ended. Upsetting the white mistress's plans, her mother insisted that Janie attend Hampton University and learn to live and thrive in the black world, rather than move north to attend school and "escape from her race" by passing for white. In a brief sketch of Barrett's life and work, the civil rights activist Mary White Ovington suggests that what she "might have achieved as a white woman we can never know, but there is little likelihood that she would have been given the impulse to service that came from Hampton Institute." Indeed, Barrett emerged from Hampton as a leader in Virginia's black community. She was a central figure in developing settlement houses, organizing clubwomen, and advancing race-related juvenile justice reforms.[25]

Barrett's reform efforts reveal the centrality of black individual agency to social reform efforts. Her settlement activity began in her home. Barrett and her husband (Hampton University's cashier) opened it to black neighborhood women and children who asked for assistance. Around 1905, she began to transform the administration of juvenile justice by organizing clubwomen to "carry food, clothing and bedding to inmates [and took] the students and women of the clubs with her [to] get firsthand knowledge of the existing conditions." On these occasions, she "became shockingly aware of the number of small children housed in the jails." Like other black civic actors and associations in the period, Barrett "made it her business to get every child out of jail and into local homes where they could be cared for as growing citizens should [be]." She brought black youths into her home and persuaded other black and white allies to do so as well.[26]

After helping organize the Virginia State Federation of Colored Women's Clubs in 1907 and becoming its first president, Barrett put juvenile justice reform at the top of the organization's agenda. She led a petition drive among black and white citizens to establish a juvenile court and then raised funds and other support to establish a reformatory for black girls.

A distinguishing characteristic of the black child-saving movement, and of Progressive Era black leaders generally, was the formidable challenge posed by institution building. White women had ties and access to white men in government, industry, and philanthropy who provided ample financial and other (i.e., legal) support. In contrast, Barrett and other black child-savers had to raise initial funding through private and often very small donations, mostly from other black people. They had no guarantees that authorities in the white parental state would recognize or utilize their services and institutions. To overcome these constraints, Barrett organized collections of ten-dollar donations from each club affiliated with the state federation and used the proceeds as seed funding for a reformatory. The remaining funds came from a prominent black attorney and the first black social worker affiliated with the Virginia Board of Charities and Corrections. When the Industrial Home for Wayward Girls finally opened in 1915, it admitted twenty-eight black girls ranging in age from eleven to eighteen. They likely constituted only a fraction of the black girls sanctioned in Virginia courts that year.[27]

It is not surprising that the home's organization would reflect the Hampton Institute's model of industrial education and its ideology of racial uplift since Barrett was a Hampton graduate. Alabama's Tuskegee Institute, the black college founded and headed by Booker T. Washington, recruited Barrett to serve as a dean, but she declined. As superintendent of the industrial home, she could bring about racial uplift through industrial education. The small and modest home (fig. 5.2) emphasized "ideas of home, industry, and school" (fig. 5.3), rather than what Barrett held as impractical goals of reform and correction.

Contrary to common impressions of early reformatories and evidence from other black-operated institutions, Barrett rejected the use of corporal

Figure 5.2. The Industrial Home for Wayward Girls (Virginia, ca. 1915). William A. Aery,
"Helping Wayward Girls: Virginia's Pioneer Work," *Southern Workman* 44 (1915): 599.

punishment at her industrial home. She explained that, "if it produced virtue to be whipped, these children would be angels . . . [having] had little but that sort of discipline at home"—and in other institutions. Instead, control and discipline were encouraged through a credit-based system. At age seventeen, girls were released; however, Barrett and her staff supervised their community placement and reintegration since the state provided no parole officers. With an eventual return to the community in mind, the industrial home shunned physical punishment and rewarded good conduct. It also sought to provide adequate housing, a healthy balance of work and leisure, and remuneration through wages rather than "in board and old clothes only."[28]

The Virginia Industrial Home operated for its first two years without state support. Perhaps in response to increased demand for youth services during

Figure 5.3. Farming at the Industrial Home for Wayward Girls (Virginia, ca. 1915). William A. Aery, "Helping Wayward Girls: Virginia's Pioneer Work," *Southern Workman* 44 (1915): 598.

World War I, in 1917 the state legislature and federal government began to subsidize it. An evaluation of all reformatories in Virginia at that time gave the school an A. Despite relatively limited resources and programming, the review claimed that "in spirit it has the highest rating of them all."[29] One of the institution's original employees reviewed it positively, recalling in 1954: "The girls appreciated what was being done for them. They had the feeling that they had a home and were being cared for." The staff, she recalled, constantly reminded the girls "of the good women (Negro and White) laboring for them and striving to have them help make the world better by having lived in it." Janie Porter Barrett remained superintendent of the Virginia Industrial School for Colored Girls (in Peak's Turnout, Virginia) until about 1930, when the segregated reformatory came under the authority of the Department of Public Welfare.[30]

"The Angel of Beale Street": Black Child-Saving in Memphis

In 1914, Florence Kelley—a major white child-welfare reformer and NAACP cofounder—vividly highlighted racial disparities in the Memphis juvenile justice system through the absurd case of a four-year-old black boy. Having stolen a pair of shoes from a store window, he was criminally charged with burglary, larceny, and prowling. Kelley ripped into the separate and unequal worlds of juvenile justice in Memphis. Although black child-savers had been opposing these oppressive conditions for a decade, Kelley had national visibility. Thus, her attention to this inequality was instrumental to intensifying collective action, especially through the NAACP.

Kelley found vast disparities in provisions for white and black delinquents that recalled structural distinctions between white and black houses of refuge. "The city of Memphis," she wrote in *The Survey*, "gives its white juvenile offenders six teachers, and establishes their Juvenile Court in a beautiful building once a school house," including in her article a photograph of the well-appointed white court (fig. 5.4). A caption notes the "separate detention rooms for delinquent and dependent children," "a large gymnasium," "a model cottage" where girls learned cooking and other aspects of household management, and various well-equipped shops for the industrial training of white boys expected to graduate into the labor market. Meanwhile, Kelley protested, Memphis "afforded no teacher for colored delinquent children." Its separate "colored juvenile court" was in a "shabby six-room wooden cottage . . . badly equipped, [with just] its sewer connection in the back yard." This side of the Jim Crow ordeal for juveniles was captured in a provocative image of the four-year-old burglar, clutching a teddy bear, on the dilapidated front porch of the black court and detention facility (fig. 5.5). Notwithstanding these structural and programmatic deficiencies, Kelley noted that the colored juvenile court was "kept clean as hands can make it with plants in pots here and there by the unwearied effort of Mrs. Julia Hooks," a local black woman leader who along, with her husband, were the only staff of the black court.[31] The modest but humanizing touch, seen in the background of the image of the black court, reveals the contested nature of racialized juvenile social control as well as the limited collective efficacy of the early black child-savers.

Julia Hooks became involved in juvenile justice reform in the later stages of a long career in which she worked to improve the well-being of black Memphis. Born free in Lexington, Kentucky, in 1852, she was the daughter of two recently manumitted house slaves who were "spared the unspeakable hardships of working in the field, [but] shared the collective, excruciating indignities that all blacks were forced to endure."[32] Julia lived a relatively privileged life but was never far away from the racial tyranny of her time.

Julia's parents were determined to enrich her life with art and education. She became an acclaimed pianist by age nine and attended private primary and secondary schools in Louisville as there were no schools for

FOR WHITE CHILDREN

· To the white Juvenile Court, the city has just turned over a disused public school building. It houses the court, separate detention rooms for delinquent and dependent children, special school rooms for backward and truant children, a large gymnasium, a model cottage and manual training rooms. Memphis has in this building one of the best equipped juvenile courts and detention homes in the country. Until now the white Juvenile Court has been housed in a dingy and inadequate building.

Figure 5.4. The white juvenile court building in Memphis (ca. 1914). Florence Kelley, "A Burglar Four Years Old in the Memphis Juvenile Court," *The Survey*, June 20, 1914, 319.

black children in Lexington. Her talents won her admission to Berea College in Kentucky (the first integrated coeducational college in the South), and she was its first black woman student. Doubling as a music instructor while enrolled as a student, she was likely its first black teacher. Julia protested the policy of racially segregated social functions at Berea. "Her stubborn streak," according to the Reverend Benjamin Hooks, her grandson, "propelled this relatively tiny woman with a huge fighting heart to stand up against injustice wherever it raised its ugly head."[33]

In 1876, Hooks settled in Memphis, where she accepted a position as superintendent of colored schools. She quickly emerged as a leader of the black community that had settled on and around Beale Street. Over half the city's residents fled when yellow fever swept through Memphis in the summer of 1878. Those with the least means had to ride out the epidemic. Of the twenty thousand residents who remained, fourteen thousand were black. Julia Hooks was among them. She became known as "the Angel of Beale Street" owing to her efforts as a nurse's aide with the Citizens Relief Committee. Working among poor families ravaged by the epidemic, she dispensed food, clothing, and medicine. Relief work brought her together with Charles Hooks, a laborer born enslaved in Memphis around 1849. Their marriage in 1880 united a soft-spoken, literate (though not formally educated) man and a remarkably accomplished and professional woman. They collaborated in Memphis reform work for the remainder of their lives together.[34]

FOR COLORED CHILDREN

Memphis houses its Juvenile Court in two buildings in different parts of the city—one each for colored and white children. The colored court is in an old house, badly equipped, its sewer connection in the back yard. But Julia Hook, the colored probation officer in charge, keeps it clean as a whistle, with plants in pots here and there. Mrs. Hook has been a paid probation officer for three years. Before that, beginning as far back as 1876, she did volunteer work for children.

Figure 5.5. The black juvenile courthouse in Memphis (ca. 1914). Florence Kelley, "A Burglar Four Years Old in the Memphis Juvenile Court," *The Survey*, June 20, 1914, 318.

As the superintendent of and a teacher in Memphis's black public schools, Julia Hooks protested against Jim Crow segregation. Building good character was one of her particular passions. However, separate and unequal schools based on white supremacist ideology privileged white youths and communities while threatening black child development and collective well-being. Schools in Memphis's black communities had "poorly prepared teachers, lack of books and supplies, overcrowded classrooms, low standards and attendance, and inferior shelter, food and clothing." These factors mitigated against the full development of black character and capacity.[35]

Hooks was also concerned with a larger civil rights agenda. When Ida B. Wells-Barnett moved from nearby Holly Springs, Mississippi, to take a teaching job in Memphis in 1884, she soon befriended Hooks. Together, they challenged Jim Crow in education and beyond. In the 1880s, well before Rosa Parks and others strategically violated segregation laws to force civil rights reform, Hooks, Wells-Barnett, and others intentionally violated racial segregation in public transportation, theaters, and other public accommodations in Memphis, sometimes in court.[36]

Wells-Barnett was fired from her teaching position in 1891 for too sharply protesting colored schools. Turning her full attention to newspaper work, her protests became more resolute, prompting her eventual departure from Memphis. The following year, her courageous antilynching crusade began with her editorials condemning a brutal lynching in Memphis. Julia's husband, Charles, was among the black citizens falsely arrested and imprisoned when they protected a Memphis grocery store. Operated by three black businessmen, it was considered by white competitors to be too prosperous to continue. Efforts to protect the three businessmen and their property proved futile. After their arrest, a mob dragged them from jail and shot them to death.

One victim, Tom Moss, had been a childhood friend of Mary Church Terrell, a leading black clubwoman. His lynching for "succeeding too well" devastated her.[37] Ida Wells-Barnett also knew the victims. Tom Moss and his wife were her closest friends in Memphis. His killing led her to take "up the pen that would spew forth fire about the horrors of lynching for the next several decades." In her first pamphlet, she states: "The city of Memphis has demonstrated that neither character nor standing avails the Negro if he dares to protect himself against the white man or become his rival." She encouraged a mass migration to deprive Memphis of its black consumers and workers. White city leaders pleaded with her to call off the exodus. When Wells argued that the rationale that black men were lynched for raping white women was "a thread bare lie" and cover-up for the mate-selection practices of white women, a white mob burned her Memphis newspaper office and threatened her life. This forced her to move to New York.[38]

Meanwhile, carefully blending protest with moderate self-help initiatives, Julia and Charles Hooks chipped away at the built environment of American apartheid in Memphis, especially as it affected youths. In the 1890s, they founded the Hooks Cottage School, a private kindergarten and educational facility for black children, the integrated Hooks Music School, and homes for black orphans and elderly persons.[39] The institutions were partially supported through funds raised by Julia's public music performances and by soliciting help from the various black civic associations to which the Hookses belonged.

In 1902, the Hookses became probation officers in the newly established colored juvenile court in Memphis. The only paid officers, Julia and Charles supervised and maintained a facility that was built next door to their residence. During her 1914 tour of Memphis, Florence Kelley met the couple, "hands overfull with the care of boys and girls detained day and night in the [colored] Juvenile Court building," and witnessed their struggle to rearrange the color lines of a white-dominated parental state.[40]

Of Hooks's leadership of the black court and detention facility little is known. Her "compassion, gentleness, and calm manner" are said to have "gained the trust and cooperation of young and [old] inmates."[41] An essay Hooks published entitled "Duty of the Hour" provides insight into her outlook. Based on a speech she gave at the Beale Street Baptist Church in 1884, it suggests a complex view of black child-saving initiatives, where moderate, gradualist impulses of uplift ideology and industrial education are blended with notions of government responsibility and hopes for social change:

> I believe character should be considered the "Duty of the Hour." . . . There is in every child [this] divine principle awaiting development, [this] precious germ awaiting unfolding. . . . The chief factor of an advancing civilization is a sound system of instruction which every child, no matter his color or nationality, may receive. Let us make it the duty of the hour to garnish with art, strengthen with acquirement, and elevate with eloquence and good character. . . . All hail the auspicious day when the dark sons and daughters of the South shall arise to conquer the wrong. He who would cure must first cure himself.

Here, and elsewhere, Hooks emphasized the belief that industrial education is needed to uplift the race and advance American society. Private individuals and public leaders were dually bound to facilitate these advances, as self-help "must and needs be supplemented by earnest, thoughtful, careful and intelligent endeavors on the part of the State."[42]

Like other black child-savers, Julia and Charles sought to realize these ideals in the context of Jim Crow Memphis. Her critique of racial oppression and domination was subtle. By suggesting that black character building was a prerequisite to a societal "cure," Julia gained a measure of protection, access, and influence in Memphis. Three decades before Jane Bolin became the first black woman judge in the United States, Camille Kelley, Memphis's white juvenile court judge, occasionally invited Julia Hooks to sit with her and give advice on cases involving black youths.[43]

In 1917, a youth shot and killed Julia's husband during an escape attempt, and no investigation took place.[44] The event severely tested her commitment to black child-saving initiatives, but she continued her work nonetheless, joining with black clubwomen in Memphis to purchase and supply a new building for the colored juvenile court. She never discussed the tragic loss of her husband but dressed in black every day thereafter until her own death in 1942 at ninety years of age.[45]

Julia and Charles Hooks's descendants carried on their reformist spirit and efforts. The Reverend Benjamin L. Hooks took the path of civil rights and juvenile justice reform and embodied the professionalization that defined later black child-saving initiatives. After unsuccessful runs for the state legislature in 1954 and juvenile court judgeships in 1959 and 1963, he became the first black criminal court judge in Tennessee. Through a vacancy appointment in 1965, he became the state's first black judge since Reconstruction, a position he retained through election a year later. In 1977, Reverend Hooks became the executive director of the NAACP, "a fitting tribute to grandmother Julia," who, like Beale Street luminaries such as Ida B. Wells-Barnett, was a charter member of the NAACP's Memphis branch some six decades earlier.[46]

The Pride of "All-Negro Staffs": Black Child-Saving in Oklahoma

The small black population in the Plains states grew during the Progressive Era owing to migration from the South. Black youths and communities experienced ongoing denials of equal protection in the administration of juvenile justice. In the Mid-Central states, black youths were institutionalized at rates far exceeding those for white native and foreign-born youths, and 53 percent of institutionalized black youths were committed to adult jails and prisons in 1910.[47] This proportion was the highest for any region outside the South and was rooted in the exclusion of black youths from segregated white reformatories.

The Oklahoma Federation of Colored Women's Clubs (established in 1910) immediately attacked local Jim Crow juvenile justice institutions. "Since the union of Oklahoma Territory and the Indian Nation in 1907, segregation in the new state of Oklahoma created intolerable burdens for civic, religious and educational leaders among the Negro people," a historian of Oklahoma's black clubwoman's movement recalled. In response, "in 1910 the women leaders sought relief through organization of the Oklahoma Federation," affiliating with the older NACW, and joining with over twenty state federations and hundreds of local clubs.[48]

Oklahoma clubwomen benefited from a decade of related effort and the strategies of intervention forged by other clubs. In 1913, the Oklahoma Federation's first initiative placed a bill before the legislature that called for the establishment of a state training school for black male and female delinquents. With six hundred other bills that session, most with more formidable backing, the appeal died without consideration when the legislature adjourned. In the following year, the federation's self-help initiatives included visits to the state prison, where they were "disturbed to see the young boys confined with the most hardened criminals." They again petitioned the legislature for an appropriation, this time to establish a separate building for juveniles within the adult prison. It was granted. Four years later, the federation helped secure passage of a bill to establish a separate reformatory for black girls.[49]

By 1920, Oklahoma clubwomen had secured state funding for institutions that greatly expanded access for black youths. As an Oklahoma clubwoman proudly pointed out thirty years later, both institutions were "operated and superintended by All-Negro staffs, and maintained by the State of Oklahoma."[50] These victories are still little known. They indicate the development of a national movement and the evolution of a strategy from self-help to pressure group politics that would soon characterize a second wave of black child-saving initiatives.

Making Do Without: Black Child-Saving in South Carolina

Government support for black child-saving initiatives was generally not forthcoming. Sometimes a state's government denied funding for many years before assuming control of an institution and employing black clubwomen or their appointees in its administration. That was the case for

Alabama's Reformatory for Negro Boys. In Oklahoma, where reform efforts emerged later, the state subsidized black child-saving initiatives from the outset. However, as clubwomen in South Carolina realized while developing and maintaining an institution for black girls, cooperation was never assured.

In 1914, pressures associated with World War I led several local groups, including the Culture Club, to establish a home for black delinquent girls under the banner of the South Carolina Federation of Colored Women's Clubs. Their limited political influence and reform capacity were readily apparent. The federation's first appeal for state funding was unsuccessful, so it privately raised the incredible sum of $30,000 from clubwomen and other community supporters before opening the home in 1917.[51]

White officials denied appropriations requests, and white-controlled courts disallowed the use of the clubwomen's home for disposing the cases of black delinquent girls. Lacking legal and political standing, they appealed to court officials to consider their home for placements. Informal agreements were made, but they were not reliable. In at least one case, a judge undermined the pact by diverting two girls from the black reformatory to the penitentiary. In justifying the severe sanction, he observed: "The [clubwomen's] home was not officially a State Reformatory." This punished the reformers and the two girls for the state's refusal to support the private black reformatory or to provide a public reformatory for black girls.[52]

In 1925, the federation again asked the state to appropriate funds for or to assume control of its institution for black girls. The legislature made a small annual commitment of $2,000—token support that was not long lasting. Two years later, the governor questioned the value and legality of spending money on a private institution that served black delinquent girls and withdrew all funding. The federation again shouldered full responsibility, including rebuilding the reformatory after fire destroyed it during a deepening depression. Regularly shuffling the focus of its program to suit public and private funding sources, the federation supported the home until 1989.[53]

Assessing the Early Black Child-Savers:
Politics, Pragmatics, and Impacts

The social history of the black child-saving movement sets its protagonists apart from their more familiar white, northern elite counterparts, whose interests, experiences, and interventions dominate our understanding of the development of juvenile justice.[54] This initial reform wave offers insight into the unique origins, strategies, impact, and limitations of the black child-saving movement. The black movement is distinguished by its social and historical context. It began in the South, where most blacks lived until the middle third of the twentieth century, encountering separate and unequal systems of juvenile social control amid Jim Crow segregation. Typically affluent relative to other blacks, leaders of the early black child-savers remained marginalized—socially, economically, and politically—in this wider racialized social system. Their social position significantly distinguishes the movement. It is evident in the duration and scope of the black child-saving movement, which began in the Progressive Era South but grew into a national movement against Jim Crow juvenile justice at the height of the civil rights period.

Other distinctions concern the black child-saving movement's ideology and organization as well as the injustice frames and resources black leaders mobilized to counter Jim Crow juvenile justice.[55] Mainstream reforms developed new institutions to regulate delinquency and dependency, particularly among whites. In contrast, black child-saving initiatives focused on securing equal protection, opportunity, and influence within the arms of the parental state. Attention to the social status of these reformers and their oppositional politics will clarify the characteristics, impact, and limitations of the black child-saving movement.

The Social Position of Black Child-Savers

Early black women reformers resembled the white women who were leading figures of Progressive Era juvenile justice reform. Upwardly mobile, these black women chose work with children as paths to meaningful, professional employment. Their clubs, a centerpiece of the movement, were multidimensional, voluntary civic associations that facilitated a range of purposive, expressive, and status-enhancing activity. Beyond their work on behalf of dependents and delinquents, women in NACW-affiliated clubs pressed for reforms in early childhood education, provided homes for the elderly, and assisted black migrant women and their families to adjust to urban living. Clubs were also a valued social outlet, as revealed in the pomp and circumstance of national conventions and local gatherings. Clubwomen sought to advance the race through eleemosynary efforts, and their own example was a demonstration and measure of black progress.[56]

Characterizing these women as mainly self-interested, petit bourgeois catalysts of black juvenile social control misrepresents the complexity of their social position and the nature of their reforms. Equally misleading are assertions that a vast chasm of class distinctions separated child-savers from the youths and families they meant to influence.[57] Prominent among the black child-savers were individuals of considerable status and power within the black community—teachers, attorneys, and business owners—many of whom were college educated and otherwise of far greater means than most black folks in their communities. However, the rank and file of black women's clubs represented a broader cross section of the black community. As the historian Gerda Lerner writes: "Like the club movement of white women this movement was led by middle-class women, but unlike white club women, members of black women's clubs were often working women, tenant farmwives or poor women."[58]

Thus, class interests and aspirations were present but never superordinate in the politics and practices of early black child-savers. Most of them navigated a racialized social world of extreme socioeconomic and political marginalization along with the children and communities they aimed to serve. Without erasing differences, intersections of race, class, and gender narrowed the gaps between the experiences and outlooks of the reformers and those of the people they aimed to help. As Kevin Gaines has observed about black political activism: "The category of the black middle class obscures the extent to which the social position of blacks is irretrievably mired in racial and class inequalities."[59] Reformers were vested in their benevolent associations because it made them feel good about what they accomplished, because it offered a back door into a world of importance and prosperity, and because the injustices they potentially relieved were proximal group threats.

By directly threatening the black child-savers' families and the people around them in racially segregated communities, Jim Crow juvenile justice systems thus imperiled the survival and progress of their common racially defined group. They and their families were not immune to threats of racial violence or the everyday strains of segregation and exclusion. Their privilege did not burden them with abundant leisure or the desperate need to search for purpose in life, as is said to have inspired the nouveau riche within the white child-saving movement.[60] Josephine Washington, a graduate of Howard University and a leader among Alabama clubwomen, sought to correct the confusion implied by a white journalist's derogatory charge that black women's clubs in the South were consumed with frivolous, haughty affairs: "Such may be the clubs of the idle rich, of the self-indulgent votaries of fashion; and doubtless there are in some of the larger cities, Afro-American women who ape the follies of this class, but the average club woman, certainly the club woman of this section, is a creature of another type. The colored woman's organization is an eleemosynary organization. . . . [T]he main purposes are to relieve suffering, to reclaim the erring, and to advance the cause of education."[61]

Denial of education and other opportunities for self-development was a personal affront to these women and a threat to their group interests. In an earlier essay, Washington protested the practice of setting aside playgrounds in the South for the exclusive use of white children, sharing her pain and frustration at seeing the reaction of black children in her community, who "look on longingly, but dare not touch the sacred structures."[62]

Essentializing black child-savers (and their white counterparts) as self-interested bourgeois agents of social control mistakes their social position, the complexity of their oppositional consciousness, and the personal stakes and progressive politics behind many of their reform efforts. Sociologists have stressed the need for an interactional understanding of structure and agency to appreciate the standpoints of activists and the nature of their reforms. As Aldon Morris explains: "Human action cannot be reduced to social structures and impersonal social forces [since] human beings are embedded within cultural contexts that provide them with belief systems that help guide their actions and infuse them with meaning and comprehensibility." However, human beings are not simply free-willed cultural actors; "they are also embedded within [structures] that shape actions and limit options." "To understand human action," Morris notes (as have others), "attention has to center on the intersection between culture and structure."[63]

This interactional notion of political consciousness provides the necessary conceptual framework for comparing and contrasting the black child-saving movement. The intersection of race, class, and gender essentially helps explain variations between and within white and black child-saving movements across historical and social contexts. It explains the logic of white child-savers in South Carolina and elsewhere who targeted reforms at poor and immigrant white youths but were "willing to sacrifice improvements for whites if blacks would share in them."[64] The social movement of early black child-savers was born of an interactional political consciousness unique to their social position. It prioritized but lacked the power to privilege black interests, growing in reaction to the denial of opportunity and influence in Jim Crow juvenile justice. This social position, which changed over time, distinguishes the modest racial uplift agenda of early black reformers from the aims of their white counterparts and from a later wave of black child-saving that pushed more aggressively and effectively for civil rights.

Revisiting the Race and Class Politics of the Uplift Agenda

Vanguard black child-saving initiatives reflected the limits of agency in a particular time and place. Rather than a capitulation to conservative interests, the relative modesty of their racial uplift agenda was, instead, a negotiated, pragmatic expression of black progressivism. The focus of their early initiatives blended mainstream and group-specific sensibilities as well as the profound influence of rigid social exclusion. Abolitionism and the Reconstruction Era push for full citizenship rights and public education inspired them. Modern concepts of true womanhood and progressive maternalism also influenced black clubwomen and other women central to the early movement. Such ideas repositioned modern women within public and private spheres. The barriers of black disfranchisement and the terrors of white state and popular violence bound these leaders and left an imprint on the strategy and impact of the early movement.

Booker T. Washington and W. E. B. DuBois's well-known debate on the best path toward black social, economic, and political progress strongly influenced early black child-saving initiatives. Washington's Hampton-Tuskegee agenda of racial uplift through industrial education was pitted against DuBois's explicitly political idea of cultivating the race's "Talented Tenth"—black professionals and elites—to fight for social justice and civil rights. For black women activists in the South, many of whom had attended black industrial schools, the Hampton-Tuskegee model was relatively clear, safe, and familiar. As the historian Deborah White notes: "While some regional peculiarities existed, the guiding principle behind all the [women's] clubs was racial uplift through self-help."[65]

Uplift ideology proposed that black Americans should be educated to achieve industriousness. That would provide opportunities to work independently and productively as farmers and in various trades and, ultimately, to build educational, economic, and other foundations of power, including character. In contrast to full social and political equality in the New South, industriousness was more attainable and practical. The agenda was also vague and open to interpretation, including exploitative ideals such as making black delinquents useful to dominant group interests. Booker T. Washington's basic view was that "it is by means of practical education that the Negro is to be developed and made a useful citizen."[66] Vanguard black child-savers largely agreed. Their reformatories and other reform efforts envisioned industrial education as a protective and rehabilitative strategy—indeed, a citizen-building initiative—with the potential of saving black youths ensnared in Jim Crow systems of criminal social control and enhancing their ability to earn a living, maintain decent lives and households, and become credits to the future of the race.

Progressive Era black leaders, including Washington, DuBois, Anna Julia Cooper, and Ida B. Wells-Barnett, contested and debated racial uplift ideals and the model of industrial education. The group was never in concert and used various platforms to promote general ideals and strategies of progress. More radical leaders, such as DuBois, considered Washington's gradualist strategy to be foolhardy and unacceptable. Without political power, they argued, economic power was useless. Economic gains could be neither protected nor effectively leveraged without social and political influence. In a 1917 issue of *The Crisis*, DuBois and other black progressives stated that they did not oppose industrial education per se. Rather, they resented its manipulation by white authorities and others who saw it as a means of permanently assigning black people to menial labor and otherwise marginal societal roles. Washington's peers often disparaged him as the "great accommodator" and worse because he failed to aggressively challenge these approaches, all the while preaching patience.[67] Certain contemporary scholars have severely critiqued racial uplift ideology, arguing that elitism, patriarchy, and internalized racism defined its agenda. These critiques suggest that uplift ideology represented a form of false racial consciousness or, worse, a self-interested attempt at personal advancement brokered by black pawns of the white elite.[68]

Applied to the black child-savers, the critique of uplift ideology is reminiscent of critical readings of the class politics and oppression born of the bourgeois sensibilities of white child-savers in midwestern and northern cities. Owing to the ideological and institutional environment in which the black and white movements took shape, it is alleged, they were ineffective at altering social, economic, and political relations of inequality and complicit in exploiting marginalized populations. In one of the few scholarly considerations of black involvement in early juvenile justice reform, Alexander Pisciotta dismisses the significance of early black interventions on these grounds. In reference to black child-saving in Virginia and the Negro Reformatory Association specifically, Pisciotta contends: "The founding of reformatories for black children under the direction of black administrators before the turn of the century further legitimized the state's racist distortion of *parens patriae*." Black child-savers, he argues, "taught charges that hard work and submission to the white man's authority were the key to advancement." Pisciotta dismisses black American agency when he concludes:

"Whites were willing to allow blacks to run reformatories and act *in loco parentis* as long as they continued to train blacks for menial positions and perpetuated existing power relations."[69]

My own research on whether racial uplift ideology derailed the progressive potential of the black child-saving movement suggests that such dismissals confound the inevitability of racial consciousness (i.e., ongoing racial projects within a durably racialized society) with the politics of white supremacy and fail to appreciate the complexity of Progressive Era black interventions. The racial politics of early black child-saving initiatives were not overdetermined by schemes of black oppression and domination or exclusively influenced by conservative uplift ideals. If uplift ideology is a racist formation, then options other than the development of new racial projects, intended to renegotiate relations within the racialized social system, had to be available. Dismissing uplift efforts as perpetuations of existing power relations ignores the important elements of black agency and empowerment evident in early reform efforts and in their historical legacy.

An oppositional racial project meant to counter the oppression and domination of Jim Crow juvenile justice, the movement increased recognition of liberal rehabilitative ideals for black youths and communities. The intervention was meant to increase access for black youths to developmental opportunities and resources as well as to achieve participatory parity in the administration of juvenile justice. Its early phase was a modest attempt to alter existing color lines of social control by asserting black group interests in processes then dominated by whites. Although the vanguard movement was not revolutionary, it was a progressive expression of liberal idealism meant to counter Jim Crow juvenile justice through strategies of democratic inclusion.

Racial uplift ideology inspired but did not overdetermine the strategies of these early interventions. Rather, the black child-saving movement was influenced and measured by more practical concerns, including risks to movement activity, whose moderate rhetoric of uplift was more useful strategically than tactically. For social movement theorists, activism entails measurement and reaction to movement risks or potential costs. "Grievances or deprivation do not automatically or easily translate into social movement activity," especially when high risk is involved. Assessments of movement costs "may be raised or lowered by state and societal supports or repression." In the Progressive Era South, where black child-saving emerged and state and societal repression was intense, potential costs were extremely high.[70]

In the Jim Crow South and elsewhere, the threat posed by blacks who imagined or advocated equality was often met with lethal violence or other reprisals. Even modest efforts to promote individual and group standing, such as establishing a small business in Memphis, could lead to lynchings and other extreme anti–civil rights violence. Critics of such violence had their lives and property threatened, sometimes forcing them to relocate. Pursuing social justice in the South, as Julia and Charles Hooks, Janie Barrett, and numerous others did, was a high-risk proposition. W. E. B. DuBois's research on Progressive Era racial politics observes that "nigger teacher was one of the most opprobrious epithets the Southern vocabulary furnished." Oral histories convey the real dangers of black educational pursuits. In Georgia, a resident recalled, Klansmen "went to a colored man there, whose son had been teaching school, and took every book [the family] had . . . and said they would just dare any other nigger to have a book in his house."[71]

Turn-of-the-century civic leaders managed such risks through strategic decisions, including their embrace of a modest racial uplift agenda. Booker T. Washington's political philosophy acknowledged these limits and encouraged their momentary acceptance. The gesture won him considerable popularity among blacks, favors in the white world, and the scorn of black elites. "I believe it is the duty of the Negro—as the greater part of the race is already doing," Washington wrote in 1901, "to deport himself modestly in regard to political claims, depending upon the slow but sure influences that proceed from the possession of property, intelligence and high character for the full recognition of his political rights." In 1915, Washington's main nemesis, DuBois, conceded that logic. Following Washington's death, he credited Washington's emphasis on industrial education with making "the Negro patient, when impatience would have killed him."[72]

The strategic influence of uplift ideology can be overstated. It was as much an abstract rallying cry, or motto, as an influential formula for social change. Unlike subsequent liberal agendas for integration and radical freedom, early black child-saving lacked an articulated vision for racial group progress and societal transformation. Uplift ideology provided a forward-looking pedagogical framework that was intentionally vague, and its fluidity over time made it difficult to distinguish between its conservative and its liberal agendas. It lacked a clear indication of its long-term plans for American society or of how progress would be measured. A spectrum of reactionary, conservative, liberal, and progressive voices weighed in on the ideal of uplift, but none enjoyed creative control over its terms or its practical influence on black civic actors and social movements. And a black group consensus on its meaning or path never emerged, with black intellectual and political leaders making little effort before the 1920s to develop such a plan.[73]

Local black leaders and organizations were not concerned with arguments and speeches about the most promising path to freedom and equality that appeared in public forums and in the black press. For the black historian Lerone Bennett Jr., influences on the black freedom movement were far more complex and diffuse: "The Washington–Du Bois debate . . . happened onstage and was heard by a small minority. Backstage, behind the walls of thousands of homes, churches, and schools, far away from the organizational centers of Tuskegee and Atlanta and Boston, millions of blacks were making their own analyses and creating foundations for one of the most important acts in the history of Black America."[74]

The black community's colleges, churches, and presses brought competing visions of uplift to emergent leaders, but most blacks were illiterate and had negligible access to education. Most influenced by these institutions were black middle-class actors and powerful white leaders such as General Samuel Armstrong, the founder and president of Hampton Institute. Armstrong generally opposed racial equality and played a significant role in the conceptual development and institutional promulgation of a more conservative racial uplift agenda. By controlling a major black institution, his agenda became more visible and potentially influential. White northern industrialists and southern elites often channeled their influence through black leaders and institutions. In this way, they defined the modest and exploitative aims of uplift ideology and derailed a more radical Reconstruction agenda.[75]

Yet the conservative thrust of the Hampton-Tuskegee idea never dictated the interests of black leaders. At Hampton and elsewhere, students and alumni regularly questioned "the relevance of Armstrong's social philosophy to the interests and aspirations of the Afro-American South."[76] Many reflected critically on the conservative philosophy and drew their own conclusions. They lamented the lost momentum of Reconstruction and fashioned more robust freedom dreams. Those so disposed regularly followed alternative civic ideals as new initiatives took shape amid changing cultural and structural conditions.

Uplift ideology was adaptable to many pursuits and was not incompatible with calls for political action. According to the historian Elizabeth Jacoway, "industrial education" was literally translated to mean "education for life." Consistent with Julia Hooks's view of the "duty of the hour," Jacoway notes that uplift did not primarily seek to prepare black pupils for industrial labor markets but rather was "a moral program designed to inculcate the primary virtue of industry." It was not simply a capitulation to white elites but an expression of self-determination among an early generation of free black Americans intent on fully realizing black individual and group potentials.[77]

As feminist scholars argue in challenging class-centered critiques of white child-savers, early black child-saving endeavors defy zero-sum notions of progressive and conservative politics.[78] Black child-savers dealt fleetingly, creatively, and strategically with the nuances of the Washington-DuBois debate, mixing attention to morality, training in agriculture and service work, and the wholesomeness of the black family with interests in self-defense through protective services, fund-raising, lobbying government, and protest.[79] Somewhat like black power generations later or Dr. Kings' "dream," racial uplift mainly conveyed a murky but inspirational agenda for racial group action and progress. Unlike these and other more specific and forceful twentieth-century ideals, whose popularity and promise became possible with the progress of freedom struggles, racial uplift acknowledged the often violent realities of white reaction. It inspired and guided an emerging social movement, plotting a careful escape from Jim Crow juvenile justice and the abyss of the Black Nadir.

Obstacles to Collective Efficacy: The Problem of Resource Deprivation

Did the black child-savers movement substantively affect the racial democratization of American juvenile justice? Conceptual frames define the purpose and direction of social movements, but collective action requires material resources.[80] The movement's structural and institutional shortcomings, it appears, were a more undermining factor than its ideology. Early black child-savers commanded impressive and effective organizational means for efficiently mobilizing information, funds, and other essential resources. The black press, black educational institutions, and black clubwomen's associations effectively advanced their agendas. They transmitted the information needed to build an oppositional consciousness and collective action frame as well as the resources for training and organizing clubwomen, teachers, lawyers, and other community leaders. Constraining these networks internally were the limited political and economic resources available to their members, and, externally, it was their collective dependence on white authority structures. This is a key distinction between the early black and the early white child-saving movements. It defined black initiatives over time and relegated reforms to a separate and unequal realm of American juvenile justice until the 1960s.

The interlocking and cooperative structure of black women's associations facilitated early race-related juvenile justice reforms on a scale not otherwise possible. A local group like the Ten Times One Is Ten Club in Montgomery could not establish and maintain an institution on its own. By working together with other clubs under the administrative leadership of the State Federation of Women's Clubs, and with help from other affiliates of the NACW, it became possible for clubwomen statewide to realize a common goal of providing reformatories for black delinquent boys (1907) and girls (1917). This strategy prevailed throughout the South. In some states, local organizations were created solely to contribute specific resources to the child-saving initiatives of state or local clubwomen. Over the first half of the twentieth century, pooling resources made it possible for the Southeastern Association of the NACW to establish "training schools for delinquent Negro girls in every state of the South."[81]

These modest alterations of Jim Crow juvenile justice reflected the limited resources available to the early movement. Unlike northern blacks and especially their white contemporaries, black child-savers in the South worked on the extreme periphery of juvenile justice. They lacked external political and financial backing and confronted staunch white opposition. The cooperation that their white counterparts enjoyed from white police, lawyers, judges, and legislators never materialized, and they were not well connected to leading figures in mainstream political, economic, or civic affairs.

Social-structural marginalization, extreme dependence on white cooperation, and the absence of formal black influence and autonomy were serious resource deficiencies that limited meaningful change. Without the support of white legislative and court authorities for black child-saving initiatives, self-help measures would not reach court-involved black girls and boys. There were exceptions. Black clubwomen credited Alabama's Judge Feagin with demonstrating "a marked interest in the salvation of the Negro boy." South Carolina clubwomen noted the court's respect and confidence in their organization and appreciated that it had put "case after case" into their hands. In both contexts, however, this cooperation was long delayed, inconsistent in the legislature and judiciary, and fleeting.[82]

Many authorities and laypersons offered little or no cooperation to black child-saving initiatives, even when cloaked in the palatable terms of industrial education. States refused to establish institutions for black juveniles or to integrate existing ones, delayed promised resources, and committed black children to adult institutions; the white community actively opposed granting public funds and land for black reformatories. A diffuse hostility emerged in the white community toward "upstart" black Americans who challenged or sought to circumvent the boundaries of white democracy, particularly in the Jim Crow South. In the North, racialized denials of financing or regulatory licensing proved to be as effective as abject indifference or racial violence in the perpetuation of Jim Crow juvenile justice. Chicago's Louise Juvenile Home, established in 1907 by black clubwoman and a voluntary probation officer, Elizabeth McDonald, was perpetually underfunded and in debt for the six years before the state incorporated it. Writing in 1913, a Hull House leader noted: "In spite of various efforts on the part of colored people themselves to found homes for dependent and semi-delinquent colored children, the accommodations are totally inadequate."[83] It took Missouri clubwomen fifteen years to establish an industrial school for black girls. Tipton School finally opened in 1917. Their objective had been to keep black "girls of tender years out of the jails, workhouses and penitentiary." In 1908, the state legislature appropriated funds for Tipton, but its construction was delayed for nearly a decade owing to white citizen resistance.[84]

Because of limited political and financial capital, reformatories for black delinquents were financially unstable and generally very small. Rarely was there more than one institution in a state. When the Industrial Home School for (black) Girls opened in Virginia in 1915, it served two girls. Just fifteen girls were in the home by the end of its first year of operation. No record exists of another public or private institution serving black girls in the state at this time.[85] The Reform School for Negro Boys in Alabama housed twenty children during its first year of operation. It was then "filled to its utmost capacity, [with] these children to remain there until reformed, or until grown."[86] Except for a few larger black reformatories, such as the Virginia Manual Labor School, which housed 135 black children in 1904 and nearly 200 by 1916, most black child-saving institutions supported much smaller numbers of children and adolescents. Their financial straits were typically so tenuous that services were always uncertain.[87]

Black Child-Saving Initiatives: Summary and Conclusion

Early black child-savers realized that they were in for a long fight and might not live to see the end of Jim Crow segregation, in juvenile social control or otherwise. Even if every black dependent or delinquent before World War I had gained equal access to reformatories and allied services, what were the real prospects of their effective (re)habilitation and social integration? The communities to which they would return lacked equal social, economic, and political opportunities, and rigid barriers denied their black humanity and democratic standing, institutionalizing their marginalization.

Rehabilitated black youths could expect inferior education, housing, health care, and labor market opportunities. They also faced ongoing exposure to "a certain type of policeman, of juryman, and of prosecuting attorney [with] apparently no scruples in sending a 'nigger up the road' on mere suspicion."[88] Somewhere along that road, a black child-saving initiative might await them, but the modest resources and influence of these efforts, more than their ideological limitations, rendered them more palliative than ameliorative. In short, whatever transcendence black child-savers might achieve would confront the limits of the racial caste status of black youths.

These contradictions were nationwide. In Chicago's Juvenile Detention Home and other northern institutions for dependent and delinquent boys in the period surrounding World War I, officials steered black boys into futures as menial laborers and "helped them readjust mentally and morally through wood work, basket making, folksongs and patriotic singing."[89] Recalling the limits of rehabilitative initiatives in northern houses of refuge a century earlier, the relatively few black youths helped by early-twentieth-century black child-savers faced the paradox of preparing for opportunities that generally did not exist.

Limiting the prospects of early black child-saving initiatives and the life chances of black delinquents were the enduring boundaries of American democracy. Resource limitations and wider social, economic, and political realities constrained each step that first-wave black child-savers took toward more inclusionary models of juvenile justice. Consequently, their efforts were modest and uneven. Only a fraction of the black population subject to juvenile social control was affected directly by black child-saving reforms before 1920. Still fewer inroads were made by black adults seeking authority within the parental state.

Nonetheless, hope prevailed. The contradictions ultimately intensified black child-saving initiatives as early efforts to furnish modest placement alternatives and other ameliorative services gave way to more radical demands for racial integration of black youth and adult authority as well as racial equality in juvenile justice. And the early black child-savers toiled on at the speed of molasses, lifting as they climbed. The movement's impact on the color lines of juvenile social control was important but limited. Its significance would become apparent in the opportunity and influence enjoyed by generations of black stakeholders to come.

Uplift ideology was not a racist social formation or capitulation to white power. Its agenda was not that influential, particularly since white racial tyranny conditioned all possibilities. Ideologically, racial uplift did not openly advocate dramatic social and economic change and, therefore, helped appease white fears of black equality, limiting threats of violence and reprisal as black child-saving initiatives took shape.[90] Political opposition to early reforms thus diminished, and the agenda helped give common cause to black civic leaders and associations in the struggle against Jim Crow juvenile justice. Uplift ideology inspired Progressive Era black child-savers and had a strategically useful message. It was easily paired with mainstream rehabilitative ideals and other cultural notions to help fuel a new and dynamic movement to promote racially democratic practices of liberal social control.

Many black Americans accepted the gradualism of uplift ideology because it was practical and because, "despite its limitations, would permit them to upgrade the quality of their lives." Although its oppositional strategies were modest and its political and economic resources were limited, the early wave of black child-savers wielded "initiative, effort and organizational talent [to] supply what white racism sought to deny," that is, greater participatory parity in citizen-building initiatives.[91] Its modest provocations and achievements helped facilitate a slow but meaningful improvement in black collective and individual life chances in juvenile justice, education, politics, and employment. These piecemeal interventions chipped away at the dialectic of racialized exclusion by affirming black developmental capacity and establishing developmental resources. They spawned an evolving black child-saving movement and the eventual legal demise of Jim Crow juvenile justice.

SIX

Institutionalizing Racial Justice:
The Black Surrogate
Parental State, 1930–65

In the first half of the twentieth century, the color line of juvenile social control changed more than it diminished, becoming more representative of diverse racial group expectations and influences. A crucial element was the growing organization of the black freedom movement, which influenced the second wave of black child-saving. Modest efforts to improve black youth and community well-being during the middle third of the twentieth century, especially in the South, gave way to a national movement. Jim Crow juvenile justice came under direct moral, legal, and political pressure. The goal was to secure equal opportunity for black youths and equal adult influence within the parental state.

A confluence of cultural and structural changes shaped the growing impact of child-saving initiatives on the racial makeup of American juvenile justice. Midcentury demographic, cultural, and social-structural transformations in the black experience—related to migration, identity, and education—recast black civic ideals. They also fragmented black interests and involvement in juvenile justice reform (relative to the consensus of earlier movement leaders, such as the National Association of Colored Women's Clubs [NACW] affiliates). Yet black collective efficacy in American civil society was enhanced, as was the structural impact of later initiatives. The new wave brought novel ideals and resources to the old fight against Jim Crow juvenile justice. A more professional and technical approach to race-related juvenile justice reform emerged, along with a legal-bureaucratic strategy of institutionalizing racial justice. Previously, black clubwomen's associations and the black press formed the indispensable backbone of a vanguard movement that focused on voluntary, eleemosynary efforts to relieve suffering under segregation and dealt sparingly with the meaning or pursuit of formal equality in juvenile justice. In the second wave of reform, civil rights organizations, social research, pressure group politics, legal challenges, and labor force integration became more prominent. The movement retained self-help strategies that immediately improved black youths and community well-being while expanding its resource base. Equal protection of black youths and equal representation of black adults in the mainstream administration of liberal rehabilitative ideals became priorities of the movement.

Refracting the world around it, the second wave of black child-saving initiatives was a duality of structure and agency rooted within and shaping a changing racial terrain.[1] In this chapter, I stress the evolution of a distinct sense of self and society among black women and men after World War I, especially in the urban North. This played a role in the changing outlook and organization of black child-saving initiatives. A new self-concept and social consciousness blended gender, race, and class identities to shape more assertive, professional, and eclectic icons of the modern *race man* and *woman*. These identities intermixed notions such as the modern woman, the New Negro, and the race expert. This catalyzed, divided, and, eventually, isolated black civic leaders and organizations.

This chapter also focuses on the resources mobilized during the second wave. Vanguard efforts had relied almost exclusively on the social networks and resources of black clubwomen's associations. The more robust organizational and resource base of the growing civil rights establishment supported the new leadership of black professional race experts. Through their research and writing, for example, W. E. B. DuBois and Charles Johnson helped build and maintain moral, legal, and political pressure on separate and unequal juvenile justice systems. From its founding in 1910, the NAACP was involved in the black child-saving movement, first through its reporting in *The Crisis*, and later as a political and legal resource. Jane Matilda Bolin, the first black woman judge in U.S. history and one of the few black women leaders of the NAACP, also figured prominently. She fiercely pursued black child-saving initiatives from her insider position on the bench of the Manhattan Domestic Relations Court and through her wider activist network.

These actors and their resources formed a more powerful black "surrogate parental state" structure, a new social network that enhanced protections for black youths and representation of the black community in juvenile justice.[2] Their novel interventions included detailed research investigations, legislative initiatives, and court challenges. The network drew national attention and directly opposed the often local racial violence of the white-dominated parental state. In this way, the civil rights movement gained momentum and rendered Jim Crow juvenile justice unsustainable. Along the way, forceful demands were made for racially democratic access to citizen-building initiatives. Some argued that only revolutionary social change could ensure racial equality in juvenile justice. Ultimately, a compromise version of liberal civil rights reform prevailed. Equal protection for black youths and an integrated juvenile justice administration were to provide a durable legal-bureaucratic framework for institutionalized racial justice. Formal inclusion, in which racial equality represented a positive right to racial group access and influence, promised to mainstream the ethos and resources of black child-saving initiatives. That, at least, was the plan.

Shifts in Black Population, Identity Politics, and Power

The metamorphosis of black child-saving during the first half of the twentieth century was rooted in the Great Migration from the rural South to northern cities. Ideological and political efforts to racially democratize social control changed in response to shifts in black cultural orientations and socioeconomic status. Black youths, families, and civic leaders now lived where the juvenile court was most active, intensifying the conflict between unmet black community interests and the white-dominated parental state. In American cities, problems of delinquency and dependency grew alongside rising expectations of opportunities. Inevitably, pressure for equal access for black youth and adult influence in juvenile social control built.

Migratory expansion beyond the South meant that the front of juvenile justice reform had broadened nationally and movement resources, strategies, and influence were expanded. Regional variations continued to shape strategies of collective action. Yet national outlooks and interests emerged in northeastern and midwestern cities as black civil society became more robust with its politically influential and professionally trained civic leaders. No doubt, the black community was now better positioned to force structural change.

Confronting Exclusion Up North

In the early twentieth century, the rising industrial and cultural metropolis of Detroit was an important destination for black families. Connected to other major black settlements such as Chicago, St. Louis, Memphis, the Mississippi Delta, Birmingham, and Atlanta, the beaten path to Wayne County, Michigan, raised the black population from 43,000 in 1920 to over 100,000 in 1928. Nearly all newcomers settled in Detroit. In that period, Wayne County records of confined youths show skyrocketing numbers of "American colored nationality," in the strained official parlance for black people. The 100 black youths detained in the county in 1918 grew to 1,109 by 1928.[3]

Wayne County officials neglected this growing black juvenile population until the late 1930s, when black civic leaders shifted the balance of racialized social control. Black Detroit youths in detention faced long, idle waits owing to the segregation of court services. Michigan's juvenile institutions used mainly private contractors that routinely denied access to most black youths while aiding white, Catholic, and Protestant youths. The state institution at Adrian did admit black youths on a quota system. Though intended for serious cases, it was often filled to quota capacity with blacks accused of minor offenses.[4]

Race relations were about to explode given police violence, housing and employment discrimination, and juvenile injustices. Sensing the pressures emanating from the expanding dockets of black court-involved youths and the growing organization of black civil society, white city leaders began to accommodate demands for social change. "[The] rapid influx of people coming from entirely different living and working conditions, from radical differences of climate and equally violent changes of laws, ordinances and health regulations," a 1928 Detroit court study reasoned, "has imposed on this group most exacting problems of adjustment and adaptation." Noting northern hostility toward foreign arrivals and the inevitability of "race adjustment," the report acknowledged that court officials would have to amend policies and practices in light of the growing presence and demands of black people.[5] Over the next two decades, Detroit and other cities would illustrate how the growth of New Negro identity politics and political resources encouraged this realization and a gradual system response.

Emboldened Black Leadership: Racial Politics of the New Negro

The New Negro was defined by the black urban condition, and the concept enticed rural and southern blacks to move to cities. A romantic and pliable ideal of black self-realization and group progress, the notion was adaptable to the varied circumstances and outlooks of black women and men. It displaced the outdated modesty of uplift ideology by asserting an explicitly political, masculinist, and militant claim on the future of black America. The New Negro was as much a forecast as a description. It was, as Alain Locke wrote, "an augury of a new democracy in American culture."[6]

Fashioned during the Black Renaissance of the 1920s, New Negro identity rejected modesty and marginalization and was at once a defensive and an offensive statement. It challenged the defamations of black character and denials of civil standing that were still rampant in mainstream science, politics, literature, popular culture, and law. It offered a defense of black humanity, intelligence, and civil rights against white supremacist assaults, countering with a "positive public image of blacks as thinking, creative human beings." In offensive terms, it was a psychological and social strategy intended to spark the latent potential of black collective action. As the historian John Henrik Clarke writes of the broader Black Renaissance: "The movement . . . was the natural and logical result of years of neglect, suppression, and degradation. Black Americans were projecting themselves as human beings." They were also demanding that whites and nonwhites accept their humanness. For the first time in American history, Clarke writes, "a large number of Black writers, artists and intellectuals took a unified walk into the North American sun," discovering and constructing new visions for the black world.[7]

Though radiating from many urban settlements, this black declaration of rebirth was centered in the incomparable black metropolis of Harlem. During the first decades of the twentieth century, New York City had been a principal destination for black migrants from all over searching for opportunity. Owing to residential segregation, poverty, and the real estate magnate Phillip Payton Jr., many new arrivals settled in the northern Manhattan community of Harlem. It brought together a diverse mix of black social, economic, and political capital. Harlem thus became the intellectual and political heart of the black world, the "Mecca of the New Negro," as Alain Locke famously described it. It was center stage for "the greatest period of self-discovery in African-American history after the Civil War and before the start of the Civil Rights era of the 1960s."[8]

A prismatic, fragmented expression of black leadership after World War I, New Negro identity politics turned on intersecting axes of race, social class, and gender difference.[9] Relatively few black elites and charismatic leaders orchestrated much of the creative work. Figures of varied means and interests, they created and circulated symbolic and substantive expressions of new black politics. Many would make claims on the New Negro, but two especially embodied its radical turn in racial consciousness, conflict, and cooperation. Marcus Garvey founded the United Negro Improvement Association (UNIA), and the scholar-activist W. E. B. DuBois was one of few black founding directors of the NAACP as well as a vital figure in the second wave of black child-saving.[10]

In the disheartening years following World War I, the charismatic Marcus Garvey enticed the black masses with "a new dream, a new promise, and a new land," even if the black elite remained apprehensive.[11] World War I had put the enduring boundaries of the racial contract into sharp relief. During and after the war, black soldiers suffered "all forms of Jim Crow, humiliation, discrimination, slander, and . . . violence at the hands of white civilians," with little protection or recourse. The Ku Klux Klan's resurgence and the Red Summer of 1919 offered evidence that Progressive Era black advances had collapsed. Some lost whatever faith remained in their own nation and people.[12]

Garvey's powerful rhetoric and audacious plans seemed to offer concrete and accessible answers to unwavering race questions. They gave him and the UNIA a massive and enthusiastic black audience. The first UNIA convention, held in New York in 1920, was an incomparable affair. Harlem was electrified with anticipation of the event and then mesmerized by an opening parade in which "component parts of the U.N.I.A. were for the first time revealed to an astonished black world." The historian Edmund Cronon has recounted the powerful spectacle: "First came the African Legion, smartly dressed in dark blue uniforms with narrow red trouser stripes. . . . Unarmed except for the dress swords of its officers, [its] existence hinted that the redemption of the Negro people might come through force. Another group, the Black Cross Nurses, two hundred strong and neatly attired in white, indicated the readiness of the U.N.I.A. to come to the aid of stricken peoples all over the world. . . . Even children had a place . . . [marching] beside their elders in a special juvenile auxiliary." Garvey's culminating address drew an overflow crowd of over twenty-five thousand, filling Madison Square Garden, and spilling onto surrounding streets.[13]

Garvey and the UNIA cultivated the impression of emboldened race leadership and rapid race achievement through public spectacles, its newspaper (*The Negro World*), and industries such as the Black Star shipping line. These cultural symbols inspired and expanded black collective identification and action. Signaling growing black economic means and Garvey's singular mass appeal, the UNIA sold $500,000 of Black Star stock between 1919 and 1920 alone, almost exclusively to black shareholders. In its first months of operation, the UNIA drew thousands of dues-paying members; in three years, it had over one thousand divisions in forty countries. Garveyism inspired massive resistance to the oppression and domination gripping the black diaspora and, as the historian John Henrik Clarke writes, thereby "shook the foundations of three empires," including the United States.[14]

Neither Garvey nor the UNIA were significantly involved in juvenile justice reform. At the 1920 convention, however, the Declaration of Rights of the Negro Peoples of the World addressed the human and civil rights of criminally condemned black youths. "In order to encourage our race all over the world and to stimulate it to a higher and greater destiny," the declaration begins, "we demand and insist on the following Declaration of Rights." Article 44 identifies juvenile justice reform as a component of elevating the race. "We deplore and protest against the practice of confining juvenile prisoners in prisons with adults," the article declares, "and we recommend that such youthful prisoners be taught gainful trades under humane supervision."[15] Though it reinforced long-standing concerns of earlier black child-saving initiatives, no intervention in juvenile justice policy or practice seems to have resulted.

Garvey's significance to juvenile justice reform was, thus, general or contextual. As an incomparable force in the black world and the leader of one of the largest mass movements the United States had ever seen, Garvey shaped impressions of what was possible and the kind of leadership that would be required. Particularly relevant to the second wave of reforms were his calls for racial pride and self-government. He often declared his intention to remake the black world by elevating representative black leadership. In one of his first speeches, he highlighted the absence of a black political power base and vowed to create it. "Where is the black man's government?" he asked. "Where is his president, his country, and his ambassadors, his army, his navy and his men of big affairs?" Playing to black yearnings for national standing, he promised "a new world of black men, not peons, serfs, dogs and slaves, but a nation of sturdy men making their impress upon civilization and causing a new light to dawn upon the human race."[16]

Garveyism focused on reclaiming continental Africa, but it furnished more omnibus race pride even among black Americans who never intended to leave the United States. As such, it was an early radical foil that inspired and likely aided more liberal efforts to frame and negotiate concessions in domestic human and civil rights.[17] Garvey's ideals resonated with the desires of many black moderates and progressives, including the rising educated and professional class, to seize opportunities within the capitalist democracy, rather than radically redefine social relations in America or globally. They inspired legions of New Negro women and men to join in remaking the cultural and institutional boundaries of American democracy as their "ambitions and wishes [grew to] demand a wider field of social participation than permitted within the traditional Negro status." Garvey staged ceremonial rituals of black authority. At the 1920 UNIA convention, he was elected "provisional president of Africa," and troops marched through the streets of Harlem. Yet his empowering message of a black renaissance inspired diverse efforts to claim modest, proximal power within American society.[18]

Power Moves: The Expansion of Political Strategy

The later wave of black child-saving was a calculated reaction to evolving social and political opportunities available through educational attainment, professional integration, and political participation. Pioneer black child-savers dreamed of empowering black adults in the administration of juvenile justice. Despite making some inroads, they generally leveraged limited resources in self-help efforts. Relations of racial domination and oppression in juvenile social control thus remained intact. Disfranchised black child-savers and constituencies found pressure group politics impossible. This limited their influence on decisionmaking and the structural impact of their opposition. Exclusion weakened between World Wars I and II owing to the black exodus, New Deal programs, advances in education, and expansions of civil rights.

One key to this changing opportunity structure was the passage in 1920 of the Nineteenth Amendment. Despite lacking explicit regional or race-based limits on women's suffrage, extensions of the franchise pertained only to black populations outside the South. Northern and typically urban community activists could now use pressure group politics to force structural reforms in juvenile justice. In the small but rapidly growing northern black settlements, some black women's clubs immediately began to leverage this new political influence. In 1925, when Ohio's Federation of Club-women attempted to extend services to black girls in juvenile institutions, it focused on securing black adult influence within the state administration of juvenile justice rather than creating its own institutions. It aimed to position black teachers and administrators for work in state facilities, supplementing the effort by "keeping up with all the bills that vitally affected [blacks] as a group, as well as all state institutions." A federation circular coordinated political action by publicizing bills deserving consideration and instructing members on "how to vote intelligently." Partisanship was of little use to southern NACW federations, but, in the urban North after 1920, it became a viable strategy for redistributing status and power in the parental state.[19]

Because northern black populations were not powerful voting blocks, the vote remained a limited instrument for changing the racial politics of juvenile justice. Moreover, little pertaining to juvenile justice was subject to popular vote. Occasionally, the black vote did influence the national, state, or local leadership of key government offices and even choices in policy-making, regulation, and appropriation. Yet these were distant and unreliable forms of indirect representation, especially before the 1970s.

Since power was dispersed throughout various agencies and authorities of the parental state, reformers embraced diverse political interventions, especially through education and labor. For later black child-savers, education, professional training, and employment were more direct and reliable paths to political influence within juvenile social control. They reasoned that enduring freedom depended on ending segregation through ballot booths and legal reforms. Educational preparation could prepare race-conscious black women and men for key roles in services and the professions as they slowly opened along the way. Lasting recognition of black interests in American juvenile justice would require an active black presence among authorities, not merely changes in formal law or policy.

A new political strategy for racially democratizing social control required education, professional employment, and the organization of black professional and service workers to be interdependent parts.[20] A major test of this strategy came in the mid-1920s, when the NACW and NAACP co-founder Mary Church Terrell pressed the Coolidge administration to create a "division of colored women" within either the Women's Bureau or the Children's Bureau of the Labor Department. As director of such a division, Terrell explained, she could advise the administration on what more "might and should be done for colored women and children where they get little protection from the law."[21]

The Department of Labor declined Terrell's request, saying that she lacked the credentials necessary for appointment to an executive position. A federal classifications board determined the bureau to be a "Professional and Scientific Service." As such, administrators were required to have technical skills and credentials in medicine, law, economics, sociology, statistics, etc. All nonclerical positions in either bureau now required a college education and years of professional experience, both of which Terrell possessed. In reply to Terrell, Mary Anderson, the head of the Women's Bureau, noted previous efforts to include black workers, especially in a defunct Division of Negro Economics during World War I. Anderson then admitted that there was neither black representation currently nor interest in Terrell's proposal. She did not think much of Terrell's qualifications. She wrote to the secretary of labor that "her greatest effort has been spent in the League of Peace and Freedom and I do not feel Mrs. Terrell has the special . . . qualifications and technical knowledge which are essential," adding that she "doubt[s] very much if [Terrell] could pass the special examination which our investigators have to pass." In her letter to Terrell, Anderson was more evasive. Establishing a division of colored women would be impossible owing to lack of funds, "unless a special emergency arises to employ a colored woman, a trained investigator, to do emergency work." Other officials such as Children's Bureau director Grace Abbott received Terrell more favorably, as did President Coolidge's personal secretary. Both encouraged her to take the civil service exam and to apply for an existing position.[22]

Demonstrating her emboldened leadership, Terrell replied that, in light of her accomplishments and the agencies' own standards, she was already well qualified and it was "useless to take an examination." She added:

> If my record, my training . . . , my travels, my life-long interest in the welfare of the race, my indefatigable labors along all lines, and the many offices of trust and honor heaped upon me by white and black do not entitle me to recognition, to say nothing of my work for the Republican Party in the last two campaigns, nothing that I can write on paper in an examination will do me any good. . . . Neither Miss Anderson . . . nor Miss [Grace] Abbott in the Children's Bureau had to take an examination. My training and record certainly compare favorably with theirs.

Insisting that "colored women should be allowed to assist in promoting the welfare of their group in the government," the sixty-two-year-old veteran of black child-saving initiatives persisted in requesting that the administration provide a position commensurate with her stature and ability.[23] Terrell was refused positions in both bureaus, but her attitude signaled the new political maneuvering of black juvenile justice reformers. Black clubwomen and other second-wave leaders continued to prioritize educational preparation and formal qualification for various positions of influence. This rising generation of race-expert leaders gradually penetrated the base of parental state authority, shifting the balance of racial group power in American juvenile justice.

Black Activist Professionals, 1920–50

The diversified intervention strategy eventually yielded a black surrogate parental state. A novel and formidable apparatus, this refuge for black youths and representation would oppose Jim Crow oppression and domination in juvenile justice. This section will survey the shifting strategy and growing impact of black child-saving initiatives through the second quarter of the twentieth century.

Detailing the Crisis: Enter the NAACP

Histories of American juvenile justice regularly overlook the major contributions of black civic associations, including black women's clubs and civil rights organizations. For black America, however, these nongovernment organizations were essential to the nineteenth- and twentieth-century development of juvenile justice—none more so than the NAACP. The association's determination to eliminate the separate but equal doctrine, as well as its focus on equality in education and the courts, meshed well with the rights of criminally accused and condemned black youths. The early leadership of the NAACP was largely white, with Dr. W. E. B. DuBois the sole black American on the original executive board. All strata of the black world became card-carrying members. Its first black director came in 1975, in the person of the Reverend Benjamin Hooks. The grandson of the Memphis black child-savers Julia and Charles Hooks, he was elected executive director. Marcus Garvey and other black nationalists believed the prominence of white leadership to be to the organization's discredit, but the NAACP's integrationist agenda was calculated to offer political cover and enhance its effectiveness in the early years.[24]

The NAACP's visibility and influence grew dramatically. By 1914—its fourth year in operation—the association had around six thousand members in forty branches nationwide. Its periodical, *The Crisis: A Record of the Dark Races*, edited and largely written by W. E. B. DuBois, had over thirty thousand readers.[25] Along with black newspapers in Chicago, New York, Pittsburgh, and Cleveland, *The Crisis* became a key source of information on black cultural, socioeconomic, and geopolitical interests. Nearly 100,000 copies were sold monthly by 1919. "In an era of rampant illiteracy, when hard labor left Afro-Americans little time or inclination for reading Harvard-accented editorials," the historian David Levering Lewis writes, *The Crisis* "found its way into kerosene-lit sharecroppers' cabins and cramped factory worker's tenements. In middle-class families it lay next to the bible."[26]

The Crisis informed many readers and future civil rights leaders of the collective violence of Jim Crow juvenile justice. Its second issue weighed in on the issue, briefly noting the work of black child-savers in the South. A section titled "A Colored Reformatory" reported that the North Carolina legislature was to consider a proposal for a black reformatory. The proposal came from a local organization formed after a black woman, who had been raised in Greensboro but migrated to New York, bequeathed a tract of 365 acres for this purpose. The land had been purchased with savings from years of domestic work, and her will instructed that it be sold to raise funds for the establishment and operation of a black reformatory in the state. Excerpts from a black Kentucky paper on Louisville's police department were circulated nationally. They criticized the "systematic process of bulldozing the Negro population [with] causeless arrests." DuBois subtly connected the abuse of white police power to the *Dred Scott* (1857) decision. Noting the "offensive and illegal commands thrown at quiet, inoffensive Negro citizens on the street," he protested that "policemen acted upon the assumption that the Negro had no rights, civil or political, that a police bully was bound to respect."[27]

A 1912 issue of *The Crisis* extensively covered the murder conviction and pending execution in Virginia of a sixteen-year-old black girl, Virginia Christian. The white woman she allegedly killed had employed her as a servant. "It was Christian Virginia against Virginia Christian," DuBois announced, "a Christian Virginia which does not even provide a reformatory for colored girls." DuBois argued that clemency was warranted because of evidence of self-defense, the girl's age, her diminished mental capacity, and other mitigating factors. He blasted the state for its handling of this case and its treatment of black delinquents generally. "It was the social organization of white Virginia that made this girl what she was and then brutally killed her for it," he wrote. "It is a disgrace to civilization for any modern State to put to death a mental child, whatever her color or race, when that child has been the product of adverse conditions for which the society is to blame." All efforts to spare her life failed, but the NAACP became more deeply involved in the fight against "social conditions which produce Virginia Christians in a race which obtains neither justice nor fair play in so many States of the Union."[28]

Similar reports on racial injustice in juvenile social control appear in a section within *The Crisis* called "The Burden." A 1912 issue protested the arrest and imprisonment of a sixteen-year-old girl for fighting in Montgomery, noting the generational impact of her mistreatment. The girl, Daisy Bell, spent a year and six months on the chain gang for this conviction, during which time she became pregnant by one of the white guards. By age eighteen, Daisy had been arrested and sentenced to the chain gang for fighting once again, leaving "her sickly baby in the shanty of a poor woman who is so busy trying to earn food that she can no more care for it than Daisy's mother could care for her." "The family history seems likely to proceed in the same vicious circle," noted DuBois. Tragically, he continued, "Daisy Bell, aged 18, untaught, neglected, outraged, has had no worse fate than befalls thousands of unhappy colored girls under the 'protection' of the white man's laws and 'superior civilization.'" He linked this burden in part to the lack of equal educational opportunities in the state, including the denial of access to reformatories. "The number of colored children brought before the [Alabama] court is rather larger than the number of white," he observed, but "apparently they are left to reform themselves as best they may, with the exception of the few who can be sent to Mount Meigs, the reformatory started by the colored women's clubs of Alabama." A 1914 issue covered the lynching of a seventeen-year-old girl in Oklahoma and the sentencing of a nineteen-year-old Virginian to ninety-nine years in prison for the status offense of having "illicit relations with a young white woman." In that year, a Los Angeles doctor appealed to the NAACP national office to investigate the case of "a young negro . . . sentenced to thirty years imprisonment on conviction of having robbed a white girl of a kiss."[29]

The NAACP's earliest involvement in juvenile justice reform raised consciousness of racial inequality in criminal and juvenile justice and highlighted the ameliorative efforts of others. *The Crisis* delivered news of countless instances of injustice to tens of thousands of readers nationwide. Its politicized crime and justice log recorded absurd, mundane, and horrific dimensions of Jim Crow justice and reflected on their injury to the race.

By World War I, the NAACP and other civil rights and social-welfare groups had become more directly involved in race-related juvenile justice reform. Reporting on events and activities around the country shifted to more detailed empirical investigations, advocacy of black representation, and leadership of direct action. The advance of empirical research was important, for it clarified the dynamics of racialized social control and focused attention on Jim Crow juvenile justice and other social problems. This work informed the development of protests and other social action.[30]

DuBois began to research and write on racialized crime control before the turn of the twentieth century. His sense of the political significance of the immortal youth, whose future shaped group fate, naturally progressed to an empirical study on Jim Crow juvenile justice.[31] The catalyst was Florence Kelley's field report on separate and unequal conditions of juvenile justice in Memphis. DuBois and other NAACP leaders planned a national study of Jim Crow juvenile justice. "As the result of another case which was brought to our attention," DuBois announced in 1914, "the [association] is making a study of the Relation of the Colored Child to the Juvenile

Courts of the United States." The board approved a motion by Mary Wright Ovington to appoint a committee led by DuBois, then director of publicity and research, to conduct a national study of race and juvenile justice. Committee correspondence suggests that the study was to include a survey of juvenile law in various states, compilation of data on the development of juvenile courts, identification of cities and states where black children were provided for separately, and data on outcomes for black youths processed in segregated and integrated courts. "It is impossible to make an exhaustive investigation," DuBois acknowledged, "but enough representative cities will be included to give a fair idea of actual conditions."[32]

What remains of the NAACP study in organizational records are handwritten field notes on formal structures of juvenile justice systems in a few states and indications of progress reports.[33] Around the time of the study, DuBois and the NAACP were inundated with efforts to combat black disfranchisement. DuBois investigated the cases of two Oklahoma black children reported to be "wealthy in oil lands and [being] defrauded and neglected by their white guardians." In 1914, the association launched a protest of segregation in federal government agencies and became embroiled in its first major legal campaign when it challenged the infamous "grandfather clause." Another major protest and legal fight was against *Birth of a Nation* in 1915, the blockbuster film that fueled racial violence nationwide. Internationally, World War I erupted just as the juvenile court study was to commence. The NAACP and DuBois were consumed with the local and transnational implication of the conflict. Given all these efforts, the NAACP may have likely tabled or abandoned the ambitious study. Despite being concerned with youths, crime, and justice throughout his long and closely studied career, DuBois left no written commentary or reference to the study or to data obtained from it.[34]

Empirical studies by other civil rights and social-welfare organizations after World War I did advance the understanding of, and opposition to, Jim Crow juvenile justice. In 1926, the Department of Research of the National Urban League, along with the Women's City Club of New York and other parties, formed the Joint Committee on Negro Child Study in New York City. The committee included three dozen black and white members. They represented the NAACP, the Empire State Federation of Colored Women's Clubs, the New York Urban League, the Brooklyn Urban League, the Utopia Neighborhood Club, and several other groups. Charles S. Johnson, another black sociologist (then heading the National Urban League's research department), directed the committee, which produced *A Study of the Delin-*

quent and Neglected Negro Children Before the New York City Children's Court
(1927). Six recommendations addressed problems that black youths encountered in the court and the community, black delinquency and neglect
cases, and inadequacies in institutional provision. They called for increased
city efforts to prevent black delinquency and dependence (i.e., after-school
programs and recreation), improved social work services, and better access
to segregated institutions for court-involved black youths.[35]

Beyond New York, the committee thought that its research findings
would benefit social workers and reformers "in those cities . . . facing the
problems arising from recently arrived groups of people differing in race
from the dominant group, as with the Mexican in the west and the Negro
in the north." The report speaks to how professional research and reporting
through multiracial collaborations can help advance social change. Calling
for more coalitions like its own, the committee thought that the approach
demonstrated the value of "accumulating and examining existing information upon a special subject with the purpose of securing action regarding
it." It acknowledged that social change often depends on dominant group
support. "Only as a large group of publicly minded citizens of both [*sic*]
races becomes interested in giving the Negro child a better opportunity will
the specific recommendations of the report be carried out."[36]

In North Carolina, a diverse committee of social researchers and community organizers conducted a collaborative study of Jim Crow juvenile justice
to advance social change. It discovered nearly complete government neglect
of black youth and family justice issues in the state before the mid-1920s as
"lack of funds and perhaps a more or less indifferent attitude on the part of
county and city officials prevented the development of any specialized effort
in the field of Negro Welfare." Change began in 1925 with the establishment
of an interracial committee, the Division of Work among Negroes, within the
North Carolina Board of Public Charities. The first of its kind in the South, the
committee's accomplishments under the black social work pioneer Lawrence
Augusta Oxley led several states to adopt the model.[37]

Prospects for formal integration were slim, so the division believed that
"the only practical approach to the Negro community lies through the machinery the Negroes themselves have set up." Its information was intended
to assist efforts to expand the state's black social and child-welfare services.
It developed a detailed empirical study of racialized juvenile social control
in North Carolina. Half the study's $10,000 budget was provided by the
Rosenwald Fund. The School of Public Welfare and the Institute for Research in Social Science at the University of North Carolina provided pro

bono services, and the remainder, nearly $2,000, "came in gradually in gifts, ranging from pennies of Negro school children to $100 checks from organizations and citizens of both races."[38]

In work leading up to its publication of *Negro Child Welfare in North Carolina* (1933), this group of white and black social workers and social researchers amassed ethnographic data, court transcripts, interviews, case records, and commitment records. Together, they offer a rare perspective on the specific needs and experiences of black youths in southern juvenile court communities. The authors asked whether the "social institutions of North Carolina function for the protection and development of the Negro child" and whether this can "foster a more thorough, systematic and intelligent care of the Negro child of the future." The answers were not encouraging. Yet the study's empirical basis for opposing Jim Crow juvenile justice morally and politically exceeded all previous and most future attempts. By the time Lawrence Oxley left North Carolina to join the Department of Labor in 1934, he had used the study to secure new positions for black juvenile probation officers in thirty North Carolina counties and to professionalize social work education by developing black college programs.[39]

Mobilizing the Black Race Relations Expert

Midcentury advances in education and the professions propelled black child-saving initiatives. They affected movement strategies and capacities as well as structural or institutional reform. Partly due to the skills and services of black professionals, civic leaders became better informed about civil rights and wrongs in juvenile justice. By the 1920s and 1930s, scholars, lawyers, social workers, and others skillful at measuring, critiquing, and challenging Jim Crow juvenile justice were the backbone of black civic associations. Service workers within agencies of the parental state, including the juvenile courts, were now better positioned to influence decisionmaking.

After World War I, it was not uncommon to find one or two black probation officers, and perhaps some black police officers, handling cases in large, urban black communities. Typically, their resources and influence were extremely limited.[40] Many cities initially hoped that probation officers would assume social work functions for juvenile courts to help manage the growing caseloads of black youths. According to a 1928 study, Birmingham, Atlanta, Savannah, Richmond, Baltimore, New York, Cleveland, Chicago, and Louisville had "Negro probation officers for work with juveniles."[41] Black women and men long relegated to the margins of juvenile social control or operating exclusively through black community institutions were now increasingly employed in the formal legal and bureaucratic apparatus of juvenile justice. As the economic and political position of blacks strengthened, service workers and professionals experienced expanded influence, became more representative of organized black interests, and became seen as vital resources for institutionalizing racial justice.[42]

Black professionals were idealized as expert race leaders. They were seen to possess a unique capacity to "voice protest against racial barriers" and "perform the necessary and complimentary task of *race adjustment* in the best tradition of the struggle against discrimination and segregation." The so-called race relations expert was envisioned as a specialized analyst of race relations distinguished by professional skills, access to information, and the ability to mobilize "techniques for race adjustment" (i.e., reforms). These experts' professional insights and political access positioned them better "than the nonprofessional constantly to know the status quo of those interests bearing upon [their] particular field of action." Thus, they had "a more inclusive and detailed view of the 'interests' which really motivate change." This logic owed much to the marginalization of black communities and the inevitability of negotiating compromises with white power structures through incremental assertions of black interests. Race relations experts would theoretically represent black interests through involvement in "the making of policy; the development of procedures and techniques; the observation and review of operations; and the development and distribution of information."[43] All the while, they had to balance professional obligations, competing political agendas, and other practical considerations.[44]

Earlier black clubwomen had used similar resource mobilization strategies. Professionals were expected to be vehicles of concentrated influence and, like women's clubs, to maximize collective efficacy by pooling limited group resources. By this logic, professionalization created individual leaders whose advanced education and formal employment propagated group influence, and compounding group benefits were expected from training individuals for employment in social work, education, law, and other fields. One professional school graduate became another potential educator and professional contact who would expand the presence and ranks of race experts.

Efforts of idealized black race relations experts to engage in progressive interventions and social change were circumscribed by dominant group influence over professional selection, which favored politically moderate blacks, and limits on black institutional influence. However, mobilizing black professionals was essential to the growing scope and impact of black child-saving initiatives in extending services to black youths and giving voice to black constituents.

Racial Politics of Professional Integration: From Tokenism to Race Brokering

White domination of juvenile justice administration kept black candidates out of decisionmaking positions, filtered the black representatives who did gain entry, and limited their roles, resources, and authority. Black juvenile justice professionals thus had few of the tools needed to redefine the racial politics of juvenile social control. The reign of "Mother Bowles," a somewhat infamous black authority of Missouri's parental state, illustrates the uncertain progressive significance of black professional integration, given structural constraints and the shortcomings of particular leaders.

Through much of the 1930s, a black woman named Ethel Bowles, but known as Mother Bowles, led Missouri's Tipton School for Girls. Appointed by the state's Democratic governor, Bowles was a climber who failed to lift black spirits or circumstances along the way. She is remembered for relishing, mismanaging, and abusing her limited authority, which compounded problems of deprivation at the school.[45]

When Bowles arrived, over eighty black girls were committed to Tipton. She started with enlightened strategies, such as a merit system for good behavior, but eventually took shorter routes to inmate management and control. As institutional pressures grew, Bowles and her staff (all black) "found themselves unable to be more than custodians of a building full of troubled girls. . . . Their priority became the smooth running of the institution, not the rehabilitation of its inhabitants."[46] Faced with overpopulation, insufficient staff, and too few resources to provide services, Bowles and her staff turned to corporal punishment. Describing it as plain abuse, one girl was moved by pain and fear to craft an ominous parody of the Twenty-third Psalm, kept hidden in her Bible in quiet protest at Tipton: "Mother Bowles is my shepherd. I am in want. She maketh me lie down on the floor. She leadeth me beside starvation. She torments my soul. . . . Yea tho' I walk through the valley of death I fear evil for she is with me. Her rod and her staff they beat me. She breaks down my defense in the presence of mine enemies. She anoints my head with whelps. My cup is empty, surely hatred and revenge shall follow me all the days of my life and I shall dwell in hell forever and ever."[47]

Bowles viewed the threat and the act of whipping as an effective control strategy. This was not because it harkened to slavery, as officials in 1930s North Carolina saw it, but because she could manipulate the girls' fear in attempting their reform. To break through to girls, "we have found that the nearest approach to them is through fear," she explained; "then we are able to develop 'Pride' and 'Self Respect' and . . . [obedience to] authority. If not, they will be hurt physically [since] their bodies are the only things they are conscious of, apparently."[48]

Poor leadership contributed to the ordeals at Tipton, but so did persistent denials of resources for the institution's programming, supply, and staffing needs. From its opening through the 1950s, resource deprivations affecting supplies, wages, and services were far greater at Tipton than at the reformatory for white girls in Chillicothe, Missouri. Bowles's biennial report for 1933–34 notes the state's irregular annual appropriations for Tipton's operating budget. Amounts steadily declined from an initial sum of $64,000 in 1915, to $40,000 in 1929, to $27,000 in 1933. The governor vetoed a planned $5,000 appropriation for Tipton School in 1943, claiming that it "exceeded the girls' needs by $4,297."[49]

Consequently, Tipton could not adequately clothe, feed, educate, or provide health care to the girls, much less recruit and maintain adequate personnel. Owing to chronic clothing shortages, the girls' school uniforms were characterized as "rags"; they had too few coats to go around and wore shoes with worn-out soles. "Old and ragged" textbooks were too few in number, limiting their education to lectures. This "handicapped" the teaching of younger girls. Medical supplies were unaffordable, and there were no resident health services. Such deprivations at an institution filled beyond capacity compounded difficulties, likely hastening desperate control measures such as physical punishments.[50]

When black child-savers envisioned integration, they idealized the official position and influence of people like Ethel Bowles and her staff. Although run by an all-black staff, Tipton paid salaries that remained "considerably lower than those paid at Chillicothe." The superintendent was forced to hire "any who applied," not those whose training and temperament would most benefit the institution. Bowles thanked clubwomen in Missouri for helping shore up Tipton's resource deficit by "lending valuable aid in finding work and providing homes for girls released from the School, and promising to be 'Big Sisters' to them until paid social workers or parole officers can be supplied."[51]

Given these considerations, it is not surprising that so many girls who left Tipton soon returned or wound up in the penitentiary. Mother Bowles patiently indulged these disparities and was selected more for her "political loyalty than . . . [her] professional training in how to deal with juvenile delinquents." The suffering of Tipton's black youths thus demonstrates the limits of black professional influence and effectiveness.[52]

Another early and influential advocate of the liberal agenda of professional integration was Mary McLeod Bethune. With her, more representative black leadership showed progress but also ongoing constraints. Bethune was a former president of the NACW (1924–28) and the founding president of the National Council of Negro Women (NCNW) (1935). The NCNW surpassed the NACW to become the most influential and longest-lived national black women's organization in the post–World War I period, and the shift belied the New Negro politics of later black child-saving initiatives.

In contrast to NACW clubs, which emphasized self-help efforts, the NCNW prioritized "networking with an eye to influence and hiring in [state agencies]." The NCNW was a new "voice for Negro womanhood in all the new agencies of the Roosevelt administration." In 1938, it "asked the Children's Bureau, Women's Bureau, Bureau of Education, Federal Housing Authority, and Social Security board to hire black women." It offered to improve their capacities for understanding and addressing black interests by coming to work with them.[53] Bethune and her contemporaries were not the first to promote professional integration of child- and social-welfare agencies. Black representation in government was recognized as important at least as far back as Reconstruction, and DuBois and other black leaders pressed for inclusion during the Progressive Era.

Owing to persistence and modest gains in black social and political capital, race women and men were better able to attain administrative positions. The strategy remained unreliable, however. Mary Church Terrell's experience showed the limits of black reliance on the state. Blacks lacked the leverage to have their favored representatives appointed or to assure sufficient access to needed resources and influence.[54] Formal credentials and experience were important, but they were not the primary factors governing the selection and influence of early black authorities of juvenile social control.

In 1935, Mary McLeod Bethune became the first black woman appointed to a federal office when President Roosevelt named her director of the new Division of Negro Affairs, which was created within his National Youth Administration (NYA). Terrell had coveted such an executive position, but the internal and external realities of segregation overshadowed Bethune's leadership of this New Deal agency. She accepted separate accommodations for black youths if black leaders were equally involved. Her concern was, not to integrate youth programs, but to ensure black supervision of black programs, to increase black participation in policymaking, and to force NYA programs to train black youths for more rewarding services and occupations than were traditionally prescribed under Jim Crow. As national director of "Negro affairs," Bethune struggled to impose these ideas on the NYA's state and local leaders and on others in Roosevelt's Black Cabinet. She became a high-profile adviser with little official influence.[55]

Representative Managers of Race Adjustment: Negotiating Liberal Reform

By World War II, black social, economic, and political advances were reducing white control over black leadership and increasing black professional influence. Black race relations experts emerged who were increasingly agents "selected and controlled by the group [they profess] to represent," especially in the urban North.[56] By the 1930s, a new arrangement had emerged between black, white, and other constituents of urban juvenile court communities. It was not participatory parity, but liberal black professional leaders increasingly served as arbiters of black community interests, deliberating and bargaining with dominant white counterparts over racial politics of juvenile justice.

By pressing for access to higher education and employment opportunities and extending the popular call for service to the race, the burgeoning civil rights movement encouraged black civic leaders to formulate innovative responses to the problems of black youths and families. A deepening pool of educated black activists included social and behavioral scientists, social workers, and lawyers and a growing array of black and interracial civic and professional associations. Collectively, they furnished a formidable base of information, strategy, technical skill, and influence to leverage in opposition to Jim Crow juvenile justice.[57]

Progress toward a negotiated racial order became apparent in Detroit. Detroit's growing black population had been denied resources and influence in juvenile justice administration. By the summer of 1943, however—a year after major race rioting in Detroit and other cities—the situation was ripe for change. The Council of Social Agencies (CSA) called meetings with Wayne County juvenile court authorities and service providers to assess the need for a new institution for black girls. Although the public facility at Adrian was filled to capacity, the CSA concluded that it was "unnecessary and uneconomic to create a new agency for Negro girls when there are now enough beds to accommodate them" in private, church-run facilities. Private institutions were urged to accept black youths.[58]

Detroit's white churches held firm to their segregation practices, despite receiving public funding and having vacancies in their reformatories. "Although the boards of these agencies did not originally set [them] up on a segregated basis," a CSA official explained, "the policy has gradually excluded Negro girls from the training and protection they require." Pressed by the growing black population and the scrutiny of civic leaders, the board of the League of Catholic Women affirmed a policy of serving "white, Roman Catholic girls only." Protestant churches likewise refused appeals to integrate, suggesting that black Detroit girls be sent three hundred miles south, to Carthage, Ohio, where a church-run institution for serious delinquents already held twenty-five black girls, mostly from Detroit.[59]

At a second CSA meeting, city leaders from the Detroit Urban League, the Department of Public Welfare, and the Detroit Council of Churches reflected on segregated services for girls to find new solutions. Black race leaders pressed hard for integration. Noting the success of interracial programming at other Michigan institutions, including a training school in Lansing, they protested that "arguments for exclusion and segregation appear as rationalizations of prejudice to the Negro group." "Since Negroes have the deep conviction that [integration] is and can be [effective]," they explained, "they resent the artificial barriers of color that deprive them from full participation in community life." They reminded participants that denial of full societal participation was at the core of racial conflict, including urban rebellion. The Urban League and others advocated "complete interracial integration of Negroes and whites in social agency programs as being the soundest policy for democratic and Christian practice." White church leaders resisted, insisting that Catholic and Protestant agencies were reasonable in "providing girls with an opportunity to retain their own faith if they wished."[60]

No compromise was in sight. In January 1944, the CSA sidestepped the issue with an "interracial policy" that required new agencies to be integrated. What to do with black girls now involved in Detroit's court remained unresolved. Antiracism among white Detroiters was so rare, a frustrated board member concluded, and seemingly limited to "professional social workers and the medical groups," that integration remained impossible. To diffuse the issue, the CSA appealed to black self-help initiatives, promising public funding, technical assistance, and formal control that had rarely existed in the past if a black "nationality organization" would step in.[61]

The Urban League declined because it was interested in working toward economic and social policy change rather than service delivery. Answering the call was the Detroit-based alumni chapter of Delta Sigma Theta, a black sorority dating to 1913 and symbolizing the evolution of black women's leadership, including the prominence of professionals. The chapter, established in 1939, already had over one hundred "professional women" among its members when the city called for help.[62]

The CSA's new interracial policy posed a barrier to this solution since the Deltas would have to offer services to black and white girls. They balked, considering the acute paucity of services for black girls and their interest in *treating* the race issues black girls faced. They hoped to provide services that addressed the "additional burden of the disturbed adolescent needing to deal with racial discrimination" but, ultimately, agreed to establish an integrated program.[63] White race leaders rejected the interracial plan anyway. Private foundations rejected funding proposals, and church leaders threatened to withdraw their support; an unsolicited private donor pledged $20,000 if the Delta institution were restricted to black girls.[64]

To move forward on the Delta project, the CSA's integration agenda had to be jettisoned. To offset continued denials of public and private support outside the black community, the Wayne County juvenile court judge pledged a court payment of $10.00 per week for each girl committed to the Delta facility and appeased the white community by promising to "never send a white girl to the home against her or her parents' wishes." The council quietly waived its interracial policy and the one-year probationary period for new state-contracted agencies. To reduce the Deltas' program costs, the city purchased the home. Race expert researchers at the Urban League gave technical assistance, using their residential segregation data to locate a site within a neighborhood with the right racial mix. In June 1947, the Deltas opened the Delta Home for Girls. The institution had twenty-five beds and remained in operation into the 1960s.[65]

Slow, steady efforts delivered the city's first black-led reformatory and elevated black adult authority within Wayne County's juvenile court community. Closely cooperating with the CSA and the court, the Deltas established a professional board of directors to oversee the operation. They assembled a biracial board with twenty-one members. Most of them were black women affiliated with the sorority, but many were drawn from the growing local ranks of black women social workers. The council also helped locate a Delta Home director with relevant training in child and social welfare. It proposed Mary O. Waters, a black woman previously interested in helping the council provide services to black girls. She had social work credentials and a graduate degree in education from the University of Michigan. After becoming founding director, Waters was credited with bringing a "creative spark theretofore missing in the study of this problem."[66]

In Detroit, the second wave of reform advanced politically and professionally to challenge Jim Crow juvenile justice. The movement to racially democratize youth justice was explicitly political, more technical, and diversified. From the 1930s to the 1940s, this loose network created a new social movement, a black surrogate parental state, that gave black youths and communities unprecedented access to social services, legal representation, and political advocacy in juvenile justice. Eventually, liberal reformers would try to blend this entity into a racially integrated parental state, as the representational basis of institutionalized, ongoing racial justice. In the meantime, the black surrogate parental state became a formidable force in the fight against Jim Crow juvenile justice.

Growing Leverage: The Foil of Radical Demands

Liberal reform efforts in the 1930s and 1940s progressed partly from the growing radicalism and nationalism of black political culture. According to the sociologists St. Clair Drake and Horace Cayton, the black freedom struggle was not "a monolithic unity" in the movement, advancing instead owing to the "diversity of competing leaders stimulating each other to win gains for the Negro people." "There [was] a kind of informal and even unplanned division of labor," they explain, "with the 'accepted leaders' negotiating and pleading for Negroes, while the radicals turned on the heat."[67]

The existence of more radical demands offered liberal, black child-saving initiatives leverage. From at least the 1930s, national and global injustices promoted revolutionary change over piecemeal social reform. Outrageous incidents of racial violence against black youths also fueled radical demands. Although lynch law declined in the 1930s, over one hundred lynchings, mostly of black Americans, took place. As expressions of popular, overt racial violence diminished, state violence increased under the auspices of criminal social control, including juvenile whippings and executions.[68]

In early 1930, nine black youths were falsely accused of gang raping two white girls on a Memphis-bound freight train. Ranging in age from twelve to nineteen, they were tried in Scottsboro, Alabama, twelve days after their arrest. "Guilty or not guilty," the prosecution told an all-white jury, "let's get rid of these niggers."[69] Three days later, all nine were found guilty. Eight were sentenced to death, and one of the youngest, a thirteen-year-old, received life imprisonment. Owing to protests and appeals by the NAACP, the Communist Party, the celebrity attorney Clarence Darrow, and others, the U.S. Supreme Court overturned the convictions and ordered retrials in 1932.[70] Reconvicted in two subsequent trials, four of the Scottsboro boys were finally acquitted in 1936 and four more in 1940. Sentenced to death in four trials, the remaining defendant escaped and fled to Detroit. He was captured in 1950, but the governor of Michigan refused extradition.[71]

Others did not fare as well as the Scottsboro Boys. In the middle third of the twentieth century, scores of black adolescents and young adults were killed legally and extralegally for offenses that defy neat distinctions in criminal and civil law. Nearly one hundred black youths were executed between 1931 and 1959, constituting over 80 percent of all youths executed in the

United States. That was nearly half of all black youth executions recorded in U.S. history to that date.[72] Other state executions that provoked national and international outrage were those of George Stinney in South Carolina and Charles Trudell and James Lewis Jr. in 1940s Mississippi. These events intensified the determination to advance racially democratic relations, whether through civil rights or radical social change.

Divisions between the NAACP's old and new guard reflected the growing radicalism of the 1930s and 1940s. The former allied with white liberals and worked through formal and professional channels. The latter became more vested in local leadership and self-determination. In 1934, W. E. B. DuBois broke with the old guard, resigning as editor of *The Crisis* after failing to seize greater control of the NAACP. He had hoped to break its dependence on white philanthropy and leadership, diminish the role of the national office, and increase "democratic control" of the board through elections by NAACP members. Blacks, he insisted, must replace whites in determining their own destiny. Frustrated by Depression Era economic and organizational tensions and the slow pace of social change, he sought to revive earlier plans for a segregated black economy. College-educated black "technical engineers" were to create manufacturing and distribution systems to support a black economy. The falling out with the NAACP and the black nationalist plan were part of a radical third stage of his "Evolving Program for Negro Freedom." It was dedicated to "scientific investigation and organized action among Negroes, in close co-operation, to secure the survival of the Negro race, until the cultural development of America and the world is willing to recognize Negro freedom."[73]

Other black race leaders also embraced more radical and nationalist politics. In 1935, Ralph Bunche, A. Phillip Randolph, and other "new crowd leaders" organized the National Negro Congress, whose militancy attracted more than five thousand largely middle-class black women and men—"secretaries and social workers, labor leaders and preachers, politicians and doctors"—to its first convention in Chicago. The black press announced "a new race leadership in the making," hoping that this generation would be "free of the inhibitions which have tended to distort the thinking or seal the lips of the older generation."[74]

The shifts reinforced the cultural and political repositioning of the New Negro and reflected the generally dynamic nature of race consciousness and leadership. Still, divisions between the old and the new guards were not always clear-cut. Tired of foot dragging by race experts in the national office, NAACP chapters in several cities collaborated with the National Negro Congress to advance labor interests.[75]

The national NAACP maintained a moderate, liberal integrationist agenda, but its journal gave voice to more radical political agendas. In 1937, with Roger Wilkins in charge, *The Crisis* published "Our Delinquent Children," its most radical critique of Jim Crow juvenile justice to date. Expanding on DuBois's race-specific notion of the immortal youth, it characterized the criminalization of black youths as a "Fascist threat to the working class and to the Negro race." Its author, Elaine Ellis, insisted that equality in juvenile justice would depend, not on socialization through institutions, such as the integration of black youths and workers, but rather on "the economic level of the people [being] raised."[76] Associating Jim Crow juvenile justice with the racist eugenics movement, Scottsboro, and the political economy of capitalism, she cited fascism as the common ingredient. Socialist revolution would be the only realistic cure.

Liberal black leaders did see the need for fundamental change. Structural transformation, however, would come through formal legal protections and professional representation. The experiences of Mother Bowles at Tipton and Mary Bethune in the Roosevelt administration exposed the limits of relying on institutional integration. Detroit's Deltas and others illustrated the measured but important impact of representation among authorities. Promising or not, liberal demands for equal youth protection and participatory parity in juvenile justice gained traction amid calls for socialist revolution.

Black Child-Saving from the Bench: The Honorable Activist Jane Bolin

The liberal race-expert leadership of Judge Jane Matilda Bolin illustrates the midcentury evolution of black child-saving initiatives and the more robust resource base of the black surrogate parental state. A leading member of the NAACP, Bolin was the first black woman judge in the United States. She agitated constantly and effectively against white racial tyranny by mixing incisive and often radical political rhetoric with an ability to broker liberal reforms through her professional and activist network. From her 1939 appointment to the juvenile court until her retirement forty years later, Bolin was instrumental in numerous victories against Jim Crow juvenile justice. Her career is emblematic of the second wave of black child-saving.

Born in 1908, Jane Bolin was the youngest of four children in an activist family that had lived free in and around Poughkeepsie, New York, for two centuries. Her mother, Matilda Bolin, a white woman born to English parents in Ireland, died when Jane was eight years old. Her father, Gaius Bolin, of black and Native American ancestry, never remarried. He had a distinguished legal and activist career in Poughkeepsie, and his household became a headquarters for the burgeoning black freedom movement. Both he and his oldest son were lawyers, perhaps inspiring Bolin's own civil rights leadership and professional achievement through law.

Gaius Bolin was an "earnest supporter of the NAACP from its beginning." He stocked his home with issues of *The Crisis* and other black periodicals and helped establish the local NAACP branch in 1931, naming his oldest son after its president.[77] Judge Bolin reflected on how DuBois's work in *The Crisis* blended with more local, family influences to define her political consciousness and professional career:

> It was *The Crisis* and conversations in my home which brought my first awareness that by a superficial difference of skin color some people are treated differently. . . . This is a shocking realization for a child, especially a child who was fascinated and made to glow by American history and took literally our Declaration of Independence and Constitution. I recall the horror with which I learned mainly through *The Crisis* and also through Negro newspapers the meaning of the brutal word "lynching." I remember the shock and dismay and anger I experienced when first I heard of the compulsory racial segregation. I was confused by these realities and the teachings I had at home, in school and in church about the dignity of man and the equality of all people. As I grew an older child I was prevented from feeling hopeless and helpless only because I knew there were people like Dr. Du Bois on a larger scale and my father on a smaller scale who were uncompromising and tireless in fighting for the democratic ideal my school taught and for the brotherhood my religion taught.[78]

In 1923, the fifteen-year-old Jane Bolin sent a letter to Poughkeepsie's daily newspaper protesting its failure to capitalize *Negro*, its practice of indicating racial or ethnic background only in matters involving black Americans, and the "use of a southern dialect in all its reporting about black persons." Three years earlier, the UNIA's Declaration of Rights of the Negro Peoples of the World had emphasized these points. Bolin likely read it. The newspaper printed her letter, capitalizing the word *Negro*, but the daily practice of maligning black people in the news continued unabated.[79]

Despite the isolation and the discouragement from advisers that black women routinely experienced in mainstream schools of her time, Bolin graduated from Wellesley College and went on to become the first black woman graduate of the Yale University Law School in 1931. After passing the New York bar, she briefly returned to Poughkeepsie to practice law with her father and brother. In 1932, she left for New York City. Drawn by her marriage to a black New York City lawyer and love for the big city, she also sensed that "fascist" Poughkeepsie would waste her life and leadership potential.[80]

Denied a position at a New York City firm "as much for her gender as skin color," Bolin struggled to develop a private law practice with her husband. In 1936, she accepted a last-minute invitation to run on the Republican ticket for a seat on the New York State Assembly. It was offered, she said, "for dearth of another candidate." Although the entire Republican ticket lost in a landslide, she gained valuable exposure and political capital. In 1937, she was appointed assistant corporation counsel in the New York City Law Department. Her assignment was to defend indigents in the Family Division of the Domestic Relations Court. In 1939, her friend and colleague Judge Rosalie Whitney recommended Bolin to Mayor LaGuardia, a Republican, for a vacant judgeship in the Domestic Relations Court.[81]

The ascendance of black juvenile justice professionals relied on earlier and concurrent agitation, making Bolin's candidacy timely. By the 1930s, NAACP strategy was to pressure the state to abolish separate and unequal treatment in juvenile social control. Aiming to abolish Jim Crow juvenile justice, the New York–based national office litigated in the courts, made legislative appeals, and otherwise attempted to change formal policies and practices. In 1935, the NAACP and other New York City–based organizations opposed discrimination against black girls at the state reformatory. They challenged segregation in the institution and disparities between services in white and black facilities. Black girls in New York's juvenile court communities suffered fewer educational opportunities, inferior vocational training, far more crowded conditions (i.e., access to two cottages, as compared to fifteen designated for white girls), and frequent corporal punishment.[82]

The NAACP and its allies brought these concerns to the governor. Indicating the small but meaningful gains in black standing, he assigned an investigative committee. It exonerated the institution but recommended that segregation be gradually phased out. Forced to revise its formal policies and practices, by the end of the year the institution had, according to the white press, introduced "administrative changes . . . at the school, and efforts to place the Negro girls on an equal footing with the white girls [had] been successful." Black papers and race leaders were more circumspect. They acknowledged some changes, but the NAACP called the white press account "as perfect an example of punch-pulling and whitewashing as ever seen," declaring it too soon to measure success.[83]

The Harlem riots of 1935, one of many urban rebellions in the period, added weight and urgency to the demands of the moderate civil rights establishment to racially integrate public administration. Inroads became evident federally in the mid-1930s with Mary Bethune, Lawrence Oxley, and others. In 1937 came the appointment of the first black federal judge and in 1939 the creation of the Civil Rights Section of the U.S. Justice Department. By 1941, for the first time in history, black representation in (mainly service-related) government occupations exceeded the black proportion of the U.S. population. Mayor LaGuardia's reputation among black leaders was that of an ally in the fight against segregation and employment discrimination. With local and national pressures growing, Bolin's candidacy was almost certain to be seriously considered.[84] Her appointment to the Children's Division of the Manhattan Domestic Relations Court in 1939 began the first of four consecutive ten-year terms. She was the first black woman judge in the history of the Republic. That year she was elected first vice president of the NAACP's New York City branch, making her one of the few black women leaders in this increasingly influential association. She personified the growing political, professional, and service network in the emerging civil rights movement.[85]

Bolin quickly confronted the workings of Jim Crow juvenile justice. She discovered that black dependents and delinquents in New York City, as elsewhere, were commonly denied placements on the bases of race and religion. Urban League researchers had documented the problem a decade earlier, and more recent studies confirmed it. Ongoing denial of court services weighed heavily on the black population. A 1934 report revealed that crime rates for black youths had increased by over 200 percent since 1920. One in four juveniles arraigned in Manhattan's children's court were now black, and over one-fourth of all dependency cases in the city involved black families. Still, the court systematically denied services to black youths and families.[86]

Her presence as a black activist judge, however, allowed Bolin to observe and counter the mechanics of exclusion and pursue institutional change. The idealized race expert had materialized. By reviewing cases and files, she discerned how Jim Crow worked in the Manhattan juvenile court community of the early 1940s. All court-involved black youths were exclusively assigned to the two black probation officers employed in the court, limiting their access to court services and support. Cover sheets of case files for black and Puerto Rican youths were subtly coded to guide race-based probation assignment. This discouraged the placement of nonwhite youths in public and private juvenile institutions whose services were reserved for white youths.[87]

Bolin's response combined old and new tactics of self-help initiatives, professional intervention, and political protest. To alleviate suffering and ensure that services would be available to these youths, she joined other civic leaders to save Wiltwyck School, a juvenile institution in upstate New York. Opened originally in 1936 through the New York Protestant Episcopal City Mission Society, it was among the few to offer black and Puerto Rican dependent and delinquent children in New York City access to citizen-building initiatives.[88] When lack of funding and disrepair threatened the school with closure, Bolin joined the philanthropist and first lady Eleanor Roosevelt (whose family home faced Wiltwyck from across the Hudson River), her colleague and friend Judge Polier, and "other forward thinking people" to reestablish the school as an interracial treatment facility for court-involved boys.[89]

Using pressure group politics, Bolin got government officials to extend equal protections and opportunity to youths. She wrote to probation officials and others within the court to voice opposition to their Jim Crow practices while also alerting NAACP headquarters. Legislative change followed. In 1942, Judge Jane Bolin and NAACP president Walter White testified before the New York City Council and Board of Estimate to support a "Race Discrimination Amendment" that prohibited public funding of charitable institutions that discriminated on the basis of race. Informed by Bolin's insider perspective, White protested that "some nineteen child-care institutions in New York City receive a total of one million dollars in city subsidies . . . but exclude inmates because of color." He insisted that these institutions either "cease discriminating or get along without city funds [as] the City of New York cannot afford longer to be party to such discrimination." The amendment was formally adopted months later but was not always enforced. Bolin continued to protest discrimination in case processing and segregated court services well into the 1960s.[90]

Bolin opposed Jim Crow practices in other juvenile court communities and institutional contexts. In 1942, a book review she wrote criticized the racial and democratic politics of Memphis juvenile court judge Camille Kelley. Case histories in Kelley's book, Bolin thought, informed the public of the general ideals of the juvenile court. Yet she wished that "some histories had been included with other than happy endings, to give a more balanced and accurate picture of Children's Court problems." Cases of black youths and families had been neglected. "In view of the social pattern of the

South," she wrote, "the services provided for Negro children are of interest and importance."[91]

Bolin found Kelley's concluding chapter to be especially problematic. It called on (white) citizens to "vote intelligently" to advance good government, noting that civic action was vital to the historic development of the Memphis court. Knowing from *The Crisis* that white citizens and officials cooperated to maintain separate and unequal juvenile justice in Memphis, Bolin charged her colleague with a naive or callous embrace of hypocritical democratic ideals. "A deep social awareness on the part of Judge Kelley must be questioned," she stated, "when she can write this in a state where the poll tax prevails without . . . any efforts on her part to seek its revocation." Bolin then reflected on the traditional citizen-building ideal and the problem of white democracy: "One of the main objectives of Children's Court is the preparation of children appearing before it to become good citizens and to assume the responsibilities and duties of citizenship. Children should charge us with hypocrisy, and justly, if on becoming voting age they find themselves faced with unprogressive, undemocratic and outmoded financial restrictions which Children's Court Judges themselves have done nothing to abolish. Plato might well be paraphrased as 'the punishment suffered by the wise who refuse universal participation in government is to live under the government of bad men.'"[92]

Throughout her judicial career and NAACP leadership, Bolin raised concerns over democratic participation in speeches, letters, and official actions. Being a celebrated "first" embarrassed her, and she was more consumed with the question of succession.[93] She challenged the public, fellow activists, and officials to prioritize mass democratic participation. In a speech in Poughkeepsie meant to celebrate her life achievements, Bolin turned the spotlight on the values of her audience, declaring: "There are Negro and Jewish and Catholic and Chinese, Japanese, and Indian youngsters, who dream the same dreams I once had and who shoot at the same stars. What will you make democracy mean to them? They too study the Constitution and the history of America. They take seriously the Constitution and unlike the United States Supreme Court during much of our history, they take it literally. They mean to have liberty and a full, rich life, free of want, oppression and inequality of opportunity, whether economic, social, or political."[94]

In a 1947 letter, Bolin rejected an invitation to join the Harlem Advisory Board of the New York City Red Cross. She balked at the plan to confine black influence to "a Jim Crow Advisory Board" for a citywide agency. "I feel this all the more deeply since I am aware of the Jim Crow policy you maintain at Booth Memorial Hospital," she noted, "where you segregate the pregnant Negro girls we refer from the Court from the pregnant white girls."[95]

Bolin's democratic ethos and activism informed general strategies of the growing civil rights movement. The "Race Discrimination Act" Bolin helped develop with the NAACP and others provided a template for broader civil rights interventions. The original appeal applied to charitable institutions that denied services on the basis of race and religion. It was revised to form the Brown-Isaacs Bill, which focused on racial and religious discrimination in public housing. Bolin lobbied strongly for the housing bill, stressing the contradiction between this American practice of discrimination and America's democratic "professions." She testified concerning the impact of housing discrimination in her court. "I see daily the effects not only of inadequate housing but of segregated housing on families and children," she wrote to the comptroller. "I see little bodies dwarfed by an overcrowded, substandard home and I see little minds warped by the knowledge that 'we are somehow considered different and inferior.' With that injustice as a starting point, festering over a period of time, it is perhaps little wonder that there should be finally rebellion against law and authority."[96]

Years later, Bolin contacted a city councilor regarding the Sharkey-Brown-Isaacs Bill, which focused on discrimination in private housing. She urged support for the "justice and democracy of the bill," to help "eliminate sad and destructive effects of discrimination in housing" that daily appear in juvenile court. She attributed delinquency and dependency to "antisocial children rebelling against patent discrimination [and] unwholesome living conditions," with criminal adults reacting similarly. Compounding the problem were "segregated schools, diseases of slum living, [and] blatant exploitation of unscrupulous real estate interests of people . . . trapped because of their race, religion or nationality." The Sharkey-Brown-Isaacs Bill, she said, was "an opportunity for us to implement our religious teaching and our democratic principles." And the councilor and his colleagues ought to "meet this challenge to democracy with courage."[97]

The liberal civil rights establishment had found its stride by the 1950s, and race expert leaders like Bolin facilitated the inroads being made. In 1951, the Brown-Isaacs Bill passed, and the Sharkey Bill, which outlawed discrimination in New York housing, followed in 1957. An emboldened Bolin wrote to President John F. Kennedy a few years later as he considered an executive order barring discrimination in federally funded housing. She explained how the domestic relations court provided her the "daily occasion to observe the physical, moral and psychological destructiveness on children and families of poor housing, racially segregated housing and racial discrimination in any form." She urged Kennedy to outlaw any use of public monies "for the immoral, invidious and unjust purpose of injuring part of our citizenry."[98]

Liberal Abolition of Jim Crow Juvenile Justice: Summary and Conclusion

By the mid-twentieth century, the formal demise of Jim Crow juvenile justice was brought about by black child-saving initiatives that benefited from exhausted patience, improved resources, and growing leverage. The black surrogate parental state had become a formidable force. Its associated legal experts, including Bolin and the NAACP's legal division, proved to be effective in forcing formal institutional change. In 1952, with the landmark defeat of the separate but equal doctrine on the horizon, George Nesbitt, a black federal official, rejoiced in "the current high-level of attack of racial barriers coincid[ing] in time with the establishment and quickened growth of the race relations [expert] function at the three levels of government." Feeding into this historic meeting were the democratic contradictions of two world wars, increasingly radical social movements, and modest gains in integration. Sensing that victory might be within reach, Nesbitt cited the "improved educational opportunities, higher incomes, greater . . . cultural assimilation and enhanced self-respect obtaining" in the black population. He was confident that the black working and middle class had pulled black America to the brink of "winning complete equality, not at some remote period, but here and now."[99]

More circumspect radical black leaders insisted that full equality required more fundamental social change. In a 1950 essay entitled "Juvenile Delinquency and Civil Rights," the Communist civil rights lawyer William Patterson reasserted Elaine Ellis's position that a radical movement for democratic socialism alone would ensure black youth and community justice. As secretary of the International Labor Defense, Patterson had been involved in the Scottsboro Boys defense. His intent here was to build political will. "The deep social roots of what is termed 'juvenile delinquency' have long been known to many people," he wrote, but "few . . . have had the courage to militantly fight for a people's solution to the problem." "[This] silence as to the real issues involved," he argued, "endangers the lives of millions of youth and the future of the country."[100]

Patterson believed that black youths were alienated in America's racialized, capitalist democracy. Any real solution to delinquency must, therefore, address structural exclusion. Like Bolin, he argued that youths were not fully responsible for their delinquency, having been "set in motion by unemployment, inadequate schools and recreation . . . , by segregation, jim-crowism, and other forms of racial persecution . . . all processes that impinge on a lad's decent, normal desire to get ahead, to be somebody, to go places and be recognized." Writing at the outset of the Korean War, he condemned the nation for feeding "contempt for human life, glorify[ing] militarism and physical violence and creat[ing] emotional stresses that . . . psychologically impact youth" generally and especially poor black youths. "The ghetto-bred youth is completely thrown off balance by a call to military service from a government that jim-crows them at home and sends them abroad to some far-away land to fight for democracy of which they know little even by hear-say, and nothing through experience."[101]

Given this profound alienation, it was an error to call black delinquents "anti-social," Patterson explained. Their behavior was a logical sociopoliti-cal reaction, "the protest actions of youth to an environment over which youth has no voice and to which it could not adapt itself."[102] This radical analysis of race and social strain called for far more than equal youth pro-tection and adult integration to achieve racial equality and youth justice in the United States. The increasing rate and seriousness of delinquency repre-sented a growing indictment of society itself, Patterson argued. Stemming the tide would mean restructuring American culture and society. His list of needed changes included: "1) permanent employment . . . for heads of families; 2) job opportunities for . . . youth . . . ; 3) adequate wages; 4) vast slum clearances; 5) price and rent controls; 6) liquidation of ghettoes; 7) adequate cultural, health, [and] recreation centers and facilities; 8) a veritable holy crusade against racism and religious bigotry; [and] 9) new schools and a broad expansion of educational advantage." The following year, Patterson, Paul Robeson, and others in the Civil Rights Congress peti-tioned the United Nations for relief from the crime of black genocide in the United States but were generally ignored.[103]

Bolin and activist liberals like her scarcely disagreed with Patterson's analysis and advocated for several of these structural changes. However, they sought to negotiate a far more modest settlement of black youth and community claims. As black radical leaders turned up the heat, accepted leaders of the second wave of black child-saving prioritized integration as the object indicator and practical mechanism for sustaining racial equality in juvenile social control. Realistically, moderates maintained, radical reor-ganization of social, economic, and political relations would not produce racial justice. Instead, securing equal rights and recognition for black Americans would give them the freedom to make their own fates in a racially representative capitalist democracy.

Blind faith in the benefits of formal integration in juvenile social control would later prove costly. In the meantime, these basic demands offered effective, remediable challenges to separate and unequal juvenile justice. The liberal agenda tried to broker a middle way between two unlikely alternatives: continuation of the white racial project of selective citizen and state building through Jim Crow juvenile justice or a revolutionary push toward democratic socialism. The end of Jim Crow juvenile justice thus represented a compromise between competing interests in race adjustment, ushering in the modern era of formal integration in American juvenile justice.

The triumph of liberal reform owed much to the foil of radical demands, but it also depended on the skills, determination, and collective efficacy of black race expert leaders. By facilitating the development and deployment of social movement strategies and resources, activists in these social and professional roles helped turn civic alienation and dependency on their head. National civil rights organizations and the black freedom movement used the steadily growing black surrogate parental state and professional and social justice networks to leverage influence.[104]

The NAACP became a movement hub for the second wave of black child-saving. Uniting the diverse strands of professional and political activity among its members made them more formidable. Its influence was also symbolic. The NAACP's early work inspired Bolin's legal career and her determination to fight in her judicial capacity against Jim Crow and injustice.[105] One of the few black women to become a national NAACP leader, she leveraged relationships with the civil rights establishment, justice professionals, and other allies to challenge and reshape the racial politics of juvenile social control.

Like W. E. B. DuBois and other new guard leaders of her generation, Bolin grew disillusioned and frustrated by the national NAACP. She questioned its commitment to democratic principles. "An authoritarian set-up, whether it is Fascist, Communist or NAACP, is abhorrent to me," she wrote in a 1950 letter resigning from the executive board, "and I feel that the NAACP can ill afford to oppose democratic procedures within its own organizational set-up." However, she reserved special praise for the NAACP's recently established legal arm, the Legal Defense Fund (LDF). Its challenges of racial discrimination and segregation in New York and nationwide were chipping away at the legal and policy foundations of racial segregation. She called the LDF "the only part of the [national] NAACP which is not programmatically bankrupt," crediting it alone with "doing an important and superb job."[106]

After over a decade of court battles against segregation, LDF lawyers led by Thurgood Marshall won the *Brown v. Board of Education* (1954) case before the U.S. Supreme Court.[107] It was the result of a long, lived history of opposition to the ordeals of separate and unequal opportunity, including the efforts of turn-of-the-century black clubwomen to renegotiate the racial contract in American juvenile justice. Credit for winning *Brown* went to professional activists, including the legal strategies set in motion by Thurgood Marshall's mentor, Charles Hamilton Houston, the dean of Howard Law School (1930–35). The *Brown* ruling also reflected contributions from black scholars who detailed the crisis of Jim Crow, including evidence provided by Drs. Mamie and Kenneth Clark, race relations experts whose clinical research on the impact of segregation on children was cited in the Supreme Court decision.[108] *Brown* was a milestone in renegotiating the racial contract, but it did not signify the end of the significance of race. It was not even the beginning of the end. For reformers, the ruling pointed to a new structure of racially integrated juvenile social control that would institutionalize racial justice itself. That outcome remained to be seen.

SEVEN

The Early Spoils of Integration

In the first two decades after *Brown v. Board of Education* (1955–75), there were slow and only slight advances in institutionalizing racial equality in American juvenile justice. Scattered signs of more racially democratic relations made brief appearances. Liberal reformers thought that the sociolegal framework of integration would produce racial justice through a new bundle of rights and resources. Their hope was that formally equal protection of black youths and recognition of black authority would counter the oppression and domination characteristic of Jim Crow juvenile justice. The aftermath of these reforms thus provides insight into the impact of the black child-saving movement on the modern era of racialized juvenile social control.

An ongoing and intensified struggle over civil rights law and its enforcement occurred during the decades following *Brown*. "Massive resistance" to integration limited progress in institutionalizing racial justice in American society.[1] In the urban and rural South, black communities remained severely marginalized—socially, economically, and politically. In Northern urban contexts, recognition increased for black youths and communities in juvenile justice. There, the second wave of black child-saving established social norms, networks, and institutions that were more capable of supporting a new racial praxis of juvenile justice.[2] Oppression and domination persisted, but there were also unique signs of advances in black youth and community recognition relative to the cultural ethos and institutional resource base of the liberal rehabilitative ideal.

This chapter examines developments in postintegration juvenile justice to assess progress in institutionalizing racial justice. In the early period of integration, a racially democratic system of social control began to take shape but, ultimately, failed to materialize. At best, progress toward racial democratization of liberal rehabilitative ideals reached a plateau. It was an unfinished revolution in the relation between race and American democracy, set in the changing terrain of juvenile social control. By the end of the 1970s, the cultural and institutional foundations of this democratic experiment in juvenile justice were eroding and under attack. Three overlapping factors undermined racially democratic reform: persistent mainstream commitments to separate and unequal juvenile justice, the decline of black collective efficacy in the wake of formal inclusion, and the retraction of entitlements to liberal rehabilitative ideals.

Race and Reconstruction in the Civil Rights–Era South

Civil rights reforms of the 1950s and 1960s, such as court-ordered integration and the Civil Rights Act (1965), promised to eliminate the significance of race in juvenile justice. Beyond that, they proposed to redistribute racial group rights and recognition in juvenile court communities, changing the balance of power in racialized social control.[3] The liberal black child-saving movement idealized this formal inclusion as a legal and bureaucratic arrangement of racial justice. The movement meant to rewire race relations within the basic cultural and institutional framework of traditional American juvenile justice. Civil rights reforms, they believed, would create a basic structure of racial equality that benefited black and American civil society alike.[4] Greater legal protection of black youths and the presence of black authorities would co-opt white control over juvenile justice administration, steering citizen-building ideals and resources toward nonwhite communities. This manufactory of citizens, to recall Teddy Roosevelt's phrase, would be transformed from a cultural and institutional appendage of white democracy into a resource for a new multiracial and ethnic democracy.[5]

John Braithwaite calls this strategy a "republican disposition" toward social control. The politics of "net-widening can be a good thing," he explains, "when at the end of a fair process of community dialogue the conclusion is reached that net-widening will increase freedom" or dominion.[6] Black community opposition to Jim Crow juvenile justice represents a racial project in net widening or mending. The effort was progressive insofar as it advanced black youth and community dominion, or recognition, relative to liberal rehabilitative ideals. Rather than an end in itself, integration was a means of actively advancing black interests in justice administration by co-opting control processes long dominated by white civil society. It was expected that integration would institutionalize black dominion before and through law, replacing the white supremacist parental state with a racially democratic system defined by a new reality of participatory parity.

Sustained community participation in the praxis of juvenile justice was vital to civil rights reform. For more just race relations in American juvenile justice to emerge, black civic actors had to engage in racially conscious social control. Braithwaite and others do not idealize co-optation of government authority and are skeptical of the state. But the notion of democratic control does include representation among formal authorities, accompanied by on-going public scrutiny, input, and action.[7] By empowering black civil society and removing obstacles to influence, integration should have accelerated efforts to reconstruct juvenile justice, populating juvenile justice jurisdictions with black youths, families, and adults with recognized civil rights and authority. In reality, integrating juvenile justice and other institutions such as education, employment, and housing was fiercely contested and only sporadically delivered the cultural or institutional changes envisioned by civil rights advocates.

Ironically, the contentious and violent years between 1955 and 1975 represent an *encouraging* period of growing black community access to re-habilitative ideals and resources. The civil rights era brought heightened attention and civic action to the issues of race and juvenile justice, broader access and influence, and examples of innovation. If only as flashes in a few places, the period saw significant changes in the racial structure of juvenile justice policy and practice, for example, in terms of novel approaches to community-based delinquency prevention and intervention that promised to empower black youths and communities in the administration of reha-bilitative ideals. By the end of the 1970s, however, progress was drawing to a halt. Support for liberal rehabilitative ideals was eroding. Black civil society had grown dependent on the formally integrated parental state and disengaged from the problems of youths. Together, the decline of black collective efficacy and the rise of a new punitive agenda in juvenile justice constrained the possibilities for institutionalized racial justice.

Before considering these illustrative, albeit fleeting, signs of civil rights–era advances in black standing relative to citizen-building ambition and authority, it is important to note some of the ways in which state and local authorities resisted, undermined, and distorted civil rights reforms in the two decades following the *Brown* ruling.

Resistance to Civil Rights Enforcement Cases

The continuing significance of race after the landmark *Brown* ruling is evi-dent in local and state government resistance to court-ordered integration of juvenile court communities. For over a decade after the decision, white authorities of the parental state claimed that court-ordered integration was irrelevant to juvenile justice administration and maintained separate and unequal institutions. They also manipulated integration struggles by adjudicating young, black civil rights activists as delinquents. In civil rights battleground states, these activists were committed to juvenile institutions while the police and courts failed to punish white youths involved in anti–civil rights violence and protests. These responses illustrate the diverse strategies of massive resistance and the contested and limited impact of court-ordered integration on the administration of rehabilitative ideals, especially in the South.

Formal desegregation of juvenile justice met substantial opposition and proceeded slowly.[8] Maryland, Alabama, Florida, and Louisiana maintained segregated juvenile institutions through the 1960s and into the 1970s, forcing continued agitation for substantive civil rights reform. In February 1960, the civil rights lawyers Thurgood Marshall and Jack Greenberg (Marshall's successor as NAACP Legal Defense Fund director) filed a class-action lawsuit on behalf of a thirteen-year-old black boy and others like him against the Maryland Board of Public Welfare, the Board of Managers of the Maryland Training School, and several Maryland reformatories. The suit asked for declaratory relief from the schools' continued racial segregation policies, based on violation of the Fourteenth Amendment. A Baltimore city court agreed that the segregation policies violated the Constitution and conflicted with the Supreme Court's *Brown* decision.

Maryland officials appealed. In a harbinger of future policies, they argued that *Brown* did not apply to segregated reformatories since they resembled state prisons rather than public educational institutions. Although the rehabilitative ideal was already in decline, the argument contradicted a century of institutional history, the names of the state training schools, and prevailing popular and professional sentiment that juvenile justice systems remained reform-oriented institutions.[9] The state court ruled against the segregationist plea in *State Board v. Myers* (1961), declaring segregation in the state's juvenile reformatories to be a violation of the Fourteenth Amendment and detrimental to the educational, psychological, and social well-being of children. Along with the 1965 Civil Rights Act, this decision and similar enforcement rulings targeting segregated juvenile justice systems in Florida (1966), Alabama (1966 and 1969), and Louisiana (1969) forced the gradual integration of southern reformatories.[10]

These cases illustrate the local filtration of federally mandated integration. The Supreme Court decision outlawing separate and unequal juvenile justice institutions simply applied new and substantial pressure to end segregation. State and local governments controlled juvenile justice administration, so the forms and consequences of integration varied by community. Tests of the applicability of *Brown* thus illustrate patterns of resistance to integration in the South and how its local meaning would be negotiated.

Changes in the racial politics of juvenile justice are also highlighted by cases involving youths arrested and brought before courts for civil rights protests. Southern governments not only illegally maintained separate and unequal institutions but also used police, courts, and penal institutions to selectively criminalize black youths participating in civil rights protests and delay civil rights reform.[11]

Selective Criminalization of Civil Rights–Era Youth Activism

The structural violence inherent in Jim Crow juvenile justice threatened the linked fates of black youths and communities. Beyond symbolizing the limits of liberal ambitions in juvenile social control, inequality actively reproduced white privilege and the boundaries of white democracy by underdeveloping black youths and denying recognition of black constituent interests. Selective criminalization and sanctioning of youth activism was a persistent feature of structural violence during the civil rights movement. The police and courts often criminalized and punished the pro–civil rights activities of white and black youths and young adults. Criminal vandalism and violence by white youths who opposed such activity were typically met with relative indifference.[12] In short, civil rights–era police and courts defended white democracy instead of enforcing civil rights law.

Anti–civil rights violence by white youths dates back to their involvement in black lynchings and early-twentieth-century race riots. The national Taskforce on Violent Aspects of Protest and Confrontation during the late 1960s observed that the "historically prominent role of youth in militant white violence has received less attention than it deserves," both by researchers interested in juvenile crime and justice and by law enforcement authorities.[13] Research and news accounts confirm the predominant role of white working-class youths in racial violence in the United States, including rioting and violent attacks during the Red Summer of 1919, attacks on black families attempting to integrate white neighborhoods, and the urban rebellions of the 1960s.[14]

The psychologist Kenneth Clark's 1959 study of racism and delinquency briefly addressed white youth violence and delinquency. "The most concrete expression of this relationship in whites," he writes, "is to be found in the racial incidents wherein white youth attack Negro property or Negro individuals in tension areas. Generally, these incidents are either not recognized or recorded as part of the general delinquency statistics and the individuals involved are not brought before the courts." Extreme cases resulting in death or grave injury were an exception. Clark considered the indirect effects of racism on white delinquency "even more difficult to deal with statistically." White supremacist ideology and racial segregation within formal democracies may engender "moral confusion, conflict and cynicism" in white youths, and their deviance and delinquency represented a rejection of hypocritical societal values. Yet these acts were also likely to go unrecorded, he stressed, especially for "the privileged delinquent." Parents, schools, police, and courts worked to protect these middle- and upper-middle-class youths from formal crime and delinquency processing.[15]

Evaluating civil rights–era crime and delinquency among white youths is problematic because of distortions introduced by white power into criminology, law, and society. Police organizations and "local and state juries and courts . . . acquired an impressive record of failing to indict or convict in crimes against civil rights workers." The same is true of attacks on black bodies and property. Numerous reports and anecdotal accounts indicate that legal authorities reacted with relative indifference to the involvement of white youths in such violence.[16]

The attempted integration of schools in Little Rock, Arkansas, offers an illustration. In 1959, some two hundred whites, mostly teenagers, marched through the streets of Little Rock to protest federal orders to integrate city schools. Marchers refused orders to disperse, so police arrested one woman, two teenage girls, ten teenage boys, and eight men. All of them were quickly released. Among the white citizens who were outraged was the wife of an Arkansas congressman. Identifying herself as the chair of the "Committee of Harassed American Patriots of Little Rock," she complained to city officials that the police had reacted unjustly toward white marchers.[17]

In contrast, young black Americans pushing for expanded civil rights were harassed and experienced unequal protection from the police and courts. Daisy Bates, the NAACP's Little Rock branch president, expressed concerns to headquarters over school violence on the part of white students. The Little Rock Nine—black students who integrated Central High School in the fall of 1957—experienced violence, and school and city officials failed to offer them protection and recourse. One white girl was suspended indefinitely for pushing a black girl down a flight of stairs, but another faced only a three-day suspension for "a sneak attack perpetrated on one of the Negro boys which knocked him out, and required a doctor's attention." Propaganda scattered around the school by segregationists incited racial violence.

One pamphlet complained that integration violated white students' rights and invited violent reprisal against black students. It read like a get-out-of-jail-free card: "Good Only Until May 29, 1958 / Bearer May Kick Rumps of Each [Central High School] Negro Once Per Day Until the Above Expiration Date / Last Chance, Boys. Do Not Use Spiked Shoes." Given these threats and attacks, the school's refusal to provide adequate protection to black students, and hostile local law enforcement, Bates inquired about bringing the FBI into the school.[18]

The criminalization and sanctioning of black youth activists are well documented. In the early 1960s, a black teenager named Brenda Travis was labeled *delinquent* and committed to a reformatory to deter her and other youths from becoming involved in Mississippi's civil rights movement. In hundreds of similar cases, the white-dominated parental state used its monopoly over legal authority, including the juvenile courts, to defend against threats to white power and privilege.[19] By 1961, fifteen-year-old Brenda Travis had joined the Pike County Nonviolent Movement. She was a natural student leader at all-black Burgland High School in Macomb, Mississippi. She and other local students participated in a nonviolent sit-in to protest the segregated lunch counter at a local Greyhound bus terminal. She and four others were arrested and jailed for thirty-four days; later, they were released on bonds supplied by the NAACP and the Southern Christian Leadership Conference (SCLC).[20]

On their release, the principal refused to readmit Travis and another student to Burgland, hoping to discourage further student involvement in the Macomb movement. That provoked another school walkout. Travis and over one hundred other students marched to a nearby Student Nonviolent Coordinating Committee (SNCC) office and then to city hall, where they prayed for their classmates' reinstatement and protested the murder of a local activist, Herbert Lee, a week before. When they and some concerned SNCC companions arrived at city hall, they held banners and sang "We Shall Overcome." As they knelt to pray on the city hall steps, police began to arrest them; ninety-seven student activists under the age of eighteen were released, with the rest charged with breaching the peace and "contributing to the delinquency of a minor."[21]

Owing to white control of law enforcement in Macomb and elsewhere and the discretion of juvenile courts, these formally protected expressions of free speech and assembly could be prosecuted as civil and criminal infractions.[22] After her second arrest, Brenda Travis was given an indeterminate sentence at the reformatory for Negro delinquents at Oakley. The first reformatory for black youths in the state, Oakley had opened just twenty years earlier, and now its "delinquency services" were used to punish black youths fighting for equality. As Travis's mother aptly explained the cruel irony: "Brenda was taken away . . . because she was determined to get her rights."[23]

Brenda Travis remained at Oakley for eight months, until a sixty-four-year-old German émigré teaching at Talladega College in Alabama persuaded a local judge to release her into his custody.[24] Professor Herman Einsman had been in the United States for twelve years. He likely offered refuge to Travis because a black International Rescue Committee official had helped him enter the country. Long an opponent of racial injustice, he was disposed toward acts of black child-saving. *Jet* magazine detailed this remarkable story, noting that Einsman's father disowned him after he married a Jew. He was "court-martialed by the German Army because he objected to Hitler tactics, and fired from a post-war education job when he went to the aid of military-spawned 'Brown Babies,'" the European children of black American soldiers. After learning of Travis's plight from the SNCC chapter on his campus, Einsman asked NAACP lawyers and Mississippi officials about the possibility of her release. Having been declared an enemy of the state, she could not be released in Mississippi. Oakley lacked classes beyond the tenth grade, so Travis was not receiving an education. Einsman offered to take her and was granted custody so long as she refrained from joining further protests for integration.[25]

The courageous black youths who desegregated Little Rock's institutions and the scores of other black children who protested for civil rights sparked debate on the role of the immortal youth in the progress of the race. Black child-savers generally framed youths as victims of white supremacist systems; their underdevelopment threatened individual and group interests and required black adult opposition. When black children thus saved became adults, they would, it was assumed, help advance black community interests. But it was not envisioned that these young people would engage in civil rights activism.

By the early 1960s, the perception of civil rights leaders and the youths themselves was that young blacks were emerging as vital participants in the intensifying struggle for freedom. In the Children's Crusade of 1963, Martin Luther King Jr. and the SCLC intentionally recruited youthful protesters to advance the languishing Birmingham movement. As in Macomb, the strategy was hotly contested. King and other advocates sought to take advantage of the moral and emotional influence of youths to force the federal government into action. In King's view, young people had developed "a sense of their own stake in freedom and justice" and wished to become involved in the movement. Citing safety and other concerns, however, many black parents and community leaders opposed youth involvement. Malcolm X used the Children's Crusade to discredit the liberal strategy of nonviolent resistance, claiming: "Real men don't put their children on the firing line."[26] Despite the misgivings of those who characterized the strategy as a reckless, exploitative use of black children as political pawns, the Children's Crusade proved effective. It filled national newspapers and television screens with scenes of young, black, nonviolent activists facing fire hoses, police dogs, and imprisonment. The spectacle increased outrage and pressure against the Jim Crow South.[27]

A 1965 study documented hundreds of cases of black youths arrested, adjudicated delinquent, and institutionalized for involvement in civil rights protests. In Jackson, Mississippi, over half of all demonstrators arrested in 1963 were juveniles. The first ones were released to parents only if they agreed to do "everything in [their] power to keep [their] child from being involved in further demonstrations." In Jackson, juvenile protesters were subsequently charged and detained for extended periods, often without bail or hearings. Protests in Americus, Georgia, led to approximately 125 juvenile arrests and, according to the Civil Rights Commission, "disposed of in a unique manner": "Some of them were released from jail upon payment of a jail fee of $23.50, plus $2 per day for food. These fees were paid by parents who agreed to send their children to relatives living in the country. No court hearing was held in these cases; of those juveniles who appeared in court (approximately 75% of those arrested), about 50 were sentenced to the State Juvenile Detention Home and placed on probation on the condition that they would not associate with certain leaders of civil rights organizations in Americus."[28]

As civil rights protests grew in St. Augustine, Florida, juvenile court judge Charles C. Mathis wrote a preemptive letter to black leaders "stating that parents and other interested persons should not permit juveniles to participate in civil rights demonstrations." He warned that juveniles involved in protests would be forcibly removed by police and sent home but that they could also be arrested. Demonstrations that summer (1963) resulted in 234 juvenile arrests. In one sit-in, several black youths were charged with breaching the peace, trespassing, and violating the undesirable guest statute. After adjudicating the activists delinquent, the Civil Rights Commission reports: "Judge Mathis offered to place them on probation instead of sending them to prison, provided they [agree to] refrain from all demonstration activity for an indefinite period. These terms were accepted by the parents, but not by all the children. Four rejected the restriction and were sent to the county jail for 30 days. Subsequently they were transferred to reform schools and following extensive legal proceedings, released in . . . 1964, nearly six months after their arrest." Subsequently, dozens more black youths were arrested at St. Augustine demonstrations and sent to the county jail or the still-segregated black reform school.[29]

Federal Interventions

Despite local and state court efforts to discourage civil rights agitation, racial politics of juvenile social control were changing even in the South. Abuses of state power prompted sporadic federal intervention, including the release of youthful black activists who were wrongfully arrested and imprisoned. In St. Augustine in 1964, a federal judge ruled that since "the customary procedure with respect to juveniles in Florida charged with misdemeanors is to release them to parents' custody to await trial . . . detention [of youth activists] without bond or release was an arbitrary and capricious act of harassment and cruel and unusual punishment on the part of [Judge] Mathis." The youths were released.[30]

Desegregation enforcement cases also eroded the southern sociolegal structure of Jim Crow juvenile justice, sometimes with the aid of federal courts. An Alabama desegregation case went beyond demanding equal protection of black youths by petitioning for the integration of black authorities in juvenile justice systems. In 1967, NAACP lawyers filed a federal class-action suit against three segregated reform schools in Alabama. A judge in the U.S. District Court for the Northern District of Alabama ordered two exclusively white institutions to submit desegregation plans and gave the Alabama Industrial School for Negro Children a year to develop a plan. However, the state's desegregation plan pledged only to admit four black students to the white boys' training school and to admit black girls to the girls' school sometime in the future. NAACP lawyers appealed to the U.S. Court of Appeals for more immediate and meaningful relief. The 1969 court ruling noted that reformatories were included in the desegregation requirements of *Brown* and that the state's desegregation plans were inadequate. It required the three schools to issue a unified plan that would immediately desegregate youths and staff throughout Alabama's juvenile reformatory system.[31]

The district court rejected the resubmitted plan and ordered that the Mt. Meigs reformatory (which black child-savers had established) be closed. All remaining schools were to be operated as one "unitary system." School authorities could "in good faith take into account racial tensions in maintaining discipline and good order," but only "without racial discrimination." The schools had to admit youths and employ staff without regard to race. No later than June 1970, the order stated, the personnel employed cannot "indicate that a school is intended for Negro students or white students. Staff members who work directly with children, and professional [administrative] staff . . . shall be hired, assigned, promoted, paid, demoted, dismissed and otherwise treated without regard to race, color or national origin."[32]

Federal orders to ensure racially equal youth and adult opportunity were consistent with general ideals of antidiscrimination. Yet they were problematic given the liberal integration strategy promoted by black child-savers. Desegregation orders framed racial equality in distributive rather than deliberative terms. Integration did not necessarily need to enhance juvenile justice administration through the insight or authority of black race expert leaders. Rather, this 1970 order pledged to make race irrelevant to juvenile justice, defining *racial justice* as a negative right to diminish discrimination, rather than a positive right to establish more racially representative systems of juvenile social control.

The ruling was simply one indication that racial integration might not institutionalize racial justice in juvenile social control. Though the federal government challenged the most egregious injustices of southern juvenile justice, its narrow interpretation of equal rights suggested that the state might be an unreliable partner in efforts to establish black dominion in the administration of liberal rehabilitative ideals.

Black Dominion in the Civil Rights–Era North, 1955–75

Relatively integrated institutions, greater civil rights protections, and black political and professional representation already distinguished juvenile court communities in the urban North when the U.S. Supreme Court outlawed separate and unequal juvenile justice. Oppression and domination persisted, but integration effectively enhanced northern black youth and community standing, especially in court communities with well-established black political and professional networks of influence.

In Detroit, Delta Sigma Theta Sorority, the Urban League, and other groups had begun working with Wayne County agencies and court officials to provide services to black girls nearly a decade before *Brown*. These services continued and improved as the civil rights era advanced. In 1954, the interracial board of the Delta Home for girls felt "the need for objective evaluation of the effectiveness" of its interventions. It commissioned a study of outcomes for girls placed there since the home's opening in 1947. Though it did not adequately isolate Delta Home influences from other contributing factors, the report concluded that half the ninety-eight girls in the study "improved" during placement. Positive changes occurred in girls' lives while in the home, but an urgent need existed for case monitoring and community-based support lest these citizen-building achievements be lost. The report recommended hiring a social worker to enhance case evaluation and community reintegration because the girls improved very little after leaving Delta Home and many were unable maintain improvements gained while there.[33]

In 1961, Delta Home housed just fourteen girls. This declining population likely resulted from the integration of state and private institutions, but program changes had also been implemented. Delta's elected board remained in charge, aided by three full-time staff and three part-time workers. Girls committed to Delta Home enjoyed a wider range of services and resources after the introduction of casework interviews, psychiatric consultations, a big sister program, and medical and dental care. These services balanced attention to the girls' "personality, social, religious, educational, health, and cultural needs." In a nod to traditional liberal rehabilitative ideals, and with optimism unseen in the South, the board concluded: "With continued encouragement, constructive criticism, seasoned suggestions and advice from consultants, Delta Home will . . . help residents . . . develop into happy, useful, successful, mature, adjusted citizens."[34]

After *Brown* and other legal and policy measures outlawing discrimination, patterns of racial discrimination and segregation persisted in the North. Despite greater black recognition, where the progressive impact of integration would become most apparent, entrenched racist ideologies and structural inequalities limited substantive advances in formal civil rights. The historian Cheryl Greenberg notes that, in Harlem, "local customs and the widespread belief in black inferiority" often undermined the intended benefits of new laws, policies, and campaigns. Well-positioned black authorities "would by no means eliminate discriminatory practices." Indeed, racial discrimination and segregation in Manhattan's juvenile court did not end in the mid-1950s despite state and city legislation that outlawed discrimination in charitable institutions and federal rulings against segregation. Well into the 1960s, Jane Bolin constantly wrote to officials, imploring them to heed laws against racial discrimination in delinquency and dependency case processing and to practice the democratic principles they preached.[35]

Black child-savers envisioned such vigilance when they promoted a formal system of accountability to black youth and community interests. But they did not anticipate that the fight to secure equal protection for youths would proceed so slowly. Bolin's ability to effect such social-organizational changes through political and professional channels was limited but still unique. Black dominion (i.e., representation) and the impact of civil rights reform on juvenile justice administration in Harlem reflected the robust nature of black power there. Harlem was a unique space for racially democratic experimentation in juvenile justice reform.

The basis for the unprecedented access of black youths and black communities to juvenile justice opportunities and influence gradually eroded during the civil rights era. As black collective efficacy declined locally and postintegration child and social-welfare commitments experienced national retraction, black community influence over citizen-building ideals and resources waned. By the end of this era, Judge Bolin and other race expert leaders had become isolated and disillusioned. The black child-saving movement had forced the formal racial integration of juvenile justice, but it was failing to institutionalize racial justice in the administration of rehabilitative ideals.

Democratic Experiments in Harlem

Harlem's growing crisis in juvenile delinquency added pressure to the search for innovative local solutions. From 1951 to 1962, the delinquency rate in Harlem was more than twice that of New York City and was growing at double the rate of the city overall. Kenneth Clark, a local race relations expert, believed that even these figures were *underestimates*. Ninety percent of the "youth population in most ghettos do not come in direct conflict with law," he wrote, so "no one knows . . . from delinquency statistics alone—with which society is often preoccupied—how many other ghetto youths lead lives caught up in the tangle of antisocial activity dominated by apathy and despair."[36]

Kenneth Clark and Mamie Phipps Clark were central figures in Harlem's response to civil rights–era delinquency through more representative and innovative approaches to juvenile social control. The Clarks demonstrate the importance of political and professional networks to the experimentation in Harlem's juvenile court community and to broader midcentury developments, including growing federal intervention in juvenile justice. Exemplifying such experimental efforts are the Northside Center for Child

Development, where the Clarks first became involved in juvenile justice reform, and, later, Harlem Youth Opportunities Unlimited (HARYOU). The Clarks established the Northside Center, a child mental health and developmental services program, in Harlem in 1946. Its professionalism and focus on racial integration paralleled efforts of the NAACP and others in the second wave of the black child-saving initiative. In other ways, Northside recalled earlier voluntary, self-financed, self-help initiatives, albeit with a social and behavioral science focus. Foundations rejected funding proposals for the project, so Northside was launched in a basement apartment of the Dunbar Housing Project with a $936 loan from Mamie Clark's father. The only salaries went to its remedial teacher and secretary. Four psychiatrists, four psychologists, three pediatricians, and four psychiatric social workers were part-time volunteers drawn to the opportunity of working with the Clarks, who were gaining a reputation as race leaders in the city, and whose integrated clinic was unique.[37]

Northside was sensitive to the underserved developmental needs of Harlem's black youths. Its founders and staff, however, believed that, as the historians Gerald Markowitz and David Rosner put it, "racial integration could be a powerful factor in healing the deep wounds of racism." Therefore, they sought to diversify staff and clients alike. Client integration proved difficult given the segregation of the surrounding community and the refusal of city leaders to embrace its experimental agenda. "Northside came up against the stubborn reality that New York City's voluntary social-service system did not share its goal of integration," Markowitz and Rosner explain. Not one "white child guidance clinic was willing to send white children to a center that served primarily black children." Northside's board and staff remained integrated, and some clients were white. But most of the youths served were black or Puerto Rican residents of Harlem.[38]

By the mid-1950s, the Clarks had become increasingly visible advocates of child-welfare and social reform in Harlem and nationwide. Their psychological research and applied work in Harlem positioned them to take advantage of federal legal and policy shifts related to integration, poverty reduction, and community-based juvenile delinquency prevention and intervention. Since their time as graduate students in the late 1930s and early 1940s, they had conducted research on the impact of segregation on children. Mamie assumed control of Northside's operations, and Kenneth became a more publicly prominent race relations expert. As an assistant professor at City College in the 1940s, he published research, taught classes, and was increasingly called on to provide expert testimony or advice on NAACP cases that challenged segregation. In 1951, he became coordinator of social science testimony for the Legal Defense Fund. Two former Columbia University and Howard University professors serving on an advisory committee attached to the 1950 Mid-Century White House Conference on Children and Youth urged him to address the conference. His paper summarized research on the impact of racial prejudice and discrimination on children. It was famously cited first among several social science publications in the *Brown* decision, fueling Clark's reputation as an "the icon of integration" and the "new Gunnar Myrdal"—research interpreter of the black urban condition as American pathology incarnate.[39]

Some criticized the Supreme Court's use of clinical psychological research as legal evidence, and many vowed massive and passive resistance. Nonetheless, Clark, "the scholar of *Brown v. Board*," received a flood of congratulatory and thankful reactions.[40] A crucial supporter of Northside Center said that she and other members of the Friends of Northside were "vicariously basking in glory," adding: "Our pride knows no bounds. . . . You have contributed in a major degree to the progress of democracy in America. You have been able to influence the decision of the most authoritative body in our land. And last, but not least, you have assisted in the future development of the education, cultural, and economic life of the Negro Citizens of America." Clark replied that he had played only a "small part" and directed her attention to the lasting challenge of integration. "As momentous as that decision was," he said, "it has not solved our basic problems. It has only removed some of the obstacles in the path of the solution." "Those of us who have been working toward making a better life for our children must continue to work with the same good will, clarity, intelligence and courage," he advised, "until that decision is translated into social reality."[41]

To that end, Northside Center was meant to fill the void of child-welfare programs available to New York City's black and Puerto Rican youths. The Clarks rejected impractical or irrelevant aspects of standard psychoanalysis and clinical practice, adapting Northside's approach to the structural racism and poverty impinging on ghetto youths and families. Northside aimed to resocialize racially, ethnically, and economically marginalized youths with "compensatory doses of love and acceptance," delivered through remedial education, medical care, and emotional and family support.[42]

The Clarks located their child-guidance clinic in Harlem to respond directly to the environment of racism. Doing so countered crime and delinquency, which were among the symptoms of deprivations feeding apathy and despair. Social disorganization, poverty, and the lack of quality housing contributed to the delinquency of all children, as Chicago school criminologists and, later, Richard Cloward and Lloyd Ohlin stressed. Following

W. E. B. DuBois, Jane Bolin, William Patterson, and others, the Clark's research and Northside program also saw delinquency as a specific "reaction
to racial frustrations, deprivations, discrimination, and segregation." Their
modern, professional, and interracial intervention sought to serve as "a surrogate or supplementary parent to the children and as a concerned neighbor
to their families" that was attuned to linked human developmental and
social dynamics of poverty and racism.[43]

In a 1957 evaluation, Mamie Clark reported that Northside's client base
was 54 percent black, 26 percent Spanish, and 20 percent white. To measure the "healing value" of Northside's interracial staff and client model,
she studied the effect on treatment length and success of race in patient-
therapist relationships. She reported "a strong trend for more children to
improve when the clinic team is of mixed ethnic background or when the
ethnic background of the team is entirely different from that of the child,"
especially in the case of black children. She reasoned that mixed clinician
teams offered more effective intercultural interventions because they mim-
icked the multiracial and ethnic environment children experienced. Mixed
clinic teams might be more motivated to achieve treatment objectives given
the staff's strong commitment to Northside's interracial clinical model.[44]

Northside's model of neighborhood-based child and family services
dovetailed with a growing national movement toward community-based
juvenile delinquency prevention and intervention. The approach was not
new. Chicago's Hull House was a Progressive Era example. In the early
1930s, the Chicago Area Project popularized the strategy of saturating urban
neighborhoods with services and empowering community members to prevent and solve problems related to delinquency. The University of Chicago
sociologist Clifford Shaw conceived of that project to apply an ecological
theory of delinquency to strategies of community-based delinquency prevention. In this framework, delinquency reflects an adaptation to the social
disorganization of the environment. The Chicago Area Project sought to
disrupt and alleviate conditions giving rise to delinquency by treating the
social environment rather than merely isolating troubled youths.[45]

Civil rights–era efforts to develop community-based strategies for delinquency prevention and intervention were distinguished by their national
scope and federal support. Black civic leaders were able to develop their
own funded initiatives, particularly in Harlem. From the late 1950s to the
early 1960s, socioeconomic conditions and delinquency rates for Harlem
and New York City youths were worsening. Major philanthropic organizations and the federal government, led by the Ford Foundation and President
Kennedy's Committee on Juvenile Delinquency, committed major resources

to combat delinquency and the environmental sources of poverty and social disorganization in New York's neighborhoods and in other cities.

Richard Cloward and Lloyd Ohlin's *Delinquency and Opportunity* (1960) largely guided this infusion of concern and resources. The two Columbia University School of Social Work professors were influential community leaders. Their book updated and offered a critique of Shaw's theory, which emphasized the transmission of deviant cultural norms. For Cloward and Ohlin, criminal behavior among youths did not result simply from deviant socialization but was a rational adaptation to the lack of social and economic opportunity. The theory recalled classic anomie theory and long-standing arguments of black child-savers. But Cloward and Ohlin had the attention of mainstream liberal civic leaders, so their call for youth and community empowerment through expanded opportunity was widely embraced in the 1960s.[46]

After five years of planning, one of the first major projects based on Cloward and Ohlin's "opportunity theory" was launched on New York's Lower East Side. It attempted to alter the opportunity structure of an area with over 100,000 people, one-third of whom were black and Puerto Rican, spread across sixty-seven city blocks. By creating a coalition of programs under the banner Mobilization for Youth (MFY), the project aimed to reduce delinquency by promoting "the maximum feasible participation of residents in efforts to reshape the communities." It included educational and vocational training, services to children and families, and leadership development. The core mission was to build "the power resources of the community," that is, the capacity for residents to assume control in defining their social-welfare interests and to negotiate their fulfillment.[47]

Richard Cloward began to work closely with the Clarks. Considering their common interests and graduate educations at Columbia University, they were probably long acquainted. In 1963, Cloward joined Northside's board of directors and played a key role in internal debates over the future of this perpetually underresourced center. Northside enhanced the opportunity structure of Harlem, and introduced innovative strategies, but struggled to direct needed child- and social-welfare resources to marginalized black youths and communities.[48]

In 1964, Cloward's study of New York City child services found that downtown, white-dominated public and private agencies largely ignored the needs of uptown black and Puerto Rican neighborhoods. Of the $1.6 billion allocated to services for child and youth programs citywide, very little went to programs like Northside, which served nonwhite youths facing acute poverty, racial discrimination, and unemployment. For Cloward, this persistent neglect of nonwhite youths and Northside's innovative interracial clinic derived partly from Harlem's lack of a "strong federation that works in its behalf."[49]

Northside's directors argued that, if the clinic was to have the desired impact, its focus must begin to emphasize advocacy and organizing over direct services. After heated and protracted debate, the board and staff members agreed that a more radical community-organizing approach was needed. Ironically, the self-professed surrogate parent and neighbor now struggled to re-create the once formidable black surrogate parental state structure that drove the second wave of black child-savers. For Mamie Clark and Cloward, changing social facts had led to an evolving mission rather than an abandonment of founding principles. Northside directors and staff thus slowly steered the center toward a dual organizing and direct-service model.[50]

Kenneth Clark then devised HARYOU, an ambitious racial justice demonstration project. The plan combined elements of Northside and MFY with Clark's strategies for empowering the immortal youth—particularly those struggling with apathy and despair in the "tension areas" of black ghettos. The program, eventually merged with Adam Clayton Powell's Associated Community Teams (ACT) and renamed HARYOU-ACT, is an extreme illustration of how black civic engagement blended with liberal governmentality to produce experimentation and innovation in civil rights–era juvenile justice. It also underscores why such efforts to institutionalize racial justice failed.[51]

Things Falling Apart

Evidence of civil rights–era unequal recognition and stalled collective action around child welfare in Harlem spurred Northside and others to action. These early returns on integration warned of larger social problems, however. Liberal strategies of professional integration were generally ineffective in co-opting dominant group control of the racial politics of the parental state. Although courts ordered states to statistically integrate their juvenile justice systems, they did not stipulate the importance of a substantive infusion of black community and professional perspectives. There is no record of progress made in integrating local, state, and federal agencies and institutions. In any event, the effort did not translate into a new praxis of racially democratic juvenile social control. Opposition to even moderate social change foreclosed that development.

The jubilation after *Brown* was tempered by the realization that legal orders are not the same as social practices and that integration was a path to full equality but not freedom itself. By the end of the 1950s, it was clear that this quest was not nearly complete. Separate and unequal juvenile justice persisted for decades after *Brown*, with black youths becoming *more* alienated in legally integrated court communities. In the South, and in supposedly more racially liberal areas, such as New York City, new civil rights laws and policies went unheeded, were underenforced, and were regularly trampled. Throughout the period, leaders such as Jane Bolin were consumed by protracted efforts to enforce earlier legal and policy gains. Black child-saving remained a countermovement rather than an institutional norm, and black communities increasingly struggled to sustain and advance juvenile justice reforms.

Reformers such as the Clarks and Bolin were surprised by their limited ability to institutionalize racial justice and overwhelmed by the profound challenges posed by urban delinquency. The prescient W. E. B. DuBois had foreseen some of these challenges when he warned in 1930 of a growing and complex crisis of black urban delinquency. He anticipated that urban delinquency would grow, leading to more severe punishment of black youths and to fragmented and diminished black collective identification and action around issues of youth justice, which together would jeopardize the collective future of black civil society. DuBois called this "the tremendous problem of the next Negro city generation," explaining:

> The colored child, reared in the Northern large city, is so peculiarly a problem of parents that it deserves special thought. . . . The problem of their discipline in school and on the street and in the home is overwhelming in its complexity. The cause is their parents' attitude. In the first place, the parents have little time for the home training of their children because they are hard pressed to earn a living. Many . . . are absent during the day, and when they return tired from work, . . . only too willing to be rid of their children. . . . Moreover, in their desire to have their children self-respecting and not obsequious and fearful, parents encourage truculence and rudeness . . . [which] they mistake for natural self-assertion. . . . In the absence then of parental insistence and care, the greater part of the training of these children comes inevitably from the gutter.

If black youths determine the future of the race, as DuBois maintained, this problem threatened to unravel the fabric of black civil society. He outlined this "two-fold catastrophe":

First of all, the surrounding and dominant white world will put up with this impudence on the part of colored children to a certain point and then they will clap them in jail. The children will not deserve jail. They are not bad. They are simply untaught and their ideals are all awry. But in jail they will learn crime and thus a considerable proportion of them are destined to be driven into real crime almost before they reach manhood and womanhood.

In the second place, in their contact with their own colored people, they will, as they grow up, increase the inner hatreds, jealousies and feuds; the difficulties of attaining group action, the difficulties of maintaining proper and pleasant social intercourse. . . . They will increasingly respect nothing and nobody because they will believe that nothing is respectable. . . .[52]

Left unaddressed, DuBois warned, the growing alienation of black youths and the disorganization of black communities would trigger exclusionary sanctions within the punitive parental state. Black civil society would become weaker, and future generations of black youths would experience mass incarceration and civic exclusion.

For DuBois, this problem affected the growing black working class and middle class. They had settled in urban areas amid the rise of America's "dark ghettos" and were expected to institutionalize racial justice. It was "a problem which one can easily see among the better colored people of New York and Philadelphia, of Indianapolis and Chicago, of Pittsburgh and Baltimore, and all of our major cities." Anticipating later efforts to organize black urban responses to the problems of youths, in Harlem and elsewhere, DuBois urged a proactive response through "thoughtful individual and co-operative action."[53]

Lacking effective policies, many families moved away from the urban center during the civil rights era. Flight, not confrontation, was the response to the growing problem of "bad kids." Collective efficacy declined further, and the black working class and poor urban communities faced an intensified downward spiral in the problem of juvenile crime and the effectiveness of local responses. The popular retreat from the problem of urban delinquency compelled the black child-saving movement to devise, almost single-handedly, solutions to the full-blown "problem of the next Negro city generation."[54]

Black Collective Efficacy in the Midcentury Wind

Community strategies and resources for addressing racial inequality in juvenile justice were still needed. In 1959, Dr. Benjamin Mays, then the president of Morehouse College in Atlanta, issued an urgent critique of black community unresponsiveness to mounting challenges of delinquency and youth justice. Writing in the *Journal of Negro Education,* Mays argued that increased social class fractioning within black communities was the reason that collective responsibility was not being taken. This was especially true of the middle or professional class, which earlier reformers had relied on to lead the institutionalization of racial justice. Mays charged the growing black middle class with deflecting the problem of black delinquency to the police, courts, and social service organizations. He called for a renewal of oppositional self-help strategies. Juvenile justice reform efforts during the previous half century pursued that goal, but he was seemingly unaware of that social movement.[55]

For the integrated parental state to be effective, Mays believed, black community stakeholders, and particularly the growing black middle class, needed to be involved. "The tendency is to run from the problem. The more culturally and economically secure [black] people become," he wrote, "the more likely they are to seek refuge in an exclusive community where their children will be protected from the environment of the lower-income groups." "[The black elite] write about [delinquency], study it in college and university, discuss it casually at social gatherings and make a few speeches about it in church, school and club," he chided, "while the number of Negro delinquents increases and the problem grows in complexity."[56]

Integrating black justice professionals was not problematic for Mays, but he believed that formal control agents, agencies, institutions, and the formal law alone could not address black needs and interests concerning youth and community development. A complementary base of community support and services was equally important. The ideal of race expert leadership had neglected this practical aspect of dominion—the key feature of previous black child-saving initiatives, which lacked complementary power. As the popular base eroded, so too did the social network on which integrated race leaders depended. The drift away from solving delinquency created a generalized ecological crisis, a crack in the social foundation that drained or undermined gains in formal rights and representation.

The rise of black professional representation in child- and social-welfare agencies and institutions, as well as in law enforcement after the 1940s, partly accounts for black popular disengagement from juvenile court communities. Increased representation was especially pronounced in the administration of juvenile justice.[57] In social work, professional integration paradoxically hastened a withdrawal of popular involvement in youth and community development. Thus, informal social controls and the networks on which professional child- and social-welfare providers relied were weakened. "Although these developments brought inarguable improvements in social welfare provisions for poor and troubled people," Sandra O'Donnell writes concerning the emergence of black social work professionals, "they also set in motion a problem that persists to this day—the discouragement and resultant disengagement of communities in battling their social problems."[58]

Political deactivation of black civil society, and black child-saving initiatives in particular, also contributed to a withdrawal from the racial politics of juvenile justice. Even seasoned activists had lost sight of its group significance. William Patterson's 1950 essay "Juvenile Delinquency and Civil Rights" confesses his own slow awakening to the general connection between black youth justice and the black freedom movement. Before that, "delinquents had been abstractions—beings without name or personality—young men, women, and youth, without flesh and blood." This mild interest prompted him to follow police and the press reports on delinquency. Sensational depictions of criminal children and teenagers were the norm. "Delinquency was obviously a matter of statistical, but not grave political and social concern." A deeper political critique of this rebelliousness among youths was needed, but the issue remained marginal to his political consciousness and work. "Juvenile delinquency seemed to present no basic problems for a civil rights organization," he explained. "I was [thus] absorbed by other things: the defense of the constitutional liberties of the Negro people, of labor, and minority groups, as well as the fight against repressive legislation."[59]

Patterson's prison visits and discussions with young prisoners sensitized him to their "warped lives distorted by frustrations in the ghetto." He saw how young men had been "made expendables" and how the state wasted their lives and potential "contributions to the betterment of mankind." Black communities and American democracy could not afford this loss. "Like never before," Patterson wrote, apparently unaware of the long black child-saving movement, "youth must be regarded as one of the decisive segments of the people. Its struggles for human dignity can turn the tide for democracy."[60] That this did not transpire was due in part to the decline of popular support in black and mainstream society.

Many blacks became disconnected from youth justice and from the freedom movement. This was a logical, tragic consequence of apparent gains in civil rights, including direct and indirect representation in the authority of the parental state. Between 1955 and 1975, black Americans and others were deeply engaged in social movements, including pitched battles over education, employment, and child welfare and youth justice. Yet these decades witnessed fleeting organized responses to issues of juvenile delinquency and justice. Black civic leaders remained engaged in the politics of youth justice through the 1960s and beyond, but they rarely enjoyed the levels of shared oppositional consciousness, networking, and resource mobilization that were evident during the first and second waves of the black child-saving movement.

Local movements generally involved a small fraction of the black community; most people had little or no direct involvement in protest activity. Regular updates in the media outraged the national audience and gave the impression that matters were coming to a head. With the forces of full equality seemingly set in motion, black leaders complained that many members of the black community were sitting out the final push for freedom.[61] With professional integration, the public became dependent and disengaged with respect to managing group welfare. To the extent that figures like Jane Bolin and the Clarks gave legitimacy to an increasingly multiracial parental state, they also discouraged continued vigilance around racial equality in juvenile justice. This weakened the ability to carry out cultural and institutional change and limited the intellectual, political, and pragmatic vitality of the integrated parental state. Growing social distance also reduced levels of trust and familiarity, lessened black professional accountability to constituencies, diminished the political capital of civic leaders, and reduced court-community resources.[62] It also may have accelerated the socialization of black justice workers into dominant professional norms, dimming or erasing their identification as race relations experts or advocates of black group interests.

Activists grew frustrated and wrote scathing critiques, such as a *Negro Digest* article entitled "Negro Apathy: How to Combat It." The essay lambasted a segment of the black public it described as "civil rights non-strugglers." Members of the black elite, the author argued, were "selfishly content to enjoy the fruits of their own success" and to escape group threats rather than fight them. A less vital but far larger "complacent element" among the working and middle class "gullibly note scattered privileges at places of public accommodation, and the scant hiring of Negroes on white collar jobs and placidly resign themselves in blind faith to an unquestioned dream about things that will 'naturally' get better—because they are better now than they were fifty years ago."[63]

The decline of black civic identification and engagement concerning youth justice reflected macrosocial and adversarial influences. Among them were the growing force of federalism in juvenile justice policy and black community dissension on whether saving black delinquent youths was essential to black community well-being. Increased federal involvement in juvenile justice reform, through legislation, court rulings, and executive measures, initially bolstered efforts to reorganize civil rights–era juvenile justice. Quietly, however, it consumed a greater share of influence over local juvenile justice agendas. As diminishing numbers of black civic leaders pressed for inclusion, federal and national influences overshadowed them. Traditionally singular notions of immortal black youths were being updated by new class, kin, and even color-based classifications of black and other youths as variably threatened or threatening aspects of linked youth and community fates.[64]

Mays's proposed solution was a black community "war on juvenile delinquency among Negroes." It was an unfortunate characterization in light of a later, largely punitive war on young (black) offenders. But Mays's war entailed a liberal reconstruction that strategically leveraged unprecedented levels of black power or capacity in the prevention of delinquency.[65] It was detailed, multidimensional, and unlikely given the erosion of community-based support for black delinquents. Mays sought to mobilize unprecedented levels of black capital—intellectual, legal, financial, and institutional—in an initiative targeting children and youths, with the aim of delinquency prevention. Given acute need for recreational and other resources for black children and adolescents, especially in the dense and deprived racial ghettos of American cities, he pressed the ubiquitous black church to deepen its contribution to delinquency prevention. "Its chief function is to teach and worship," Mays wrote, and "included in teaching and worshipping is the command to reclaim, rehabilitate and to save." "To prevent a boy from wasting his life in misdemeanors and crime and thus saving him to a life of usefulness in adulthood," he submitted, "is the noblest kind of salvation." He speculated that if "a dozen churches in each metropolitan area work[ed] on this problem . . . churches . . . could reduce juvenile delinquency among Negroes by 50 percent in ten-years."[66]

Mays realized that church and moral suasion alone could not stir fragmented black communities to claim greater control over juvenile delinquency and justice. For black capital to be mobilized, the unfamiliarity, indifference, and opposition regarding delinquency had to be countered. If new resources were to be leveraged, they needed to re-create the sense of common fate and purpose that was more abundant in earlier racial formations. Mays proposed mass enlightenment as a precursor to collective action. He urged others to read the entire special issue of the *Journal of Negro Education*, where his essay appeared, as it contained "more important data on delinquency among Negroes than can be found in any other single production." Since the journal would go unread by the broad public, he recommended distributing briefs through the black press and other popular media. His caring war on black delinquency would lay the social problem squarely "upon the mind and conscience of the entire Negro community."[67]

It was an incredibly optimistic strategy since unfamiliarity was less a barrier to collective action than the lack of political will. The latter reflected a growing distinction between black youth and broader community interests. Calling for more personal commitment to the interests of troubled youths, especially among black leaders, Mays charged:

> The Negro community, particularly the leadership of the Negro community, has to be more than theoretically concerned with the excessive rate of delinquency among Negro youth. With [the reasons for delinquency] clearly known, the leadership in the Negro community all too often gets on the defensive when juvenile delinquency among Negroes is discussed or publicized. We explain the reasons for it, blame it on the environment and leave the burden of improving the situation to the courts, to welfare and character-building agencies. The Negro community rarely comes to grips with the problem except the professional leadership that is hired by the courts and other agencies to deal with it.[68]

The problem was not so much ignorance as apathy, indifference, fear, and hostility, which combined to draw new lines of social distance between poor, black, troubled youths and black civil society. The problem was less the *Journal of Negro Education*'s small readership than the shifting cultural and political meanings of equal protection, black youth opportunity, and black community well-being. Still, Mays and other black leaders struggled to rally popular support. A New York branch of the NAACP held a meeting in 1959 to address juvenile crime and advised potential attendees: "Remember: if we are to be free by '63, we must pay to pave the way" (see fig. 7.1).

Another complicating factor was the broad sociolegal retreat from a sense of civic obligations to poor and otherwise disadvantaged youths. If poverty and racism had been addressed as hoped, black community disengagement would have been less devastating. But, already by the mid-1950s, a trend toward differentiating and excluding "undeserving" black delinquents was evident. Bertram Beck's keynote address at the 1955 National Conference of Social Work drew attention to the growing alienation of black urban youths in need of social services just after court-ordered integration began. For him, the phenomenon of "the exiled delinquent" had its roots in the absence of a common commitment to child- and social-welfare issues: "The failure of the slum community stems from the presence of intergroup conflict which

THE BUFFALO BRANCH of the
N. A. A. C. P.

will have its - - MONTHLY MEETING
at the - - MICHIGAN AVENUE Y.M.C.A.

585 Michigan Avenue, Buffalo, New York

SUNDAY, SEPTEMBER 27, 1959 3:30 P.M.
A PANEL DISCUSSION -
"WHAT APPROACH
SHOULD BE USED
TO CURB
JUVENILE CRIME?"

THE PANEL

MODERATOR:
The Rev. George J. Leake, III: Pastor of Durham Memorial A.M.E. Zion Church

Mr. Horace Johnson: Detatched Worker, Buffalo Youth Board

Mrs. Archie Lewis: Youth Worker, Y. M. C. A.

Captain William J. Shaughan: Michigan Avenue Police Station

Mr. Archie Hunter: Former Detatched Youth Worker, Neighborhood House

Mr. Harold White: Project Coordinator of Buffalo Youth Board

Miss Thelma Hardiman: Teacher, Public School System

Remember: If we are to be free by '63, we must pay to pave the way!!!

JOIN THE N.A.A.C.P. TODAY!
SEE YOU THERE! EVERYONE WELCOME!

For NAACP information call MOhawk 0823 or GRant 1024

The Rev. James T. Hemphill,
Buffalo Branch President

7.1. Flyer advertising NAACP meeting to address juvenile crime (Buffalo, NY, 1959).

militates against the development of a spirit of togetherness. . . . The concomitants of delinquency, such as poor housing and poverty, are not accompanied by crime and delinquency when a collective strength amongst the persons burdened by such problems engenders positive group feelings. Such findings make it possible to see how suddenly developed middle-class communities, without community services or tradition, may be limited in their capacity to induce social conformity." With this breakdown of collective action, "each family comes to such [problems] separately, removed from contact with kith or kin, lacking any sense of 'togetherness' with neighbors."[69]

Beck indicted social workers for their role in this disassociation and for advancing the notion of undeserving youths. Thus, they failed to respond to the challenges of urban youth and community welfare. Delicately sidestepping race, he admitted that the profession had "exiled the delinquent by our overall lack of interest in the field of corrections; by maintaining services chiefly for groups that [exclude] the aggressive, the hostile, and the obstreperous." Social workers actively avoided these challenges and tensions "by closing access to casework to the heavily burdened, downtrodden, and disenchanted poor and opening it to the middle-class neurotic whose aggression, like our own, is displayed in symbols rather than in open hostility."[70] This postintegration retreat from rehabilitative ideals would later become openly hostile.

Beck desperately sought to connect the rehabilitative ideal to the lives of increasingly marginalized youths and communities. The choice, he told the gathered social workers, researchers, educators, and administrators, was "not just punishment vs. treatment for offenders; but love vs. hate in our society." He then appealed to the values of American liberal democracy: "To the extent we [social workers] can help the community in facing up to [the] problem of the delinquent, we shall be successful in creating a community in which basic religious and democratic values are both theory and practice. This is the community that cares and through caring meets its collective needs and is cared for and thus establishes a bridge between the individual and society."[71] This is the kind of black child- and social-welfare bridge that had been cobbled together over decades of black child-saving initiatives; rather than institutionalizing racial justice, the supportive structure was falling apart.

Harlem Youth Opportunity Unlimited: Dying Breaths of a Long Movement

Black social workers, lawyers, probation officers, police, judges, and others who rode the first waves of integration into positions of parental state authority entered a professional realm where key social and institutional systems were in crisis. Very few recognized the historical significance of the formal collapse of Jim Crow juvenile justice. Urban delinquency and collapsing community and institutional supports hampered their abilities to deliver on high expectations of institutionalizing racial justice in juvenile social control.

The historian John Henrik Clarke traces Harlem's deteriorating political power base to developments in the mid- to late 1950s. The election of a black city councilman and borough president gave an impression of "political fortunes on the rise." Political disillusionment and disengagement grew in tandem with passive dependence on elected race leaders. According to Clarke: "Very few demands were being made on the elected representatives [and] the people were losing confidence in politicians as a breed. [Adam Clayton] Powell was dutifully re-elected every two years . . . sent back to Washington to 'bless out the white folks in Congress.' And so long as he blessed them out loud and strong very few people cared to find out whether he was right or wrong. There was a lot of talk about his activities but very little genuine discussion and examination. In the meantime, the political deterioration of the community continued, seemingly unnoticed."[72] In this context, the Clarks and their collaborators encountered barriers to their influence. They needed to (re)build a "strong federation" of community leadership. Northside's involvement in social-welfare politics at the city, state, and federal levels allowed them to intervene in Harlem's opportunity structure, deeply aware of the problems before them.

The Clarks proposed an ambitious plan to empower Harlem and push the nation to realize its democratic creed. With a War on Poverty grant in 1962, Kenneth Clark planned HARYOU. The program, a "democratic experiment in community mental health," as Clark explained in 1963, would fuse social and behavioral science, clinical work, and political mobilization to reconstruct Harlem neighborhoods. As a demonstration project, HARYOU sought to escape a generalized American dilemma. Clark characterized the ghetto crises as "symptoms of personal pathology, emerging out of the context of societal cruelty." Harlem's poor black and Latino neighborhoods, and those in other ghettos, were landmarks of a society in crisis, "monument[s] of human cruelty, injustice and insensitivity." The nation, Clark said, "spawn[ed] human casualties."[73]

Entitled "Youth in the Ghetto: A Study of Powerlessness and a Blueprint for Change," the proposal was presented to President Johnson's Committee on Juvenile Delinquency in April 1964. HARYOU would be an atypical child- and social-welfare program:

HARYOU is not . . . geared primarily toward the saturation of services approach, to the problems of controlling delinquency or the larger problem of making the lives of youth in the Harlem community more meaningful. Rather, HARYOU . . . [will develop] programs which will seek to discourage dependency through an increasing sense of pride, confidence and initiative in the youth themselves. It would seem more important for these young people to learn how to work for social change themselves rather than to continue to have others provide them with occasional palliatives, panaceas or worse. . . . HARYOU therapy . . . combines in its treatment of individuals techniques for the treatment of society . . . contribut[ing] to the movement of society toward greater stability and justice.

The proposal combined elements of Northside Center and MFY on the scale of the Harlem community. Technically a delinquency prevention and intervention program, HARYOU was intended to demonstrate a racially democratic approach to the full development and societal mobilization of Harlem's marginalized youths. "If [HARYOU] is successful," the proposal promised, "it will be making a needed contribution to the strengthening of American democracy." The program's "inviolable theme" was that "minority youth are not expendable." This updated pledge to the immortality of youth was meant for black and nonblack stakeholders alike.[74]

The plan was to combine "skills, methods and techniques of value-sensitive social sciences, social-action-oriented clinicians and social services" with "a realistic identification, mobilization and use of the political, economic and social power within the community." It employed the popular idea of connecting youths to opportunity—entrepreneurial, educational, employment, etc.—as a method of building a network of community services and support while boosting the civic capacity and participation of black urban youths. Like Northside and MFY, HARYOU would meld activism with services in an attempted dramatic restructuring of racial group opportunity and power relations.[75]

HARYOU's community empowerment agenda met with skepticism and opposition. Urban rioting and rebellion caused liberal fervor over opportunity to give way to fears of radical democracy. By the mid-1960s, MFY came under attack for its radical and Communist empowerment agenda. It shifted its emphasis to gang work, job training, and other service provision. Any unease about HARYOU could raise questions about a Harlem program that sought large-scale mobilization and social change. Though leery of the action agenda and other aspects of the plan, the president's committee funded the proposal because of its innovative approach to urban poverty.[76]

Drafting the empowerment strategy proved easier than executing it. Even with Harlem's power base, this radical new vision of youth and community justice had to overcome incredible odds. Harlem had also experienced a decline in black collective efficacy. HARYOU's politically moderate model and conflict over the program illustrate the challenges. A power struggle soon removed Kenneth Clark from the leadership and moderated HARYOU's action plan. Clark accused the revered but sometimes autocratic Harlem Congressman Adam Clayton Powell of attempting to seize control of HARYOU's finances and development. They quarreled over whether politicians or service professionals should run the organization. Clark insisted that leadership should be independent, technical, and professional. Powell, he said, was less interested in the program than in its value as a pork barrel project and feather in his political cap.[77]

Clark lacked Powell's base of popular support. His credentials and national reputation led some to question his authenticity as a Harlem leader. The federal government considered the HARYOU model to be too radical, while some within black civil society considered the work too moderate and reformist. Harlem leaders and residents such as Malcolm X and Adam Clayton Powell questioned the scholarly Clark's identity and leadership. He was a War on Poverty hustler, too out of touch with black communities and beholden to power brokers to bring about meaningful change.[78] He was castigated as man of science *rather than* action, in contrast to the strategic blend of these social roles sought by black child-savers. Clark lost out to Powell's popularity in Harlem and influence in the federal government. He ceded authority over HARYOU around 1964. Powell's former assistant, Livingston Wingate, was named director of the $118 million antipoverty program. Several Powell supporters became board members of what was now HARYOU-ACT, and the renamed organization was reframed as a more moderate youth and community program.

HARYOU's plan had emphasized youth-based social action. HARYOU-ACT gutted this agenda, with its goal becoming urban riot prevention. During Wingate's first eighteen months as director, no community action efforts were undertaken. HARYOU planners believed that youth and community action was key to breaking the pathologies of the ghetto and changing societal power relations. HARYOU-ACT's political leadership saw radical community action as a potential threat to vested interests. They prioritized black juvenile social control over the empowerment of Harlem youths and communities. According to the social work historian Mary Day, the major programmatic thrusts became "the provision of social services and those programs thought to hold promise for containing the riot potential of Harlem—

junior cadet corps, arts, educational and vocational training, and employment placement." For the new leadership, participation of Harlem youths in a parade was "the essence of community action." They declared HAROU-ACT a success because no riots occurred in Harlem during the summer of 1965.[79]

A defeated and frustrated Clark predicted that this failure to empower ghetto inhabitants and restructure power relations would mean that the programs would have little lasting impact. Writing later on the "pathos of power" inside and outside black communities, he located this failure of reconstruction in the "controlling and inhibiting fact that those human beings with power are deeply unwilling or unable to share even a modicum of real power with those who have been powerless": "The poor and the powerless are objects to be manipulated, taunted, played with and punished by those with power. . . . Antipoverty programs based upon these social realities were doomed to failure because they reflected a total lack of commitment to eliminate poverty, to share power with the powerless. . . . These programs did not want to, and would not, operate in terms of the [expectation] of the potential equality of all human beings. They did not seek to accept and strengthen the humanity of the deprived through compassion, empathy, and a serious sharing of power."[80]

Conclusion: The Collapse of Liberal Racial Reconstruction

This chapter has examined how formal integration altered black youth and community involvement in juvenile social control. The period from 1955 to 1975 combined intense and often violent protests for and against civil rights. It featured a liberal reconstruction of juvenile justice. Attempts to institutionalize racial justice were typically thwarted by resistance to civil rights reform, especially in the urban and rural South, but also in Northern cities, where more subtle discrimination endured. Midcentury gains extended greater protection to black youths and representation to black adults but failed to institutionalize a racially democratic approach to administering liberal rehabilitative ideals.

Federal legal and executive interventions and the determination of a dwindling black child-saving movement brought about scattered but noteworthy changes in the racial politics of American juvenile justice. These gains are most apparent in integrated court communities where the black surrogate parental state had made earlier inroads in black youth and community empowerment. In the case of Harlem, for example, there was an unprecedented effort to rearrange racial group power relations in juvenile social control. Programs such as Northside Center for Child Development, MFY, and HARYOU illustrate this effort to redefine child- and social-welfare services through innovative, race-conscious strategies of delinquency prevention and intervention.

The racial reconstruction of juvenile justice was a contested, ongoing process. In the later phases, the negotiated reform of integration faltered and declined in significance. Liberal reformers envisioned early self-help efforts and the more politicized black surrogate parental state as temporary, transitional resources of refuge and representation. These remedies were to yield to a formally integrated parental state in which black race experts (i.e., integrated professionals and service workers) would institutionalize black child-saving initiatives—and, thus, racial justice. In reality, advances in integration coincided with the erosion and fragmentation of black community engagement in juvenile justice reform. Black collective efficacy diminished in terms of shaping the present and future of juvenile social control.

Toppling Jim Crow juvenile justice meant that the dominant parental state formally adopted black youths and communities in a legal sense. This did not guarantee a lasting love or civic embrace of black delinquents. Segregationist officials in Maryland, Florida, Mississippi, and elsewhere undermined integration by enlisting the authority of the parental state to selectively punish black youths, committing young civil rights activists to newly established reformatories. In places such as New York, which were relatively racially progressive, uptown black civic actors and white-dominated downtown agencies battled over a more benign neglect of black youth and community interests and the hoarding of service resources. Integration thus had many faces, but each poorly resembled what black child-savers had envisioned as institutionalized racial justice.

After generations of organized efforts to expand civil rights and advance black youth and community interests in citizen-building initiatives, black youths and adults grew isolated in formally integrated juvenile court communities, and new forms of racialized exclusion began to characterize juvenile justice. A diminished group of black child-savers struggled to revitalize the movement in the late 1950s and early 1960s, but to little effect. Owing to the apparent success of liberal civil rights reforms, many black citizens and civic leaders withdrew, and the link between black youth and community interests grew subject to debate. This disengagement and discord weakened the intellectual, political, and pragmatic vitality of the integrated parental state. Growing social distance reduced levels of trust and familiarity, limited professional accountability to constituent communities, and diminished the political capital of civic leaders and the resources of court communities. Northside's experience revealed the importance of continued local community support for securing access to resources, such as political influence, funding, programs, and the client base needed for large-scale innovation.

Disengagement likely accelerated the socialization of black justice workers into dominant professional norms, and it clearly affected the memory of the black child-saving movement. Black justice workers grew unfamiliar with their idealized role as expert advocates of black group interests. Black leaders in the 1950s and 1960s became unaware of the black child-saving movement. Faced with growing crises of black urban delinquency, their calls for child-saving civic action ignored earlier precedents and belied their limited legacy. As black collective efficacy weakened and the movement continued to decline, the "exile" of recently incorporated black delinquents became an enduring feature of the postintegration period.[81]

Compounding the reduced capacity for local control were a national backlash and the growing federal role in previously local juvenile justice systems. Between 1950 and the early 1970s, federal involvement was largely beneficial and, perhaps, ideal for the liberal reconstruction envisioned by black child-savers. Civil rights laws, desegregation enforcement rulings, increased due process protections, War on Poverty programs, and other federally backed reforms liberalized the racial politics of the parental state. But New Frontier and Great Society programs would be rolled back by national fears of (black) urban youths, a contraction of the welfare state, and militarist wars on urban crime and delinquency. The benefits of formal integration and federal engagement rapidly diminished. Despite gains that had been made, black communities were now ill equipped to counter the coming storm of punitive redemption.

Writing on the aftermath of struggles for equal rights, Herbert Marcuse captured this tragic dimension. The sought-after rights and liberties "served to promote and protect—essentially critical ideas," he wrote. Moreover, the activation or deployment of new rights and liberties would "replace an obsolescent material and intellectual culture by a more productive and rational one." Yet the apparent achievement of new rights and liberties "cancels the premises" of their importance, "and their critical role is lost in new forms of control."[82] Black child-savers idealized the postintegration, multiracial parental state as a more legitimate and productive system of racially democratic control. They assumed that the rights and liberties of formal inclusion would be actively leveraged to advance more progressive racial politics within juvenile justice. Kenneth Clark warned that the *Brown* ruling removed obstacles to participation in a more robust racial democracy, but this was only the beginning. Formal inclusion appears to have canceled the critical premise of racially equal protection and representation in postintegration juvenile justice. Deactivation of black child-saving initiatives left formally integrated black youths and authorities and less organized black communities exposed to "new forms of control."

The conclusion considers this tragic turn in the racial history of juvenile justice. It focuses on the subtle racial oppression and domination of the modern era of accountability-based juvenile justice. Redefined social-contractual terms of juvenile justice altered the civic entitlements and duties of youth and adult authorities within integrated juvenile justice systems. This compromised the real value of equal protection and representation. The transition negated new claims to citizen-building ideals and resources, such that visible racial integration in juvenile justice became a poor simulation of racially democratic control.[83]

The Declining Significance of Inclusion

Generations of black child-savers shaped the juvenile justice system into the racially integrated institution it is today, yet their movement failed to institutionalize equal black youth and community access to rehabilitative ideals and resources. White resistance to integration and declining black collective efficacy undermined progress in reinventing and maintaining more representative models of juvenile justice administration. Rather than celebrating the achievement of formal integration, veterans of the black child-saving movement watched in dismay as the punitive reconstruction of the multiracial parental state reasserted familiar patterns of exclusion.

This conclusion examines how the significance of formal inclusion diminished in the postintegration period, especially in the wake of the punitive turn in juvenile justice. I argue that the formally multiracial parental state declined in significance for two reasons in particular. First, penal-managerial policies and practices that emerged in the final decades of the twentieth century redefined the social contractual terms of youth justice by bracketing citizen-building ideals. A new emphasis on penal classification identified a new breed of delinquent, one who was uniquely dangerous, morally depraved, and, therefore, justifiably excluded from citizen-building ambitions and, ultimately, civil society.[1] Being classified as a serious delinquent triggered the loss of presumptive rights to developmental opportunity and civic reintegration within the legal structure and administrative practices of the parental state. Normal delinquents retained previous rights as citizens, including access to rehabilitative resources and sanctions, while serious delinquents, as one governor put it, would "forfeit childhood." While the normal delinquent might still enjoy access to the fabled manufactory of citizens, the serious delinquent faced a loss of civil standing through more severe and exclusionary sanctions.[2]

Data on youth sanctioning since 1970 reveal a pattern of racially differential selection into the categories of *normal* and *serious* delinquents. White youths tend to be categorized as normal delinquents, while black and other nonwhite youths are assigned to the undeserving status of serious offenders. Racialization of these classifications is clearly indicated by studies that observe the significance of racial status to offender classification and sanctioning. However, even where the patterns do not specifically violate legal rights to equal protection, it should be noted that the practice denies access to citizen-building initiatives to black youths and communities. This was the substantive concern of black child-savers regarding equal protection for black youthful offenders and the fate of black civil society.[3]

Second, formal integration lost significance because of renewed black community alienation in the governance of juvenile justice. Although physically present, recently incorporated black decisionmakers became marginalized in deliberative milieus of postintegration juvenile justice. Recognition of black adults was partly limited by the erosion of community-based controls, which, I have argued, constrained the practical utility of professional integration as a means of brokering group influence. However, the reorganization of parental state authority through accountability reform further alienated black publics and justice workers alike, making federal, state, and local political structures less accountable to black community interests.

Powerful citizen groups and political actors moved to the fore of juvenile justice policy reform through the accountability movement. Court community practices of structured and guideline sanctioning were instituted, and juvenile justice policy became increasingly nationalized and federalized. Consequently, juvenile justice became less responsive to the interests of marginal groups. Among the constituencies with limited political capital were black urban communities and local black government authorities and service workers whose capacity to determine juvenile justice policy and practice had diminished.[4]

Black adults within juvenile justice had been envisioned as representatives of group interests—as race-conscious operatives who would enlighten the racial politics of the multiracial parental state. Under accountability-based juvenile justice, however, the potential of race expert leaders to determine social policy was limited. Accountability-based juvenile justice restructured power relations through new legislative codes, federal and state funding structures, efforts to rationalize local decisionmaking, and other means.

Standardized decisionmaking technologies and federal policies regarding racial justice illustrate how altered power relations diminished the substantive significance of integration. To limit bias, discretionary or individualized justice was replaced by standardized or structured decisionmaking (SDM). This diluted the relevance of difference or multiculturalism among arbiters of justice. Although black child-savers sought to embed architects of race adjustment who would enlighten race relations in juvenile justice, federalization of reform efforts diminished the role of courts in regulating racial equality. In 1982, the centerpiece of federal race policy was a mandate to address disproportionate minority contact. Equality became narrowly defined as racially proportional sanctioning outcomes. The commitment bears little resemblance to the original goal of recognizing black youth and community interests in citizen-building initiatives.

Ultimately, the rise of penal managerialism turned the integration of juvenile justice into a more symbolic than substantive achievement of racially democratic social control. Federalization initially advanced the black child-saving agenda. But, as community control diminished and the dependence on federal, state, and local authority grew, the historic progress in accessing citizen-building ideals and authority was undermined. By the end of the twentieth century, that progress was all but erased from the political culture and national memory. Anniversaries of the *Brown* ruling became occasions to lament the unfulfilled expectations of integration. Veteran black child-savers grieved over the failure to institutionalize racial justice in juvenile social control. They watched as a wave of law-and-order reform washed away their once nuanced and vibrant movement and black youths and communities became subject to new modes of exclusion. Faint new black community calls to mobilize in the name of the immortal youth recall the origins of the early movement and betray a lack of any sense that black child-savers ever existed.

Empty Promised Lands of Integration

The twentieth-century profile of race and juvenile institutionalization helps illustrate the persistence of racial inequality amid appearances of inclusion. Over the past several decades, much research and numerous policies have dealt with race and juvenile institutionalization. Given the incredible rise of black and Latino youths in juvenile and adult detention, jails, and prisons, federal efforts concentrated on explaining this disproportionate minority contact. As figure 8.1 shows, increasingly disproportionate confinement of minority youths (in relation to the general population) is the dominant trend in juvenile justice from 1950 to 2000. Researchers and policymakers have scrambled to measure, explain, and reduce this growing inequality.[5]

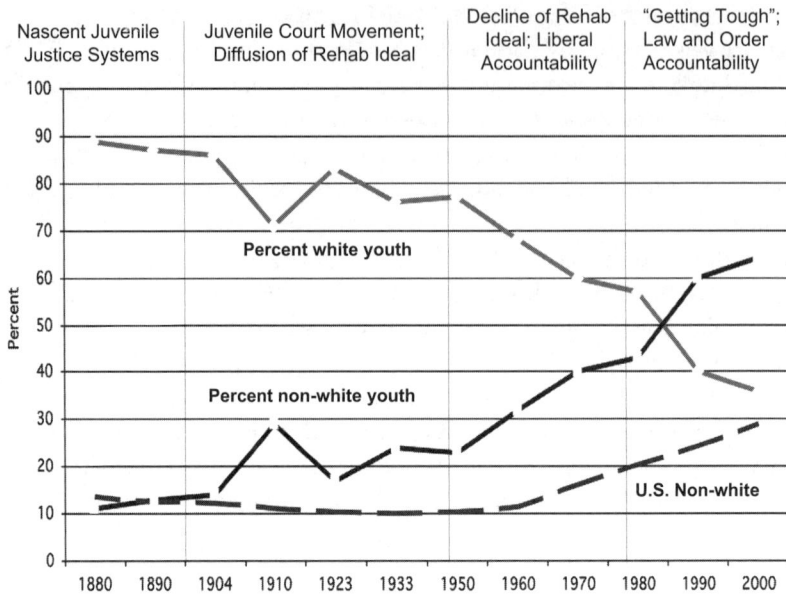

| Nascent Juvenile Justice Systems | Juvenile Court Movement; Diffusion of Rehab Ideal | Decline of Rehab Ideal; Liberal Accountability | "Getting Tough"; Law and Order Accountability |

8.1. Racially disproportionate confinement by period.

This picture of racial disparity distorts the racial politics of youth justice, giving a misleading impression of the nature and extent of inequality, historically and today. From a distributive perspective, in which racially proportional distributions of commitment decisions or other sanctions indicate equality, race relations in juvenile justice were most equal at the outset of the juvenile court movement. Then, inequality dramatically worsened over the past half century. Yet racial and ethnic inequality in juvenile justice has been a fundamental feature throughout this institutional history. Since the nineteenth century, the politics of white privilege and inequalities in power have defined juvenile justice policy and practice. This yielded a contested agenda of juvenile social control in which preparing white and potentially white youths for societal reintegration was the priority. The success of this agenda is evident in *lower* and more proportional rates of nonwhite youth institutionalization in the preintegration period.

The migration of black Americans to more inclusive or integrated urban and northern juvenile court communities lessened the historic imbalance with whites. Had these institutions remained committed to citizen-building ideals, increased access of nonwhite youths to juvenile institutions would have been considered a civil rights success. In terms of racial justice, proportional group representation within juvenile institutions should be read in relation to expressed racial group interests and the historically situated meaning of *institutionalization*.

After the fall of Jim Crow systems, the racial composition of juvenile institutions changed during two waves of accountability-based reform in the fifty years leading to the millennium. The initial wave (1955–75) was generally liberal and less politicized. It focused on system responsibilities to youths, such as civil rights and due process protections, as well as on access to developmental resources. Black and other nonwhite youths experienced better access to public juvenile institutions, along with innovations and increased investments in child and social welfare (i.e., community-based delinquency prevention). Racial justice advanced to the extent that juvenile justice systems were beginning to provide for the needs of all members of society.

But unintended consequences of the collapse of Jim Crow and the first wave of accountability reform undermined longer-term prospects for institutionalizing racial justice. Support for traditional rehabilitative ideals weakened in terms of community social structures (i.e., sustained civic engagement), as did popular and political sentiment toward rehabilitative ideals. Moreover, the liberal critique of rehabilitation, including discretion in juvenile courts and reformatory institutions, created a legitimacy crisis for the juvenile justice system. The challenge to the cultural and institutional bases of rehabilitative ideals created an ideological vacuum regarding the future of juvenile and criminal justice. A search for new organizing principles pushed aside the once dominant "penal-welfare paradigm."[6]

The public, mainstream academics, and policymakers had long expressed confidence in the state's civic obligation and capacity to pursue enlightened rehabilitative interventions, especially in the case of white youths. In the post–civil rights period, however, many civic actors rejected the liberal child- and social-welfare agenda. They lost faith in the authority of an integrated parental state and abandoned its traditionally utilitarian, rehabilitative agenda. After a decade of forced integration and growing problems of juvenile crime and violence (often attributed to black youths in urban settings), advocates of greater punishment and control unleashed a backlash. Their response was a new punitive paradigm and policy framework of accountability-based juvenile justice.[7]

The second wave of accountability reform (post-1975) was part of a comprehensive conservative attack on the legitimacy and reach of the welfare state. It discredited the broad application of traditional rehabilitative ideals. Citing youthful indiscretion, it shifted the logic of civic responsibility in juvenile social control. Heretofore, enlightened juvenile justice had stressed the civic duty to protect the best interests of youths and to deliver these embryonic citizens into the body politic. The punitive turn instead identified deserving and undeserving delinquents. Proponents pursued deinstitutionalization and dedicated the remaining, often privatized citizen-building resources to the former. The latter faced more exclusionary sanctions, or variations on what Bertram Beck had termed *exile*.[8] Punitive accountability reform was more explicit and politicized. Certain youths should be held criminally responsible, proponents argued, reserving the severe sanction of institutionalization for serious delinquents, subtly racialized figures who were less entitled to rehabilitative ideals and resources.

In the twentieth century, nonwhite youths gained greater access to institutions, but what did *inclusion* mean? The time line on disproportionate minority contact (see fig. 8.1 above) reveals white inclusion and black exclusion across eras of racialized citizen building but not a growing problem of racial inequality. It reflects the imbalance in racial group privileges and power that characterized Jim Crow juvenile justice, which predominated in the most ambitious era of citizen-building initiatives (1900–1950). Revealed as well are mass black migration to the urban North and West, where opportunity was thought to abound, and a brief period of civil rights reconstruction (1955–75). In the last period, black youths and communities gained unprecedented but limited access to rehabilitative ideals and institutions. Finally, it signals the end of experiments in racially democratic control and redemption through citizen building. Postintegration practices adapted: white youths were still constructed as more deserving of social support and diverted toward inclusionary sanctions, but black and other nonwhite youths were reconstituted as undeserving delinquents and subject to familiar patterns of neglect and severe sanctioning.

Limiting Rights to Rehabilitation

Racial inequality in juvenile justice today is neither new nor more intense than in earlier years. Rather, it is uniquely organized in relation to systems of juvenile social control.[9] Formal integration of the parental state created new crises in delinquency and new expressions of well-known patterns of racial oppression and domination. The black child-saving movement did not anticipate the organizing principles that emerged in juvenile justice in the late 1970s. In particular, the punitive accountability movement weakened the already limited ability of formal integration to institutionalize black community access to citizen-building ideals and resources.

In her final years on the Manhattan juvenile court, Judge Jane Bolin noted the tragic consequences of the postintegration punitive turn for black youth and community opportunities. For decades, her civil rights activism and judicial influence had sought to equalize the benefits of liberal-democratic rehabilitative ideals. Her court community had once been in the forefront of changing racial group relations of opportunity and influence, but, when she retired, it was taking the lead in punitive accountability reform.[10] In the late 1970s, Bolin lamented that labeling black and Latino youths as seriously delinquent constituted a new mechanism of exclusion. "Just before I left the bench," the eighty-two-year-old jurist recalled in 1990, "the whole philosophy of the Children's Court was changed. Philosophy from the last century had been that children were not to be treated as adult criminals." This presumption of limited criminal culpability, by virtue of age, was now in decline. "The year before I left the bench," she continued, "the whole philosophy of the Children's Court was changed. New York State passed laws which permitted children, as young as 13, to be taken to the Criminal Court to be tried as adults for certain felonies."[11]

Bolin was not naive about the modern challenges of juvenile justice. On the bench since 1939, she was concerned about the growing seriousness of juvenile crime and that even among "younger children, for some reason, some of them have become violent." Acknowledging that cases involving "guns, arson and rape, and other violent crimes have increased very much in numbers since I first started to preside in court," she considered this "a reflection of our society . . . [which has also] become very much more violent." Bolin was more concerned about the choices civic leaders were making in response to these problems and the resort to severe sanctioning rather than preventive and supportive measures:

> It's true that many . . . or some of the young people today are very violent. It's reflected in our society, or the violence in our society is reflected in them. They do need serious attention. They need a better education than many of them are getting. There needs to be a curb on drugs. There needs to be more help for families, particularly poor families. Young people need guidance. . . . We haven't met all our obligations to young people by any means. There's not . . . enough understanding of them, and their desires and influences, and enough hasn't been done to get them through adolescence and young adulthood successfully.[12]

As was often the case, Bolin's civic convictions were sidelined as a minority view, finding little support in the dominant culture or institutional

practice. The mainstream notion limited civic obligations to deserving categories of delinquents, a selection process that routinely excluded black
and Latino youths. In 1967, President Lyndon Johnson's Commission on
Law Enforcement and the Administration of Justice proposed a bimodal
categorization of young offenders and their entitlements. It advocated a
two-track approach to juvenile justice administration that was tailored to
criminal and noncriminal jurisdictions. The noncriminal, or delinquency,
track was still defined by rehabilitative ideals and sought to limit formal intervention (i.e., court processing and commitment) in favor of informal and
community-based strategies. The criminal track embraced the penal logic
of just deserts in juvenile justice administration, subjecting boys and girls
labeled as more serious delinquents to greater punishment and control.[13]

This distinction surfaced in state legal codes and local practices related
to juvenile justice administration. Punishment became a core component
of juvenile justice that defined mechanisms or procedures for assigning
youths to treatment and punishment tracks. In the mid-1970s, state legislatures revised their statutes to stress juvenile culpability, with an emphasis on punishment and public safety over the best interests of the child. A
review of these changes concluded that "an interest in treating youths as
responsible actors can be discerned as a unifying theme of the reformed
juvenile codes." These new principles clashed with expectations that civil
rights reform would improve access to citizen-building institutions and
with commitments that black juvenile justice professionals made regarding
rehabilitative ideals.[14]

The state of Washington's Juvenile Justice Act of 1977 was among the
first to adopt retributive accountability ideals. It called for "punishment
commensurate with the age, crime, and criminal history of the juvenile
offender" and required that a youth be held "accountable for his or her
criminal behavior." California soon revised its codes along similar lines but
specified that juvenile sanctions should not be retributive in purpose and design. In other states, retribution was a prominent rationale. Accountability-
based juvenile justice gained national momentum toward the end of the
1970s and into the 1980s.[15] In 1978, New York governor Hugh Carey signed
the Juvenile Offender Act, which stipulated that juveniles who were age
thirteen or older and accused of murder be charged and sentenced as adults.
Waiver provisions such as these had always existed in juvenile justice for
the most serious, violent cases. But, in the accountability era, there was an
expansion of transfer provisions covering younger children and a wider variety of offenses.[16]

Criminal accountability measures of the late 1960s and the 1970s pres-aged the flood of political rhetoric, legislation, and public policy that crimi-nalized delinquency in the 1980s. Federal and state governments countered a juvenile crime epidemic that promised to get worse. In 1985, the admin-istrator of the federal Office of Juvenile Justice and Delinquency Prevention wrote an article provocatively titled "Getting Away with Murder: Why the Juvenile Justice System Needs an Overhaul." Wielding the "tough on crime" rhetoric common to the period, it said: "The juvenile justice system, which is supposed to act only in the 'best interest of the child,' serves neither the child, his victim, nor society. Juvenile crime rates since the 1950s have tri-pled, yet the theories and policies we use to deal with such crime fail to hold offenders accountable and do not deter crime. At best, they are outdated; at worst, they are a total failure, and may even abet the crimes they are supposed to prevent." In short, the intent was to shift from accountability *to* youths toward the accountability *of* youths. The rehabilitative ideal was rendered a naive, dangerous, and presumptive sanctioning orientation that society could no longer afford. Government's role was, not to safeguard the interests of troubled youths, but to protect society from them.[17]

Sensationalist forecasts of juvenile superpredators flooding the nation's streets encouraged this shift, gaining wide visibility in the 1980s and 1990s in the news media. The resulting hysteria over this "teenage time bomb" spawned a cottage industry of investigative reporting and films about dan-gerous children and youths.[18] Ambitious politicians declared war on these menaces to society. In his 1995 State of the State Address, Michigan's Re-publican governor, John Engler, promised protection from this new threat: "There are young people who put the rest of us at risk. They have no concept of personal responsibility, and no compunction about preying on others. Our message to these thugs and punks must be unambiguous. They not only forfeit their childhood; they forfeit their right to privacy and special treatment. . . . No longer will acts of 'youthful indiscretion' be erased from their records, while leaving permanent scars on their victims. The public is demanding—and I concur—that young punks be treated as adults." The public had grown leery of traditional rehabilitative ideals, especially where serious delinquents were concerned. A 1993 *USA Today*, CNN, and Gallup poll showed that 73 percent of adults favored treating juveniles who had committed violent crimes as adults.[19]

Governor Engler signed a twenty-one-bill package that established "re-sponsibility, deterrence, accountability and punishment [as] basic compo-nents of Michigan's juvenile justice system." Michigan's laws were among the most retributive in the country. Aspiring to national office, Engler dramatized his crusade by promoting a private maximum-security "punk prison" for violent youths; it opened in 1999. There were too few violent youths to fill it, so it housed black and less serious delinquents from Detroit and other cities. Engler's Democratic successor ended the costly and repressive spectacle by quietly closing it six years later.[20]

Although this penal-managerial policy was ostensibly race neutral, the undeserving delinquents or "thugs" being contemplated were black, urban youths. The caricature was subtler than the one deployed under Jim Crow juvenile justice. Yet this "Willie Hortonization" of modern juvenile justice plays on historically familiar race-linked themes of moral depravity and incorrigibility to render modern (black) delinquents undeserving of liberal citizen-building programs.[21] John C. Watkins Jr., a former chair and founding member of the Department of Criminal Justice at the University of Alabama, closes the preface of his 1998 *The Juvenile Justice Century* with this question: "Can society adapt a court whose original mission was to deal with the marginal delinquent and un-socialized children and their parents to the likes of predatory urban inner-city gang delinquents?" He does not think so, arguing: "The juvenile court envisaged by the Illinois founders to deal largely with Caucasian, immigrant-driven, culture-conflict criminality is not the court that can realistically deal with the often amoral delinquents of the contemporary teenage 'hood.'"[22]

Mass Incarceration of Black Citizens Marked Serious Delinquent

In the 1950s and 1960s, the capacity of black child-welfare advocates to limit or counter the racial discourse of just deserts and undeserving delinquents had diminished markedly. Black civil society's growing dependence on the formally integrated parental state fostered passivity. In the post–civil rights period, access for black youths to inclusionary juvenile justice sanctions had *diminished*, and integrated local court communities had *lost* authority over the administration of rehabilitative ideals. Juvenile courts and institutions disproportionately processed black and Latino youths, but declining commitments to citizen building decoupled the integrated parental state from the project of racially democratic reform.

By the 1950s, statistical overrepresentation of black youths was already becoming apparent. In the 1980s, the gap between white and black youth confinement rates grew sharply. Initially, overt oppression and white domination of juvenile justice had kept black youths out of institutions. So the early incremental growth in youth institutionalization owing to the black freedom movement and court-ordered integration represented progress. By the final quarter of the twentieth century, however, penal classifications of deserving and undeserving youths reversed these democratizing trends. In this "no longer separate, not yet equal" system, white and nonwhite youths continued to be systematically tracked through inclusionary and exclusionary sanctions.[23]

The demographic shift in institutionalization since the mid-1970s reveals this pattern of racially differential sanctioning. In the liberal and subsequent conservative phases of accountability reform, white youths appear to have been privileged. In 1987, the criminologist Barry Krisberg and his colleagues reported that, from 1977 to 1979, when deinstitutionalization was most pronounced, the populations of public juvenile correctional institutions in the United States declined by 7 percent, from 43,659 to 40,751. Confinement of white youths declined markedly. Selectively classified as nonserious delinquents, they could better afford private diversion alternatives to formal court processing and commitment. Deinstitutionalization of white youths accounts for about 75 percent (2,184) of the decline in the population of youths committed to public institutions.[24]

Liberal calls to limit incarceration, along with other formal interventions, benefited "deserving" white youths. Bearing the brunt of subsequent punishment and control initiatives were black and other nonwhite youths. This outcome reflected their racialized (re)construction as a distinct breed of dangerous, undeserving, and incorrigible offenders. Several states sentenced serious offenders to longer periods of institutionalization and introduced more severe penalties (i.e., adult institutions) under accountability-based juvenile justice. Youth institutionalization grew dramatically, as did the proportion of nonwhite youths in juvenile reformatories, adult jails, and prisons. Between 1979 and 1982, the juvenile reformatory population alone rose 15 percent—from about 40,751 to 46,929. Ninety-three percent of the increase came from the confinement of black and Latino/Latina youths. Twenty-three percent of youths in reformatories nationwide were nonwhite in 1950. The proportion approached 60 percent in 1990. By 1996, the proportion of nonwhite youths among institutionalized delinquents exceeded 70 percent in many states.[25]

Severe accountability-based sanctioning has uniquely affected black girls and boys. In Los Angeles during the early 1990s, a study of delinquency case processing found that the two-track (treatment vs. punishment) approach was mainly reserved for white girls. Their black and Latina counterparts were more likely to face punishment. Seventy-five percent of white girls were recommended for placement in treatment-oriented programs, compared to

34 percent of Latinas and 20 percent of black girls. A 1993 study in a midwestern state illustrates how class interacts with racialized placement patterns. Few offense differences were evident in the population of white and black girls committed to public and private institutions in the state. However, the population of more treatment-oriented private facilities was entirely white, while the population of public institutions was 61 percent black.[26]

This increase in racial and ethnic disparity is partly attributable to differential involvement in violent juvenile crime, especially relating to gangs, weapons offenses, and the drug trade. There are many caveats since race and ethnicity frame law enforcement responses, including arrest and charging decisions. Studies suggest that youths demonstrating similar behavior receive different treatment, depending on race. The limitations of official data make it difficult to determine the factors behind racial disparities in the severity of sanctioning.[27] Societal choices regarding the proper response to the social problems of nonwhite youths and communities determine the severity of punishment for serious minority youth crime and delinquency. Solid research reveals that racial and ethnic group distributions of severe sanctions reflect discrimination in justice administration. Quantitative and qualitative studies of legal decisionmaking as well as experimental and attitudinal research show that black youths are systematically constructed as more serious and culpable offenders than are their white counterparts, regardless of offense characteristics. They are likely to be subjected to severe and civically exclusionary sanctions partly on the basis of race.[28]

The Deep End of Civic Exclusion: Race and the Forfeiture of Childhood

The two-track approach to sanctioning in juvenile justice grew more pronounced from the mid- to the late 1970s. In this context, a commitment to a juvenile institution itself became a judgment of severe delinquency and more punitive response. Yet the racialization of serious delinquency and severe sanctioning is most dramatically revealed in the cases of juveniles legally classified and punished as adults. These youths are more completely stripped of moral or legal entitlements to welfare considerations and subjected to the full force of punitive sanctioning. Overrepresentation of nonwhite youths is most pronounced at this "deep end" of accountability-based juvenile justice, where children and youths are transferred to adult courts and correctional systems.[29]

Treating young people as adults under the law is not a new phenomenon. The novel features in the punitive accountability era are the breadth and discretion attached to these policies, the frequency of their use, and the resulting increase in the number of youths criminally sanctioned as adults.[30] Dramatic racial disparities exist in the population of youths punished as adults. New York legislated juvenile transfer procedures as early 1943, when its Youthful Offender Statute empowered judges to differentiate between "youthful" or normal delinquents worthy of lenience and more serious counterparts who were undeserving of rehabilitative ideals and would be legally treated as adults. In 1978, following a high-profile case of extreme juvenile violence, the statute was revised to lower the age of automatic adult jurisdiction for homicide. It provided greater discretion to deny youthful offender status even for less serious offenses. The sociologist Ruth Peterson studied the relevance of race and gender to these classifications in the early 1980s. Black and Latino youths were substantially more likely to be stripped of youthful offender status and subjected to more frequent and lengthier incarceration than similarly situated white youths were.[31]

In Michigan in the mid-1990s, nonwhite and black youths were primarily sanctioned as adults under Republican governor John Engler's policy of getting tough on young "punks."[32] In 1982, the Michigan Department of Corrections housed 29 individuals for offenses committed while juveniles; in 1998, the number rose to 207. Blacks made up around 15 percent of Michigan's population, but, each year, between 56 and 83 percent of prison commitments involved black juvenile offenders, with a median of 68 percent over the sixteen-year stretch.[33] A waiver study in Illinois reported that black and Latino youths were involved in 85 percent of all automatic (i.e., legislative) transfers to adult courts and that 99 percent of waivers related to drug offenses involved black and Latino youths.[34]

National juvenile waiver studies consistently show that black and Latino youths are most often subject to this severe sanction.[35] According to Sickmund et al., about half of all waivers authorized by judges between 1989 and 1998 involved black youths.[36] The criminologist Donna Bishop researched prosecutorial involvement in juvenile transfers after 1980 and its *increasingly* selective impact on nonwhite youths. Black youths made up around 67 percent of juvenile offenders transferred to adult criminal justice systems between 1990 and 1994.[37] State studies reveal that between 90 and 95 percent of juvenile waivers nationwide involve boys. Blacks and Latinas predominate among girls punished as adults. Sixty-eight percent, or 23, of the 34 females and 65 percent, or 1,028, of the 1,573 males sentenced as juveniles to the Michigan Department of Corrections between 1982 and 1998 were black.[38]

Even if racially biased administration of punitive measures were absent, exclusionary juvenile sanctioning in the contemporary period contrasts with expressed black interests in more inclusionary approaches to juvenile social control, denying representation of these interests.[39] Formal integration coincided with the bifurcation of juvenile sanctioning—the designation of treatment and punishment tracks—and recently incorporated minority youths still enjoy limited access to the traditional treatment track. Instead, they remain subject to the historical ordeal of racialized, exclusionary sanctioning.

Adverse individual and group implications that motivated reformers in the past continue today. For example, transfer to criminal court has adverse collateral consequences for these immortal youths and their communities. The likelihood of reoffending increases (i.e., happening sooner and more often), and prospects for employment, voting, and family involvement diminish. Race-linked criminalization and severe sanctioning of youths are factors in the crime and punishment of black adults and the social, economic, and political impact of mass incarceration on black civil society.[40]

Quieting Multiculturalism in the Multiracial Parental State

The era of mass incarceration and its impact on black youths and young adults are relatively well documented. Less attention has been given to how the punitive turn affected arbiters of juvenile and criminal justice or the issue of representation in justice administration. Assessing racial injustice in the contemporary period requires attention to the reassertion of racial domination in juvenile social control. Punitive reconstruction of juvenile justice not only diminished black youth access to developmental opportunity, reasserting oppression, but also limited black community recognition in the law, policy, and practice of juvenile social control. This reassertion of domination has reduced the racially democratic accountability of the formally integrated parental state.

Black community and professional estrangement takes a few forms. Racial integration of local juvenile court authority coincided with the federalization and nationalization of crime control agendas. Thus, the influence of the black public and professionals over juvenile justice policies and practices diminished locally. Then, decisionmaking within accountability-based juvenile justice was rationalized. Delimiting and relocating discretion diminished the substantive significance of diversity, or multiculturalism, among statistically diverse juvenile justice authorities. Through integration, black professionals were expected to enlighten juvenile justice administration with unique standpoints and informed decisions. With standardized decisionmaking, the identities of authorities became less meaningful, as was their impact on justice processes and outcomes. These developments are also revealed in attempts to police racial inequality in contemporary juvenile justice. When the federal government seized greater control over the agenda of racial justice, it defined the problem of injustice and established protocols or procedures for intervention. The definition and approach neglect issues of representation, or the problem of racial domination central to the black child-saving movement.

These developments illustrate what the political philosopher Nancy Fraser has described as the redistribution-recognition dilemma, in which attempts to eradicate the significance of racial or other group difference (i.e., efforts to achieve race neutrality in sanctioning) clash with simultaneous interests in promoting racial group recognition. In this case, recognition refers to black adult influence in an idealized multiracial, rather than color-blind, parental state. Instead, new policies, procedures, and funding developments have rewired the administration of juvenile justice in ways that undermine black representation. Rigid principles of accountability-based juvenile justice, standardized decisionmaking technologies, and a narrowly redistributive agenda of racial justice are examples of developments that have limited the potential for black communities to impose their concerns, insights, and judgments on modern ideas and practices of American juvenile justice.

Renewing Racial Domination

Several assumptions concerning the impact of integration on the racial democratization of juvenile justice administration were, perhaps, unrealistic. In any case, these expectations were undermined by the federalization and nationalization of accountability-based juvenile justice. Black communities were expected to continue to reflect on their collective interests and effectively express these interests through political participation and representation among juvenile justice authorities. Race and other status characteristics would continue to link the identities and policy inclinations of community members and legal decisionmakers, and both would remain capable of expressing these orientations through decisions that affect system outcomes.[41] But the erosion of black collective identity and action during the civil rights era significantly compromised any capacity to co-opt systems of juvenile social control. Nationalization and federalization of juvenile crime control limited the power of black constituencies and authorities even further.

Federalization of juvenile crime control initially buoyed efforts to combat the dominance of Jim Crow at the state and local levels. Local or county control of juvenile justice administration had facilitated the underdevelopment of black youths and white community domination of social control resources. This began to change during the civil rights era. Early federal interventions emphasized liberal regulation of local authority, including legal decisions, policies, and programs beneficial to the racial democratization of juvenile social control. Reduced local control empowered more organized and influential national citizen groups and even invalidated the racially conscious control measures envisioned by black child-savers. Ultimately, it limited their capacity to institutionalize racially democratic control.

Early federal desegregation rulings invalidated the black agenda of race-conscious professional leadership. While ordering the integration of black youth and adult workers in the Alabama juvenile justice system, the federal court held that race must be substantively irrelevant to justice administration.[42] Racial justice was defined as a negative right—a protection from discrimination—rather than as an affirmative right to the race-conscious representation idealized by liberal integration strategies.

Notwithstanding the federal government's advocacy of color blindness, Americans remained highly attuned to racial issues and implicitly maintained racial preferences that favored racial "in-groups" and disadvantaged "others." Research on the racial identities and attitudes of juvenile and criminal justice workers, though limited, suggests that race is salient to preferences and practices in crime control. Diverse groups of decisionmakers, including blacks, are less inclined to advantage white youths and adults in sanctioning than are their white counterparts or less diverse groups of authorities.[43] By limiting the local influence and discretion of black juvenile justice authorities, federalization restricted the possibilities for more inclusive racial politics.

The diminished role of local authorities and the marginalization of less powerful constituencies is key to the resurgence of racial domination in juvenile justice. The political scientist Lisa Miller notes that few congressional hearings on crime dealt with juveniles before World War II. In the 1950s and early 1960s, attention to juvenile delinquency and violence drove the upsurge in federal crime control hearings and legislation. In gun control, she argues, local citizen groups and governments tend to be squeezed out of deliberations as more powerful citizen groups and federal and state government authorities seize control over criminal justice agendas. Marginalization is especially pronounced for the most powerless segments of the polity, such as poor black Americans in high-crime urban areas, whose appeals have relatively little bearing on national debates on crime control policy and practice.[44]

Black officials are also often marginalized and limited in their capacity to function as race leaders. Increases in black representation in government positions are most evident in local bureaucracies (i.e., city councils, mayoral offices, and juvenile courts). These actors exercise the least influence over national and federal agendas of accountability-based control. Black officials in state and national offices are more beholden to those larger constituencies, where civil rights groups and local black citizen groups are marginalized. Thus, even when so inclined, black authorities have little capacity to serve as representative race relations experts. The rise of color-blind racial ideology, which associates race consciousness with racial discrimination, has threatened to invalidate the idea of professional or expert race leadership.[45]

National media and federal hearings on delinquency created tremendous political and financial incentives for states to adopt accountability-based reforms. Governor Engler's retributive policy in Michigan was but one example of the national politicization of juvenile crime. State politicians sought "tough-on-crime" credibility through punitive juvenile justice reforms. Federal and state funding structures imposed national accountability agendas on state and local juvenile justice systems. In 1997, the Republican-controlled Congress considered a Violent and Repeat Juvenile Offender Act (S. 10) and a Juvenile Crime Control Act (H.R. 3), which sought to institutionalize this punitive policy and philosophy in American juvenile justice. Republican sponsors of S. 10 promised that it would "ensure that young people be held accountable for their criminal or delinquent acts from the start . . . [by making accountability] . . . a central feature of the Federal juvenile justice system in prosecuting violations of Federal law." The legislation expanded the criminal responsibility of young offenders, defined by the certainty of punishment, relaxed prohibitions on juvenile commitments to jails and prisons, and limits on traditional protections from criminal stigma since members of society should know "who among them are repeat and violent offenders."[46]

Those bills and the related Violent and Repeat Juvenile Offender Accountability and Rehabilitation Act of 1999 (S. 254) never became law. Retributive notions of accountability-based juvenile justice were, nonetheless, imposed on state governments and local juvenile court communities. Inroads were made, in part, through appropriations bills that funded programmatic aspects of proposed bills, including a provision of $250 million for the Juvenile Accountability Incentive Block Grant program described in Title III of H.R. 3. Increases in youth violence were framed as threats to public safety. State governments were offered funding to develop and administer accountability-based sanctions for juvenile offenders. Given their financial needs and pressures to address juvenile crime, they did not have much choice. So local government agencies and court workers became parties to such reforms. In this political environment, local black authorities lost control over juvenile justice policies and practices.[47]

The Standardization of Accountability-Based Sanctioning

The racial history of American juvenile justice, including the black child-saving movement, indicates that transforming the structure of racialized social control hinges on contextual factors related to resources and influence. This duality of structure and agency remains evident in the post–civil rights period. It is reflected, not only in the marginalization of local influence through nationalization and federalization, but also in attempts to rationalize or structure sanctioning through formal procedures and technologies that constrain the ability of black court authorities to affect the administration of justice.

Attempts to regulate authorities in juvenile social control are as old as the juvenile court. However, the widespread use of formalized procedures for classifying and sanctioning delinquents is unique to the postintegration period.[48] For example, in the early twentieth century, the Ohio Boy's Industrial School sought to develop inmate classification systems. Psychological screening tools developed by the Ohio Bureau of Juvenile Research were employed to rationalize placement decisions. Because treatment resources were not specialized or diverse enough to provide a range of interventions, however, this information was not very useful to industrial school superintendents. Ultimately, early SDM techniques failed, and the "assignment of boys to institutional programs or living quarters proceeded according to traditional criteria such as age, race, religion, and offense."[49]

Renewed effort to structure juvenile justice decisionmaking surfaced in the 1930s. Court and corrections officials advocated for "youth correction authorities" (YCAs) that would rationalize and coordinate efforts to rehabilitate youths. In their view, "a scattered unregulated judiciary" was making commitment decisions that were deleterious to youths and society. Beyond centralizing commitment procedures, the YCA could facilitate objective decisionmaking that was rooted in expert psychiatric, psychological, medical, and social work assessments. With California in the lead, Minnesota, Wisconsin, Massachusetts, and Texas created YCAs in the 1930s and 1940s. They developed security and treatment classification tools that prescribed sanctions and services. Decisionmaking was being standardized just as initial progress was being made in racially integrating juvenile justice authority.[50]

Standardization gained further momentum as juvenile justice systems came under pressure to restore waning confidence in their authority and discretion. SDM tools, such as formal instruments and protocols for guiding individual case evaluations and processing, appealed to liberal and conservative accountability agendas in juvenile justice since they promised to guide sanctioning according to case factors, law, and policy.[51] Like adult sentencing guidelines, juvenile SDM technologies were developed as bureaucratic tools for standardizing the use of discretion. For liberal advocates, SDM could help guarantee appropriate treatment and reduce bias and arbitrariness in sanctioning. Conservatives saw SDM as a measure to ensure proportionality and certainty of punishment (i.e., graduated sanctioning and just deserts). It promoted public safety by constraining liberal authorities and automating the classification and sanctioning of serious delinquents. By the 1980s, SDM was being widely embraced as an institutional remedy.[52]

Research in several juvenile court contexts has noted irregularities in the adoption and utilization of SDM technologies. Courts commonly claim to have adopted assessment and classification schemes, but many fail to stipulate formal procedures, and few use empirically validated instruments to identify and weigh factors relevant to assessment and sanctioning. Utilization of risk- and need-assessment tools is also inconsistent. This is especially apparent in the case of more powerful court actors, such as judges and prosecutors, who retain greater discretion within the rigid legal and policy bounds of federal and state accountability reforms. They also resist controls on their discretion by overriding or avoiding the use of SDM procedures when perceiving them to be burdensome or ineffective or when there is incentive to do so.[53]

A 1997 study of minority youth confinement in the Midwest found that most counties reported using formal risk-assessment tools to guide sanctioning decisions. In one county with a majority black population, however, judges overrode nearly half of all SDM recommendations. Most overrides escalated sanctions and resulted in institutionalization, even though SDM procedures recommended noninstitutional placements. Youths with low to moderate risk scores were committed to secure institutions because county resources for community-based sanctions were limited and a state copay arrangement created an incentive to use more severe institutional sanctions.[54]

SDM technologies are concentrated in larger urban courts where decisionmaker diversity is greatest. Since lower-level caseworkers (i.e., probation and intake officers) more commonly use them, they may uniquely constrain the discretion of nonwhite court workers.[55] National data on racial and ethnic group representation across juvenile court roles does not exist, but evidence from select jurisdictions shows that black juvenile court workers occupy service rather than professional roles in courts. In 2000, several hundred juvenile court workers (judges, prosecutors, defense lawyers, and probation officers) in four midwestern states were surveyed. Results showed that 83 percent of black workers were in probation, compared to 70 percent of white workers. Ninety-one percent of black respondents were familiar with SDM instruments, compared to 62 percent of white workers. Black court workers were also significantly more likely to indicate frequent use of these tools, probably owing to their concentration in probation roles and large urban courts, where SDM instruments were more frequently employed as case management tools.[56]

If the accountability movement diminished the influence of less powerful local groups over juvenile justice, it elevated the discretion and influence of other court authorities such as prosecutors. Since formal charging decisions largely determine jurisdiction and standardized recommendations, this shift is key to the reorganization of power and influence. Restrictions on discretion and the elevation of the prosecutorial role especially affect waivers, through which children and youths are transferred to criminal courts. Despite variations, transfer provisions typically establish waiver eligibility and the process by which a waiver is enacted. Certain cases must be automatically removed from the juvenile court (i.e., a legislative waiver). Other transfer policies empower prosecutors or judges to decide which cases should be referred to adult courts. The essential distinction is whether judges or prosecutors play a primary role in the transfer decisions.[57] In either instance, waiver provisions markedly reduce the discretion of integrated juvenile court authorities, who negotiate the fates of disproportionately black, waiver-eligible youths.

As the twenty-first century neared, governments expanded the use of waiver even though there was no proof that it reduced serious juvenile crime and evidence showed that youths subjected to adult sanctions were adversely affected. Between 1992 and 1997, legislatures in forty-four states and the District of Columbia enacted provisions to facilitate the removal of young offenders to criminal court. To make transfer more certain and expedient, many states established categorical offense-based waiver provisions while extending the list of offenses and lowering age limits. Several states adopted sweeping provisions that lowered the maximum age of the juvenile court's original jurisdiction. Thus, the court's involvement in cases of juvenile crime and delinquency narrowed, regardless of the seriousness of offense. Michigan's Juvenile Waiver Law of 1997 eliminated the lower age limit on trying a juvenile as an adult (previously thirteen years) and transferred certain offenses automatically. With Florida in the lead, other states shifted discretion in juvenile transfer decisions from judges to prosecutors so that prosecutors could "direct file" certain cases in the adult court. A study of Florida waiver policy revealed that, in 1995 alone, "Florida prosecutors sent 7,000 cases to adult court, nearly matching the number of cases [9,700] judges sent to the criminal justice system nationwide that year."[58]

Black youths are dramatically overrepresented among young people committed to adult jails and prisons, just as was the case with incarceration and other adult sanctions (i.e., execution) over the past century. That this problem persists is emblematic of the evolution of oppression and domination in American juvenile justice. The black child-saving movement sought to abolish the "slavery of iniquitous justice systems" through equal protection for black youths and equal community representation. Nonetheless, the modern social contract provides a new moral and political structure for limiting youth access to and community influence over citizen-building ideals. The consequence is a familiar pattern of black youth and community alienation from liberal citizen-building ideals and authority.

Limited Rights to Recognition: The DMC Mandate

Finally, current federal efforts to regulate race relations in juvenile justice exemplify the failure of the black child-saving movement to establish normative cultural expectations and institutional practices of racially democratic control. A primary objective of the movement had been to establish participatory parity. However, current federal policy ignores this expectation. In 1974, Congress passed the Juvenile Justice and Delinquency Prevention Act. To be eligible for federal block grant funding, states had to meet several mandates. They needed to deinstitutionalize status offenders and other less serious delinquents, separate juveniles from adults in long-term confinement, and remove juveniles from adult jails and lockup facilities. These were elements of the initial phase of accountability reform. In 1988, disproportionate minority confinement (DMC) became a condition of formula grant funding. By 1992, minority overrepresentation was clearly evident, and groups such as the National Council of Juvenile and Family Court Judges lobbied Congress to elevate the DMC mandate to a core requirement for funding (tying 25 percent of funding to compliance). A 2002 amendment expanded the mandate to monitor proportionality in arrest, detention, and probation, rather than merely confinement.[59]

Federal efforts to improve race relations in juvenile justice are a legacy of liberal civil rights reform. The late Judge Romae T. Powell of the Fulton County Juvenile Court became the first black American to be appointed to the bench of a Georgia court. Judge Powell served as National Council of Juvenile and Family Court Judges president from 1988 to 1989 and is credited with drawing federal attention to DMC.[60] States must investigate and work to reduce disproportionate minority youth representation in juvenile and adult correctional institutions as well as at other points of system contact. Compliance involves problem identification, assessment, intervention, evaluation, and monitoring. Overrepresentation exists in every state with a significant minority population. Measures to eliminate racial disparities include prevention efforts to reduce the likelihood of minorities entering the system, community-based alternatives to institutional placement, classification systems that might reduce decisionmaker bias, and, to a lesser extent, efforts to increase the "cultural competency" of juvenile justice authorities.[61]

DMC has not received unanimous or unwavering support. The notion that disproportionate contact reflects unwarranted disparities has been consistently challenged. Conservative legislators have tried to eliminate or weaken the DMC requirements of the Juvenile Justice and Delinquency Prevention Act. Between 1999 and 2001, House and Senate committees proposed revisions that would have prohibited numerical standards or quotas from being established, replaced the word *minority* with the phrase *segments of the juvenile population*, disallowed DMC reduction efforts that would have resulted in the release of offenders or prevented their detention, and reduced by half the proportion of block grant eligibility contingent on DMC compliance.[62]

While the mandate has so far survived, it is itself limited by its conceptualization of racial justice. The mandate reduces racial equality in juvenile social control to the narrower issue of distributive equality in youth experiences and outcomes. It is, thus, misaligned with long-standing efforts to promote equal youth and community *recognition* in a multiracial parental state. The black child-saving movement was essentially a struggle to advance democratic accountability in American juvenile justice. Distributive equality was never its objective. Instead, the goal was to empower black youths and communities in the administration of rehabilitative ideals. DMC pays little attention to these interests. Assessments of racial and ethnic group representation among authorities are not required. And the DMC mandate's goal of racial *insignificance* undermines the claim to racial group recognition. Historically complex race questions rooted in power relations are reduced to assessments of the relative distribution of youths at different points of criminal justice system contact. Equality is defined by the absence of racial significance, as indicated by racially proportional youth outcomes. The mandate idealizes the nonracial, not racially and ethnically inclusive, juvenile justice system.

Limitations of the DMC mandate reflect more than narrow perspectives or policy preferences of juvenile justice officials. They are emblematic of a broader retreat from a politics of racial group reconciliation and inclusion to an ideology of color blindness. The DMC mandate narrowly applies neoliberal notions of racial equality. The result is a disjuncture between the historic pursuit of a more robust system of racially representative social control and the present limited commitment to distributive parity in often exclusionary sanctioning outcomes.

The differences and tensions between the goals of the DMC mandate and the black child-saving movement reflect what the political philosopher Nancy Fraser describes as a nearly implacable "redistribution-recognition dilemma." Social injustices exist, she argues, within distinct but interrelated societal spheres or structures. Socioeconomic injustices involving exploitation, economic marginalization, and deprivation are rooted in the political-economic structure of society. Remedies are available through *redistributions* of political and economic opportunity (i.e., welfare transfers, a minimum wage, or new legal rights). Injustices related to recognition are rooted in the "cultural-symbolic" realm, or the cultural system of the society. They involve denials of societal standing and voice through patterns of cultural domination, nonrecognition, and disrespect and call for cultural transformations rather than redistributions of existing rights or resources. For status groups such as the poor, Fraser argues, redistributive remedies are often sufficient, since eliminating group difference is consistent with the ideal of social justice. But women and racial and ethnic groups require a "bivalent" approach to remedying social injustice. Such groups have interests in redistribution (i.e., equal protection under the law and equal compensation), where status should be insignificant. Yet they have *simultaneous* interests in recognition, such as positive portrayals in the media and substantive representation in government, where status remains salient.[63]

The dilemma lies in how each approach to remedying social injustice deals with difference (i.e., the salience of gender and race). Remedies such as the DMC mandate tend to prioritize socioeconomic aspects of injustice involving the denial of rights and resources while ignoring racial group interests in recognition in the cultural practice of juvenile justice. The mandate merely aims to make group status *insignificant* and ensure that race is not relevant to the practice of juvenile justice. Remedies of recognition, in contrast, promote cultural change through efforts that revalue and empower subjugated groups or *reorient* the significance of status group membership. The black child-saving movement sought such recognition. It succeeded in promoting black youth and community standing in the cultural-valuational structure of American juvenile justice and sought to institutionalize a more actively representative, multiracial parental state.

There is a tension or contradiction between redistribution and recognition (i.e., eliminating vs. recasting difference). This is evident in the opposition to affirmative action policies. Such race-conscious remedies, which promote group access, have been characterized as *reverse racism*. For Fraser and others, the redistribution-recognition dilemma cannot be avoided but must be addressed to achieve social justice for status groups with bivalent societal interests. A causal link ties racialized misrecognition—or racially differential valuation and influence—to unequal distributive outcomes for individuals and communities.[64] The absence of black recognition enabled decades of Jim Crow juvenile justice and, perhaps, the retributive turn during the postintegration period. Social-organizational interventions were vital to black community progress in altering cultural-valuational practices of American juvenile justice and improving the life chances of black youths. Through their movement for recognition, black child-savers sought to revalue and empower black delinquents and black civil society, within a new cultural and political structure of citizen-building initiatives.

By contrast, the DMC mandate aims to eliminate the significance of race in crime control processes and outcomes through redistributive means and obscures broader meanings and requirements of racial equality. As Iris Young points out, distributive formulations characterize institutional structures as given background conditions "whose justice is not [in] question." By limiting the analysis of injustice to distribution, the approach serves an ideological function, supporting the very cultural and institutional relations that were of primary concern to the struggle against separate and unequal juvenile justice.[65]

The Declining Significance of Inclusion: Summary and Conclusion

Twentieth-century civil rights reforms gradually expanded black access and influence in American juvenile justice but fell short of institutionalizing racial justice in the administration of rehabilitative ideals. There was some experimentation with a more racially democratic model of juvenile social control, which brought signs of a new power-sharing arrangement where white privileges and prerogatives of Jim Crow juvenile justice gave way to more equal group recognition in liberal rehabilitative ideals. This hopeful, uneven, and often violent phase of changing race relations in juvenile justice proved transitional. New structures of racialized social control emerged with updated features of black youth and community exclusion.

As we have seen in this conclusion, the punitive turn in juvenile justice over the final decades of the twentieth century redefined the opportunities and authority of formally integrated black youths and adults. These changes diminished the welfare entitlements of racialized serious delinquents, limited the resources and influence of black authorities, and, thereby, drained the substantive value of formal inclusion in relation to long-standing black youth and community interests. By the mid-1970s, juvenile justice policy began to emphasize the moral and criminal responsibility of youths over traditional rehabilitative ideals. Formally race neutral, the shift was packaged as a modern accountability-based approach to juvenile justice and a logical response to the crisis posed by serious delinquency.[66] This conservative penal-managerial agenda reorganized the cultural ideals and institutional structure of juvenile justice in ways that undermined the utility of liberal civil rights reforms. Access to liberal citizen-building ideals and resources was no longer implied by integration, and the accountability ideal introduced new mechanisms of racial oppression and domination. The decline of the black child-saving movement and strategic overreliance on formal integration left black communities with little capacity to counter these developments and dependent on a federal remedy that frames racial justice as a distributive problem rather than a more fundamental question of racially democratic control.

Race, Justice, and Juvenile Social Control: The Benefits of a Long View

Racial inequality in juvenile justice did not increase as much as it persisted and mutated over the course of the past century. Social changes such as the rise of the black child-saving movement, migration, court-ordered integration, declining black collective identification and action, and the collapse of the welfare state shaped the dynamic racial terrain of juvenile social control. Representation of black youths in juvenile institutions increased slowly as the juvenile court model developed and expanded geographically. Yet, even into the 1960s, black youths and communities were denied equal opportunity and influence within juvenile court communities. The normative oppression and domination of Jim Crow juvenile justice briefly receded but found new life in the postintegration period.

Black community exclusion has manifested historically in the denial of black youth access to more inclusionary juvenile sanctions and the denial of black representation among juvenile justice authorities. Progressive change seemed tangible when black reformatory commitments and employment as court authorities rose. Racial power sharing slowly emerged through waves of brokered reforms. In the 1970s, however, juvenile justice policy and practice were reorganized in ways that weakened the value of civil rights reforms and renewed expressions of racial oppression and domination in juvenile social control. Formal integration devolved into a poor simulation of racially democratic inclusion.

Since at least the 1960s, activists, practitioners, and the lay public have been unaware of the personalities, strategies, and organizations behind the black child-saving movement.[67] This anonymity stems in part from their neglect in prior historical research, but it also reflects their failure to institutionalize racial justice. Despite achieving greater participatory parity in the state sector, balanced developmental opportunities and deliberative influence in juvenile justice did not materialize. Racially selective citizen-building initiatives were reintroduced through racialized notions such as "serious delinquents," which limited the influence and resources available to local communities and court workers. Powerful national constituencies and authorities unraveled the gains generations of reformers had negotiated, and neoliberal conceptions of racial justice challenged the idea of race leadership.

The limited impact and legacy of the black child-savers must be attributed in part to the limits of movement strategy. To democratize justice processes, John Braithwaite insists that it is essential to co-opt state control, rather than merely winning state supports. Liberal black child-savers believed that formalizing equal protection and representation would institutionalize racial justice in the administration of rehabilitative ideals. Collective action dissipated owing to expectations that formal integration would make racial justice routine. In the late 1950s, and throughout the 1960s, telltale signs appeared that this would not happen. Overt and subtle aspects of the anti–civil rights movement played a role, but black collective efficacy also declined, while delinquency became an increasingly serious issue. W. E. B. DuBois had warned that such a development would prove costly to black youths and black civil society. It would undermine black collective identification and action and trigger a backlash of retributive control measures.[68] In the 1970s, a punitive reconstruction of juvenile justice was coupled with a wider, racialized attack on liberal child- and social-welfare ideals. The rise of accountability-based juvenile justice over the final quarter of the twentieth century remixed the racial politics of the formally integrated parental state in ways that diminished black youth and community access to citizen-building ideals and authority. Unprecedented numbers of black and other nonwhite youths poured into juvenile courts and reformatories after 1970, along with black workers, but they integrated a system with retreating and soon bracketed philosophical, legal, and resource commitments to liberal citizen-building ideals.

Except for the brief, tumultuous period of liberal accountability reform (especially 1960–70), black youths and communities have endured the worst of two worlds in the social and institutional history of American juvenile justice. Shut out of the initial era of citizen building, black youths and communities have borne the brunt of the severe sanctioning and regulated discretion characteristic of later accountability reforms. The racial politics of postintegration and Jim Crow juvenile justice systems do differ in terms of community recognition. Ultimately, however, each is characterized by diminished access for black youths and communities to liberal citizen-building ideals, resources, and authority.

Did high rates of black victimization owing to juvenile crime lead influential black citizens to issue appeals for protection that were consistent with the punitive accountability agenda? If the punitive turn reflects the political will and interests of black civil society and, perhaps, its most dominant constituencies (i.e., elites and older blacks), this would indicate that it is rooted in the stratification of black interests and collective action rather than in a misrecognition or denial of participatory parity. Research and anecdotal evidence suggest that, while blacks have supported punitive policies, they idealize rehabilitative and preventative approaches to juvenile crime and that system fairness and accountability are priorities. High-profile black conservatives have loudly embraced punitive policies in juvenile justice. More typical liberal observers favor traditional citizen-building ideals over punishment and civic exclusion, in part owing to lingering distrust of the police and courts. Many black civic leaders have been concerned with violent juvenile crime and the denial of developmental opportunity. They call for renewing the forgotten black child-saving movement, not exiling black delinquents.[69]

Black civil society neither orchestrated nor broadly supported the penal-managerial turn in American juvenile justice. A product of conservative law-and-order politics, it is largely unaccountable to black youth and community interests. Its success stems from a weakening of the black community infrastructure that had brokered group interests prior to formal integration. This alienation was aggravated by a racialized moral panic over dangerous, undeserving delinquents, a backlash against liberal governmentality, and the retraction of the social safety net. As more powerful citizen groups and political elites seized control of the increasingly nationalized and federalized juvenile crime control agenda, they imposed a more penal managerial model of juvenile social control on recently integrated systems of American juvenile justice. The administration of punitive juvenile justice reveals a particular fear and loathing of black citizens who become labeled *delinquent*.[70]

Mass incarceration of black youths and the marginalization of black constituencies were not the will of black Americans. Rather, these renewed a long history of exclusion of black youths and communities from enlightened social control. Indeed, the problem of race in juvenile justice today is, not that so many black youths and adults are tied to the integrated parental state, but that they have become marginal clients and custodians of largely shuttered manufactories of citizens.

The history of juvenile justice in the black experience is an epic tragedy whose lessons remain instructive today. Its ongoing significance owes much to the unique relation between race, juvenile justice, and American liberal democracy. Examining the contested and shifting racial politics of juvenile justice extends the historiography of this institution. This study places in a new light the many profiles of the white experience with the parental state that have preceded it. It reveals how white power and privilege accompanied class domination and patriarchy to shape a white supremacist system of citizen-building initiatives, or Jim Crow juvenile justice. Traditional liberal rehabilitative ideals and institutional resources effectively reproduced a white democracy, and the two-track (treatment and punishment) system of the postintegration period evidences similar racial group relations and outcomes.

Not only does this detailed racial history of juvenile justice help us understand the past, but it is also relevant to present and future research, policy, and, perhaps, civic engagement. This history provides deeper insight into the nature and mechanisms of racial oppression and domination in a context of social control and, thus, a perspective on the meaning, requirements, and possibilities of racial justice. Tracing the racial history of juvenile justice in the black experience not only helps fill a remaining void in historical research on the origins and organization of American juvenile justice but also uncovers the contours of racialized social control, offering theoretical and practical insights into the pursuit of racial justice.

In research and policy on race and juvenile or criminal justice, nonwhite racial and ethnic groups are often reduced to subjects of justice processes. They are criminal populations, victims of crime, or victims of discrimination. My study suggests the need for a more nuanced perspective on racial group identification, subjugation, and agency and attention to be paid to how these play out along dynamic color lines of social control. More comparative research on other racial and ethnic group experiences and interventions in the history of American juvenile justice would extend and deepen this insight.

This study illustrates the sociologically layered and historically shifting significance of race in American juvenile justice. It raises important and unsettled questions for research, policy, and advocacy. Most pressing is the question of what we mean by *racial justice* and how it will be achieved. This was the constant concern of the black child-savers. Their struggle settled on a vague and retrospectively naive answer: black youth and community integration. Yet integration proved a poor proxy for black youth and community empowerment. It removed obstacles to inclusion, as Kenneth Clark stressed, but did not facilitate the articulation and recognition of black community interests in deliberations of the parental state. Moreover, since integration (e.g., formally equal protection and representation) was often falsely equated with institutionalized racial justice, it undermined more vital resources of collective identification and action on behalf of troubled youths and, thus, the cultural and material base of racially democratic control.

Back to the Future: Stirrings of the Unfulfilled-Promises Camp

Protagonists of the once formidable black child-saving movement watched as the apparent spoils of integration turned into bitter fruit. They witnessed postintegration juvenile justice come unhinged from historical efforts to ensure its racially democratic accountability. They watched the decline of black collective efficacy and mainstream retreat from the citizen-building agenda and saw integrated, wayward black youths redefined as undeserving serious delinquents. As the twentieth century drew to a close, they saw racial oppression and domination being reorganized within a formally integrated parental state stripped of its liberal utility to black youths and communities.

Veteran black child-savers lamented the continued refusal of citizen-building ideals and resources. They recognized that separate and unequal juvenile justice had evolved and survived into the civil rights era. Kenneth Clark grieved over this development following the death of his wife and collaborator, Mamie Clark, in 1983. At a 1986 conference on the legacy of *Brown*, Clark acknowledged the couple's deep sense of frustration and powerlessness as they watched the continued tracking of black youths into second-class citizenship: "I must accept the fact that my wife left this earth despondent at seeing that damage to children is being knowingly and silently accepted by a nation that claims to be democratic." He had lost faith in American democratic culture: "Thirty years after *Brown*, I feel a sense of hopelessness, rather than optimism, because the underlying theme of *Plessy* and the explicit statements of *Dred Scott* persist. The majority of Americans still believe in and vote on the assumption that Blacks are not worthy of the respect, and the acceptance of their humanity, which our democracy provides to others." Deepening his malaise were deprivations in education, housing, and labor as well as the mass incarceration of black citizens considered seriously delinquent.[71]

The more recent fiftieth anniversary of *Brown v. Board of Education* was another occasion for somber reflection rather than celebration. Several leaders remarked stoically that the achievement was important, but limited. Skeptics, whom the historian V. P. Franklin characterized as the "unfulfilled promises camp," cited ongoing inequality in income, wealth, education, employment, criminal justice, health, and other contexts to indicate that civil rights reforms had failed to equalize status and power relations among racial and ethnic groups. Franklin challenged that camp to mobilize in the pursuit of unrealized aspirations, as generations before them had done. "It was the agency and activism of African Americans that laid the groundwork for the [*Brown*] ruling," he said, referring to civil rights organizations. In the case of juvenile justice, a black child-saving movement stretching back to the 1890s had helped stage later civil rights reforms, and the decline of this collective action limited its long-term impact. To the extent that promises of integration remained unfulfilled, Franklin noted, "it will take agency and activism among African Americans to bring these promises to fruition, not just for people of African descent in the U.S., but for poor and oppressed people in this society and people of color throughout the world."[72]

For advances in racially democratic relations of social control to occur—that is, the reorganization of juvenile justice to align with multiple racial group needs and interests—diverse constituencies must actively negotiate ideals, resources, and authority. Racial justice is "an endless meeting," as another civil rights movement scholar has stressed, rather than a static sociolegal end state.[73] Freedom itself derives from the activity of deliberative democracy, where racial group rights and recognition in juvenile justice are exercised through the intentional performance of racially democratic control. It requires far more, culturally and institutionally, than a redistribution of outcomes.

Interestingly, though not surprisingly, the unfulfilled promises camp faintly echoes early black child-saving ambition. Since the 1960s and 1970s, black civic leaders have struggled to rebuild the collapsed community infrastructure of juvenile justice reform, and this struggle continues today. In 2005, the 21st Century Black Massachusetts Conference gathered in Boston under the familiar banner "Unity + Strategy = Power." The conference was sponsored by Diane Wilkerson, a black former member of the state legislature, and was attended by a cross section of Boston's black leadership and community members. The slogan of the meeting brought to mind the organizing logic of the Ten Times One Is Ten Club and efforts of early black clubwomen and later organizations and practitioners to impress racial group threats in juvenile justice on the conscience of black America.

After a century of related activism and limited impacts, juvenile justice reform remains high on the agenda for black empowerment. At this conference, a panel entitled "Race and Juvenile Justice" featured a speaker whose charges of black genocide in juvenile justice were met with polite nods and applause. Dr. Rosa Smith's address, "The Pampers to Prison Pipeline," unknowingly channeled the outrage of vanguard black clubwomen, DuBois's racial logic of the immortal youth, and the racially democratic values of Judge Jane Bolin into a critique of the renewed crisis along the color line of social control. She characterized the mass incarceration of black youths amid declining rehabilitative ideals and resources as a problem of "educational genocide," a systematic underdevelopment of black youths that amounted to "killing the seeds of a people." The crisis was "criminal on their part," she insisted, "and criminal on ours for letting it happen." Smith understood racial inequality in juvenile justice to be a threat to black democratic aspirations and survival. Her definition of the problem led to a familiar call for a "new movement to save our black boys [sic]" and, thus, to save the race.[74]

ACKNOWLEDGMENTS

This book could not have been written without the support and assistance of so many of my family members, colleagues, and friends. Given the amount of time spent developing this study, beginning in graduate school and continuing through several academic appointments, the list is too long to fully recount here. I do want to acknowledge and thank several key people who contributed to this work.

I must begin by thanking my parents, Cheryl and Michael Ward, whose love, sacrifice, and support first materialized in their decision to adopt me as an infant. Without this support and their own examples, I likely would not have aspired to or attained an advanced education and might have a more personal story to tell about American juvenile justice, that is, as a longtime ward of the parental state. In many ways, this book is about the spirit of caring for other people's children, and my own parents have exemplified that beautiful and vital spirit. My larger family is as much a part of this foundation of support, and my stepmother, Tigi, my sisters Tamiyah, Caryn, and Nisa, and my brothers Toussaint and Stephen also provided valuable support over the years, often with the gentle prod, "How goes the book?" My older brother, Stephen, deserves special mention here as he set an early (and then bizarre) model of scholarly endeavor as an adolescent and is now a historian with similar interests in the black freedom movement. Our conversations about this research and other academic experiences have helped shape my work and career.

Numerous faculty mentors, colleagues, and friends have also contributed to the development of this research. My professors at Hampton University, especially Beverly John and Steven Rosenthal, introduced me to the critical analysis of race and class, leaving a lasting imprint on my approach to sociological inquiry. At the University of Michigan, Rosemary Sarri introduced me to juvenile justice research as her research assistant and became a key support. My visits to Michigan prisons to interview young men while working on her project convinced me of the need to study the problem of racial inequality in criminal and juvenile justice. She along with Alford Young Jr., James Jackson, Mayer Zald, and George Steinmetz advised my initial research on the black child-savers. Tyrone Forman, Donald Deskins, Eduardo Bonilla-Silva, Lester Monts, Amanda Lewis, Sherri-Ann Butterfield, and many others provided support and helpful insight during those Michigan days and since.

This book took incremental steps forward over a series of academic appointments, beginning with a Mellon postdoctoral fellowship at the Vera Institute of Justice, which began the day before the attacks of September 11, 2001. I wish to thank the Mellon Foundation and Vera's former director Christopher Stone for their support of this research and Chris for his understanding when I responded to this terrible event by shifting attention from my intended solitary, archival research on black child-saving in Harlem toward more contemporary and engaged initiatives. I found this outlet for engaged scholarship at the Institute for Research in African American Studies (IRAAS) at Columbia University, where the late Manning Marable hired me to coordinate a project addressing the crisis of mass incarceration. Manning was a great activist-intellectual and human being, and it was a pleasure and honor to work with him. Besides his feedback on this project, his energy, versatility, and spirit have been inspirations. I still managed to conduct some archival research on black child-saving in Harlem at this time, thanks in part to a student at IRAAS, Anna Martinez, who helped me review the papers of Judge Jane Bolin.

The book finally took shape during faculty appointments at Northeastern University and my current institution, the University of California, Irvine. At Northeastern, Jack Greene, Margaret Burnham, Amy Farrell, Nicky Rafter, Simon Singer, and Donna Bishop lent key insight and support as the project inched along. Nicky Rafter's keen insights and calm urges to press on with the grind of historiography were especially helpful and refreshing. Amy Farrell aided development of this book as a collaborator on related research. Our research on representation brought peace of mind, easing pressure to force the book along, and also helped clarify and focus ideas I began developing here. Similarly, years of collaboration with Aaron Kupchik helped me develop ideas that, for me, originate in my study of the black child-saving movement.

My research on the black child savers would not have gotten very far without the generosity and support of a number of other crime and justice scholars. As I note in the introduction, Vernetta Young shared personal copies of several pamphlets illustrating black clubwomen's involvement in Progressive Era juvenile justice reform, giving my research an early footing. Tony Platt became an early and most helpful adviser in my development of this research, and he and his partner, Cecilia O'Leary, gave generously of their time (and guest room) as I worked through finalizing the manuscript. Barry Feld, Scott Decker, David Tanenhaus, and Miroslava Chávez-García also aided the development of this work through their own research and feedback. The Racial Democracy, Crime, and Criminal Justice research network has provided an important outlet for this research and more general support; Ruth Peterson and Laurie Krivo deserve special thanks for their leadership of this wonderful group. I also want to thank my colleagues in the Department of Criminology, Law, and Society at the University of California, Irvine, for their interest and faith in this book project and for providing such a collegial and stimulating intellectual environment.

Several research and advocacy organizations must also be acknowledged. Working with the boards of the Ruffin Society and Roxbury Youthworks in Boston provided unique perspective on the racial politics of juvenile and criminal justice and the pleasure of working closely with their founder, Judge Julian Houston, a modern black child-saver. Similarly, I must thank James Bell, director of the Hayward Burns Institute, for engaging my historical research in the institute's vital work to eliminate racial inequality in juvenile justice today. The friendly staff and my fellow haunts at the Boston Athenaeum, where much of the book was drafted, made wrestling with the manuscript a more pleasant and inspired experience. The staffs of the Spingarn Archive at Howard University, the Schomburg Center in New York City, the Library of Congress, and the Walter P. Reuther Library at Wayne State University provided valuable research assistance.

At the University of Chicago Press, I wish to thank my editor, Douglas Mitchell, for taking an interest in this book from an unknown author before it was even written and for his patience with its development. For this I must also thank Mary Pattillo, whose endorsement got Doug's attention. Doug and his assistant, Tim McGovern, have been a pleasure to work with. The manuscript reviewers provided valuable pages of feedback that I have attempted to translate into a better book, and the editing assistance of Joseph Brown and Greg Shank has been indispensable here.

Finally, I must thank my loving wife and best critic, Cynthia Feliciano, who was happy to read the draft-after-draft with editing pen in hand and forthcoming with heaping doses of enthusiasm, support, and suggested deletions. Notwithstanding the patience I have taken in developing this study and all the contributions others have made, I might still be writing (and then cutting) were it not for Cynthia's insights and assistance, her prods to "finish the book," and the wonderful balance created by our lives coming together.

NOTES

INTRODUCTION

1. W. E. B. DuBois, "The Immortal Child," *The Crisis* 12, no. 6 (1916): 267–71. Volumes 1–25 (1910–22) of *The Crisis* are available online through the Modernist Journals Project (http://dl.lib.brown.edu/mjp/render.php?view=mjp_object&id=crisiscollect ion). Most of these and later volumes are available through Google.books.

2. Roosevelt quoted in Jack Holl, *Juvenile Reform in the Progressive Era: William R. George and the Junior Republic Movement* (Ithaca, NY: Cornell University Press, 1971), 9.

3. See Office of Juvenile Justice and Delinquency Prevention, *Disproportionate Minority Contact Technical Assistance Manual*, 4th ed. (Washington, DC: Office of Justice Programs, 2009).

4. See Anthony M. Platt, *The Child Savers: The Invention of Delinquency* (1969), 40th anniversary ed. (New Brunswick, NJ: Rutgers University Press, 2009). See also Ellen Ryerson, *The Best-Laid Plans: America's Juvenile Court Experiment* (New York: Hill & Wang, 1978); and Randall G. Shelden and Lynn T. Osborne, "'For Their Own Good': Class Interests and the Child Saving Movement in Memphis, Tennessee, 1900–1917," *Criminology* 27, no. 4 (1989): 747–67. For an overview of the contribution of *The Child Savers* and a critique, see Miroslava Chávez-García, "In Retrospect: Anthony M. Platt's *The Child Savers: The Invention of Delinquency*," in Platt, *The Child Savers*.

5. Several studies have moved beyond the black/white binary but are generally focused on the contemporary period. See, e.g., Francisco A. Villarreal and Nancy E. Walker, *¿Dónde está la justicia? A Call to Action on Behalf of Latino and Latina Youth in the U.S. Justice System* (Washington, DC: Building Blocks for Youth, 2002); Barry Krisberg, *Juvenile Justice: Redeeming Our Children* (Thousand Oaks, CA: Sage, 2005), chap. 5; and Nancy Rodriguez, "Juvenile Court Context and Detention Decisions: Reconsidering the Role of Community Characteristics in Juvenile Court Processes," *Justice Quarterly* 24, no. 4 (2007): 629–56. For recent historical research on juvenile justice in the Mexican American experience, see Miroslava Chávez-García, "Youth, Evidence, and Agency: Mexican and Mexican American Youth at the Whittier State School, 1890–1920," *Aztlán: A Journal of Chicano Studies* 31, no. 2 (2006): 55–83, and "Intelligence Testing at Whittier School, 1890–1920," *Pacific Historical Review* 76, no. 2 (2007): 193–228.

6. William H. Sewell Jr., "Three Temporalities: Toward a Sociology of the Event," in *The Historic Turn in the Human Sciences*, ed. Terence J. McDonald (Ann Arbor: University of Michigan Press, 1996), 207. See also William H. Sewell, *Logics of History* (Chicago: University of Chicago Press, 2005).

7. The terms *exclusionary* and *inclusionary* distinguish the impact of criminal sanctions on societal participation. *Exclusionary* sanctions aim to diminish or break social ties, prioritizing the removal of offenders from society, and eschewing reform or reintegration (i.e., extended detention and incarceration, deportation, or death). *Inclusionary* sanctions seek to maintain or strengthen social ties, prioritizing reform, stigma avoidance, and societal reintegration (i.e., counseling, vocational training, and drug treatment). I use the terms to compare race-linked sanctioning orientations and outcomes in American juvenile justice and to contrast the racially exclusionary orientation of Jim Crow juvenile justice from the inclusionary agenda of the black child-saving movement. See Theodore N. Ferdinand, "Juvenile Delinquency or Juvenile Justice: Which Came First?" *Criminology* 27, no. 1 (1989): 79–106.

8. See Darnell F. Hawkins and Kimberly K. Leonard, *Our Children, Their Children: Confronting Racial and Ethnic Differences in American Juvenile Justice* (Chicago: University of Chicago Press, 2005); Jeffrey Fagan and Franklin E. Zimring, eds., *The Changing Borders of Juvenile Justice: Transfer of Adolescents to the Criminal Court* (Chicago: University of Chicago Press, 2000); George S. Bridges and Sara Steen, "Racial Disparities in Official Assessments of Juvenile Offenders: Attributional Stereotypes as Mediating Mechanisms," *American Sociological Review* 63, no. 4 (1998): 554–70; and Jerry G. Miller, *Search and Destroy: African-American Males in the Criminal Justice System* (New York: Cambridge University Press, 1997).

CHAPTER ONE

1. Philippe Ariès, *Centuries of Childhood: A Social History of Family Life* (New York: Vintage, 1962); Stanford J. Fox, "Juvenile Justice Reform: An Historical Perspective," *Stanford Law Review* 22, no. 6 (1970): 1187–1239.

2. For a review of research on families and children since the Middle Ages, see Linda A. Pollock, *Forgotten Children: Parent-Child Relations from 1500 to 1900* (New York: Cambridge University Press, 1983).

3. Ariès, *Centuries of Childhood*; Pollock, *Forgotten Children*; Barry C. Feld, *Bad Kids: Race and the Transformation of the Juvenile Court* (New York: Oxford University Press, 1999).

4. Ariès, *Centuries of Childhood*, 9–11.

5. Thomas J. Bernard, *The Cycle of Juvenile Justice* (New York: Oxford University Press, 1992), 51–52.

6. Ibid., 54.

7. Hugh Cunningham, *The Children of the Poor: Representations of Childhood since the Seventeenth Century* (Cambridge, MA: Blackwell, 1991), and *Children and Childhood in Western Society since 1500* (New York: Longman, 2005); Pollack, *Forgotten Children*.

8. Pollock, *Forgotten Children*, 269.

9. William A. Corsaro, *The Sociology of Childhood*, 2nd ed. (Thousand Oaks, CA: Pine Forge, 2005), 64.

10. Ariès, *Centuries of Childhood*, 403.

11. Ibid., 404. Ariès argues that, though originating among elites, the modern concept of the family-child relationship "finally embraced nearly the whole of society, to such

an extent that people have forgotten its aristocratic and middle-class origins," especially in the new industrial centers of the late eighteenth century and the nineteenth (ibid.).

12. Victor Bailey, *Delinquency and Citizenship: Reclaiming the Young Offender, 1914–1948* (New York: Oxford University Press, 1987); Linda Mahood and Barbara Littlewood, "The 'Vicious' Girl and the 'Street-Corner' Boy: Sexuality and the Gendered Delinquent in the Scottish Child-Saving Movement, 1850–1940," *Journal of the History of Sexuality* 4, no. 4 (1994): 549–78; Mary Carpenter, *Juvenile Delinquents: Social Evils, Their Causes and Their Cure* (London: W. & F. G. Cash, 1853); E. C. Wines, *The State of Prisons and of Child-Saving Institutions in the Civilized World* (Cambridge, MA: J. Wilson & Son, 1879), 67–85.

13. Anthony Platt, "The Child-Saving Movement and the Origins of the Juvenile Justice System," in *The Sociology of Juvenile Delinquency*, ed. Ronald J. Berger (Chicago: Nelson- Hall, 1991), 5. See also David J. Rothman, *The Discovery of the Asylum* (Boston: Little, Brown, 1971); and Robert M. Mennel, *Thorns and Thistles: Juvenile Delinquents in the United States, 1825–1940* (Hanover, NH: University Press of New England, 1973).

14. Bernard, *The Cycle of Juvenile Justice*, 43–48; Clifford Shaw and Henry McKay, *Juvenile Delinquency and Urban Areas* (Chicago: University of Chicago Press, 1942).

15. *First Survey of Juvenile Delinquency in London, 1815–1816*, Report of the Committee for Investigating the Causes of the Alarming Increase of Juvenile Delinquency in the Metropolis (London, 1816), and *Further Description of Juvenile Delinquency in London, 1818*, Report of the Committee of the Society for the Improvement of Prison Discipline and for the Reformation of Juvenile Offenders (London, 1818), both reproduced in Wiley B. Sanders, ed., *Juvenile Offenders for a Thousand Years: Selected Readings from Anglo-Saxon Times to 1900* (Chapel Hill: University of North Carolina Press, 1970), 102–4, 112.

16. Charles Loring Brace, *The Dangerous Classes of New York, and Twenty Years' Work among Them* (1853), 3rd ed. (New York: Wynkoop & Hallenbeck, 1880), quoted in Platt, "The Child-Saving Movement," 8–9.

17. Sanders, ed., *Juvenile Offenders for a Thousand Years*, xviii. See also Mennel, *Thorns and Thistles*, xvii–xxvii; and Anthony M. Platt, *The Child Savers: The Invention of Delinquency* (1969), 40th anniversary ed. (New Brunswick, NJ: Rutgers University Press, 2009).

18. Bernard, *The Cycle of Juvenile Justice*, 69.

19. *Ex Parte Crouse*, 4 Wharton 9 (1839), quoted in Stanford J. Fox, *Cases and Materials on Modern Juvenile Justice* (St. Paul, MN: West, 1972), 26, 28.

20. Ben Lindsey and Rube Borough, "Juvenile Court and the Artistry of Approach," in *Childhood in America*, ed. P. Fass and M. Mason (New York: New York University Press, 1931), 566. This authority was not substantially curtailed until 1967, when the U.S. Supreme Court began extending constitutional due process protections to youths in juvenile court.

21. Robert H. Bremner, introduction to *Children and Youth in America: A Documentary History*, ed. Robert H. Bremner, 3 vols. in 5 (Cambridge, MA: Harvard University Press, 1970–74), 1:21.

22. Daniel Webster, "The First Settlement of New England," in *The Works of Daniel Webster*, ed. Edward Everette (Boston, 1851), reproduced in Bremner, ed., *Children and Youth in America*, 1:451.

23. Benjamin Labaree, "The Education Demanded by the Peculiar Character of Our Civil Institutions," in *The Lectures Delivered Before the American Institute for Instruction, 1849* (Boston, 1950), in Bremner, ed., *Children and Youth in America*, 1:457–58.

24. James Simmons, "Address Delivered at the Opening of the Free Schools in Charleston," *Southern Quarterly Review*, vol. 6 (1852), in Bremner, ed., *Children and Youth in America*, 1:472.

25. Editorials, *Philadelphia National Gazette*, July 10, 12, August 19, 1830, reproduced in John R. Commons et al., eds., *A Documentary History of American Industrial Society*, 10 vols. (Cleveland: Arthur H. Clark, 1910), 5:107–12.

26. George Fitzhugh, *Sociology for the South; or, The Failure of Free Society* (Richmond, VA: A. Morris, 1854), 147, in Bremner, ed., *Children and Youth in America*, 1:423.

27. On the racial politics of early public education, see W. E. B. DuBois, *Black Reconstruction in America, 1860–1880* (New York: Harcourt, Brace, 1935); and James D. Anderson, *The Education of Blacks in the South, 1860–1935* (Chapel Hill: University of North Carolina Press, 1988).

28. Cesare Beccaria, *On Crimes and Punishments* (1764), trans. David Young (Indianapolis: Hackett, 1986), 7, quoted in Piers Beirne, "Inventing Criminology: The Science of Man in Cesare Beccaria's *Dei delitti e delle pene* (1764)," in *The Criminology Theory Reader*, ed. Stuart Henry and Werner Einstadter (New York: New York University Press, 1998), 21, 30–31. See also Rothman, *The Discovery of the Asylum*, 59.

29. Michael Ignatieff, *A Just Measure of Pain: The Penitentiary in the Industrial Revolution, 1750–1850* (New York: Pantheon, 1978), 94; Adam Hirsch, "From Pillory to Penitentiary: The Rise of Criminal Incarceration in Early Massachusetts," *Michigan Law Review* 80 (1982): 1264.

30. Rothman, *The Discovery of the Asylum*, 79; Hirsch, "From Pillory to Penitentiary," 1263; David Garland, *Punishment and Modern Society* (Chicago: University of Chicago Press, 1990), 180–89.

31. Garland, *Punishment and Modern Society*, 182.

32. Hirsch, "From Pillory to Penitentiary," 1263 (first quote); Samuel Walker, *Popular Justice: A History of American Criminal Justice* (New York: Oxford University Press, 1998), 80–81 (second quote).

33. Jeff Manza and Chris Uggen, *Locked Out: Felon Disenfranchisement and Democracy in America* (New York: Oxford University Press, 2006), 26.

34. Brockway quoted in David J. Rothman, *Conscience and Convenience* (Boston: Little, Brown, 1980), 33. See also Manza and Uggen, *Locked Out*, 298n57; and Norval Morris and David J. Rothman, eds., *The Oxford History of the Prison: The Practice of Punishment in Western Society* (New York: Oxford University Press, 1995).

35. Quoted in Barbara M. Brenzel, "Lancaster Industrial School for Girls: A Social Portrait of a Nineteenth-Century Reform School for Girls," *Feminist Studies* 3, no. 1 (1975): 41, 45.

36. Gustave de Beaumont and Alexis de Tocqueville, *On the Penitentiary System in the United States, and Its Applications in France* (Philadelphia, 1833), 118–20.

37. Mary Carpenter, *Juvenile Delinquents: Their Conditions and Treatment* (London: W. & F. G. Cash, 1853), 13. Carpenter is credited with helping pass the Juvenile Offender Act in 1854, which officially recognized the need to establish reformatories in England (see J. Manton, *Mary Carpenter and the Children of the Streets* [London: Heinemann, 1976]). This recognition apparently had little impact on the confinement of youths as thousands were annually committed to prisons following passage of the act (see William Osborn, *The Cry of 10,000 Children; or, Cruelty towards the Young* [London:

Adams & Co., 1860], reproduced in Sanders, ed., *Juvenile Offenders for a Thousand Years*, 267–68). For a review of child-saving in multiple nation-states, see Wines, *The State of Prisons and of Child-Saving Institutions*, 67–85.

38. See, e.g., *Childhood's Appeal* (Massachusetts Society for the Prevention of Cruelty to Children), no. 1 (December 8, 1880).
39. Jack Holl, *Juvenile Reform in the Progressive Era: William R. George and the Junior Republic Movement* (Ithaca, NY: Cornell University Press, 1971), 186.
40. Roosevelt quoted in ibid., 9.
41. David S. Tanenhaus, "Degrees of Discretion: The First Juvenile Court and the Problem of Difference in the Early Twentieth Century," in *Our Children, Their Children*, ed. D. F. Hawkins and K. Kempf Leonard (Chicago: University of Chicago Press, 2005).
42. Quoted in John C. Watkins, *Juvenile Justice Century: A Sociological Commentary on American Juvenile Courts* (Durham, NC: Carolina Academic, 1998), 51. See also LeRoy Ashby, *Saving the Waifs: Reformers and Dependent Children, 1890–1917* (Philadelphia: Temple University Press, 1984), 7.
43. Dean Roscoe Pound, "Future Challenges Judges," *Juvenile Court Judges Journal* 1, no. 4 (1950): 21–23, 28, reproduced in Robert E. Shepherd, "The Juvenile Court at 100 Years: A Look Back," *Juvenile Justice* 6, no. 2 (1999): 17.
44. Mark Harrison Moore with Thomas Bearrows et al., *The Mandate for Juvenile Justice*, vol. 1 of *From Children to Citizens* (New York: Springer, 1987); Francis X. Hartmann, ed., *The Role of the Juvenile Court*, vol. 2 of *From Children to Citizens* (New York: Springer, 1987); James Q. Wilson and Glenn C. Loury, eds., *Families, Schools, and Delinquency Prevention*, vol. 3 of *From Children to Citizens* (New York: Springer, 1987).
45. Moore, *The Mandate for Juvenile Justice*, xiv.
46. David S. Tanenhaus, *Juvenile Justice in the Making*, Studies in Crime and Public Policy (New York: Oxford University Press, 2004). For a study of this liberal juvenile justice agenda in England, see Bailey, *Delinquency and Citizenship*.
47. Ashby, *Saving the Waifs*, 7.
48. Doug McAdam, Sidney Tarrow, and Charles Tilly, *Dynamics of Contention* (Cambridge: Cambridge University Press, 2001); Michael Omi and Howard Winant, *Racial Formation in the United States from the 1960s to the 1990s* (New York: Routledge, 1994). Omi and Winant define *racial projects* as efforts to establish or transform the social meaning and significance of race through "interpretation, representation, or explanation of racial dynamics, and efforts to reorganize and redistribute resources along racial lines" (ibid., 56).
49. See, e.g., Mennel, *Thorns and Thistles*; Platt, *The Child Savers*; and Ashby, *Saving the Waifs*. More recent works by David Tanenhaus (*Juvenile Justice in the Making*) and Jennifer Trost (*Gateway to Justice: The Juvenile Court and Progressive Child Welfare in a Southern City* [Athens: University of Georgia Press, 2005]) address black youth experiences but neglect black community involvement in juvenile justice reform by focusing on white civic leaders.
50. Bernard, *The Cycle of Juvenile Justice*, 50.
51. See Wilma King, *Stolen Childhood: Slave Youth in Nineteenth-Century America* (Bloomington: Indiana University Press, 1995), xx.
52. *M'Vaughters v. Elder*, 2 Brevard 307, April 1809, quoted in E. Franklin Frazier, *The Negro Family in the United States* (Notre Dame, IN: University of Notre Dame Press, 2001), 45.
53. Jefferson quoted in King, *Stolen Childhood*, 2. Eugene Genovese (*Roll, Jordan, Roll: The*

World the Slaves Made [New York: Vintage, 1972]) explains that "better impulses of the master class combined with a good deal of economic rationality to bring slave children to maturity slowly and in a manner designed to guarantee their eventual maximum productivity" (508).

54. Genovese, *Roll, Jordan, Roll,* 504–5, 508.

55. King, *Stolen Childhood,* 32.

56. Ibid., 2, 32; Genovese, *Roll, Jordan, Roll,* 502.

57. Bernard, *The Cycle of Juvenile Justice,* 50.

58. King, *Stolen Childhood,* xvii.

59. Orlando Patterson, *Slavery and Social Death: A Comparative Study* (Cambridge, MA: Harvard University Press, 1982); Frazier, *The Negro Family in the United States.*

60. Alexis de Tocqueville, *Democracy in America,* trans. Henry Reeve, 2 vols. (New York: Appleton, 1899), 1:360; Ariès, *Centuries of Childhood,* 402. On resistance to the impositions of slavery on black family life, see Deborah G. White, *Ar'n't I a Woman? Female Slaves in the Plantation South* (New York: Norton, 1999).

61. Tocqueville, *Democracy in America,* 1:415n31; Phillip S. Foner, ed., *The Life and Writings of Frederick Douglass,* 4 vols. (New York: International, 1950–55), 1:102–5.

62. Charles W. Mills, *The Racial Contract* (Ithaca, NY: Cornell University Press, 1997). On the relation between race and the civic exclusion of "subpersons" in terms of the social contract, Mills writes: "The racial contract is explicitly predicated on a politics of the body . . . which is related to the body politic through restrictions on which bodies are 'politic.' There are bodies impolitic whose owners are judged incapable of *forming* or fully *entering into* a body politic" (ibid., 53).

63. Tocqueville, *Democracy in America,* 1:459.

64. Hinton R. Helper, *The Negroes in Negroland, the Negroes in America, and Negroes Generally* (New York: G. W. Carleton, 1868), v–vi. *Negroland* refers to continental Africa. The term was commonly enough used that it appears without quotes in an academic book review fifty years later. See Albert Gilbertson, review of *The Negro Races: A Sociological Study* by John Dowd, *American Journal of Psychology* 26, no. 2 (April 1915): 308–10.

65. Sir Charles Lyell, *A Second Visit to the United States,* 2 vols. (New York: Harper & Bros., 1849), 1:105, quoted in Helper, *Negroland,* 165. See also Sir Edward Bailey, *Charles Lyell,* British Men of Science Series (London: Thomas Nelson, 1862).

66. Henry Latham, *Black and White: A Journal of a Three Months Tour in the United States* (London: Macmillan/Philadelphia: Lippincott, 1867), 16–17.

67. Helper, *Negroland,* 212, quoted in Charles H. Wesley, "The Concept of Negro Inferiority in American Thought," *Journal of Negro History* 25, no. 4 (1940): 556.

68. Helper declared: "Any and every white person who does not think and act in strict accordance with the just and pure promptings indicated [in *Negroes in Negroland*] . . . is a most unworthy and despicable representative of his race" (*Negroland,* xiii). For an analysis of Hinton Helper's life and influence, see George M. Fredrickson, *The Arrogance of Race: Historical Perspectives on Slavery, Racism, and Social Inequality* (Hanover, NH: University Press of New England, 1988), chap. 2.

69. Lee Baker, *From Savage to Negro: Anthropology and the Construction of Race, 1896–1954* (Berkeley and Los Angeles: University of California Press, 1998), 14–17, 29–30. See also Khalid Muhammad, *The Condemnation of Blackness: Race, Crime and the Making of Modern Urban America* (Cambridge, MA: Harvard University Press, 2010).

70. Fitzhugh, *Sociology for the South,* reproduced in Bremner, ed., *Children and Youth in America,* 1:423; William Winwood Reade, *Savage Africa* (1863), 399, quoted in Helper, *Negroland,* 166.

71. Joel Olson, *The Abolition of White Democracy* (Minneapolis: University of Minnesota Press, 2004).

72. Mills, *The Racial Contract*; Leon Litwack, *Trouble in Mind: Black Southerners in the Age of Jim Crow* (New York: Vintage, 1998); Douglas A. Blackmon, *Slavery by Another Name: The Re-Enslavement of Black People in America from the Civil War to World War II* (New York: Doubleday, 2008).

73. Taney quoted in Leon Litwack, "The Federal Government and the Free Negro, 1790–1860," *Journal of Negro History* 43, no. 4 (1958): 274.

74. Eric Foner, *Reconstruction: America's Unfinished Revolution, 1863–1877* (New York: Harper, 2002).

75. *Dred Scott v. Sanford*, 19 Howard 407–10, 412–16, quoted in Litwack, "The Federal Government and the Free Negro," 276.

76. Eric Foner, *The Story of American Freedom* (New York: Norton, 1998), 74–75. See also Helen Fein, *Accounting for Genocide* (New York: Free Press, 1979), 4.

77. Thomas Jefferson, *Notes on the State of Virginia* (1782), quoted in Emmanuel C. Eze, *Race and the Enlightenment: A Reader* (Malden, MA: Blackwell, 1997), 103; Abraham Lincoln, "Address to a Deputation of Negroes, June 1862," quoted in Helper, *Negroland*, 182.

78. Cecil Frey, "The House of Refuge for Colored Children," *Journal of Negro History* 66, no. 1 (1981): 17–18.

79. Olson, *The Abolition of White Democracy*; Mills, *The Racial Contract*.

80. Nancy Fraser, "From Redistribution to Recognition? Dilemmas of Justice in a 'Post-Socialist' Age," *New Left Review* 212 (1995): 212; Iris M. Young, *Justice and the Politics of Difference* (Princeton, NJ: Princeton University Press, 1990).

CHAPTER TWO

1. Charles Dickens, *American Notes: For General Circulation* (New York: Appleton & Co., 1942), 24.

2. On the English common law origins of the legal jurisdiction of American juvenile justice, see Anthony M. Platt, *The Child Savers: The Invention of Delinquency* (1969), 40th anniversary ed. (New Brunswick, NJ: Rutgers University Press, 2009), app. For a review of the theological and legal origins of English common law principles of diminished criminal responsibility, see Anthony Platt and Bernard L. Diamond, "The Origins of the 'Right and Wrong' Test of Criminal Responsibility and Its Subsequent Development in the United States: An Historical Survey," *California Law Review* 54, no. 3 (1966): 1227–60.

3. Platt, *The Child Savers*, 196–97, 246–48, 262.

4. A study of early Chicago juvenile court transfer practices between 1906 and 1930 found 24 cases of juveniles accused of homicide, or just over 1 case per year (David S. Tanenhaus and S. A. Drizin, "'Owing to the Extreme Youth of the Accused': The Changing Legal Response to Juvenile Homicide," *Journal of Criminal Law and Criminology* 92, nos. 3–4 [2002]: 648–49). In contrast, from 1992 to 2000, there were 535 cases of homicide involving juvenile suspects reported to the Chicago police, about 66 cases per year (John Boulahanis and Martha Heltsley, "Perceived Fears: The Reporting Patterns of Juvenile Homicide in Chicago Newspapers," *Criminal Justice Policy Review* 15, no. 2 [2004]: 141). The increase is largely attributed to unprecedented gun violence (Alfred Blumstein, "Youth, Guns, and Violent Crime," *The Future of Children* 12, no. 2 [2002]: 39–53).

5. Platt, *The Child Savers*, 243.

6. *Godfrey v. State*, 31 Ala. 323 (1858).
7. Platt, *The Child Savers*, 262.
8. Edward L. Ayers, *Vengeance and Justice: Crime and Punishment in the Nineteenth Century American South* (New York: Oxford University Press, 1984); Robert M. Mennel, *Thorns and Thistles: Juvenile Delinquents in the United States, 1825–1940* (Hanover, NH: University Press of New England, 1973), 75.
9. Platt, *The Child Savers*, 262.
10. The New Jersey legislature passed "An Act for the Gradual Abolition of Slavery" in 1804, establishing that females born to enslaved parents after July 4, 1804, would be free at twenty-one years of age, males at age twenty-five. Guild was about twelve years shy of freedom when he met his end, and he was possibly already a formally free black ward of the state. A provision in the act allowed owners to manumit children sooner by turning them over to the state social-welfare agency, which received a monthly subsidy for managing slave wards. The subsidy loophole was widely used, the line item for "abandoned blacks" growing to 40 percent of the state budget by 1809. In Alabama, where Godfrey was executed, slavery was not formally abolished (or was elaborately masked) until 1865. See Edgar J. McManus, *Black Bondage in the North* (Syracuse, NY: Syracuse University Press, 1973), 178–79. See also Douglas A. Blackmon, *Slavery by Another Name: The Re-Enslavement of Black People in America from the Civil War to World War II* (New York: Doubleday, 2008).
11. On the role of white mobs in hastening executions or "legal lynchings," see James W. Clarke, "Without Fear or Shame: Lynching, Capital Punishment and the Subculture of Violence in the American South," *British Journal of Political Science* 28, no. 2 (2001): 269–89. Studies of slave executions in the United States find that they were more likely in cases involving violation of racial etiquette, such as miscegenation or interracial violence. See Adalberto Aguirre and David Baker, "Slave Executions in the United States: A Descriptive Analysis of Social and Historical Factors," *Social Science Journal* 36, no. 1 (1999): 1–31.
12. On the differential valuation of crime victims by race, see Michael L. Radelet, "Racial Characteristics and the Imposition of the Death Penalty," *American Sociological Review* 46, no. 6 (1981): 918–27; and Jennifer Eberhardt et al., "Looking Deathworthy," *Psychological Science* 17, no. 5 (2006): 383.
13. Victor Streib, *Death Penalty for Juveniles* (Bloomington: Indiana University Press, 1987), 78. For discussions of other macabre executions of black children and youths, see Christopher Hitchens, "Old Enough to Die," *Vanity Fair*, June 1999, 76–80; and Gilbert King, *The Execution of Willie Francis: Race, Murder, and the Search for Justice in the American South* (New York: Basic Civitas, 2009).
14. Mennel, *Thorns and Thistles*; Priscilla F. Clement, "The Incorrigible Child: Juvenile Delinquency in the United States from the 17th through the 19th Centuries," in *History of Juvenile Delinquency: A Collection of Essays on Crime Committed by Young Offenders, in History and in Selected Countries* (2 vols.), ed. Albert G. Hess and Priscilla F. Clement (Aalen: Scientia, 1990–93), 2:462; Alexander W. Pisciotta, "*Parens Patriae*, Treatment and Reform: The Case of the Western House of Refuge, 1849–1907," *New England Journal on Criminal and Civil Confinement* 10 (1984): 65–68.
15. Alexander W. Pisciotta, "Treatment on Trial: The Rhetoric and Reality of the New York House of Refuge, 1857–1935," *American Journal of Legal History* 29 (1985): 154–55.
16. Clement, "The Incorrigible Child," 478. A traveler to New York in 1866 observed: "The Penitentiary to-day contains five hundred and seventy-one prisoners, the largest number they have ever had within the walls; all of them men, except about twenty

women. They only keep here a sufficient number of women to do the necessary washing and mending for the male prisoners" (quoted in Henry Latham, *Black and White: A Journal of a Three Months' Tour in the United States* [London: Macmillan/ Philadelphia: Lippincott, 1867], 18).

17. William Crawford, *Report on the Penitentiaries of the United States* (1835; reprint, Montclair, NJ: Patterson Smith, 1969), 45, quoted in Alexander W. Pisciotta, "Race, Sex, and Rehabilitation: A Study of Differential Treatment in the Juvenile Reformatory, 1825–1900," *Crime and Delinquency* 29, no. 2 (1983): 260.

18. Cecil Frey, "The House of Refuge for Colored Children," *Journal of Negro History* 66, no. 1 (1981): 12–13.

19. Dickens, *American Notes*, 24.

20. Nathaniel C. Hart to Stephen Allen, December 17, 1834, Allen Papers, New York Historical Society, reproduced in Robert H. Bremner, ed., *Children and Youth in America: A Documentary History*, 3 vols. in 5 (Cambridge, MA: Harvard University Press, 1970–74), 1:687.

21. Pennsylvania Society for Promoting the Abolition of Slavery, *Review of a Pamphlet, Entitled An Appeal to the Public on Behalf of a House of Refuge for Colored Juvenile Delinquents* (Philadelphia: W. H. Brisbane, 1847); James J. Barclay, *An Address Delivered at the Laying of the Corner Stone of the House of Refuge for Colored Juvenile Delinquents* (Philadelphia: T. K. & P. G. Collins, 1848). For the *Appeal* itself, see *An Appeal to the Public on Behalf of a House of Refuge for Coloured Juvenile Delinquents* (Philadelphia: T. K. & P. G. Collins, 1846).

22. *Thirtieth Annual Report of the Philadelphia House of Refuge* (Philadelphia: Ashmead, 1858).

23. Clement, "The Incorrigible Child," 477.

24. Ibid.

25. Barclay, *Address*, 6. White supremacist rhetoric often referenced God's will. In this vein, Thomas Dew, a professor of history at and later the president of William and Mary College, insisted: "It is the order of nature and of God that the being of superior faculties and knowledge and therefore of superior power should control and dispose of those who are inferior" (quoted in Charles H. Wesley, "The Concept of Negro Inferiority in American Thought," *Journal of Negro History* 25, no. 4 [1940]: 547).

26. Pisciotta, "Race, Sex, and Rehabilitation," 261–62.

27. Black boys and perhaps girls at the Philadelphia refuge were also assigned menial labor on the grounds of the house of refuge for whites. This division of labor appeared in many segregated reformatories well into the twentieth century (Frey, "The House of Refuge for Colored Children," 18).

28. Edward S. Abdy, *Journal of Residence and Tour in the United States* (London: John Murray, 1835), 5, quoted in Pisciotta, "Race, Sex, and Rehabilitation," 262.

29. Charles Loring Brace, *First Circular of the Children's Aid Society of New York* (March 1853), quoted in Mennel, *Thorns and Thistles*, 37–38.

30. Clement, "The Incorrigible Child," 482.

31. Pisciotta, "Race, Sex, and Rehabilitation," 262.

32. Robert S. Pickett, *House of Refuge: Origins of Juvenile Reform in New York State, 1815–1857* (Syracuse, NY: Syracuse University Press, 1969), 76; Philip L. Reichel, "Nineteenth Century Societal Reactions to Juvenile Delinquents: Preliminary Notes for a Natural History," *Mid-American Review of Sociology* 4, no. 2 (1979): 47.

33. Quoted in Mennel, *Thorns and Thistles*, 39. See also Frey, "The House of Refuge for Colored Children," 20.

34. Elijah Devoe, *The Refuge System; or, Prison Discipline Applied to Juvenile Delinquents* (New York: J. B. McGown, 1848), 24–28.
35. Clement, "The Incorrigible Child," 481–82.
36. *Thirty-third Annual Report of the Board of Managers of the Refuge* (Philadelphia: Ashmead, 1861), 11, 12, quoted in Frey, "The House of Refuge for Colored Children," 17–18.
37. Ibid., 11, quoted in Frey, "The House of Refuge for Colored Children," 17–18. In debates over Emancipation and its aftermath, the idea of jettisoning free blacks from the Republic appealed to many white and some black leaders. According to Senator Montgomery Blair: "All the early patriots of the South—Washington, Jefferson, Madison, Monroe, Jackson, Clay, and others—were advocates of Emancipation and colonization. The patriots of the North concurred in the design. . . . The author of the Declaration of Independence and his associates declared equal rights impracticable in a society constituted of masses of different races. . . . In such communities, reason and experience show that one or the other race must be the dominant race, and that democracy is impossible" (Montgomery Blair, speech at Concord, NH, June 17, 1863, quoted in Helper, *Negroland*, 182–83). Black nationalists, including Martin Delany, also championed colonization, doubting prospects for full citizenship in a Republic where "the most ordinary white person is almost revered, while the most qualified colored person is totally neglected." "We love our country, dearly love her," Delany wrote, "but she don't love us—she despises us, and bids us be gone, driving us from her embraces." Ultimately, Delany, resolved to struggle for full citizenship, a commitment fueled by his service as the first black field officer in the U.S. Army during the Civil War. See Martin Delany, *The Condition, Elevation, Emigration, and Destiny of the Colored People of the United States* (Philadelphia, 1852), 109, 203.
38. Nathaniel C. Hart, *Documents Relative to the House of Refuge, Instituted by the Society for the Reformation of Juvenile Delinquents in the City of New York, in 1824* (New York: M. Day, 1832), 180.
39. About 90 percent of black Americans lived in southern states in 1900. By the end of World War I, that figure had decreased to 80 percent. Only in 1950 did the proportion of blacks living in the South fall below 70 percent. Most blacks who left the South settled in northern, midwestern, and eastern urban centers. By 1970, 80 percent of black Americans lived in urban areas, and half were in northern or western cities. See Campbell Gibson and Kay Jung, *Historical Census Statistics on Population Totals by Race, 1790 to 1990, and by Hispanic Origin, 1970 to 1990, for the United States, Regions, Divisions, and States*, Population Division Working Paper no. 56 (Washington, DC: U.S. Census Bureau, 2002).
40. See M. Louise Jenkins, "Do We Need Reformatories?" *National Notes* (National Association of Colored Women's Clubs) 3, no. 8 (1900): 1, 3. The house of refuge at Glen Mills was characterized as a model institution.
41. Margaret W. Cahalan, *Historical Corrections Statistics in the United States, 1850–1984* (Washington, DC: U.S. Department of Justice, Bureau of Justice Statistics, 1986), 129; Mennel, *Thorns and Thistles*; David J. Rothman, *The Discovery of the Asylum* (Boston: Little, Brown, 1971), 209.
42. Vernetta D. Young, "Punishment and Social Conditions: The Control of Black Juveniles in the 1800's in Maryland," in Hess and Clement, eds., *History of Juvenile Delinquency*, vol. 2; Mennel, *Thorns and Thistles*, 75 (quote).
43. Clement, "The Incorrigible Child," 478.
44. Mennel, *Thorns and Thistles*, 75. See also Leon Litwack, *Trouble in Mind: Black South-*

erners in the Age of Jim Crow (New York: Vintage, 1998); and Randall G. Shelden, "From Slave to Caste Society: Penal Changes in Tennessee, 1830–1915," *Tennessee Historical Quarterly* 38 (1979): 462–78.

45. Robin D. G. Kelley, *Freedom Dreams: The Black Radical Imagination* (Boston: Beacon, 2002). The following states had majority black populations: Louisiana (until 1900), South Carolina (until the early 1920s), and Mississippi (until the early 1940s). Until the 1940s, black Americans were just under half the population of Georgia, Alabama, and Florida. See Gibson and Jung, *Historical Census Statistics on Population Totals by Race*.

46. Bremner, ed., *Children and Youth in America*, 1:345 (introductory material).

47. Young, "Punishment and Social Conditions," 563.

48. Ibid.

49. Christopher Adamson, "Punishment After Slavery: Southern State Penal Systems, 1865–1890," *Social Problems* 30, no. 5 (1983): 557–58.

50. Mennel, *Thorns and Thistles*, 73–75. See also Edward Franklin Frazier, *Negro Youth at the Crossways: Their Personality Development in the Middle States* (1940; reprint, New York: Schocken, 1967).

51. Shelden, "From Slave to Caste Society," 463; Clement, "The Incorrigible Child," 478.

52. Adamson, "Punishment After Slavery," 557–58. See also Mark Colvin, *Penitentiaries, Reformatories, and Chain Gangs: Social Theory and the History of Punishment in Nineteenth-Century America* (New York: St. Martin's, 1997); and Fox Butterfield, *All God's Children: The Boskett Family and the American Tradition of Violence* (New York: Avon, 1995).

53. Adamson, "Punishment After Slavery," 558.

54. William S. Myers, *The Self-Reconstruction of Maryland, 1864–1867* (Baltimore: Johns Hopkins University Press, 1909), 22, quoted in Young, "Punishment and Social Conditions," 568. See also Paul S. Peirce, *The Freedmen's Bureau: A Chapter in the History of Reconstruction* (Iowa City: University of Iowa Press, 1901), 147.

55. Eric Foner, *Reconstruction: America's Unfinished Revolution, 1863–1877* (New York: Harper, 2002), 201.

56. Mary Ellen Curtin, *Black Prisoners and Their World, Alabama, 1865–1900* (Charlottesville: University Press of Virginia, 2000), 44.

57. Constitutional historians have found little to clarify the intentions of this language, but courts construe the amendment as authorizing the treatment of prisoners as slaves. See Kamal Ghali, "No Slavery Except as a Punishment for Crime," *UCLA Law Review* 55 (2007): 607–42. See also *Morales v. Schmidt*, 489 F.2d 1335, 1338 (7th Cir., 1973): "The Thirteenth Amendment, if read literally, suggests that the States may treat their prisoners as slaves." See also *Ruffin v. Commonwealth*, 62 Va. (21 Gratt) 790, 796 (1871): "For the time being, during his term of service in the penitentiary, he is in a state of penal servitude to the State. He has, as a consequence of his crime, not only forfeited his liberty, but all his personal rights except those which the law in its humanity accords to him. He is for the time being the slave of the State."

58. Steven Hahn, *A Nation under Our Feet: Black Political Struggles in the Rural South, from Slavery to the Great Migration* (Cambridge, MA: Harvard University Press, 2003), 243–44. See also M. D. Cobb and J. A. Jenkins, "Race and the Representation of Blacks' Interests during Reconstruction," *Political Research Quarterly* 54, no. 1 (2001): 181–204; and Foner, *Reconstruction*.

59. Peirce, *The Freedmen's Bureau*, 43–45, 143.
60. Ibid., 147–48. Eric Foner reports: "Maryland and North Carolina courts [had] bound out thousands of black children to white 'guardians' without the consent, sometimes without the knowledge, of their parents" (*Reconstruction*, 201).
61. Litwack, *Trouble in Mind*, 249.
62. Colvin, *Penitentiaries, Reformatories, and Chain Gangs*, 219 (quotation); Foner, *Reconstruction*, 201. In his classic study of vagrancy law in England and the United States, William Chambliss notes that Maryland expressly "restricted the application of vagrancy laws to 'free' Negroes." This use of vagrancy laws in the antebellum and post-Emancipation periods is consistent with Chambliss's emphasis on the role of "vested interest groups" in the emergence and application of law, including vagrancy laws to "provide powerful landowners with a ready supply of cheap labor." See William J. Chambliss, "A Sociological Analysis of the Law of Vagrancy," *Social Problems* 12, no. 1 (1964): 67–77, 75, 77.
63. David M. Oshinsky, *Worse Than Slavery: Parchman Farm and the Ordeal of Jim Crow Justice* (New York: Free Press, 1996), 40.
64. Matthew J. Mancini, *One Dies, Get Another: Convict Leasing in the American South, 1866–1928* (Columbia: University of South Carolina Press, 1996), 136.
65. Ayers, *Vengeance and Justice*, 151.
66. Oshinsky, *Worse Than Slavery*, 29.
67. Mancini, *One Dies, Get Another*, 99–100.
68. Shelden, "From Slave to Caste Society," 464 (first quote); Adamson, "Punishment After Slavery," 556 (second quote).
69. W. E. B. DuBois, *Black Reconstruction in America, 1860–1880* (New York: Harcourt, Brace, 1935), 167; Litwack, *Trouble in Mind*, 249; Foner, *Reconstruction*.
70. Alex Lichtenstein, *Twice the Work of Free Labor: The Political Economy of Convict Labor in the New South* (New York: Verso, 1996), 3. On the use of convict labor to break strikes and thwart attempted labor organization, see Mancini, *One Dies, Get Another*, 53.
71. Litwack, *Trouble in Mind*, 271–72. Lichtenstein notes over twenty strikes against the use of convict labor, including armed confrontations with convicts and leaseholders (*Twice the Work of Free Labor*, 96).
72. Litwack, *Trouble in Mind*, 274. See also Wiley B. Sanders, *Negro Child Welfare in North Carolina* (Chapel Hill: University of North Carolina Press, 1933).
73. Oshinsky, *Worse Than Slavery*, 47–48.
74. Colvin, *Penitentiaries, Reformatories, and Chain Gangs*, 246; Mancini, *One Dies, Get Another*, 22–23; Oshinsky, *Worse Than Slavery*.
75. Mancini, *One Dies, Get Another*, 100, 136.
76. Low convict-labor costs were fixed, "a serious liability when production had to be halted because of a lack of markets. [Only f]irms that maintained a balance of forced and free labor—the former operating as a predictable and fixed cost and . . . the later allowing the flexibility of wage reductions, rent increases in company housing, or lay-offs—could successfully exploit convict labor" (Lichtenstein, *Twice the Work of Free Labor*, 108).
77. Quoted in Adamson, "Punishment After Slavery," 566.
78. Quoted in Litwack, *Trouble in Mind*, 273.
79. Oshinsky, *Worse Than Slavery*, 56 (first quote); Litwack, *Trouble in Mind*, 273 (other quotes; death rate figures).

80. Mark T. Carleton, *Politics and Punishment: The History of the Louisiana State Penal System* (Baton Rouge: Louisiana State University Press, 1971), 37 (quotes); Mennel, *Thorns and Thistles*, 76 (on Hampton). On the predation of older convicts, see Litwack, *Trouble in Mind*, 273–74.

81. Charles Harris Wesley, ed., *The History of the National Association of Colored Women's Clubs: A Legacy of Service* (Washington, DC: National Association of Colored Women's Clubs, 1984), 41–43, 45.

82. Jenkins, "Do We Need Reformatories?" 1.

83. Ibid., 1, 3.

84. Ibid., 3.

85. The political scientist Michael C. Dawson defines *linked fate* as the "sense that race [is] the defining interest in individuals' lives and that the well-being of blacks individually and as a group [can] be secured only by continued political and social agitation" (*Behind the Mule: Race and Class in African-American Politics* [Princeton, NJ: Princeton University Press, 1994], 51). See also Lani Guinier and Gerald Torres, *The Miner's Canary: Enlisting Race, Resisting Power, Transforming Democracy* (Cambridge, MA: Harvard University Press, 2003).

86. Jenkins, "Do We Need Reformatories?" 3; Pisciotta, "Race, Sex, and Rehabilitation," 256.

87. Josephine T. Washington, "Child Saving in Alabama," *Colored American Magazine* 14 (1908): 48–51.

88. See David McLeod, *The Age of the Child: Children in America, 1890–1920* (New York: Twayne, 1998), 27–29; and Joel Olson, *The Abolition of White Democracy* (Minneapolis: University of Minnesota Press, 2004), 16.

89. Oshinsky, *Worse Than Slavery*, 28. See also DuBois, *Black Reconstruction in America*, 709 (who discusses southern jails "bursting with black prisoners incarcerated on trivial and trumped up charges").

90. Carleton, *Politics and Punishment*, 15.

91. DuBois, *Black Reconstruction in America*, 506.

92. Vernetta D. Young, "Race and Gender in the Establishment of Juvenile Institutions: The Case of the South," *Prison Journal* 73, no. 2 (1994): 249.

93. Foner, *Reconstruction*, 201.

94. Quoted in Young, "Punishment and Social Conditions," 569.

95. House of Reformation for Colored Children, *Second Annual Report, 1875* (Baltimore: Price Current Printing, 1875), 7, quoted in Pisciotta, "Race, Sex, and Rehabilitation," 261.

96. Quoted in Young, "Punishment and Social Conditions," 570.

97. Young similarly argues that the house of reformation aimed to "neutralize the political and social impact of [Emancipation] by socializing free black children into continued subordination" ("Punishment and Social Conditions," 570). White youths were often engaged in similar labor roles, but accounts of early reformatory plans suggest that this was often accompanied by educational programming less common in the black experience (see Pisciotta, "Race, Sex, and Rehabilitation"; and Hilda Jane Zimmerman, "The Penal Reform Movement in the South during the Progressive Period, 1890–1917," *Journal of Southern History* 17 [1951]: 462–92, 478–79).

98. W. E. B. DuBois, "Hampton," *The Crisis* 15, no. 1 (1917): 11.

99. Young, "Race and Gender in the Establishment of Juvenile Institutions"; Zimmerman, "The Penal Reform Movement in the South during the Progressive Era."

100. Zimmerman, "The Penal Reform Movement in the South during the Progressive Era," 478–79.

CHAPTER THREE

1. See David S. Tanenhaus, *Juvenile Justice in the Making,* Studies in Crime and Public Policy (New York: Oxford University Press, 2004); Anthony M. Platt, *The Child Savers: The Invention of Delinquency* (1969), 40th anniversary ed. (New Brunswick, NJ: Rutgers University Press, 2009); and Michael Willrich, *City of Courts: Socializing Justice in Progressive Era Chicago* (New York: Cambridge University Press, 2003).

2. William Ayers, *A Kind and Just Parent: The Children of Juvenile Court* (Boston: Beacon, 1997), 25.

3. Juvenile Court of Cook County, *First Annual Report* (Chicago, 1900), quoted in ibid., vii. See Katharine Lenroot and Emma Lundberg, *Juvenile Courts at Work: A Study of the Organization and Methods of Ten Courts* (Washington, DC: U.S. Department of Labor, Children's Bureau, 1925).

4. Ayers, *A Kind and Just Parent.* See also Orlando Patterson, *Slavery and Social Death: A Comparative Study* (Cambridge, MA: Harvard University Press, 1982); and Frances Joseph-Gaudet, *He Leadeth Me: African American Women Writers, 1910–1940* (1913; reprint, New York: Prentice-Hall, 1996).

5. Nicholas Lemann, *The Promised Land: The Great Black Migration and How It Changed America* (New York: Vintage, 1991).

6. The Negro question has been summarized as follows: "Shall the Negro, individually, enjoy equally, and only equally, with the white man individually, that full measure of an American citizen's public rights, civil and political, decreed to him both as his and as an essential to the preservation of equal rights between the States; or shall he be compelled to abandon these inalienable human rights to the custody of . . . [a] 'white man's government'?" (George W. Cable, *The Negro Question* [New York: Scribner's, 1890], 100).

7. See W. E. B. DuBois, *Black Reconstruction in America, 1860–1880* (New York: Harcourt, Brace, 1935); and Eric Foner, *Reconstruction: America's Unfinished Revolution, 1863–1877* (New York: Harper, 2002).

8. On Reconstruction Era legislative changes, see DuBois, *Black Reconstruction in America*; John Hope Franklin and Alfred A. Moss, eds., *From Slavery to Freedom* (1947), 6th ed. (New York: Knopf, 1988); Leon F. Litwack, *Been in the Storm So Long: The Aftermath of Slavery* (New York: Knopf, 1979); and Foner, *Reconstruction*.

9. James D. Anderson, *The Education of Blacks in the South, 1860–1935* (Chapel Hill: University of North Carolina Press, 1988), 154 (first quote); Deborah G. White, *Too Heavy a Load: Black Women in Defense of Themselves, 1894–1994* (New York: Norton, 1999), 25 (second quote); Rayford Logan, *The Negro in American Life and Thought: The Nadir, 1877–1901* (New York: Dial, 1954).

10. Leon Litwack, *Trouble in Mind: Black Southerners in the Age of Jim Crow* (New York: Vintage, 1998), 284.

11. Franklin and Moss, eds., *From Slavery to Freedom,* 235–38.

12. *Plessy v. Ferguson,* 163 U.S. 537 (1896); *Williams v. Mississippi,* 170 U.S. 213 (1898).

13. William Christopher Handy, *Father of the Blues: An Autobiography* (New York: Macmillan), 80–81, quoted in Litwack, *Trouble in Mind,* 89. (Handy is recalling a candidate's speech.)

14. See DuBois, *Black Reconstruction in America,* 645–46; and Litwack, *Trouble in Mind,* 87–88.

15. Anderson, *The Education of Blacks in the South*, 154.
16. Vardaman quoted in Dunbar Rowland, *Encyclopedia of Mississippi History Comprising Sketches of Counties, Towns, Events, Institutions, and Persons* (Madison, WI: S. A. Brant, 1907), 854.
17. Frank Johnston, "Treatment of Juvenile Offenders in Mississippi," *Journal of Criminal Law and Criminology* 1 (1910): 946–47. The juvenile court model depended on reformatory placement options, so failure to develop a black reformatory greatly diminished the significance of juvenile court reform for black youths and their communities.
18. *Mississippi's Boy Delinquents* quoted in David M. Oshinsky, *Worse Than Slavery: Parchman Farm and the Ordeal of Jim Crow Justice* (New York: Free Press, 1996), 266n37. See also Mississippi Association on Crime and Delinquency, *The Rehabilitation of Mississippi's Delinquent Children* (Jackson, MS: MACD, 1947), 97.
19. Robert Whitaker, *On the Laps of Gods: The Red Summer of 1919 and the Struggle for Justice That Remade a Nation* (New York: Random House, 2008); Mark Ellis, "J. Edgar Hoover and the 'Red Summer' of 1919," *Journal of American Studies* 28, no. 1 (2009): 39–59.
20. The substantive impact of early juvenile court reform on juvenile justice administration is questionable. A 1918 study found that many reportedly "specially organized" courts operated much like the adult criminal courts they were meant to replace (Evelina Belden and Emma Octavia Lundberg, eds., *Courts in the United States Hearing Children's Cases: Results of a Questionnaire Study Covering the Year 1918* [Washington, DC: U.S. Government Printing Office, 1920]). Recent research suggests that juvenile court officials lacked the skills and service resources necessary for a more individualized and treatment-based approach to juvenile justice (see Barry C. Feld, *Bad Kids: Race and the Transformation of the Juvenile Court* [New York: Oxford University Press, 1999], chap. 2). However, this analysis is concerned with black youths and community contact with juvenile courts and, regardless of the innovative distinctions of these courts, how racial privilege and discrimination were manifested in attempts to deliver liberal juvenile justice reform.
21. See Florette Henri, *Black Migration: Movement North, 1900–1920* (Garden City, NY: Anchor, 1975); and Lemann, *The Promised Land*.
22. Earl R. Moses, *The Negro Delinquent in Chicago* (Washington, DC: Social Science Research Council, 1936), 14. The Chicago juvenile court was established in 1900, one year after the first juvenile court in Denver.
23. Harry Hill, *Annual Report of the Chief Probation Officer of the Juvenile Court*, Charity Service Reports, Cook County, IL (Chicago, 1927), 364.
24. Anne M. Knupfer, *Toward a Tenderer Humanity and a Nobler Womanhood: African American Women's Clubs in Turn-of-the-Century Chicago* (New York: New York University Press, 1996), 41; Charles S. Johnson, *A Study of Delinquent and Neglected Negro Children Before the New York City Children's Court* (New York: Joint Committee on Negro Child Study, 1925), 1.
25. Hill, *Annual Report of the Chief Probation Officer of the Juvenile Court*, 364.
26. Bureau of the Census, *Prisoners and Juvenile Delinquents in the United States, 1910* (Washington, DC: Department of Commerce, 1918).
27. In these calculations, 1904 and 1910 are used since they are the only years during the Progressive Era for which national data on race, age, and incarceration are available. On the limits of historical data for race and justice, see Thorsten Sellin, "The Negro and the Problem of Law Observance and Administration in the Light of Social

Research," in *The Negro in American Civilization*, ed. C. S. Johnson (New York: Henry Holt, 1930).

28. Julia Sudbury, "Celling Black Bodies: Black Women in the Global Prison Industrial Complex," *Feminist Review* 70 (2002): 57–74.

29. See, e.g., Platt, *The Child Savers*; David J. Rothman, *The Discovery of the Asylum* (Boston: Little, Brown, 1971); Robert M. Mennel, *Thorns and Thistles: Juvenile Delinquents in the United States, 1825–1940* (Hanover, NH: University Press of New England, 1973); and Steven Schlossman, "Delinquent Children: The Juvenile Reform School," in *The Oxford History of the Prison: The Practice of Punishment in Western Society*, ed. Norval Morris and David J. Rothman (New York: Oxford University Press, 1995).

30. See Charles W. Mills, *The Racial Contract* (Ithaca, NY: Cornell University Press, 1997); and Winthrop D. Jordan, *White over Black: American Attitudes toward the Negro, 1550–1812* (New York: Norton, 1968).

31. See David R. Roediger, *The Wages of Whiteness: Race and the Making of the American Working Class* (New York: Verso, 1991); Noel Ignatiev, *How the Irish Became White* (New York: Routledge, 1995); and St. Clair Drake and Horace Cayton, *Black Metropolis* (New York: Harcourt, Brace & World, 1945).

32. Ignatiev, *How the Irish Became White*, cited in Bronwen Walter, *Outsiders Inside: Whiteness, Place, and Irish Women* (New York: Routledge, 2001), 66.

33. A speech by Montgomery Blair, a U.S. district attorney, mayor of St. Louis, and judge in the court of common appeals, illustrates a belief in the greater potential and priority of Americanizing European immigrants. Speaking in Concord, NH, on June 17, 1863, against black voting rights, Blair compared black freedmen to European immigrants and described democracy and freedom as "instincts" unique to people of European ancestry and unknown to blacks. "To compare the civilized European, accustomed to free labor, to self-support, and self-government, to all the duties and responsibilities of a freeman . . . with the poor degraded mass of Africans, plantation slaves just set free," Blair argued, "is an atrocious libel upon ourselves, upon our ancestors, upon the results of Christian civilization, and upon the Caucasian race which for thousands of years has ruled the world" (quoted in Helper, *Negroland*, 184–85).

34. Steven Schlossman and Stephanie Wallach, "The Crime of Precocious Sexuality: Female Juvenile Delinquency in the Progressive Era," in *The Sociology of Juvenile Delinquency*, ed. Ronald J. Berger (Chicago: Nelson-Hall, 1991); Meda Chesney-Lind, "Judicial Paternalism and the Female Status Offender: Training Women to Know Their Place," *Crime and Delinquency* 23, no. 2 (1977): 121. On the willingness to sacrifice the well-being of black girls to protect white womanhood, see Wiley B. Sanders, *Negro Child Welfare in North Carolina* (Chapel Hill: University of North Carolina Press, 1933), 193–95.

35. *Second generation* refers to native-born children of immigrant parents, while *third generation* refers to native-born children of native parents and immigrant grandparents.

36. National and regional data are not available on the types of institutions to which girls were committed. Many black girls were committed to adult jails and prisons far more often than their white counterparts. The initial focus of early black child-saving initiatives, addressed in the second section of this book, was to provide rehabilitative services for black girls, who were explicitly neglected in the South and afforded inferior services elsewhere.

37. Later research casts doubt on the *effectiveness* of juvenile court innovation and rehabilitative intervention and suggests that youths were often abused and neglected

within juvenile reformatories and training schools (see Belden and Lundberg, *Courts in the United States Hearing Children's Cases*; and Feld, *Bad Kids*). However, this analysis is concerned with the *intentions* of Progressive Era juvenile court reform and how choices of contemporaries charged with developing and administering these systems were framed by racial politics.

38. Bureau of the Census, *Prisoners and Juvenile Delinquents in the United States, 1910.*

39. Between 1906 and 1930, only twenty-four juveniles were accused of homicide in Chicago, an average of roughly one per year (see David S. Tanenhaus and S. A. Drizin, "'Owing to the Extreme Youth of the Accused': The Changing Legal Response to Juvenile Homicide," *Journal of Criminal Law and Criminology* 92, nos. 3–4 [2002]: 648–49). Detailed data from North Carolina also suggest comparable patterns of white and black youths offending and low levels of serious crime (see Sanders, *Negro Child Welfare in North Carolina*). Overall rates of and racial disparities in serious juvenile crime increased in the second half of the twentieth century (see Alfred Blumstein, "Youth, Guns, and Violent Crime," *The Future of Children* 12, no. 2 [2002]: 39–53; and Feld, *Bad Kids*).

40. Sellin, "The Negro and the Problem of Law Observance and Administration," 75. The Census Bureau points out: "While these [penal] figures will probably be generally accepted as indicating that there is more criminality and lawbreaking among Negroes than among whites . . . it should be borne in mind that the difference between the two races in this respect may very well be less than . . . commitments to prison or jail would indicate. The difference shown . . . may to some extent [be] the result of discrimination in the treatment of white and Negro offenders on the part of the community and courts. . . . Although these are questions on which no statistical data can be presented and in regard to which opinion may differ . . . it must always be borne in mind that the amount of crime punished in different classes or communities may not bear a fixed or unvarying ratio to the amount of crime committed" (Bureau of the Census, *Prisoners and Juvenile Delinquents in the United States, 1910*, 91).

41. The term *dark figure* describes the unrecorded criminal offenses in official police and court data. On the age-crime curve, see Rob J. Sampson and John H. Laub, *Crime in the Making: Pathways and Turning Points through Life* (Cambridge, MA: Harvard University Press, 1995).

42. Sherrilyn A. Ifill, *On the Courthouse Lawn: Confronting the Legacy of Lynching in the Twenty-first Century* (Boston: Beacon, 2007), 59; Ralph Ginzburg, *100 Years of Lynchings* (Baltimore: Black Classic, 1997), 55; W. Fitzhugh Brundage, *Lynching in the New South: Georgia and Virginia, 1880–1930* (Urbana: University of Illinois Press, 1993), 2.

43. Sanders, *Negro Child Welfare in North Carolina*, 185.

44. Ibid.

45. Ibid., 193; Wiley B. Sanders and William C. Ezell, *Juvenile Court Cases in North Carolina, 1929–1934* (Raleigh, NC: State Board of Charities and Public Welfare, 1937).

46. Sanders and Ezell, *Juvenile Court Cases in North Carolina.*

47. Ibid.

48. Ibid.

49. Sanders, *Negro Child Welfare in North Carolina*, 197.

50. Ibid., 193.

51. Ibid. (quotes).

52. Sanders, *Negro Child Welfare in North Carolina*, 194. See also Schlossman and Wallach, "The Crime of Precocious Sexuality"; Mary E. Odem, *Delinquent Daughters: Protecting*

and Policing Adolescent Female Sexuality in the United States, 1885–1920 (Chapel Hill: University of North Carolina Press, 1985); and Chesney-Lind, "Judicial Paternalism and the Female Status Offender."

53. Sanders, *Negro Child Welfare in North Carolina*, 194–95.

54. Ibid., 192.

55. Ibid., 192–93, 195.

56. For related discussions of the negotiated order of social control, see Mary Ellen Curtin, *Black Prisoners and Their World, Alabama, 1865–1900* (Charlottesville: University Press of Virginia, 2000); and Michael Ignatieff, "State, Civil Society and Total Institutions: A Critique of Recent Social Histories of Punishment," in *Crime and Justice* 3 (1981): 153–92.

57. Tennessee Board of Prison Commissioners, *Report to the Governor*, quoted in Randall G. Shelden, "From Slave to Caste Society: Penal Changes in Tennessee, 1830–1915," *Tennessee Historical Quarterly* 38 (1979): 470. See also Donald G. Nieman, ed., *Black Southerners and the Law, 1865–1900* (New York: Garland, 1994), 308; Bureau of the Census, *Prisoners and Juvenile Delinquents in the United States, 1910*; and Mark T. Carleton, *Politics and Punishment: The History of the Louisiana State Penal System* (Baton Rouge: Louisiana State University Press, 1971), 96.

58. Oshinsky, *Worse Than Slavery*, 149–52, 46–48; Mennel, *Thorns and Thistles*, 76.

59. Sanders, *Negro Child Welfare in North Carolina*, 263. See also John Dittmer, *Black Georgia in the Progressive Era, 1900–1920* (Urbana: University of Illinois Press, 1980); and Douglas A. Blackmon, *Slavery by Another Name: The Re-Enslavement of Black People in America from the Civil War to World War II* (New York: Doubleday, 2008).

60. Matthew J. Mancini, *One Dies, Get Another: Convict Leasing in the American South, 1866–1928* (Columbia: University of South Carolina Press, 1996), 222.

61. Alex Lichtenstein, *Twice the Work of Free Labor: The Political Economy of Convict Labor in the New South* (New York: Verso, 1996), 180–82. See also Hilda Jane Zimmerman, "The Penal Reform Movement in the South during the Progressive Period, 1890–1917," *Journal of Southern History* 17 (1951): 462–92; and J. H. Jones, "Penitentiary Reform in Mississippi," *Publications of the Mississippi Historical Society* 6 (1902): 111–28.

62. Vardaman quoted in Rowland, *Encyclopedia of Mississippi History*, 391; Carleton, *Politics and Punishment*; Lichtenstein, *Twice the Work of Free Labor*, 166, 181 (last quote); Mancini, *One Dies, Get Another*, 23.

63. Cited in Alex Lichtenstein, "Good Roads and Chain Gangs in the Progressive South: 'The Negro Convict Is a Slave,'" *Journal of Southern History* 59, no. 1 (1993): 107. See also Blackmon, *Slavery by Another Name*.

64. Convict work gangs took several forms, ranging from road gangs in the Southeast, to penal farms in the Southwest, to factories in border states (Lichtenstein, *Twice the Work of Free Labor*).

65. Lichtenstein, *Twice the Work of Free Labor*, 180. Of course, black contemporaries were outraged. See, e.g., M. Louise Jenkins, "Do We Need Reformatories?" *National Notes* (National Association of Colored Women's Clubs) 3, no. 8 (1900): 1, 3; W. E. B. DuBois, "Crime," *The Crisis* 8, no. 2 (1914): 64; and Josephine T. Washington, "Child Saving in Alabama," *Colored American Magazine* 14 (1908): 48–51.

66. David Wolcott and Steven Schlossman, "Punishing Serious Juvenile Offenders: Crime, Racial Disparity, and the Incarceration of Adolescents in Adult Prison in Late Nineteenth- and Early Twentieth-Century Pennsylvania," in *Beyond Empiricism: Institutions and Intentions in the Study of Crime*, ed. J. McCord (New Brunswick, NJ: Transaction, 2004), 44–45, 47.

67. Shelden, "From Slave to Caste Society," 476. These practices persisted at this training school until criticisms and civil rights agitation forced its integration in 1967, after which conditions are said to have improved (ibid.).

68. John Dittmer, *Black Georgia in the Progressive Era, 1900–1920* (Urbana: University of Illinois Press, 1977), xi.

CHAPTER FOUR

1. Iris M. Young, *Justice and the Politics of Difference* (Princeton, NJ: Princeton University Press, 1990), 38. Young states that oppression "consists in systematic institutional processes which prevent some people from learning and using satisfying and expansive skills in socially recognized settings, or institutionalized social processes which inhibit people's ability to . . . express their feelings and perspectives on social life in contexts where others can listen." Others characterize oppression as a systematic denial of conditions for "capability." See Amartya Sen, *Inequality Reexamined* (New York: Oxford University Press, 1992); and Martha C. Nussbaum, *Sex and Social Justice* (New York: Oxford University Press, 1999). For a review of these perspectives, see Iris M. Young, *Inclusion and Democracy* (New York: Oxford University Press, 2002), chap. 1.

2. According to Young, domination "consists in institutional conditions which inhibit or prevent people from participating in determining their actions or the conditions of their actions. Persons live within structures of domination if other persons or groups can determine without reciprocation the conditions of their actions, either directly or by virtue of structural [conditions]" (*Justice and the Politics of Difference*, 38). Other deliberative theories of social justice define freedom, in part, as a condition of "nondomination" (Philip Pettit, *Republicanism: A Theory of Freedom and Government* [New York: Oxford University Press, 1997], 26) or "participatory parity" (Nancy Fraser, "Rethinking the Public Sphere: A Contribution to the Critique of Actually Existing Democracy," *Social Text*, nos. 25–26 [1990]: 74).

3. Young, *Justice and the Politics of Difference*, 9.

4. Steven Hahn, *A Nation under Our Feet: Black Political Struggles in the Rural South, from Slavery to the Great Migration* (Cambridge, MA: Harvard University Press, 2003); Douglas Flamming, *Bound for Freedom: Black Los Angeles in Jim Crow America* (Berkeley and Los Angeles: University of California Press, 2005), 47; Lawrence B. De Graaf, "The City of Black Angels: Emergence of the Los Angeles Ghetto, 1890–1930," *Pacific Historical Review* 39, no. 3 (1970): 323–52.

5. The limited historical work on juvenile justice in the American West has dealt sparingly with race and ethnicity and emphasized Mexican and Mexican American youth experiences. See Mary E. Odem, *Delinquent Daughters: Protecting and Policing Adolescent Female Sexuality in the United States, 1885–1920* (Chapel Hill: University of North Carolina Press, 1985); Miroslava Chávez-García, "Youth, Evidence, and Agency: Mexican and Mexican American Youth at the Whittier State School, 1890–1920," *Aztlán: A Journal of Chicano Studies* 31, no. 2 (2006): 55–83, and "Intelligence Testing at Whittier School, 1890–1920," *Pacific Historical Review* 76, no. 2 (2007): 193–228; and William S. Bush, "James Dean and Jim Crow: Boys in the Texas Juvenile Justice System in the 1950s," in *Lost Kids: Vulnerable Children and Youth in North America, 1900 to the Present*, ed. Mona Gleason, Tamara Myers, Leslie Paris, and Veronica Strong-Boag (Vancouver: University of British Columbia Press, 2009), 72–94.

6. See Quintard Taylor, *In Search of the Racial Frontier: African Americans in the American West, 1528–1990* (New York: Norton, 1999); Lawrence B. De Graaf, "Race, Sex, and

Region: Black Women in the American West, 1850–1920," *Pacific Historical Review* 49, no. 2 (1980): 285–313, and "The City of Black Angels"; and Flamming, *Bound for Freedom*.

7.   See W. E. B. DuBois, *Black Reconstruction in America, 1860–1880* (New York: Harcourt, Brace, 1935); Leon Litwack, *Trouble in Mind: Black Southerners in the Age of Jim Crow* (New York: Vintage, 1998); and James D. Anderson, *The Education of Blacks in the South, 1860–1935* (Chapel Hill: University of North Carolina Press, 1988).

8.   Margaret W. Cahalan, *Historical Corrections Statistics in the United States, 1850–1984* (Washington, DC: U.S. Department of Justice, Bureau of Justice Statistics, 1986), 113.

9.   Eileen Boris, "Reconstructing the 'Family': Women, Progressive Reform, and the Problem of Social Control," in *Gender, Class, Race, and Reform in the Progressive Era,* ed. Noralee Frankel and Nancy S. Dye (Lexington: University Press of Kentucky, 1991), 73–86.

10. Miroslava Chávez-García writes: "Much of the African American reform school population had recently migrated to California. In the early 1900s, that populace in southern California was relatively small, though it expanded significantly from 1900 to 1920 as a result of migration. . . . Similarly, a significant proportion of [black] youth who ended up at Whittier [reformatory] came to the golden state during this period. Yet, many did so with few immediate family members—some even came alone, 'bumming' on railroad cars—indicating that they had little, if any, sources of support in the region. Doubtless, African American children and adolescents, who knew they had few immediate or extended family members or friends from whom to seek assistance, thought twice about running away" ("Youth, Evidence, and Agency," 65–66).

11. George B. Nesbitt, "The Negro Race Relations Expert and Negro Community Leadership," *Journal of Negro Education* 21, no. 2 (1952): 148–60; Dorothy C. Salem, *To Better Our World: Black Women in Organized Reform, 1890–1920* (Brooklyn, NY: Carlson, 1990); Deborah G. White, *Too Heavy a Load: Black Women in Defense of Themselves, 1894–1994* (New York: Norton, 1999).

12. Odem, *Delinquent Daughters,* 120.

13. Blacks averaged 17 percent of the Texas population from 1900 to 1940, compared to 1 percent of the California population in the same span (Campbell Gibson and Kay Jung, *Historical Census Statistics on Population Totals by Race, 1790 to 1990, and by Hispanic Origin, 1970 to 1990, for the United States, Regions, Divisions, and States,* Population Division Working Paper no. 56 [Washington, DC: U.S. Census Bureau, 2002]). Many black Texans later migrated to California (Flamming, *Bound for Freedom*).

14. Quoted in Lee F. Gustafson, "An Historical and Network Analysis of the Juvenile Justice System in the Austin, Texas Metropolitan Area" (Ph.D. diss., University of Texas at Austin, 1997), 25.

15. Ibid. Another leading member of the University of Texas law faculty, W. S. Simkins, a former Confederate general and founding member of the Ku Klux Klan, delivered a rallying speech entitled "Why the Ku Klux Klan" at the law school. It was printed in the 1916 alumni newsletter. The school was not integrated until 1950, when the U.S. Supreme Court ruled against its segregation policy in the case of *Sweatt v. Painter* (see Dwonna N. Goldstone, "Heman Sweatt and the Racial Integration of the University of Texas School of Law," *Journal of Blacks in Higher Education* 54 [Winter 2006]: 88–97).

16. Gustafson, "Historical and Network Analysis of the Juvenile Justice System," 25–27. In Houston alone, 25 percent of the 4,287 delinquents reported during the period 1939–42 were black (Herb A. Bloch and Frank T. Flynn, *Delinquency: The Juvenile Offender in America Today* [New York: Random House, 1956], 47).

17. On the characterization of *colored* as a foreign nationality, see Sherman Kingsley, "Study of Several Departments of Work Carried on by the Juvenile Court of Wayne County, Michigan and Its Relationship to Various Public and Private Agencies Which Cooperate Actively with the Court" (1928), folder 8, box 157, United Community Services Central Files, Archives of Labor and Urban Affairs, Walter P. Reuther Library, Wayne State University; and Bloch and Flynn, *Delinquency*. One of the earliest anti-slavery tracts (1737) characterized blacks as a foreign species or "extravasat Blood" within the nation that could not be assimilated and would have to be expelled: "There is such a disparity in their Conditions, Colour & Hair, that they can never embody with us, and grow up into orderly Families, to the peopling of the land [and yet] still remain in our Body Politick as a kind of extravasat Blood" (Samuel Sewall, *The Selling of Joseph: A Memorial* [1700], ed. Sidney Kaplan [Amherst: University of Massachusetts Press, 1969], 10).

18. Raymond L. Manell, "Racially Integrating a State's Training Schools," *Children* 11, no. 2 (1964): 49–54; Gustafson, "Historical and Network Analysis of the Juvenile Justice System." See also Bush, "James Dean and Jim Crow."

19. Quoted in Anne M. Knupfer, *Toward a Tenderer Humanity and a Nobler Womanhood: African American Women's Clubs in Turn-of-the-Century Chicago* (New York: New York University Press, 1996), 41.

20. Mary Lynn McCree Bryan and Allen F. Davis, eds., *100 Years at Hull House* (Bloomington, Indiana University Press, 1990), 134 (quote); Margaret K. Rosenheim, Franklin F. Zimring, David S. Tanenhaus, and Bernardine Dohrn, eds., *A Century of Juvenile Justice* (Chicago: University of Chicago Press, 2002), 287. See also M. A. Flanagan, "The Predicament of New Rights: Suffrage and Women's Political Power from a Local Perspective," *Social Politics: International Studies in Gender, State and Society* 2, no. 3 (1995): 305–30.

21. Robert Gould Shaw House, *Robert Gould Shaw House: A Social Settlement Primarily for Negroes*, First Annual Report (Boston: Robert Gould Shaw House, 1908), 1–2. See also Lawrence J. Vale, *From the Puritans to the Projects: Public Housing and Public Neighbors* (Cambridge, MA: Harvard University Press, 2000), 84.

22. See Tera Hunter, "Historical Note on 'Special Report on Negro Domestic Service in the Seventh Ward,'" in W. E. B. DuBois, *The Philadelphia Negro: A Social Study* (1899; reprint, Philadelphia: University of Pennsylvania Press, 1996), 425–26.

23. Robert Gould Shaw House, *Robert Gould Shaw House*. By the 1920s and 1930s, Shaw House was jointly led by white and black Bostonians. See Elisabeth Lasch-Quinn, *Black Neighbors: Race and the Limits of Reform in the American Settlement House Movement, 1890–1945* (Chapel Hill: University of North Carolina Press, 1993), 29; Inabel B. Lindsay, "Adult Education Programs for Negroes in Settlement Houses," *Journal of Negro Education* 14, no. 3 (1945): 347–52; W. E. B. DuBois, "Looking Glass," *The Crisis* 22, no. 1 (1921): 227; and Vale, *From the Puritans to the Projects*, 84–86.

24. Charles S. Johnson, *A Study of Delinquent and Neglected Negro Children Before the New York City Children's Court* (New York: Joint Committee on Negro Child Study, 1925), 13.

25. Ibid., 1.

26. Ibid., 26.

27. Ibid., 28, 11.

28. Davis quoted in Robert M. Mennel, *Thorns and Thistles: Juvenile Delinquents in the United States, 1825–1940* (Hanover, NH: University Press of New England, 1973), 121. This race-linked division of labor and education was common to early integrated reformatories. See Alexander W. Pisciotta, "Race, Sex, and Rehabilitation: A Study of Differential Treatment in the Juvenile Reformatory, 1825–1900," *Crime and Delinquency* 29, no. 2 (1983): 254–69; and Randall G. Shelden, "From Slave to Caste Society: Penal Changes in Tennessee, 1830–1915," *Tennessee Historical Quarterly* 38 (1979): 462–78.

29. Wiley B. Sanders, *Negro Child Welfare in North Carolina* (Chapel Hill: University of North Carolina Press, 1933), 198.

30. Ibid., 197–99.

31. Ralph Ginzburg, *100 Years of Lynchings* (Baltimore: Black Classic, 1997), 90; W. Fitzhugh Brundage, *Lynching in the New South: Georgia and Virginia, 1880–1930* (Urbana: University of Illinois Press, 1993), 30, 258.

32. Several researchers note the specific role of all-white juries in discriminatory capital sentencing decisions (for a review, see Sherri L. Johnson, "Black Innocence and the White Jury," *Michigan Law Review* 83, no. 7 [1985]: 1611–1708). It is also well established that black Americans are generally opposed to the death penalty (see Robert L. Young, "Race, Conceptions of Crime and Justice, and Support for the Death Penalty," *Social Psychology Quarterly* 54, no. 1 [1991]: 67–75). This opposition is based largely on concerns about discrimination.

33. M. Watt Espy and John Ortiz Smykla, *Executions in the United States, 1608–2002*, database/computer file (Ann Arbor, MI: Inter-University Consortium for Political and Social Research, 2004).

34. Of the 15,269 executions recorded in Espy and Smykla, *Executions in the United States, 1608–2002*, age data are missing for 52 percent, or 7,958 cases. Nearly half these cases (3,645) occur in the pre-1865 period, where age is unknown in 91 percent of executions. Age data improve over time, with age unknown in 67 percent of period 2 cases, 47 percent of period 3 cases, and 15 percent of period 4 cases. Age data are missing in black executions (60 percent) more often than in white executions (39 percent) for the entire reporting period and within each defined subperiod. The Espy and Smykla data thus provide the most comprehensive basis for estimating racial disparity in juvenile executions, despite being limited and conservative.

35. These racial group differences and historical patterns remain when limiting the class of executed "youths" to offenders under age eighteen. In the period considered, 159 such executions occurred, with 67 percent involving black youths. Eighteen-year-olds are included because of the sheer number of such cases and because age markers reference the date of execution rather than age at the time of offense, when most were likely under eighteen years of age.

36. Espy and Smykla, *Executions in the United States, 1608–2002*. Texas reported three Latino youth executions. Remaining executions in this group of southern states involved black youths.

37. John Dittmer, *Local People: The Struggle for Civil Rights in Mississippi* (Urbana: University of Illinois Press, 1995). "Although blacks were not yet organized to demand their rights," Dittmer writes, "rumors spread across the state that they were stockpiling weapons . . . for use in a race war now that so many white men were away [at war]" (ibid., 14).

38. Ibid., 14–15.

39. Christopher Hitchens, "Old Enough to Die," *Vanity Fair*, June 1999, 76–80; Victor Streib, *Death Penalty for Juveniles* (Bloomington: Indiana University Press, 1987).

40. Following Emile Durkheim's thesis of legal rationalism, several researchers suggest that racist applications of capital punishment, or "legal lynchings," "substituted" for racially motivated lynching. See Emile Durkheim, "The Evolution of Punishment" (1901), in *Durkheim and the Law*, ed. Steven Lukes and Andrew Scull (New York: St. Martin's, 1983). See also Stewart Tolnay and E. M. Beck, *A Festival of Violence: An Analysis of Southern Lynchings, 1882–1930* (Urbana: University of Illinois Press, 1995); Franklin E. Zimring, *The Contradictions of American Capital Punishment* (New York: Oxford University Press, 2003); and James W. Clarke, "Without Fear or Shame: Lynching, Capital Punishment and the Subculture of Violence in the American South," *British Journal of Political Science* 28, no. 2 (2001): 269–89. Evidence also exists of a relation between historical lynchings and later interracial southern homicides, including police killings. See Steven F. Messner, R. D. Baller, and M. P. Zevenbergen, "The Legacy of Lynching and Southern Homicide," *American Sociological Review* 70, no. 4 (2005): 633–55; and Brundage, *Lynching in the New South*, 252–56.

41. Following a 1917 race riot in Houston where seventeen whites were killed, thirteen black soldiers were sentenced to hang and another forty-one received life sentences. Baltimore's black newspaper, the *Daily Herald*, reported: "The thirteen unfortunates died because southern prejudice, hatred, and brutality clamored for Negro blood in revenge for the shedding of the blood of white men, and no penalty short of death would appease their gory thirst" (quoted in W. E. B. DuBois, "The Houston Horror," *The Crisis* 15, no. 4 [1918]: 188).

42. Roy Wilkins, "The Battle to Save Sharecropper Waller," *The Crisis* 48, no. 1 (1941): 23; Gloria J. Browne-Marshall, *Race, Law, and American Society: 1607 to Present* (New York: Routledge, 2007), 165; J. Douglas Smith, *Managing White Supremacy: Race, Politics, and Citizenship in Jim Crow Virginia* (Chapel Hill: University of North Carolina Press, 2002), 52; Albert French, *Billy: A Novel* (New York: Penguin, 1993).

43. "Execution of Two Youths Halted," *Chicago Defender* (national ed.), January 25, 1947. The convictions and sentences were affirmed by the Mississippi Supreme Court, and the U.S. Supreme Court denied review of the cases (Mary L. Dudziak, "Desegregation as a Cold War Imperative," *Stanford Law Review* 41, no. 1 [1988]: 61–120).

44. William L. Patterson, *We Charge Genocide* (New York: Civil Rights Congress, 1951), 63. Mississippi representative John Rankin sought to rebuff international and national condemnation, including opposition from some members of Congress, by dismissing the protestors as "a few communistic intermeddlers" ("Rankin Raves at Effort to Save Boys from Death," *Chicago Defender* [national ed.], January 25, 1947).

45. "Boys, 15, to Die Jan. 17," *Chicago Defender* (national ed.), January 18, 1947.

46. "Execution of Two Youths Halted," *Chicago Defender* (national ed.), January 25, 1947; "Boy Victims of Caste System Slain by Law in Mississippi," *Chicago Defender* (national ed.), August 2, 1947; Angela Y. Davis, *Abolition Democracy: Beyond Empire, Prisons, and Torture* (New York: Seven Stories, 2005), 36–37; Tolnay and Beck, *A Festival of Violence*.

47. Mark Colvin, *Penitentiaries, Reformatories, and Chain Gangs: Social Theory and the History of Punishment in Nineteenth-Century America* (New York: St. Martin's, 1997), 231–33.

48. Litwack, *Trouble in Mind*, 249.

49. W. E. B. DuBois, *Efforts for Social Betterment among Negro Americans* (Atlanta: Atlanta University Press, 1909), 127.

50. W. E. B. DuBois, "Editorial," *The Crisis* 6, no. 4 (1913): 184–86, cited in Irene Diggs, "Du Bois and Children," *Phylon* 37, no. 4 (1976): 379–80. See also Elliott M. Rudwick, "W. E. B. Du Bois in the Role of *Crisis* Editor," *Journal of Negro History* 43, no. 3 (1958): 215.

51. See Geoff Ward, "Race and the Justice Workforce: A System Perspective," in *The Many Colors of Crime: Inequalities of Race, Ethnicity, and Crime in America*, ed. Ruth D. Peterson, Lauren J. Krivo, and John Hagan (New York: New York University Press, 2006); W. Marvin Dulaney, *Black Police in America, Blacks in the Diaspora* (Bloomington: Indiana University Press, 1996); and J. Clay Smith, *Emancipation: The Making of the Black Lawyer, 1844–1944* (Philadelphia: University of Pennsylvania Press, 1993).

52. See Elliott M. Rudwick, "The Negro Policeman in the South," *Journal of Criminal Law, Criminology, and Police Science* 51 (1960): 273–76, and "The Southern Negro Policeman and the White Offender," *Journal of Negro Education* 30, no. 4 (1961): 426–31; Dulaney, *Black Police in America*; Inabel Burns Lindsay, "Race as a Factor in the Caseworker's Role," *Journal of Social Casework* 28, no. 3 (1947): 101–7.

53. Moya Woodside, *Sterilization in North Carolina: A Sociological and Psychological Study* (Chapel Hill: University of North Carolina Press, 1950), 83.

54. Ibid., 150.

55. Ibid., 38–39.

56. Ibid., 170.

57. On the concept of structural violence, see Johan Galtung, "Violence, Peace, and Peace Research," *Journal of Peace Research* 6, no. 3 (1969): 167–91; and Giovanna Borradori, *Philosophy in a Time of Terror: Dialogues with Jürgen Habermas and Jacques Derrida* (Chicago: University of Chicago Press, 2003), 63. For a critique, see C. A. J. Coady, "The Idea of Violence," *Journal of Applied Philosophy* 3, no. 1 (1986): 3–19. The concept of power threat has typically been used to theorize white racial group mobilization against threats to whites' dominant social status. See Allen E. Liska, *Social Threat and Social Control* (Albany: State University of New York Press, 1992).

CHAPTER FIVE

1. Fortune quoted in Charles Harris Wesley, ed., *The History of the National Association of Colored Women's Clubs: A Legacy of Service* (Washington, DC: National Association of Colored Women's Clubs, 1984), 24. See also Josephine T. Washington, "Child Saving in Alabama," *Colored American Magazine* 14 (1908): 48–51.

2. See W. E. B. DuBois, *Black Reconstruction in America, 1860–1880* (New York: Harcourt, Brace, 1935); and John Hope Franklin and Alfred A. Moss, eds., *From Slavery to Freedom* (1947), 6th ed. (New York: Knopf, 1988).

3. "Our Correspondents Interview a Catholic Priest and Find the Church Does Discriminate," *Cleveland Gazette*, October 26, 1886, 1; Wesley, ed., *The History of the National Association of Colored Women's Clubs*, 296.

4. Deborah G. White, *Too Heavy a Load: Black Women in Defense of Themselves, 1894–1994* (New York: Norton, 1999), 27 (motto quoted); Mark R. Schneider, *Boston Confronts Jim Crow, 1890–1920* (Boston: Northeastern University Press, 1997), 96. See also Dorothy C. Salem, *To Better Our World: Black Women in Organized Reform, 1890–1920* (Brooklyn, NY: Carlson, 1990).

5. Darlene C. Hine, Elsa B. Brown, and Rosalyn Terborg-Penn, eds., *Black Women in*

America, 3 vols. (New York: Oxford University Press, 1993), 3:88–91; Schneider, *Boston Confronts Jim Crow*, 95–98.

6. Louis R. Harlan and Raymond W. Smock, eds., *The Booker T. Washington Papers, 1899–1900*, 14 vols. (Urbana: University of Illinois Press), 5:560n2; "Address of Josephine St. Pierre Ruffin, President of Conference, August 1895 [to the National Conference of Colored Women, Boston, July 29–August 1, 1895," *Woman's Era* 2, no. 5 (1895): 14 (quotes). The *Women's Era* is available online at http://womenwriters .library.emory.edu/toc.php?id=era2.

7. "Address of Josephine St. Pierre Ruffin, President of Conference, August 1895," 14. See also White, *Too Heavy a Load*; Julia Sudbury, *Other Kinds of Dreams: Black Women's Organisations and the Politics of Transformation* (New York: Routledge, 1998); and Cecilia O'Leary, *To Die For: The Paradox of American Patriotism* (Princeton, NJ: Princeton University Press, 1999).

8. White, *Too Heavy a Load*, 27–35; Wesley, ed., *The History of the National Association of Colored Women's Clubs*, 51–53.

9. M. Louise Jenkins, "Do We Need Reformatories?" *National Notes* (National Association of Colored Women's Clubs) 3, no. 8 (1900): 3 (quotes); Wesley, ed., *The History of the National Association of Colored Women's Clubs*, 41–43 (on the conference resolution).

10. On the class structure of black communities and related distinctions in the class politics of black clubwomen, see Adam Fairclough, *Better Day Coming: Blacks and Equality, 1890–2000* (New York: Penguin, 2002), 32; Katrina Bell McDonald, *Embracing Sisterhood: Class, Identity, and Contemporary Black Women* (Lanham, MD: Rowman & Littlefield, 2007), 53–56; Gerda Lerner, "Early Community Work of Black Club Women," *Journal of Negro History* 59, no. 2 (1974): 158–67; Anne M. Knupfer, *Toward a Tenderer Humanity and a Nobler Womanhood: African American Women's Clubs in Turn-of-the-Century Chicago* (New York: New York University Press, 1996), 21–26; and Anne F. Scott, "Most Invisible of All: Black Women's Voluntary Associations," *Journal of Southern History* 56, no. 1 (1990): 3–22.

11. Hine, Brown, and Terborg-Penn, eds., *Black Women in America*, 1:661.

12. Frances Joseph-Gaudet, *He Leadeth Me: African American Women Writers, 1910–1940* (1913; reprint, New York: Prentice-Hall, 1996), 141 (quote); Hine, Brown, and Terborg-Penn, eds., *Black Women in America*, 1:661; Dorothy C. Salem, ed., *African American Women: A Biographical Dictionary*, 2 vols. (New York: Garland, 1993), 2:295–96.

13. Lee McCrae, "Birmingham's Probation Plan for the Little Negro," *Charities and Commons: A Weekly Journal of Philanthropy and Social Advance* 19 (1908): 1729.

14. Ibid.

15. Josephine T. Washington, "What Our Women in Alabama Have Done," *National Notes* (National Association of Colored Women's Clubs) 15, no. 5 (February 1912): 10–13.

16. McCrae, "Birmingham's Probation Plan for the Little Negro," 1729; Washington, "What Our Women in Alabama Have Done."

17. McCrae, "Birmingham's Probation Plan for the Little Negro," 1730.

18. Washington, "Child Saving in Alabama," 48–51.

19. Racial violence was often directed at black educational reformers and institutions in the Progressive Era South. See DuBois, *Black Reconstruction in America*, 645–46; and Leon Litwack, *Trouble in Mind: Black Southerners in the Age of Jim Crow* (New York: Vintage, 1998), 87–88.

20. Washington, "Child Saving in Alabama," 48–51.

21. Cornelia Bowen, "Club Life in Alabama," *National Notes* (National Association of Colored Women's Clubs) 16, no. 5 (May 1913); White, *Too Heavy a Load*, 28.

22. L. H. Hammond, "Negro Boys Make Good," *Survey* 32 (1914): 603.

23. John H. Smyth, "Negro Delinquent Children in Virginia," address presented at the Twenty-fifth National Conference of Charities and Correction, New York, May 19, 1898, reproduced in Isabel Barrows, ed., *Proceedings of the National Conference of Charities and Correction at the 25th Annual Session Held in the City of New York, May 18–25, 1898* (Boston: Geo. H. Ellis, 1899), 471–73.

24. Ibid.

25. Mary W. Ovington, *Portraits in Color* (New York: Viking, 1927), 181–82.

26. Winona Hall, "Janie Porter Barrett, Her Life and Contributions to Social Welfare in Virginia" (M.S.W. thesis, Howard University School of Social Work, 1954), 15.

27. William A. Aery, "Helping Wayward Girls: Virginia's Pioneer Work," *Southern Workman* 44 (1915): 598–604; Hall, "Janie Porter Barrett," 15–17.

28. Ovington, *Portraits in Color*, 190.

29. Ibid., 186.

30. Hall, "Janie Porter Barrett," 19; personal correspondence with E. Franklin Frazier, folder 18, box 131–39, E. Franklin Frazier Papers, Moorland-Spingarn Research Center, Howard University.

31. Florence Kelley, "A Burglar Four Years Old in the Memphis Juvenile Court," *The Survey*, June 20, 1914, 318.

32. Benjamin L. Hooks and Jerry Guess, *The March for Civil Rights: The Benjamin Hooks Story* (Chicago: American Bar Association, 2003), 2.

33. Ibid., 3.

34. Hine, Brown, and Terborg-Penn, eds., *Black Women in America*, 1:572; Hooks and Guess, *The March for Civil Rights*, 4–5.

35. Hine, Brown, and Terborg-Penn, eds., *Black Women in America*, 1:572; Hooks and Guess, *The March for Civil Rights*, 7–8.

36. James W. Davidson, *"They Say": Ida B. Wells and the Reconstruction of Race* (New York: Oxford University Press, 2007), 64–82; Trudier Harris, introduction to *Selected Works of Ida B. Wells-Barnett*, comp. Trudier Harris (New York: Oxford University Press, 1991), 4–6.

37. Harris, introduction to *Selected Works of Ida B. Wells-Barnett*, 5. As Herbert Shapiro notes, Mary Terrell's reaction to the lynching suggests the multidimensional impact of racial violence. Terrell gave birth to a child shortly after the lynching, but her newborn died a few days later. She attributed the premature death to stress and depression caused by the lynching. Terrell also wondered whether it was divine intervention, saving the child from "the horror . . . and bitterness which filled her soul, [and] might have seriously affected the unborn child . . . if he had lived." See Herbert Shapiro, *White Violence and Black Response: From Reconstruction to Montgomery* (Amherst: University of Massachusetts Press, 1988), 479.

38. Harris, introduction to *Selected Works of Ida B. Wells-Barnett*, 5–6.

39. Hine, Brown, and Terborg-Penn, eds., *Black Women in America*, 1:572–73; Harris, introduction to *Selected Works of Ida B. Wells-Barnett*, 4–5.

40. Kelley, "A Burglar Four Years Old in the Memphis Juvenile Court," 318.

41. Hine, Brown, and Terborg-Penn, eds., *Black Women in America*, 1:572–73.

42. Julia Hooks, "Duty of the Hour" (1894), reproduced in *Afro-American Encyclopedia; or, The Thoughts, Doings, and Sayings of the Race*, comp. James T. Haley (Nashville:

Haley & Florida, 1895), 332–39. See also Hooks and Guess, *The March for Civil Rights*, 7–8; Hine, Brown, and Terborg-Penn, eds., *Black Women in America*, 1:572–73; and Julia Hooks, "Industrial Education for Negroes" (1895), reproduced in Haley, comp., *Afro-American Encyclopedia*, 170–73.

43. "Julia Hooks: An Activist and Educator with a Passion," African American Registry, http://www.aaregistry.org/historic_events/view/julia-hooks-activist-and-educator-passion (copy in author's files).

44. The date of death is reported by Officer Down Memorial Page as August 29, 1917. See http://www.odmp.org/officer/17579-detention-officer-charles-f.-hooks. On the lack of a criminal investigation, see Hooks and Guess, *The March for Civil Rights*, 5.

45. Kelley, "A Burglar Four Years Old in the Memphis Juvenile Court," 319; Hooks and Guess, *The March for Civil Rights*, 8. See also Jennifer Trost, *Gateway to Justice: The Juvenile Court and Progressive Child Welfare in a Southern City* (Athens: University of Georgia Press, 2005).

46. Hine, Brown, and Terborg-Penn, eds., *Black Women in America*, 1:573.

47. Bureau of the Census, *Prisoners and Juvenile Delinquents in the United States, 1910* (Washington, DC: U.S. Department of Commerce, 1918).

48. "History of the Oklahoma Federation of Colored Women's Clubs, Inc., 1900–1982" (n.p., n.d.), 4 (quote) (copy in author's files); W. H. Tatum, "Oklahoma," *National Notes* (National Association of Colored Women's Clubs) 18, no. 2 (1915); H. P. Jacobson, "From Oklahoma," *National Notes* (National Association of Colored Women's Clubs) 16, no. 5 (1913): 5; "Tulsa: History of City Federation of Colored Women," *Sooner Woman* 2, no. 2 (1951).

49. "History of the Oklahoma Federation of Colored Women's Clubs."

50. Mildred P. Williams, "Forty Years of Climbing," *Sooner Woman* 1 (June 1950): 5.

51. Etta B. Rowe, "Fairwold Industrial School for Colored Girls," *National Notes* (National Association of Colored Women's Clubs) 28, no. 6 (March 1926): 11–12.

52. Joan Marie Johnson, "The Colors of Social Welfare in the New South: Black and White Clubwomen in South Carolina, 1900–1930," in *Before the New Deal: Social Welfare in the South, 1830–1930*, ed. E. C. Green (Athens: University of Georgia Press, 1999), 173.

53. Ibid.; Rowe, "Fairwold Industrial School for Colored Girls."

54. See Geoff Ward, "The 'Other' Child Savers: Racial Politics of the Parental State," in Anthony M. Platt, *The Child Savers: The Invention of Delinquency* (1969), 40th anniversary ed. (New Brunswick, NJ: Rutgers University Press, 2009).

55. Sociologists use the concept of *collective action frames* or *injustice frames* to describe the ideological, constructionist ingredients present in any social movement. These frames organize movement adherents by inspiring and legitimating their activity and are, therefore, useful to understanding the organization of movements themselves. See Doug McAdam, ed., *Political Process and the Development of Black Insurgency, 1930–1970* (Chicago: University of Chicago Press, 1982).

56. White, *Too Heavy a Load*; Knupfer, *Toward a Tenderer Humanity and a Nobler Womanhood*.

57. Ellen Ryerson, *The Best-Laid Plans: America's Juvenile Court Experiment* (New York: Hill & Wang, 1978), 49–50. See also Platt, *The Child Savers*; Anthony Salerno, "The Child Saver Movement: Altruism or a Conspiracy?" *Juvenile and Family Court Journal* 42, no. 3 (1991): 37–49; and Randall G. Shelden and Lynn T. Osborne, "'For Their Own Good': Class Interests and the Child Saving Movement in Memphis, Tennessee, 1900–1917," *Criminology* 27, no. 4 (1991): 747–67.

58. Gerda Lerner, *Black Women in White America: A Documentary History* (New York: Vintage, 1992), 437.

59. Kevin Gaines, *Uplifting the Race: Black Leadership, Politics, and Culture in the Twentieth Century* (Chapel Hill: University of North Carolina Press, 1996), 15.

60. Anthony Platt, "The Child-Saving Movement and the Origins of the Juvenile Justice System," in *The Sociology of Juvenile Delinquency*, ed. Ronald J. Berger (Chicago: Nelson-Hall, 1991), 7.

61. Washington, "Child Saving in Alabama," 48–49.

62. Josephine Washington, "Impressions of a Southern Federation," *Colored American Magazine* (November 1904), quoted in Hine, Brown, and Terborg-Penn, eds., *Black Women in America*, 2:1233.

63. Aldon D. Morris, "Political Consciousness and Collective Action," in *Frontiers in Social Movement Theory*, ed. Aldon D. Morris and Carol McClurg Mueller (New Haven, CT: Yale University Press, 1992), 351. See also William H. Sewell, *Logics of History* (Chicago: University of Chicago Press, 2005). Morris suggests that the cultural and institutional dynamics of the black American experience have produced a race and class interaction in black political consciousness. Overlooking gender dimensions, he notes: "Blacks have been the victims of two vicious systems of human domination, one based on race and the other on class. They have developed a two-pronged oppositional consciousness because their very survival has depended on their understanding and combating both kinds of oppression." He continues: "Attainment of high class positions . . . has not cushioned [blacks] from harsh racial oppression. And their common oppression on the basis of race and class has always linked poor and working-class blacks" ("Political Consciousness and Collective Action," 365–66). See also Kimberle Crenshaw, "Mapping the Margins: Intersectionality, Identity Politics, and Violence against Women of Color," *Stanford Law Review* 43, no. 6 (1991): 1241–99; Patricia Hill-Collins, *Black Feminist Thought: Knowledge, Consciousness, and the Politics of Empowerment* (Boston: Unwin Hyman, 1990); and Doug McAdam, Sidney Tarrow, and Charles Tilly, *Dynamics of Contention* (New York: Cambridge University Press, 2001).

64. Johnson, "The Colors of Social Welfare in the New South," 169.

65. White, *Too Heavy a Load*, 27. On the Washington-DuBois debate, see David Levering Lewis, *W. E. B. Du Bois: Biography of a Race* (New York: Henry Holt, 1993); and Louis R. Harlan, *Booker T. Washington: The Wizard of Tuskegee, 1901–1915* (New York: Oxford University Press, 1986).

66. Booker T. Washington, review of *The Negro in the New World* by Sir Harry Johnston, *Journal of the Royal African Society* 10, no. 38 (1911): 177. See also Cynthia Neverdon-Morton, *Afro-American Women of the South and the Advancement of the Race, 1895–1925* (Knoxville: University of Tennessee Press, 1989); and James D. Anderson, *The Education of Blacks in the South, 1860–1935* (Chapel Hill: University of North Carolina Press, 1988).

67. W. E. B. DuBois, *The Souls of Black Folk* (1903; reprint, New York: Signet Classics, 1995), and "Hampton," *The Crisis* 15, no. 1 (1917): 11; Lewis, *W. E. B. Du Bois: Biography of a Race*, 238; Langston Hughes, introduction to *Up from Slavery*, by Booker T. Washington (New York: Dodd, Mead, 1965), vi.

68. According to Gaines: "The problem of racial uplift ideology is one of unconscious internalized racism. The racist and antiracist preoccupation with the status of the patriarchal family among blacks and the notion of self-help among blacks as building black homes and promoting family stability came to displace a broader vision of uplift as group struggle for citizenship and material advancement. At worst, this

misplaced equation of race progress . . . seemed to forget that it was the state and the constant threat of violence, not some innate racial trait, that prevented the realization of black homes and families" (*Uplifting the Race*, 6). White similarly stresses the "debilitating" character of uplift ideology (*Too Heavy a Load*, 270n11). See also Jeffrey Williams, "Benjamin Brawley and the Aesthetics of Racial Uplift," in *Race Struggles*, ed. Theodore Koditschek, Sundiata Keita Cha-Jua, and Helen A. Neville (Urbana: University of Illinois Press, 2009), 184; and Charles F. Peterson, *Dubois, Fanon, Cabral: The Margins of Elite Anti-Colonial Leadership* (Lanham, MD: Rowman & Littlefield, 2007), 52–53.

69. Alexander W. Pisciotta, "Race, Sex, and Rehabilitation: A Study of Differential Treatment in the Juvenile Reformatory, 1825–1900," *Crime and Delinquency* 29, no. 2 (1983): 262–63.

70. Mayer N. Zald, "Looking Backward to Look Forward: Reflections on the Past and Future of the Resource Mobilization Research Program," in Morris and Mueller, eds., *Frontiers in Social Movement Theory*, 332.

71. DuBois, *The Souls of Black Folk*, 645–46; Litwack, *Trouble in Mind*, 87–88 (Georgia resident quote).

72. Booker T. Washington, *Up from Slavery* (New York: A. L. Burt, 1901), 235; W. E. B. DuBois, "Education and Work," *Journal of Negro Education* 1, no. 1 (1915): 65.

73. Gaines, *Uplifting the Race*, 1.

74. Lerone Bennett Jr., *Before the Mayflower: A History of the Negro in America, 1619–1964* (New York: Penguin, 1968), 339–40.

75. See Lewis, *W. E. B. Du Bois: Biography of a Race*, 238; and Gaines, *Uplifting the Race*, xiv.

76. Anderson, *The Education of Blacks in the South*, 59–63.

77. Elizabeth Jacoway, *Yankee Missionaries in the South: The Penn School Experiment* (Baton Rouge: Louisiana State University Press, 1980), cited in Elisabeth Lasch-Quinn, *Black Neighbors: Race and the Limits of Reform in the American Settlement House Movement, 1890–1945* (Chapel Hill: University of North Carolina Press, 1993), 79–80.

78. See Mary E. Odem, *Delinquent Daughters: Protecting and Policing Adolescent Female Sexuality in the United States, 1885–1920* (Chapel Hill: University of North Carolina Press, 1985), 99; Linda Gordon, "The New Feminist Scholarship on the Welfare State," in *Women, the State and Welfare*, ed. Linda Gordon (Madison: University of Wisconsin Press, 1990); and Regina Kunzel, *Fallen Women, Problem Girls: Unmarried Mothers and the Professionalization of Social Work, 1890–1945* (New Haven, CT: Yale University Press, 1993).

79. Knupfer, *Toward a Tenderer Humanity and a Nobler Womanhood*, 11. See also Anderson, *The Education of Blacks in the South*, 59–63; and Douglas Flamming, *Bound for Freedom: Black Los Angeles in Jim Crow America* (Berkeley and Los Angeles: University of California Press, 2005), 31.

80. As Zald notes, social-psychological shifts are "a resource as well as an outcome of social movements" ("Looking Backward to Look Forward," 330).

81. Wesley, ed., *The History of the National Association of Colored Women's Clubs*, 281, 246; White, *Too Heavy a Load*, 32.

82. Washington, "Child Saving in Alabama," 50 (first quote); Rowe, "Fairwold Industrial School for Colored Girls," 11 (second quote).

83. Knupfer, *Toward a Tenderer Humanity and a Nobler Womanhood*, 72–74.

84. Gary Kremer, "System Failed Residents of Home for Negro Girls," *Jefferson City (MO) New Tribune*, June 21, 1998.

85. Aery, "Helping Wayward Girls," 603.

86. Washington, "Child Saving in Alabama," 51

87. Helen H. Ludlow, "Virginia's Negro Reform School: A Drop out of the Bucket," *Southern Workman* 33 (1904): 609; Negro Reformatory Association of Virginia, *Seventeenth Annual Report to the Board of Trustees* (Hanover, VA, 1916); Knupfer, *Toward a Tenderer Humanity and a Nobler Womanhood.*

88. W. E. B. DuBois, "Crime," *The Crisis* 8, no. 2 (1914): 64.

89. Knupfer, *Toward a Tenderer Humanity and a Nobler Womanhood,* 75 (quote); Louise D. Bowen, *The Colored People of Chicago* (Chicago: Juvenile Protective Association, 1913).

90. Neverdon-Morton, *Afro-American Women of the South and the Advancement of the Race,* 10–11. See also Adam Fairclough, "'Being in the Field of Education and Also Being a Negro . . . Seems . . . Tragic': Black Teachers in the Jim Crow South," *Journal of American History* 87, no. 1 (2000): 73–75; Gunnar Myrdal, *An American Dilemma: The Negro Problem and Modern Democracy* (New York: Harper & Bros., 1944), 881; and Donald J. Calista, "Booker T. Washington: Another Look," *Journal of Negro History* 49 (October 1964): 240–55.

91. Lerner, *Black Women in White America,* 451.

CHAPTER SIX

1. William Sewell Jr., "A Theory of Structure: Duality, Agency, and Transformation," *American Journal of Sociology* 98, no. 1 (1992): 1–29; Anthony Giddens, *The Constitution of Society* (Berkeley and Los Angeles: University of California Press, 1984). See also William H. Sewell, *Logics of History* (Chicago: University of Chicago Press, 2005).

2. George S. Nesbitt, "The Negro Race Relations Expert and Negro Community Leadership," *Journal of Negro Education* 21, no. 2 (1952): 148–60.

3. Sherman Kingsley, "Study of Several Departments of Work Carried on by the Juvenile Court of Wayne County, Michigan and Its Relationship to Various Public and Private Agencies Which Cooperate Actively with the Court" (1928), folder 8, box 157, United Community Services Central Files, Archives of Labor and Urban Affairs, Walter P. Reuther Library, Wayne State University.

4. Ibid., 4.

5. Ibid., 3–4 (quote); Nesbitt, "The Negro Race Relations Expert."

6. Alain Locke, "Enter the New Negro," in "Harlem: Mecca of the New Negro," ed. Alain Locke, special issue, *Survey Graphic* 6, no. 6 (1925): 632.

7. Lionel Bascom, *A Renaissance in Harlem* (New York: Amistad, 2001), 3–6 (first quote); John Henrik Clarke, ed., *Harlem: A Community in Transition* (New York: Citadel, 1964), 46.

8. Locke, ed., "Harlem: Mecca of the New Negro"; Bascom, *A Renaissance in Harlem,* 4 (second quote). James Weldon Johnson depicted Harlem as "the great Mecca for the sight-seer, the pleasure-seeker, the curious, the adventurous, the enterprising, the ambitious, and the talented of the whole Negro world; for the lure of it has reached down to every island of the Carib Sea and has penetrated even into Africa" ("The Making of Harlem," in Locke, ed., "Harlem: Mecca of the New Negro," 635).

9. Though a galvanizing force and inspiration to seize power, New Negro politics also created wedges in black leadership, fragmenting the notion of legitimate black representation, and weakening the cross-gender and -class alliances characteristic of the vanguard black child-saving movement. For discussions of gender and race divisions,

see White, *Too Heavy a Load*, 112, 120–32; and T. G. Standing, "Nationalism in Negro Leadership," *American Journal of Sociology* 40, no. 2 (1934): 180–203, 188–89. Initially, the divisions may have expanded the base of black leadership, but they proved costly to the long-term prospects of the black child-saving movement, especially as class divisions destabilized the foundations of black collective identification and efficacy.

10. Standing distinguished two types of "new black radicalism," of which DuBois and Garvey were representative. "One demands unconditional equality with the whites, and seeks this end through alliance with the communist movement, or such other similar organizations as welcome Negro support," he wrote, referencing DuBois. "The second division of the radical group," which Garvey represented, "has no patience with futile demands for racial equality, but advocates the frank repudiation of white standards and the substitution, where possible, of black ones." Standing, "Nationalism in Negro Leadership," 187.

11. Clarke, ed., *Harlem*, 14. Standing notes: "Garvey's success in winning over the Negro masses was in striking contrast with his failure to attract the clergy and the intelligentsia" ("Nationalism in Negro Leadership," 191). W. E. B. DuBois, Garvey's primary critic, accused him of seeking to "oppose white supremacy and the white ideal by a crude and equally brutal black supremacy and black ideal." "His mistake did not lie in the utter impossibility of this program," DuBois argued, "but rather in its spiritual bankruptcy and futility; for what shall this poor world gain if it exchanges one race supremacy for another?" W. E. B. DuBois, "Back to Africa," *Century Magazine* 105 (1923): 539–48, cited in David Levering Lewis, ed., *W. E. B. Du Bois: A Reader* (New York: Henry Holt, 1995), 337.

12. Roi Ottley, *"New World a-Coming": Inside Black America* (Boston: Houghton Mifflin, 1943), cited in Clarke, ed., *Harlem*, 15.

13. E. David Cronon, *Black Moses: The Story of Marcus Garvey and the Universal Negro Improvement Association* (Madison: University of Wisconsin Press, 1969), 62–64. See also Clarke, ed., *Harlem*, 14.

14. Clarke, ed., *Harlem*, 14. See also Mary W. Ovington, *Portraits in Color* (New York: Viking Press, 1927), 22.

15. Marcus Garvey and Anne J. Garvey, *Philosophy and Opinions of Marcus Garvey; or, Africa for the Africans* (2 vols., 1923–25), 2 vols. in 1 (New York: Macmillan, 1992), 141. Other articles condemning lynching, "the atrocious crime of whipping," racially discriminatory court sanctions, and unequal educational opportunities also applied to youths.

16. Garvey and Garvey, *The Philosophy and Opinions of Marcus Garvey*, 126.

17. Clarke, ed., *Harlem*, 14. See also Adam Clayton Powell, *Marching Blacks: An Interpretive History of the Rise of the Black Common Man* (1943), rev. ed. (New York: Dial, 1973); and St. Clair Drake and Horace Cayton, *Black Metropolis* (New York: Harcourt, Brace & World, 1945).

18. Standing, "Nationalism in Negro Leadership," 184 (see also 187–90); Garvey and Garvey, *The Philosophy and Opinions of Marcus Garvey*, 135 (on Garvey's appointment as provisional president).

19. Ohio Association of Colored Women's Clubs, *The Queen's Gardens* (Delaware: Ohio Association of Colored Women's Clubs, 1955), 3 (quotes); White, *Too Heavy a Load*, 147. For discussion of similar responses to suffrage among black women leaders in Chicago, see M. A. Flanagan, "The Predicament of New Rights: Suffrage and Women's Political Power from a Local Perspective," *Social Politics: International Studies in*

Gender, State and Society 2, no. 3 (1995): 305–30. Notwithstanding this political mobilization, black youths and communities remained excluded from Ohio juvenile court communities for much of the twentieth century. M. J. Morton, "Institutionalizing Inequalities: Black Children and Child Welfare in Cleveland, 1859–1998," *Journal of Social History* 34, no. 1 (2000): 141–62.

20. Adam Fairclough, "'Being in the Field of Education and Also Being a Negro . . . Seems . . . Tragic': Black Teachers in the Jim Crow South," *Journal of American History* 87, no. 1 (2000): 90–91. Dorothy Salem described the shift away from charity work toward a broader range of social reforms and institution building, which she says helped establish the earliest "foundations for major social services in [black] communities." See Dorothy C. Salem, *To Better Our World: Black Women in Organized Reform, 1890–1920* (Brooklyn, NY: Carlson, 1990), 68, 100. Evelyn Higginbotham observes a shift in emphasis among black women activists in the Baptist Church, for whom "rescue constituted the older form of service, which relieved and aided people already in distress, while the updated and preferable form sought preventive remedies for social ills through (as [Nannie] Burroughs noted) a 'larger sociological direction.'" Evelyn B. Higginbotham, *Righteous Discontent* (Cambridge, MA: Harvard University Press, 1993), 176.

21. See the correspondence collected in "Mary Church Terrell, 1924–25," ser. 1, case file 2689, microfilm accession no. 12,731 (reel 170), Calvin Coolidge Papers, Library of Congress, Washington, DC, http://memory.loc.gov.

22. Ibid.

23. Ibid.

24. The ability to raise financial support, wield influence, and avoid white interference was expected to be enhanced by the white leadership and apparent moderation of the new civil rights organization. See Elliott Rudwick, "W. E. B. Du Bois: Protagonist of the Afro-American Protest," in *Black Leaders of the Twentieth Century*, ed. John Hope Franklin and August Meier (Urbana: University of Illinois Press, 1982); Eugene Levy, "James Weldon Johnson and the Development of the NAACP," in ibid.; and Benjamin L. Hooks and Jerry Guess, *The March for Civil Rights: The Benjamin Hooks Story* (Chicago: American Bar Association, 2003).

25. Mia Bay, *To Tell the Truth Freely: The Life of Ida B. Wells* (New York: Hill & Wang, 2009), 297; Lewis, *W. E. B. Du Bois: A Reader*, 513. DuBois edited *The Crisis* continually until 1934. Aptheker concludes that "the longest sustained piece of work by Du Bois was his editorship of the *Crisis* . . . [where] in the early volumes, very nearly the entire magazine was written by him." Herbert Aptheker, ed., *Annotated Bibliography of the Published Writings of W. E. B. Du Bois* (Millwood, NY: Kraus-Thomson, 1973), 120.

26. David Levering Lewis, *When Harlem Was in Vogue* (New York: Oxford University Press, 1981), 7.

27. W. E. B. DuBois, "Opinion," *The Crisis* 1, no. 2 (1910): 11–15, 14–15. Ruling against the fugitive slave Dred Scott (1857), Chief Justice Taney held that "[black Americans] had no rights which the white man was bound to respect."

28. W. E. B. DuBois, "Christian Virginia vs. Virginia Christian," *The Crisis* 4, no. 5 (1912): 236–39.

29. W. E. B. DuBois, "The Burden," *The Crisis* 4, no. 2 (1912): 90–91, and "Crime," *The Crisis* 8, no. 2 (1914): 64; J. A. Sommerville to National Association for the Advancement of Colored People, March 12, 1914, and "30 Year Sentence for Negro Who Stole Kisses," *New York World*, March 5, 1914, both National Association for the

Advancement of Colored People Collection (hereafter NAACP Collection), Library of Congress.

30. For the role of social research in opposing Jim Crow, see Nesbitt, "The Negro Race Relations Expert," 156.

31. See W. E. B. DuBois, *The Philadelphia Negro: A Social Study* (1899; reprint, Philadelphia: University of Pennsylvania Press, 1996), chap. 13, *Efforts for Social Betterment among Negro Americans* (Atlanta: Atlanta University Press, 1909), 127, and "The Immortal Child," *The Crisis* 12, no. 6 (1916): 267–71.

32. DuBois, "Crime," 292.

33. May Nerney to NAACP Attorney Chapin Brinsmade, June 19, 1914, NAACP Collection, Microfilm Edition, pt. 8, Discrimination in Criminal Justice (1910–1955), reel 15; Minutes, Meeting of the Board of Directors, July 7, 1914, NAACP Collection, Microfilm Edition, pt. 1, Meetings of the Board of Directors (1909–1950), reel 3.

34. Minutes, Meeting of the Board of Directors, June 2, 1914, NAACP Collection, Microfilm Edition, pt. 1, Meetings of the Board of Directors (1909–1950), reel 3; Diggs, "Du Bois and Children," 372.

35. Charles S. Johnson, *A Study of Delinquent and Neglected Negro Children before the New York City Children's Court* (New York: Joint Committee on Negro Child Study, 1925).

36. Ibid., 46.

37. Wiley B. Sanders, *Negro Child Welfare in North Carolina* (Chapel Hill: The University of North Carolina Press, 1933), 4.

38. Ibid., 5, vi.

39. Ibid., vi. See also N. Yolanda Burwell, "Lawrence Oxley and Locality Development: Black Self-Help in North Carolina, 1925–1928," *Journal of Community Practice* 2, no. 4 (1995): 49–70; and Inabel B. Lindsay, "Race as a Factor in the Caseworker's Role," *Journal of Social Casework* 28, no. 3 (1947): 101–7.

40. See W. Marvin Dulaney, *Black Police in America*, Blacks in the Diaspora (Bloomington: Indiana University Press, 1996); Harry Hill, *Annual Report of the Chief Probation Officer of the Juvenile Court*, Charity Service Reports, Cook County, IL (Chicago, 1927); and Herb A. Bloch and Frank T. Flynn, *Delinquency: The Juvenile Offender in America Today* (New York: Random House, 1956), 47.

41. Eugene K. Jones, "Social Work among Negroes," *Annals of the American Academy of Political and Social Science* 140 (1928): 287–93.

42. On the growing importance of these authorities and their perceived role in institutionalizing equality, see Myrdal, *An American Dilemma*, 816–17; Nesbitt, "The Negro Race Relations Expert"; and Drake and Cayton, *Black Metropolis*, 732. For a related discussion of the "social democratic conception of [social work] service," see Wendy Sarvasy, "From Man and Philanthropic Service to Feminist Social Citizenship," *Social Politics: International Studies in Gender, State and Society* 1, no. 3 (1994): 306–25.

43. Nesbitt, "The Negro Race Relations Expert," 148, 157, 153. Nesbitt was a federal race expert himself, possessing the cumbersome title of special assistant to the director of the Division of Slum Clearance and Urban Redevelopment, Housing and Home Finance Agency, Washington, DC.

44. On this balancing act today, see C. Watkins-Hayes, "Race-ing the Bootstrap Climb: Black and Latino Bureaucrats in Post-Reform Welfare Offices," *Social Problems* 56 (2009): 285–310.

45. Ida A. Walker, "Industrial School for Girls in Missouri," *National Notes* (National Association of Colored Women's Clubs) 19, no. 4 (January 1917): 3; Gary R. Kremer

and Linda R. Gibbens, "The Missouri Home for Negro Girls: The 1930s," *American Studies* 24, no. 2 (1983): 77–93. "The position of superintendent at Tipton was the most prestigious public job available to Black American women in the state at the time," Kremer writes, and "the Democrat Bowles eagerly sought it." Gary Kremer, "System Failed Residents of Home for Negro Girls," *Jefferson City (MO) New Tribune*, June 21, 1998.

46. Kremer and Gibbens, "The Missouri Home for Negro Girls," 90.

47. Quoted in ibid., 87–88.

48. Quoted in ibid., 85.

49. Ethel Bowles, "Biennial Report of the State Industrial Home for Negro Girls," in *Biennial Report of the Department of Penal Institutions, 1933–1934* (Jefferson City: Missouri Department of Penal Institutions, 1934), 435, 437; Douglas E. Abrams, *A Very Special Place in Life: The History of Juvenile Justice in Missouri* (Jefferson City: Missouri Juvenile Justice Association, 2003), 106 (quote).

50. Abrams, *A Very Special Place in Life*, 105–6.

51. Bowles, "Biennial Report of the State Industrial Home for Negro Girls," 437.

52. Kremer and Gibbens, "The Missouri Home for Negro Girls," 90.

53. White, *Too Heavy a Load*, 148–52.

54. See Michael C. Dawson, *Behind the Mule: Race and Class in African-American Politics* (Princeton, NJ: Princeton University Press, 1994), 54.

55. B. Joyce Ross, "Mary McLeod Bethune and the National Youth Administration: A Case Study of Power Relationships in the Black Cabinet of Franklin D. Roosevelt," in Franklin and Meier, ed., *Black Leaders of the Twentieth Century*, 201, 207.

56. Nesbitt, "The Negro Race Relations Expert," 151. See also Harry J. Walker, "Changes in the Structure of Race Relations in the South," *American Sociological Review* 14, no. 3 (1949): 380.

57. Walker, "Changes in the Structure of Race Relations in the South," 380–81.

58. Council of Social Agencies (CSA), "Facilities for Delinquent Girls" (March 24, 1944), folder 11, box 157, United Community Services Central Files, Archives of Labor and Urban Affairs.

59. CSA, "Institutions for Delinquent Girls: Summary Notes" (Fall 1943), and Memorandum (June 27, 1944), both folder 11, box 157, United Community Services Central Files, Archives of Labor and Urban Affairs.

60. CSA, "Institutions for Delinquent Girls: Summary Notes" (Fall 1943); Robert H. MacRae, Managing Director, Board of the Council of Social Agencies of Metropolitan Detroit, to Mrs. Wm. Kales, Board of the Council of Social Agencies (Detroit), October 23, 1943, folder 1, box 23, United Community Services Central Files, Archives of Labor and Urban Affairs.

61. Robert H. MacRae to Mrs. Wm. Kales, Board of the Council of Social Agencies (Detroit), October 23, 1943; Kingsley, "Study of Several Departments of Work."

62. CSA, Memorandum (June 27, 1944); Harvey C. Jackson, "Delta Home for Girls: Summary of a Study Covering the Years 1947–1954" (1957), folder 7, box 23, United Community Services Central Files, Archives of Labor and Urban Affairs.

63. CSA, Memorandum (June 27, 1944).

64. CSA, "A Proposal for a New Agency to Provide Semi-Custodial Care to Negro Girls Who Are Wards of the Juvenile Court: A Progress Report" (1944–45), folder 11, box 159, United Community Services Central Files, Archives of Labor and Urban Affairs.

65. Jessica Kimball, "Delta Sigma Theta Home for Girls" (November 1945), folder 5, box 23, United Community Services Central Files, Archives of Labor and Urban Affairs.

66. CSA, "A Proposal for a New Agency to Provide Semi-Custodial Care to Negro Girls Who Are Wards of the Juvenile Court."

67. Drake and Cayton, *Black Metropolis*, 731–32. Emphasizing the practical role of liberal race expert leadership, Nesbitt writes: "Gains against Jim Crowism [were] not the results of protest alone, despite its vigor and repetition. Gains . . . emerge from a complex of processes, including protest, but also: the discovery, identification, and amassing of the facts involved; the development of an understanding of the adverse effects of the particular antiracial practice upon the whole as well as the Negro community; the alignment of the constructive forces in the community in support of corrective action; the identification, exposure, and immobilization of reactionary forces; good timing; appropriate tactics; and the prompt and skillful implementation of the decision makers, once they have moved forward" ("The Negro Race Relations Expert," 156).

68. Randall Kennedy, *Race, Crime, and the Law* (New York: Pantheon, 1997), 42. See also Angela Y. Davis, *Abolition Democracy: Beyond Empire, Prisons, and Torture* (New York: Seven Stories, 2005), 37.

69. Haywood Patterson and Earl Conrad, *Scottsboro Boy* (New York: Doubleday, 1950), 13.

70. The Alabama Supreme Court had affirmed seven of the death penalty convictions earlier that year, though one of the condemned (Eugene Williams) was determined to have been a juvenile and ordered to receive a juvenile hearing. He was finally acquitted of all charges with the other very young accused youth, Roy Wright, in 1937. James R. Acker, *Scottsboro and Its Legacy: The Cases That Challenged American Legal and Social Justice* (Westport, CT: Praeger, 2008), 44–45, 53, 95, 179.

71. The remaining defendant, Haywood Patterson, escaped custody and fled to Detroit. The FBI captured him in Detroit in 1950, but Michigan's governor refused Alabama's extradition request, and a federal judge ordered his release. By the time Alabama pardoned the Scottsboro nine in 1976, all but one of the victims of injustice had died. See Acker, *Scottsboro and Its Legacy*, 189, 192–93.

72. M. Watt Espy and John Ortiz Smykla, *Executions in the United States, 1608–2002*, database/computer file (Ann Arbor, MI: Inter-University Consortium for Political and Social Research, 2004).

73. Elliott M. Rudwick, "W. E. B. Du Bois in the Role of *Crisis* Editor," *Journal of Negro History* 43, no. 3 (1958): 237 (first two quotes); W. E. B. DuBois, "My Evolving Program for Negro Freedom," in *What the Negro Wants*, ed. R. W. Logan (Chapel Hill: University of North Carolina Press, 1944), 70 (last two quotes).

74. B. T. Bates, "A New Crowd Challenges the Agenda of the Old Guard in the NAACP, 1933–1941," *American Historical Review* 102, no. 2 (1997): 341, 360.

75. Cheryl Lynn Greenberg, *Or Does It Explode? Black Harlem in the Great Depression* (New York: Oxford University Press, 1991), 120; Bates, "A New Crowd Challenges the Agenda of the Old Guard in the NAACP," 368–69.

76. Elaine Ellis, "Our Delinquent Children," *The Crisis* 44, no. 12 (1937): 362, 363.

77. Jane Bolin, "Speech at Schomburg Dedication of Du Bois Bust" (May 7, 1957), box 3, Jane Bolin Papers, Schomburg Center for Research in Black Culture, New York. See also Jacqueline McLeod, "Persona Non-Grata: Judge Jane Matilda Bolin

and the NAACP, 1930–1950," *Afro-Americans in New York Life and History: An Inter-disciplinary Journal* 19, no. 1 (2005): 1–29.

78. Bolin, "Speech at Schomburg Dedication of Du Bois Bust."

79. Jane Bolin, to Judge Justice Polier, October 24, 1978 (quote), box 3, Bolin Papers; Garvey and Garvey, *The Philosophy and Opinions of Marcus Garvey*, 135–43.

80. "When I am asked why I left such a beautiful town as Poughkeepsie," she explained to an audience there a decade after leaving, "I am forced to answer: 'Yes it is physically beautiful, but I hate fascism wherever it is practiced, by Germans, Japanese, or by Americans. Poughkeepsie is fascist to the extent of deluding itself that there is a superiority among human beings by reason solely of color or race or religion." Jane M. Bolin, Oral History Interview (by Jean Rudd and Lionel Bolin), June 4, 1990, box 1, Bolin Papers. See also "Judge Bolin Declares Brotherhood Pointless Unless Poughkeepsie Ends Its Intolerance," *Poughkeepsie New Yorker*, February 23, 1944, box 1, Bolin Papers.

81. "The Wellesley College Graduate Who Was the Nation's First Black Woman Judge," *Journal of Blacks in Higher Education* 34 (2002): 37; Bolin, Oral History Interview, 8–9 (quotes).

82. M. E. Ross to Governor Herbert Lehman (New York), July 18, 1936, NAACP Collection, Microfilm Edition, pt. 8, Discrimination in Criminal Justice (1910–1955), reel 15.

83. "Equality Is Won by Negro Girls in State School," *New York Herald-Tribune*, November 20, 1936; Walter White to Hon. David C. Adie (Commissioner of Public Welfare), November 19, 1936, NAACP Collection, Microfilm Edition, pt. 8, Discrimination in Criminal Justice (1910–1955), reel 15.

84. Greenberg, *Or Does It Explode?* 85, 163.

85. Bolin, Oral History Interview, 10, 12. Bolin was also a director of the Child Welfare League, the Wiltwyck School for Boys, United Neighborhood Houses, and the New York Urban League (ibid., 12).

86. Katherine Hildreth, "The Negro Problem as Reflected in the Functioning of the Domestic Relations Court of the City of New York" (report of the special examiner, New York City Children's Court, June 1934), cited in Greenberg, *Or Does It Explode?* 171.

87. Nesbitt, "The Negro Race Relations Expert," 156; Bolin, Oral History Interview, 10, 31.

88. Wiltwyck's founding charter described "a constructive program of moral and spiritual enlightenment, character development, correction of behavior problems, education and training for good citizenship" (cited in *Wiltwyck School for Boys v. Hill*, 11 N.Y.2d 182 [1962]).

89. Bolin, Oral History Interview, 30. See also "Wiltwyck School for Boys," in *The Eleanor Roosevelt Encyclopedia*, eds., Maurine H. Beasley, Holly C. Shulman, and Henry R. Beasley (Westport, CT: Greenwood, 2001), 567–69.

90. Walter White, "Statement by Walter White to the Board of Estimate of New York City in Support of Race Discrimination Amendment to Prohibit Payment of Public Funds to Charitable Institutions which Discriminate Because of Color," April 16, 1942, NAACP Collection, Microfilm Edition, pt. 8, Discrimination in Criminal Justice (1910–1955), reel 15. See also Jane Bolin to John A. Wallace, Director of NYC Office of Probation for the Courts of New York City, July 31, 1963, box 3, Bolin Papers.

91. Jane M. Bolin, "A Friend in Court" (book review), *Lawyers Guild Review* 48, no. 6 (1942): 47–48.

92. Ibid., 48.
93. Asked how she felt about being the first black woman judge, Bolin replied: "As time went by, I was embarrassed by it because it was years after I went on the bench before another African American woman went on the bench" (Bolin, Oral History Interview, 74).
94. "Judge Bolin Declares Brotherhood Pointless."
95. Jane Bolin to Ernest Pugmire, Territorial Commander, Salvation Army, February 4, 1947, box 3, Bolin Papers.
96. Jane Bolin to Lazarus Joseph, December 18, 1950, box 3, Bolin Papers.
97. Jane Bolin to Robert E. Barnes, City Councilor, September 9, 1957, box 3, Bolin Papers.
98. Jane Bolin to President John F. Kennedy, October 24, 1961, box 3, Bolin Papers.
99. Nesbitt, "The Negro Race Relations Expert," 154.
100. William L. Patterson, "Juvenile Delinquency and Civil Rights" (n.d.), 1, folder 7, box 208–10, William L. Patterson Papers, Moorland-Spingarn Research Center, Howard University. The essay is undated but archived with files from 1950.
101. Ibid., 4, 14.
102. Ibid., 3. Patterson's argument recalls Robert Merton's classic theory of anomie (see Robert K. Merton, "Social Structure and Anomie," *American Sociological Review* 3, no. 5 [1938]: 672–82) and relates to Cloward and Ohlin's later theory of delinquency and opportunity (Richard A. Cloward and Lloyd E. Ohlin, *Delinquency and Opportunity: A Theory of Delinquent Gangs* [Glencoe: Free Press, 1960]).
103. Patterson, "Juvenile Delinquency and Civil Rights," 14–15.
104. Black professional networks in education and the professions, including social work, law, and other fields, as well as outlets for news, editorials, and social and behavioral science research helped shape and propel the movement. In 1932, a few years before establishing its School of Social Work, Howard University established the *Journal of Negro Education* (*JNE*), a scholarly journal that provided black social researchers with unmatched exposure to studies broadly related to race, education, and racial justice. Like older black periodicals—*The Crisis* (est. 1910), the *Journal of Negro History* (1916), and *Phylon* (1940)—*JNE* became an integral source of information on child welfare and juvenile justice. Most of the empirical research published before 1970 on black experiences of juvenile justice appears in *JNE*, including a special 1959 issue dedicated to "Juvenile Delinquency among Negroes in the United States." It featured essays and articles by an array of black professionals affiliated with government agencies, academic institutions, and social justice organizations. One of the most important articles in *JNE* was Kenneth B. Clark and Mamie P. Clark's "Emotional Factors in Racial Identification and Preference in Negro Children" (*The Negro Child in the American Social Order* 22, 19, no. 3 [Summer 1950], 341–50), cited in *Brown v. Board of Education*.
105. Jane Bolin to Judge Justice Polier, October 24, 1978. "From my childhood, I read the *Crisis* magazine and Black newspapers and periodicals to which my father subscribed," Bolin told colleagues at her retirement. "I was horrified and transfixed by pictures and news stories of lynchings and other atrocities against blacks solely because of their race. It is easy to imagine how a young, protected child who sees portrayals of brutality is forever scarred and becomes determined to contribute in her own small way to racial justice" (ibid.). See also Bolin, "Speech at Schomburg Dedication of Du Bois Bust."
106. Jane Bolin to Arthur Spingarn, President, NAACP Board of Directors, March 9, 1950, box 3, Bolin Papers. See also McLeod, "Persona Non-Grata."

107. *Brown* (1954) combined cases challenging discrimination in educational provisions in Kansas and other states—*Davis v. County School Board of Prince Edward County* (filed in Virginia in 1951), *Briggs v. Elliott* (filed in South Carolina in 1952), *Gebhart v. Belton* (filed in Delaware in 1952), *Bolling v. Sharpe* (filed in Washington, DC, in 1954), and *Brown v. Board of Education of Topeka* (filed in Kansas in 1954). The *Brown* ruling established that segregation violated the Fourteenth Amendment, overturning the ruling in *Plessy v. Ferguson* (1896) that established the legal doctrine of separate but equal. Importantly, *Brown* was part of a larger set of Supreme Court rulings that forced the integration of primary and secondary education as well as other institutions. *Smith v. Allwright*, 321 U.S. 649 (1944), *Sweatt v. Painter*, 339 U.S. 629 (1950), and *McLaurin v. Oklahoma State Regents*, 339 U.S. 637 (1950) were especially instrumental in increasing black adult access to professional education and political influence (see Michael J. Klarman, *From Jim Crow to Civil Rights: The Supreme Court and the Struggle for Racial Equality* [New York: Oxford University Press, 2006]). On *Brown*'s limited impact on school desegregation, see Gerald N. Rosenberg, *The Hollow Hope: Can Courts Bring about Social Change?* (Chicago: University of Chicago Press, 2008); and Thomas J. Espenshade and Alexandria W. Radford, *No Longer Separate, Not Yet Equal: Race and Class in Elite College Admission and Campus Life* (Princeton, NJ: Princeton University Press, 2009).

108. Kenneth B. Clark, "The Effects of Prejudice and Discrimination on Personality Development," in *Toward Humanity and Justice: The Writings of Kenneth B. Clark, Scholar of the 1954 Brown v. Board of Education Decision*, ed. Woody Klein (Westport, CT: Praeger, 2004), app. 2.

CHAPTER SEVEN

1. See Clive Webb, ed., *Massive Resistance: Southern Opposition to the Second Reconstruction* (New York: Oxford University Press, 2005); and Gene Roberts and Hank Klibanoff, *The Race Beat: The Press, the Civil Rights Struggle, and the Awakening of a Nation* (New York: Knopf, 2006), chap. 8.

2. I use the term *recognition* to describe group standing or voice within the democratic culture and institutions. Nancy Fraser explains this meaning in her comparison of social injustices based on "cultural valuational" vs. "political-economic" structures of society and the different remedies each requires. Injustices rooted in the cultural valuational structure (i.e., the domain of cultural representation and constructed meaning) require "remedies of recognition," such as "revaluing disrespected identities and the cultural products of maligned groups; . . . recognizing and positively valorizing cultural diversity; . . . or, the transformation of social patterns of representation, interpretation, and communication" (Nancy Fraser, "From Redistribution to Recognition? Dilemmas of Justice in a 'Post-Socialist' Age," *New Left Review* [1995]: 15). Black child-savers envisioned recognition (i.e., black authority and valorization of the immortal youth) as a principle means of redistributing rights and resources and, thus, achieving the political restructuring of American juvenile justice.

3. On the general theory of racial group power threat in criminal social control, see Hubert M. Blalock, *Toward a Theory of Minority-Group Relations* (New York: Wiley, 1967); Allen E. Liska, *Social Threat and Social Control* (Albany: State University of New York Press, 1992); and Geoff Ward, Amy Farrell, and Danielle Rousseau, "Does Racial Balance in Workforce Representation Yield Equal Justice?" *Law and Society Review* 43, no. 4 (2009): 757–806.

4. Rawls uses the term *basic structure* to characterize the core institutional arrangement

regulating distributions of societal opportunity or advantage. See John Rawls, *A Theory of Justice* (Cambridge, MA: Harvard University Press, 1999), 10.

5. Roosevelt quoted in Jack Holl, *Juvenile Reform in the Progressive Era: William R. George and the Junior Republic Movement* (Ithaca, NY: Cornell University Press, 1971), 9.

6. John Braithwaite, "Thinking Harder about Democratizing Social Control," in *Family Conferencing and Juvenile Justice: The Way Forward or Misplaced Optimism?* ed. C. Alder and J. Wundersitz (Canberra: Australian Institute of Criminology, 1994), 201–2. On dominion and related theories in critical criminology, see also John Braithwaite, "Charles Tittle's Control Balance and Criminological Theory," in *Criminological Theories: Bridging the Past to the Future*, ed. S. Cote (Thousand Oaks, CA: Sage, 2002); John Braithwaite and Philip Pettit, *Not Just Desserts: A Republican Theory of Criminal Justice* (New York: Clarendon, 1990); and William J. Chambliss, "A Sociological Analysis of the Law of Vagrancy," *Social Problems* 12, no. 1 (1964): 67–77.

7. "As communities start taking responsibility for the social vulnerabilities of young offenders and start talking about these vulnerabilities, instead of leaving them for the police and courts to sweep away," Braithwaite writes, "they become more engaged with the deeper institutional sources of the problems" ("Thinking Harder about Democratizing Social Control," 201–2).

8. Charles Ogletree Jr., *All Deliberate Speed* (New York: Norton, 2004).

9. See Francis A. Allen, ed., *The Decline of the Rehabilitative Ideal: Penal Policy and Social Purpose* (New Haven, CT: Yale University Press, 1981); and Barry C. Feld, *Bad Kids: Race and the Transformation of the Juvenile Court* (New York: Oxford University, 1999), chap. 3.

10. Raymond L. Manell, "Racially Integrating a State's Training Schools," *Children* 11, no. 2 (1964): 49–54, 51; *State Board v. Myers*, 167 A.2d 765 (1961), available as document no. JI-MD-0002-7500 at http://clearinghouse.net. See also *Singleton v. Board of Commissioners of State Institutions*, 356 F.2d 771 (5 Cir. 1966), available as document no. JI-FL-0001 at http://clearinghouse.net; *Washington v. Lee*, 263 F. Supp. 327 (M.D. Ala. 1966), available as document no. PC-AL-0020 at http://clearinghouse.net; *Crum v. State Training School for Girls*, 413 F.2d 1348 (5th Cir. 1969), available as document no. JI-AL-0002 at http://clearinghouse.net; *Board of Managers of the Arkansas Training School for Boys at Wrightville v. George*, 377 F.2d 228 (8 Cir. 1967), available as document no. JI-AR-0002 at http://clearinghouse.net; and *Major v. Sowers*, 297 F. Supp. 664 (E.D. La. 1969).

11. U.S. Commission on Civil Rights (USCCR), *Law Enforcement: A Report on Equal Protection in the South* (Washington, DC: U.S. Government Printing Office, 1965).

12. On the legal impunity of white (including youth) involvement in anti–civil rights violence, see USCCR, *Law Enforcement*, chap. 2; Kenneth B. Clark, "Color, Class, Personality and Juvenile Delinquency," *Journal of Negro Education* 28, no. 3 (1959): 248–51; and Jeremy H. Skolnick, *The Politics of Protest* (New York: Simon & Schuster, 1969), 228.

13. Skolnick, *The Politics of Protest*, 228.

14. For accounts of white youth involvement in anti–civil rights violence, see Skolnick, *The Politic of Protest*, 228–29; Arthur Waskow, *From Race Riot to Sit In: A Study in the Connections of Conflict and Violence* (New York: Doubleday, 1966), chaps. 3–4; and Elizabeth Jacoway, *Turn Away Thy Son: Little Rock, the Crisis That Shocked the Nation* (New York: Free Press, 2007).

15. Clark, "Color, Class, Personality and Juvenile Delinquency," 249.

16. Skolnick, *The Politic of Protest*, 222.

17. Jacoway, *Turn Away Thy Son*, 345–46.
18. Cited in Carlotta W. Lanier and Lisa F. Page, *A Mighty Long Way: My Journey to Justice at Little Rock Central High School* (New York: Random House, 2009), 118 (second quote); Daisy Bates to Roy Wilkins, December 17, 1957 (first quote), NAACP Collection, Library of Congress, http://www.loc.gov/teachers/classroommaterials/primary-sourcesets/naacp/pdf/daisybates.pdf.
19. USCCR, *Law Enforcement*, 80–83.
20. John Dittmer, *Local People: The Struggle for Civil Rights in Mississippi* (Urbana: University of Illinois Press, 1995), 107–14.
21. Ibid., 110–11; Charles M. Payne, *I've Got the Light of Freedom: The Organizing Tradition and the Mississippi Freedom Struggle* (Berkeley and Los Angeles: University of California Press, 1995), 124; Robert Moses, *Radical Equations: Civil Rights from Mississippi to the Algebra Project* (Boston: Beacon, 2001), 53.
22. "Since juvenile proceedings are designed only to educate and rehabilitate and not to punish," the Civil Rights Commission (1965) explained, "constitutional safeguards assured those accused of crimes generally are not applicable. In the areas studied . . . local authorities used the broad discretion afforded them by the absence of safeguards to impose excessively harsh treatment on juveniles. . . . Juveniles who had been arrested in demonstrations were threatened with imprisonment and, as a condition of exoneration or release, were forced to promise that they would not participate in future civil rights activities." USCCR, *Law Enforcement*, 80.
23. Larry Still, "White Family in Ala. Gets Custody of Miss. Negro: Sit-In Student to Live, Study," *Jet*, May 10, 1962, 16.
24. Dittmer, *Local People*, 111–14.
25. Still, "White Family in Ala. Gets Custody of Miss. Negro," 16–19.
26. Quoted in Harvard Sitkoff, *King: Pilgrimage to the Mountaintop* (New York: Hill & Wang, 2008), 101. See also Stephen B. Oates, *Let the Trumpet Sound: A Life of Martin Luther King, Jr.* (New York: Harper Perennial, 1994), 251.
27. On black community opposition to the Children's Crusade, see Dittmer, *Local People*, 111; Payne, *I've Got the Light of Freedom*, 120; Raymond Arsenault, *Freedom Riders: 1961 and the Struggle for Racial Justice* (New York: Oxford University Press, 2006), 402, 449; and Robert Parris Moses and Charles E. Cobb, *Radical Equations: Civil Rights from Mississippi to the Algebra Project* (Boston: Beacon, 2002), 52–55.
28. USCCR, *Law Enforcement*, 81, 80.
29. "Racial and Civil Disorders in St. Augustine" (report of the Florida Legislative Investigation Committee, 1965), 30, cited in USCRC, *Law Enforcement*, 82–83. The commission reports that reform schools in Florida remained segregated under the law (Fla. Stat. §955.12 [1944]). According to the commission report: "One of the [committed] girls was a senior in high school. Since the classes at the [black] reform school only went to 10th grade, she missed an entire term of school" (USCRC, *Law Enforcement*, 83n150).
30. *Johnson v. Davis*, 9 Race Rel. L. Rep. 814 (M.D. Fla. 1964), cited in USCCR, *Law Enforcement*, 83.
31. *Crum v. State Training School for Girls*, 413 F.2d 1348 (5th Cir. 1969), available as document no. JI-AL-0002-7500 at http://clearinghouse.net.
32. "Order, *Crum v. State Training School for Girls*" (1970), available as document no. JI-AL-0002-0001 at http://clearinghouse.net.
33. Harvey C. Jackson, "Delta Home for Girls: Summary of a Study Covering the Years 1947–1954" (1957), folder 7, box 23, United Community Services Central

Files, Archives of Labor and Urban Affairs, Walter P. Reuther Library, Wayne State University.

34. "1961 Annual Report of Delta Home for Girls" (draft, May 17, 1961), folder 4, box 23, United Community Services Central Files, Archives of Labor and Urban Affairs.

35. Cheryl Lynn Greenberg, *Or Does It Explode? Black Harlem in the Great Depression* (New York: Oxford University Press, 1991), 163, 202. See also Jane Bolin to Henry Mc-Carthy, Commissioner of Welfare, March 1, 1955, and Jane Bolin to John Wallace, Director, New York City Office of Probation, July 31, 1963, both box 3, Jane Bolin Papers, Schomburg Center for Research in Black Culture, New York.

36. Kenneth Bancroft Clark, *Dark Ghetto: Dilemmas of Social Power* (New York: Harper & Row, 1965), 87.

37. Susan Ware and Stacy Lorraine Braukman, eds., *Notable American Women: A Biographical Dictionary Completing the Twentieth Century* (Cambridge, MA: Belknap Press of the Harvard University Press, 2004), 126; Ludy T. Benjamin, *A History of Psychology in Letters* (1993), 2nd ed. (Malden, MA: Blackwell, 2006), 216.

38. Gerald E. Markowitz and David Rosner, *Children, Race, and Power: Kenneth and Mamie Clark's Northside Center* (Charlottesville: University Press of Virginia, 1996), 54, 183; Mamie Phipps Clark, "Evaluation of an Inter-Racial Guidance Clinic" (March 1957), cited in Ben Keppel, *The Work of Democracy: Ralph Bunche, Kenneth B. Clark, Lorraine Hansberry, and the Cultural Politics of Race* (Cambridge, MA: Harvard University Press, 1995), 280.

39. See Kenneth B. Clark, *Prejudice and Your Child* (Middletown, CT: Wesleyan University Press, 1988), xx; and Kenneth B. Clark, *Toward Humanity and Justice: The Writings of Kenneth B. Clark, Scholar of the 1954 Brown v. Board of Education Decision*, ed. Woody Klein (Westport, CT: Praeger, 2004). On Clark's renown post-*Brown* as "the new Myrdal, an interpreter of the ghetto to the nation's conscience," see Keppel, *The Work of Democracy*, 101–2. See also Clark, *Toward Humanity and Justice*, xxiii; and Benjamin, *A History of Psychology in Letters*, 216.

40. Roberts and Klibanoff, *The Race Beat*, 109.

41. Alberta C. J. Lewis, Secretary, Friends of the Northside Center for Child Development, to Kenneth Clark, May 27, 1954, and K. B. Clark to Alberta C. J. Lewis, June 16, 1954, both cited in Benjamin, *A History of Psychology in Letters*, 226.

42. Markowitz and Rosner, *Children, Race, and Power*, 65; Shafali Lal, "Giving Children Security: Mamie Phipps Clark and the Racialization of Child Psychology," *American Psychologist* 57, no. 1 (2002): 25 (quote).

43. See Clark, "Color, Class, Personality and Juvenile Delinquency," 240 (first quote); and Markowitz and Rosner, *Children, Race, and Power*, 146 (quote), 187. The Clarks stressed that racism affected the social adjustment and, therefore, the delinquency of all youths. This perspective informed the interracial child-guidance approach at Northside.

44. M. Clark, "Evaluation of an Inter-Racial Guidance Clinic" (1957), 1, 7–8, cited in Keppel, *The Work of Democracy*, 280.

45. Barry Krisberg, *Juvenile Justice: Redeeming Our Children* (Thousand Oaks, CA: Sage, 2005), 44–50.

46. See Richard A. Cloward and Lloyd E. Ohlin, *Delinquency and Opportunity: A Theory of Delinquent Gangs* (Glencoe: Free Press, 1960). William L. Patterson characterized delinquency as a logical sociopolitical adaptation, "the protest actions of youth to an environment over which youth has no voice and to which it could not adapt itself" ("Juvenile Delinquency and Civil Rights" (n.d.), 4, folder 7, box 208–10, William

L. Patterson Papers, Moorland-Spingarn Research Center, Howard University). Jane Bolin attributed delinquency and dependency to "anti-social children rebelling against patent discrimination" (Jane Bolin to Robert E. Barnes, City Councilor, September 9, 1957, box 3, Bolin Papers). Cloward worked closely with the Clarks and other New York City leaders, and all were influenced by the others' ideas (see Markowitz and Rosner, *Children, Race, and Power*, 186–87).

47. Markowitz and Rosner, *Children, Race, and Power*, 187 (quotes); Krisberg, *Juvenile Justice*, 50–53.
48. Markowitz and Rosner, *Children, Race, and Power*, 182–84.
49. Richard Cloward, "The Administration of Services to Children and Youth in New York City" (Institute of Public Administration, New York City, 1963), cited in Markowitz and Rosner, *Children, Race, and Power*, 183.
50. Markowitz and Rosner, *Children, Race, and Power*, 144.
51. Lisa L. Miller, *The Perils of Federalism: Race, Poverty, and the Politics of Crime Control* (New York: Oxford University Press, 2008).
52. W. E. B. DuBois, "Editorial," *The Crisis* 37, no. 10 (1930): 352, cited in Irene Diggs, "Du Bois and Children," *Phylon* 37, no. 4 (1976): 387–88.
53. Ibid., 388.
54. Ibid., 387. See also Wesley G. Skogan, *Disorder and Decline: Crime and the Spiral of Decay in American Neighborhoods* (Berkeley and Los Angeles: University of California Press, 1990).
55. Benjamin E. Mays, "The Role of the 'Negro Community' in Delinquency Prevention among Negro Youth," *Journal of Negro Education* 28, no. 3 (1959): 366–70, 368–96. The novelty of the idea is telling. Mays writes: "The Negro community knows in a vague way that delinquency among Negro youth is a serious problem but the people and the leadership have not been factually and emotionally aroused to the point of assuming responsibility to do something about it. . . . There is a considerable number of Negroes in most communities who could make a valuable financial contribution toward the prevention of delinquency. In this number would be found school teachers, ministers, social workers, business men, doctors, lawyers, dentists, morticians and the like, enough in a community like New York, Atlanta, Chicago, and Birmingham to provide the means for several hundred underprivileged boys to go to camp each summer. Each city could send several hundred [boys] without anybody being hurt. Suppose the idea could become nation-wide! Couple this idea with a crusade to get supervised recreation in the areas where the lowest-income groups live and we would go a long way toward preventing delinquency among Negroes" (ibid., 367–69).
56. Ibid., 366.
57. The racial and ethnic composition of juvenile and criminal justice–related labor is unrecorded. The most complete data are U.S. census figures that identify only general groups, such as lawyers, police, and prison guards, without respect to jurisdiction, and primarily after 1970. Personal conversations with black judges and other justice professionals suggest black justice-related labor may be concentrated in juvenile justice for three reasons: (1) black professionals' own interests in working with youths; (2) the segmentation of black labor in this relatively marginal area of law (e.g., in terms of prestige, power, and compensation); and (3) race-based barriers to professional mobility that deny black juvenile officers, lawyers, and judges equal access to higher offices and positions.

58. Sandra M. O'Donnell, "The Care of Dependent African-American Children in Chicago: The Struggle between Black Self-Help and Professionalism," *Journal of Social History* 27, no. 4 (1994): 763. See also Andrew Billingsley and Jeanne M. Giovannoni, *Children of the Storm: Black Children and American Child Welfare* (New York: Harcourt Brace, 1972).

59. Patterson, "Juvenile Delinquency and Civil Rights," 9.

60. Ibid., 4, 9–10, 12–13, 17.

61. Hosea Martin, "Negro Apathy: How to Combat It," *Negro Digest* 14, no. 5 (1965): 22–25.

62. See O'Donnell, "The Care of Dependent African-American Children in Chicago"; and Sandra M. Stehno, "The Elusive Continuum of Care: Implications for Minority Children and Youths," *Child Welfare* 69, no. 6 (1990): 551–62.

63. Martin, "Negro Apathy," 23.

64. Writing on the stratification of black orphans in New York City, David Rosner and Gerald E. Markowitz cite a 1963 Citizen's Committee for Children report finding that "the lighter the [black] child, the more Caucasian his features, the more readily he is placed" ("Race, Foster Care, and the Politics of Abandonment in New York City," *American Journal of Public Health* 87, no. 11 [1997]: 1847). See also Markowitz and Rosner, *Children, Race, and Power*, 194.

65. Mays, "The Role of the 'Negro Community' in Delinquency Prevention among Negro Youth," 366.

66. Ibid., 369. Like Ohio clubwomen in the 1920s, Mays urged intelligent use of the black vote: "If the Negro community were more vote conscious, Negroes could do much to prevent juvenile delinquency among Negroes. . . . The leadership in the Negro Community should take advantage of the ballot to get more parks and supervised play throughout the summer months, especially in areas where the lowest income groups live and where parents are unable to provide recreation" (ibid., 368).

67. Ibid., 367. Mays thought that public education on delinquency should be tailored for heterogeneous black middle-class readers. Materials would be reviewed and developed further, he imagined, in the black press, within colleges and universities, among ministerial associations, medical and dental associations, the bar association, social work organizations, parent-teacher associations, church groups, fraternities and sororities, and leaders in insurance and mortuary science—indeed, anywhere black leadership could be found—such that the problem of black delinquency would develop into a more common and advanced form of knowledge (ibid., 367–68).

68. Ibid., 366.

69. Bertram M. Beck, "The Exiled Delinquent," *Children* 2, no. 6 (1955): 209–10.

70. Ibid., 212.

71. Ibid., 212.

72. John H. Clarke, "The Early Years of Adam Powell," in *Harlem: A Community in Transition*, ed. John Henrik Clarke (New York: Citadel, 1964), 240.

73. Kenneth B. Clark, "HARYOU: An Experiment," in Clarke, ed., *Harlem: A Community in Transition*, 210.

74. Clark, "HARYOU," 212–13.

75. Ibid., 212.

76. Krisberg, *Juvenile Justice*, 51–52; Markowitz and Rosner, *Children, Race, and Power*, 199–200; Kenneth Clark and Jeannette Hopkins, *A Relevant War against Poverty* (New York: Metropolitan Applied Research Center, 1968).

77. Jerry G. Watts, *Amiri Baraka: The Politics and Art of a Black Intellectual* (New York: New York University Press, 2001), 157; Kenneth Clark, interview by Ed Edwin, April 7, 1976, interview no. 4, 147–65, Columbia University Oral History Research Office. See also Mary W. Day, "Harlem Youth Opportunities Unlimited," in *Advocacy in America: Case Studies in Social Change*, ed. Gladys Walton Hall, Grace C. Clark, and Michael A. Creedon (Lanham, MD: University Press of America, 1987), 17.

78. Day, "Harlem Youth Opportunities Unlimited," 21. For reviews of the dispute between Clark and Powell and the development of the HARYOU and ACT projects, see Herbert Krosney, *Beyond Welfare: Poverty in the Supercity* (New York: Holt, Rinehart & Winston, 1966), 36–38; and Keppel, *The Work of Democracy*, 144–52.

79. Day, "Harlem Youth Opportunities Unlimited," 20–21.

80. Kenneth B. Clark, *Pathos of Power* (New York: Harper & Row, 1974), 158–59.

81. Beck, "The Exiled Delinquent," 208–12.

82. Herbert Marcuse, *One-Dimensional Man* (Boston: Beacon, 1964), 1.

83. Jean Baudrillard, *Simulacra and Simulation* (Ann Arbor: University of Michigan Press, 1994).

CONCLUSION

1. In light of the diminished capacities and culpability of youths, the U.S. Supreme Court ruled that juvenile death sentences (*Roper v. Simmons*, 2005) and life without parole prison sentences are unconstitutional (*Sullivan v. Florida*, 130 S. Ct. 2059 [2010]; and *Graham v. Florida*, 130 S. Ct. 2011 [2010]). Youths still face civic exclusion through accountability-based sanctions, including prolonged incarceration, commitment to adult institutions, and civil penalties attaching to criminal convictions.

2. Governor John Engler, "Building on Michigan's Renaissance," State of the State Address, Lansing, MI, January 17, 1995, available at http://www.michigan.gov/formergovernors/0,1607,7-212-31303_31317-1985--,00.html. On the implications for civil status, see Devah Pager, "The Mark of a Criminal Record," *American Journal of Sociology* 108, no. 5 (2003): 937–75; Mark Mauer and Meda Chesney-Lind, *Invisible Punishment* (New York: New Press, 2002); and Jeff Manza and Chris Uggen, *Locked Out* (Oxford: Oxford University Press, 2006).

3. See George S. Bridges and Sara Steen, "Racial Disparities in Official Assessments of Juvenile Offenders: Attributional Stereotypes as Mediating Mechanisms," *American Sociological Review* 63, no. 4 (1998): 554–70; and Michael J. Leiber and Joseph D. Johnson, "Being Young and Black: What Are Their Effects on Juvenile Justice Decision Making?" *Crime and Delinquency* 54, no. 4 (2008): 560–81.

4. Following Miller, *nationalization* and *federalization* refer to the national agenda to control juvenile crime and the related political structure of juvenile justice policy and practice. Powerful federal and state governments are linked to marginalized local politicians, service professionals, and constituents. See Lisa L. Miller, *The Perils of Federalism: Race, Poverty, and the Politics of Crime Control* (New York: Oxford University Press, 2008), 5–8.

5. See Carl E. Pope and Michael J. Leiber, "Disproportionate Minority Confinement/Contact (DMC)," in *Our Children, Their Children: Confronting Racial and Ethnic Differences in American Juvenile Justice*, ed. Darnell Hawkins and Kimberly Kempf-Leonard (Chicago: University of Chicago Press, 2005); Michael J. Leiber, "Disproportionate Minority Confinement (DMC) of Youth: An Analysis of State and Federal Efforts to Address the Issue," *Crime and Delinquency* 48, no. 1 (2002): 3–45; and National Council of Juvenile and Family Court Judges, "Minority Youth in the Juvenile Justice

System: A Judicial Response," special issue, *Juvenile and Family Court Journal* 41, no. 3A (1990).

6. David Garland, *The Culture of Control: Crime and Social Order in Contemporary Society* (Chicago: University of Chicago Press, 2001), 62. See also Barry C. Feld, *Bad Kids: Race and the Transformation of the Juvenile Court* (New York: Oxford University Press, 1999), 97–99; and Simon Singer, *Recriminalizing Delinquency: Violent Juvenile Crime and Juvenile Justice Reform* (New York: Cambridge University Press, 1996).

7. On the "two-fold catastrophe" of growing urban delinquency, W. E. B. DuBois warned: "The surrounding and dominant white world will put up with this impudence on the part of colored children to a certain point and then they will clap them in jail" ("Editorial," *The Crisis* 37, no. 10 (1930): 352, quoted in Irene Diggs, "Du Bois and Children," *Phylon* 37, no. 4 [1976]: 387–88).

8. Bertram M. Beck, "The Exiled Delinquent," *Children* 2, no. 6 (1955): 208–12.

9. Disproportionate minority confinement frames racial inequality in juvenile justice as a growing late-twentieth-century problem. To encourage more historical contextualization, M. A. Bortner, Marjorie S. Zatz, and Darnell F. Hawkins write: "Race and ethnicity have always been extremely consequential in the United States, but increased levels of racial and ethnic disparity in punishment may signal a heightened significance" ("Race and Transfer: Empirical Research and Social Context," in *The Changing Borders of Juvenile Justice: Transfer of Adolescents to the Criminal Court*, ed. Jeffrey Fagan and Franklin E. Zimring [Chicago: University of Chicago Press, 2000], 279).

10. See Fox Butterfield, *All God's Children: The Boskett Family and the American Tradition of Violence* (New York: Avon, 1995); and Fagan and Zimring, eds., *The Changing Borders of Juvenile Justice*.

11. Jane M. Bolin, Oral History Interview (by Jean Rudd and Lionel Bolin), June 4, 1990, 11, box 1, Jane Bolin Papers, Schomburg Center for Research in Black Culture, New York.

12. Ibid., 14, 45–46.

13. President's Commission on Law Enforcement and Administration of Justice, *The Challenge of Crime in a Free Society: A Report* (Washington, DC: U.S. Government Printing Office, 1967), and *Task Force Report: Juvenile Delinquency and Youth Crime* (Washington, DC: U.S. Government Printing Office, 1967); Feld, *Bad Kids*, chaps. 5–6; Jody Miller, "Race, Gender and Juvenile Justice: An Examination of Disposition Decision-Making for Delinquent Girls," in *The Intersection of Race, Gender and Class in Criminology*, ed. M. D. Schwartz and D. Milanovic (New York: Garland, 1994).

14. Martha-Elin Blomquist and Martin L. Forst, "Moral and Practical Problems with Redefining the Goal of the Juvenile Justice System as Accountability," *Journal of Juvenile Law* 14 (1993): 42. According to prior research, juvenile court workers (excluding prosecutors) do not strongly support a punitive approach and continue to stress rehabilitation. Black workers are concerned with system responsibility or fairness, including racial justice. See Geoff Ward and Aaron Kupchik, "What Drives Juvenile Probation Officers? Relating Organizational Contexts, Status Characteristics, and Personal Convictions to Treatment and Punishment Orientations," *Crime and Delinquency* 56, no. 1 (2010): 35–69, and "Accountable to What? Professional Orientations towards Accountability-Based Juvenile Justice," *Punishment and Society* 11, no. 1 (2009): 85–109; and Geoff Ward, Aaron Kupchik, Lauren Parker, and Brian C. Starks, "Racial Politics of Juvenile Justice Policy Support: Juvenile Court Worker

Orientations towards Disproportionate Minority Confinement," *Race and Justice* 1, no. 2 (2011): 154–84.

15. Martin L. Forst and Martha-Elin Blomquist, "Punishment, Accountability, and the New Juvenile Justice," *Juvenile and Family Court Journal* 43, no. 1 (1992): 1–9, 2.

16. Butterfield, *All God's Children*, 227; Anthony M. Platt, *The Child Savers: The Invention of Delinquency* (1969), 40th anniversary ed. (New Brunswick, NJ: Rutgers University Press, 2009), app.; David S. Tanenhaus and S. A. Drizin, "'Owing to the Extreme Youth of the Accused': The Changing Legal Response to Juvenile Homicide," *Journal of Criminal Law and Criminology* 92, nos. 3–4 (2002): 648–49.

17. Alfred Regnery, "Getting Away with Murder: Why the Juvenile Justice System Needs an Overhaul," *Policy Review* 34 (1985): 65 (quote), 68; Ernest van den Haag, *Punishing Criminals: Concerning a Very Old and Painful Question* (New York: Basic, 1975); James C. Howell, *Juvenile Justice and Youth Violence* (Thousand Oaks, CA: Sage, 1997).

18. William J. Bennett, John J. DiIulio, and John P. Walters, *Body Count: Moral Poverty . . . and How to Win America's War against Crime and Drugs* (New York: Simon & Schuster, 1996); Justin Baer and William J. Chambliss, "Generating Fear: The Politics of Crime Reporting," *Crime, Law and Social Change* 27, no. 2 (1997): 87–107; Richard Zoglin, "Now for the Bad News: A Teenage Timebomb," *Time*, January 15, 1996, 52–53.

19. Engler, "Building on Michigan's Renaissance." See also Howell, *Juvenile Justice and Youth Violence*, 47.

20. Engler, speech delivered at the conference of the Prosecuting Attorneys Association of Michigan, Mackinac Island, MI, July 27, 1995, available at http://www.state.mi.us/migov/gov/PressReleases/199507/juvenile2.html; "Punk Prison: There Are Better Ways to Handle Young Convicts," *Detroit Free Press*, February 14, 2005. Engler was a potential vice presidential running mate for Republican nominees Bob Dole in 1996 and George W. Bush in 2000.

21. Barry C. Feld, "Transformation of the Juvenile Court, Pt. 2: Race and the Crack Down on Youth Crime," *Minnesota Law Review* 84, no. 361 (1999): 327–95; Alida V. Merlo, "Juvenile Justice at the Crossroads: Presidential Address to the Academy of Criminal Justice Sciences," *Justice Quarterly* 17, no. 4 (2000): 639–61.

22. John C. Watkins, *Juvenile Justice Century: A Sociological Commentary on American Juvenile Courts* (Durham, NC: Carolina Academic, 1998), xvii.

23. See Sidney Axelrad, "Negro and White Institutionalized Delinquents," *American Journal of Sociology* 56, no. 6 (1952): 569–74; and Thomas J. Espenshade and Alexandria W. Radford, *No Longer Separate, Not Yet Equal: Race and Class in Elite College Admission and Campus Life* (Princeton, NJ: Princeton University Press, 2009).

24. Barry Krisberg, Ira Schwartz, Gideon Fishman, Zvi Eisikovits, Edna Guttman, and Joe Karen, "The Incarceration of Minority Youth," *Crime and Delinquency* 33, no. 2 (1987): 178–79; Feld, *Bad Kids*, 180.

25. Krisberg et al., "The Incarceration of Minority Youth," 178–79; Margaret W. Cahalan, *Historical Corrections Statistics in the United States, 1850–1984* (Washington, DC: U.S. Department of Justice, Bureau of Justice Statistics, 1986); Donna Hamparian and Michael Leiber, *Disproportionate Confinement of Minority Juveniles in Secure Facilities 1996 National Report* (Champaign, IL: Community Research Associates, 1997).

26. Miller, "Race, Gender and Juvenile Justice," 18; Clemens Bartollas, "Little Girls Grown Up: The Perils of Institutionalization," in *Female Criminality: The State of the Art*, ed. C. Culliver (New York: Garland, 1993), 473; Meda Chesney-Lind, "Challenging Girls' Invisibility in Juvenile Court," *Annals of the American Academy of Political*

and Social Science 564, no. 1 (1999): 194–96; Meda Chesney-Lind and Lisa Pasko, *The Female Offender: Girls, Women, and Crime* (1997), 2nd ed. (Thousand Oaks, CA: Sage, 2004), 68–78.

27. See Feld, *Bad Kids*, 264–72; Alfred Blumstein, "Youth, Guns, and Violent Crime," *The Future of Children* 12, no. 2 (2002): 39–53; Michael K. Brown, *Whitewashing Race: The Myth of a Color-Blind Society* (Berkeley and Los Angeles: University of California Press, 2003), 139–40; and Bortner, Zatz, and Hawkins, "Race and Transfer," 278–79, 283.

28. For reviews, see Hawkins and Kempf-Leonard, eds., *Our Children, Their Children*; Barry Krisberg, *Juvenile Justice: Redeeming Our Children* (Thousand Oaks, CA: Sage, 2005), chap. 5; and Brown, *Whitewashing Race*, chap. 4. On implicit racial bias against young black offenders, see Sandra Graham and Brian S. Lowery, "Priming Unconscious Racial Stereotypes about Adolescent Offenders," *Law and Human Behavior* 28, no. 5 (2004): 483–504; and J. J. Rachlinski, S. L. Johnson, A. J. Wistrich, C. Guthrie, and M. T. Hall, "Does Unconscious Racial Bias Affect Trial Judges?" *Notre Dame Law Review* 84, no. 3 (2009): 1195–1246.

29. Donna M. Bishop, "The Role of Race and Ethnicity in Juvenile Justice Processing," in Hawkins and Kempf-Leonard, eds., *Our Children, Their Children*, 23.

30. See David S. Tanenhaus, "The Evolution of Transfer out of the Juvenile Court," in Fagan and Zimring, eds., *The Changing Borders of Juvenile Justice*.

31. Ruth D. Peterson, "Youthful Offender Designations and Sentencing in the New York Criminal Courts," *Social Problems* 35, no. 2 (1988): 114. See also Donna M. Bishop, "Juvenile Offenders in the Adult Criminal Justice System," *Crime and Justice* 27 (2000): 119. Since 1922, New York law has provided that youths sixteen to eighteen years of age are considered adults for criminal justice purposes. Only New York and three other states set sixteen years as the initial age of criminal court jurisdiction. A 1978 revision through the Juvenile Offender Statute allowed youths thirteen to fifteen years of age to be held criminally responsible for murder; fourteen- and fifteen-year-olds could be held criminally responsible for other serious offenses (e.g., manslaughter, rape, kidnapping, assault, robbery, arson, and burglary in the highest degrees). Youths convicted of serious offenses (e.g., murder, arson, kidnapping) are not eligible for youthful offender status, while first-time misdemeanants must be treated as youthful offenders. Most cases fall in between these extremes, and judges have broad discretion in granting a youthful offender designation.

32. Engler, speech delivered at the conference of the Prosecuting Attorneys Association of Michigan, and "Building on Michigan's Renaissance." See also Ward and Kupchik, "Accountable to What?" 90–91.

33. Rosemary Sarri, Geoff Ward, Jeff Shook, Mark Creekmore, Cheri Albertson, Sara Goodkind, and Jin Soh, *Decision Making in the Juvenile Justice System: A Comparative Study of Four States* (Ann Arbor, MI: Institute for Social Research, 2001). Figures reflect sentencing of individuals to the Department of Corrections who were under eighteen years old at the time of their offense. Some offenders were not admitted to adult prisons until after their eighteenth birthday.

34. Jason Ziedenberg, *Drugs and Disparity: The Racial Impact of Illinois' Practice of Transferring Young Drug Offenders to Adult Court* (Washington, DC: Justice Policy Institute/Building Blocks for Youth, 2000).

35. Bishop observes: "Almost without exception, state and local studies that have explored issues of race and waiver report disproportionate minority representation in the population of youths for whom prosecutors seek judicial waiver as well as in the population . . . waived by juvenile courts" ("Juvenile Offenders in the Adult Criminal

Justice System," 102). Researchers stress the subtle, incremental, and cumulative nature of discrimination in these and other sanctioning processes (see Bortner, Zatz, and Hawkins, "Race and Transfer"; and Brown, *Whitewashing Race*, 141).

36. Melissa Sickmund, *Juveniles in Court* (Washington, DC: U.S. Department of Justice, Office of Juvenile Justice and Delinquency Prevention, 2003), 26.

37. Bishop, "Juvenile Offenders in the Adult Criminal Justice System," 100–102, 104–8. Racial disparities in waiver have increased over time. Hamparian et al. report that 39 percent of waived youths were nonwhite in 1978, compared to 44 percent in 1985 and 54 percent by 1995 (Donna Hamparian, Linda K. Estep, Susan Muntean, Ramon Priestino, Robert Swisher, Paul Wallace, and Joseph White, *Youth in Adult Courts: Between Two Worlds* [Columbus, OH: Academy for Contemporary Problems, 1982]), 104–5. See also Melissa Sickmund, Ann Stahl, Terrence Feinnegan, Howard Snyder, Rowen Poole, and Jeffrey Butts, *Juvenile Court Statistics, 1995* (Washington, DC: U.S. Department of Justice, Office of Juvenile Justice and Delinquency Prevention, 1998).

38. Bortner, Zatz, and Hawkins, "Race and Transfer," 299; Michigan Department of Corrections (MDOC), *Selected Characteristics of Offenders of Age 14, 15, and 16 at Offense Date*, 1999, database provided by the MDOC Research Department, Lansing, MI. See also Sarri et al., *Decision Making in the Juvenile Justice System*, 72–76.

39. Bolin, Oral History Interview, 45–46. Some advocates of punitive justice policies contend that they recognize black interests by addressing victimization. See Bennett, DiIulio, and Walters, *Body Count*, 84, 162. For more critical discussions of black "underprotection" and "protectionism," see Randall Kennedy, *Race, Crime, and the Law* (New York: Pantheon, 1997); Paul Butler, "Racially Based Jury Nullification: Black Power in the Criminal Justice System," *Yale Law Journal* 105, no. 3 (1995): 677–725; and Kathryn Russell-Brown, *Protecting Our Own: Race, Crime, and African Americans* (New York: Rowman & Littlefield, 2006). Selective acknowledgment of black interests in criminal law enforcement and deemphasis of related interests in nondiscrimination, prevention, and rehabilitation is a subtle example of what Fraser terms *misrecognition*, a denial of dominion or voice in deliberations of justice system reform (Nancy Fraser, "From Redistribution to Recognition? Dilemmas of Justice in a 'Post-Socialist' Age," *New Left Review* [1995]: 68–93).

40. Charles Harris Wesley, ed., *The History of the National Association of Colored Women's Clubs: A Legacy of Service* (Washington, DC: National Association of Colored Women's Clubs, 1984), 45; Bishop, "Juvenile Offenders in the Adult Criminal Justice System," 149; Feld, *Bad Kids*; Bruce Western, *Punishment and Inequality in America* (New York: Sage, 2007).

41. Black child-savers and community stakeholders have not been alone in advancing these assumptions. By the 1940s and 1950s, legal and law enforcement entities called for increased racial diversity in the justice workforce to address substantive needs and interests of diverse constituent communities, control neighborhood crime, and bolster perceptions of legitimacy. See Geoff Ward, "Race and the Justice Workforce: A System Perspective," in *The Many Colors of Crime: Inequalities of Race, Ethnicity, and Crime in America*, ed. R. Peterson, L. Krivo, and J. Hagan (New York: New York University Press, 2006).

42. "Order, *Crum v. State Training School for Girls*" (1970), available as document no. JI-AL-0002-0001 at http://clearinghouse.net.

43. See, e.g., Ward and Kupchik, "Accountable to What?"; Ward, Kupchik, Parker, and Starks, "Racial Politics of Juvenile Justice Policy Support"; and Geoff Ward, Amy Far-

rell, and Danielle Rousseau, "Does Racial Balance in Workforce Representation Yield Equal Justice?" *Law and Society Review* 43, no. 4 (2009): 757–806.

44. Miller, *The Perils of Federalism*, 44–48, 62, 86, 113–15.

45. George B. Nesbitt, "The Negro Race Relations Expert and Negro Community Leadership," *Journal of Negro Education* 21, no. 2 (1952): 148–60. The confirmation hearings of Judge Sonia Sotomayor and right-wing attacks labeling her racist for self-identifying as a "wise Latina" are instructive here. See Carol J. Greenhouse, "Judgment and the Justice: An Ethnographic Reading of the Sotomayor Confirmation Hearing," *Law, Culture, and the Humanities*, advance online publication, 2010 (doi: 10.1177/1743872110374916).

46. U.S. Congress, Senate Committee on the Judiciary, *Violent and Repeat Juvenile Offender Act of 1997: Report of the Committee on the Judiciary, United States Senate, Together with Additional, Minority, and Supplemental Views to Accompany S. 10* (Washington, DC: U.S. Government Printing Office, 1997), 62. The Violent and Repeat Juvenile Offender Act of 1997 (S. 10) was coauthored by Senators Orrin Hatch (R-UT) and Jeff Sessions (R-AL). The Juvenile Crime Control Act of 1997 (H.R. 3) was authored by Representative Bill McCollum (R-FL).

47. 143 Cong. Rec. H2356 (daily ed. May 8, 1997).

48. Steven Schlossman, "Delinquent Children: The Juvenile Reform School," in *The Oxford History of the Prison: The Practice of Punishment in Western Society*, ed. Norval Morris and David J. Rothman (New York: Oxford University Press, 1995), 335. Schlossman notes the use of "rudimentary behavioral science methods to diagnose and classify inmates" in the earliest reformatories. These were meant to identify the treatment needs of youths and individualize interventions. However, then as now, such efforts often failed to produce the intended results. "Most reform schools were virtually impervious to change," Schlossman writes of early adopters, and, "even when serious efforts to transform correctional philosophy, design and practice were contemplated and planned, the implementation was usually so faulty as to abort the experiment" (ibid., 374).

49. Ibid., 336. SDM presumes the existence of a sanctioning and service continuum aligned with categories of classification or possible sanctioning and service recommendations. The irregular application of SDM has often been tied to resource inadequacy or incongruity. See Jeff J. Shook and Rosemary C. Sarri, "Structured Decision Making in Juvenile Justice: Judges' and Probation Officers' Perceptions and Use," *Children and Youth Services Review* 29, no. 10 (2007): 1335–51.

50. In 1941, the California Youth Authority established diagnostic centers where all delinquent youths would be sent for assessment before placement in a particular institution. The apparent sophistication and objectivity of the diagnostic centers bolstered the appearance of system accountability in the 1950s. See Schlossman, "Delinquent Children." See also Blomquist and Forst, "Moral and Practical Problems."

51. See Dean J. Champion, *Measuring Offender Risk: A Criminal Justice Sourcebook* (Westport, CT: Greenwood, 1994), 48–49; Joan Petersilia and Susan Turner, *Guideline-Based Justice: The Implication for Racial Minorities* (Santa Monica, CA: Rand, 1985); and David M. Altschuler, "Tough and Smart Juvenile Incarceration: Integrating Punishment, Deterrence and Rehabilitation," *Saint Louis University Public Law Review* 14, no. 1 (1994): 217–37.

52. In the 1980s, a survey of courts in thirty-seven states found that 47 percent used assessment tools to classify offenders and inform dispositions (W. Barton and K. Gorsuch, "Risk Assessment and Classification in Juvenile Justice" [paper presented at the

annual meeting of the American Society of Criminology, Reno, Nevada, 1989], cited in Shook and Sarri, "Structured Decision Making in Juvenile Justice," 1339). A later survey of juvenile courts in fifty states found that, although most states used some type of risk-assessment technique, only a minority used formal, empirically derived classification procedures. See Donna B. Towberman, "A National Survey of Juvenile Risk Assessment," *Juvenile and Family Court Journal* 43, no. 1 (1992): 61–67.

53. Champion, *Measuring Offender Risk*, 29; William H. Barton, "Resisting Limits on Discretion: Implementation Issues of Juvenile Dispositional Guidelines," *Criminal Justice Policy Review* 8, nos. 2–3 (1997): 169; Shook and Sarri, "Structured Decision Making in Juvenile Justice," 1344.

54. Sarri et al., *Decision Making in the Juvenile Justice System*, 81.

55. Shook and Sarri, "Structured Decision Making in Juvenile Justice," 1343. Research on racial group representation in justice-related occupations shows a general concentration of black workers in the service sector (i.e., police and prison officers, social work and security) and more limited representation in professional-administrative fields (see Ward, "Race and the Justice Workforce"). However, this pattern is likely less pronounced in juvenile justice given the diminished stature of this area of legal practice and the racial segmentation of justice-related labor.

56. Data were collected in 1999 and 2000. Race differences in occupational concentration (.01) and SDM familiarity and use (.05) are statistically significant. For further details on the survey methodology and these results, see Sarri et al., *Decision Making in the Juvenile Justice System*, 190–203; and Shook and Sarri, "Structured Decision Making in Juvenile Justice," 1340–46.

57. Franklin E. Zimring, "The Punitive Necessity of Waiver," in Fagan and Zimring, eds., *The Changing Borders of Juvenile Justice*, 208. Since prosecutors control charging decisions, they also play a primary role in legislative waiver.

58. Bishop, "Juvenile Offenders in the Adult Criminal Justice System," 84–85; Patricia Torbet and Linda Szymanski, *State Legislative Responses to Violent Juvenile Crime: 1996–97 Update* (Washington, DC: U.S. Department of Justice, Office of Juvenile Justice and Delinquency Prevention, 1998); U.S. General Accounting Office, *Juvenile Justice: Juveniles Processed in Criminal Court and Case Dispositions* (Washington, DC: U.S. Government Printing Office, 1995); Marilyn Houghtalin and G. Larry Mays, "Criminal Disposition of New Mexico Juveniles Transferred to Adult Court," *Crime and Delinquency* 37 (1991): 393–407; Vincent Schiraldi and Jason Ziedenberg, *Florida Experiment: An Analysis of the Impact of Granting Prosecutors Discretion to Try Juveniles as Adults* (Washington, DC: Justice Policy Institute, 1999), 1.

59. Howell, *Juvenile Justice and Youth Violence*, 33; Leiber, "Disproportionate Minority Confinement (DMC) of Youth." The DMC mandate originates in 1988 amendments to the Juvenile Justice and Delinquency Prevention Act of 1974 (Pub. L. No. 93-415, 42 U.S.C. 5601 et seq.). The Juvenile Justice and Delinquency Prevention Act of 2002 defined the DMC requirement as follows: "addressing juvenile delinquency prevention efforts and system improvement efforts designed to reduce, without establishing or requiring numerical standards or quotas, the disproportionate number of juvenile members of minority groups who come into contact with the juvenile justice system" (148 Cong. Rec. H6617 [daily ed. September 25, 2002]). For a review of the DMC mandate and related initiatives, see Office of Juvenile Justice and Delinquency Prevention, *Disproportionate Minority Contact Technical Assistance Manual*, 4th ed. (Washington, DC: Office of Justice Programs, 2009).

60. National Council of Juvenile and Family Court Judges, "Minority Youth in the Juvenile Justice System," iii; Judicial Council of Georgia, "Fulton County Juvenile Court: New Courthouse Keeps Kids in Mind," *Georgia Courts Journal* 4 (April 2003): 4–5; Lieber, "Disproportionate Minority Confinement of Youth."

61. Carl E. Pope, R. Lovell, and H. M. Hsia, *Disproportionate Minority Confinement: A Review of the Research Literature from 1989 through 2001* (Washington, DC: Office of Juvenile Justice and Delinquency Prevention, 2002).

62. David Teasley and Edith Cooper, *Juvenile Justice Legislation: Overview and Legislative Debate*, Report for Congress (Washington, DC: Congressional Research Service, Library of Congress, 2001), 3, 11.

63. Fraser, "From Redistribution to Recognition?" 72. See also Nancy Fraser and Alex Honneth, *Redistribution or Recognition? A Political-Philosophical Exchange* (New York: Verso, 2003); and Iris M. Young, *Justice and the Politics of Difference* (Princeton, NJ: Princeton University Press, 1990).

64. Fraser, "From Redistribution to Recognition?" 70–82; Lorne P. Foster, "Lawyers of Colour and Racialized Immigrants with Foreign Legal Degrees: An Examination of the Institutionalized Processes of Social Nullification," *International Journal of Criminology and Sociological Theory* 2, no. 1 (2009): 189–217.

65. Young, *Justice and the Politics of Difference*, 198.

66. Regnery, "Getting Away with Murder," 45; Forst and Blomquist, "Punishment, Accountability, and the New Juvenile Justice"; Ward and Kupchik, "Accountable to What?"

67. The history of the black child-saving movement was apparently unknown to figures such as Dr. Benjamin Mays and William Patterson, who called for the development of such a movement in the 1950s. It is generally undocumented in the extensive academic and policy literatures on race and American juvenile justice after 1970, including black research outlets such as the *Journal of Negro Education*.

68. W. E. B. DuBois, "Editorial," *The Crisis* 37, no. 10 (1930): 352, cited in Diggs, "Du Bois and Children," 387–88.

69. Research suggests that "racial resentments are inextricably entwined in public punitiveness," particularly among whites (see James D. Unnever and Francis T. Cullen, "The Social Sources of Americans' Punitiveness: A Test of Three Competing Models," *Criminology* 48, no. 1 [2010]: 99–129). For evidence of older blacks' resentment of young black offenders, see Larry D. Bobo and Devon Johnson, "A Taste for Punishment: Black and White Americans' Views on the Death Penalty and the War on Drugs," *Du Bois Review: Social Science Research on Race* 1, no. 1 (2004): 151–80. Other research suggests that blacks support prevention and treatment, distrust justice systems to mete out severe punishment fairly, and harbor implicit preferences that encourage more leniency toward black offenders. See, e.g., Elaine Brown, *The Condemnation of Little B* (Boston: Beacon, 2002); Ward and Kupchik, "What Drives Juvenile Probation Officers?"; Ward, Kupchik, Parker, and Starks, "Racial Politics of Juvenile Justice Policy Support"; Rachlinski et al., "Does Unconscious Racial Bias Affect Trial Judges?"; and Robert L. Young, "Race, Conceptions of Crime and Justice, and Support for the Death Penalty," *Social Psychology Quarterly* 54, no. 1 (1991): 67–75.

70. Miller, *The Perils of Federalism*; Jonathan Simon, *Governing through Crime: How the War on Crime Transformed American Democracy and Created a Culture of Fear* (New York: Oxford University Press, 2007); Western, *Punishment and Inequality in America*.

71. Clark quoted in Ludy T. Benjamin, *A History of Psychology in Letters* (1993), 2nd ed. (Malden, MA: Blackwell Publications, 2006), 228.

72. V. P. Franklin, "Introduction: *Brown v. Board of Education*: Fifty Years of Educational Change in the United States," *Journal of African American History* 90, nos. 1–2 (2005): 2–3.

73. See Francesca Polletta, *Freedom Is an Endless Meeting: Democracy in American Social Movements* (Chicago: University of Chicago Press, 2004).

74. Rose Smith, "The Pampers to Prison Pipeline: The Mis-Education of Black Boys" (speech presented at the 21st Century Black Massachusetts conference "Unity + Strategy = Power," Boston, June 3, 2005).

INDEX

positions of, 149. *See also* black child-saving movement; vanguard movement; individual organizations and institutions

Black Codes, 63–66, 74, 80; and black disenfranchising, 67

black collective efficacy: decline in, 201, 218, 228, 230–31, 233, 258

black collective identity: erosion of, 247, 257, 261

black collective responsibility: social class fractioning within, 219

black community: black church, and delinquency prevention, 222; juvenile delinquency, unresponsiveness toward, 219; juvenile delinquency, war on, 222

Black Cross Nurses, 168

black disenfranchisement, 81; and Black Codes, 67

black elites, 123–24, 127, 152; apathy of, 221; black child-saving movement, renewal of for by, 259; black delinquency, lack of responsibility of toward, 310n55; Marcus Garvey, apprehension toward, 168; juvenile crime, appeals for protection against by, 259; reform efforts of, and "linked fate," 71–72; violent juvenile crime, concern over by, 259. *See also* black race experts

black freedom movement, 156, 163, 186, 189; blacks, as disconnected from, 220; and juvenile justice reform, 124, 127; pressure group politics, 12; and racial violence, 118; self-help initiatives, 12

black incarceration: of black females, 243–44, 284n36; black youth, mass incarceration of, 246; as disproportionate minority contact (DMC), 235–36, 242; as dominant trend, in juvenile justice, 235; as "educational genocide," 263; increase in, 67–69, 85–86, 259; sanctioning of, 245–46; and social control, 260; two-track approach, 243–44; as undeserving delinquents, 238–39, 243; undeserving delinquents, and mechanism of exclusion, 239; youthful offender status, as stripped of, 245. *See also* black prison population

black juvenile delinquents: in cities, 218; as incorrigible, 242; institutions for, 75; as undeserving, 223, 242. *See also* juvenile delinquents

black migration, 257; to North, 77, 83, 238

Black Nadir, 7, 80, 127, 157

black population: as amoral, and dialectic of exclusion, justification for, 100; children of, as inferior human clay, 44; children of, as lost cause, 39; citizen building, undermining of, 38; citizenship, denial of, 42–43; developmental incapacity of, 38–40; disenfranchisement of, 81; as foreign, 110, 289n17; humanity, denial of, 10, 38, 40–42, 44, 167, 262; interests, stratification of, 259; juvenile justice policies, diminishing of, 246–47; marginalization of, 37, 248–49; oppositional consciousness of, 296n63; as police officers, 121; resistance, through self-determination, 127; sense of self, evolution of, 164; as unassimilated, 122

black prison population: 88–89, 146, in American North, 88; in American South, 47, 100; black children, as convict labor, 99; and black females, 8–9, 88, 129, 243–44, 284n36; black youths, in adult institutions, 90–91, 98, 100–101, 133; commitment rate, 89–90; as disproportionate minority contact (DMC), 235–36, 242; gap between white and black youth, 242; increase in, 86; offenses of, as more serious, 92; regional distinctions of, 88–90. *See also* black incarceration

black progressivism, 152

black race experts, 164, 178, 183, 197, 221, 230, 234, 303n67; community support, neglect of by, 219; at federal level, limited influence of, 249; isolation of, 211; and race adjustment, 179. *See also* black elites

black reformatories: as financially unstable, 159. *See also* juvenile reformatories; houses of refuge; reformatories

Black Renaissance, 167

black representation, 211; in child and social welfare institutions, and juvenile justice, 219; denial of, among juvenile justice authorities, 258; in government, 182, 249; informal social controls, as weakened, 220; national agenda, as little influence on, 249

black Republicans, 64

deserving v. undeserving categories of, 14, 86, 238, 240, 242–43; as embryonic citizens, 19, 33; exclusionary sanctions against, 233, 238; normal v. serious, 233–34; as potential citizens capable of redemption, by parental state, 33; racialized moral panic over, 259–60; as serious, 258; as undeserving, 238–39, 243. *See also* juvenile delinquency; youth violence

Juvenile Delinquents: Their Condition and Treatment (Carpenter), 31

Juvenile Detention Home (Illinois), 160

juvenile institutions: nonwhites in, as disproportionate, 5; segregated, maintaining of, 202

juvenile institutionalization, 235

juvenile justice, 22–23, 38, 229–30, 250, 254, 256, 259, 316n41; accountability movement in, 14, 232; and Americanization, 33; black genocide, charges of in, 263; black youths, as marginalized in, 260; as citizen building, 30; desegregation of, opposition to, 202; deserving and undeserving delinquents, turn to, 238; development of, 28; exclusion, of black youths from, 82, 128; federalism, as growing force, 221–22; juvenile responsibility, emphasis on, 240, 257; marginal groups, as less responsive to, 234; penal managerialism, rise of, 235; proportional group representation, 4, 236–37; punishment, as core component of, 240; punitive turn to, 15, 238, 257; race in, 1–3, 261; race relations in, inequality of, as worsening, 236; "race work" in, 129; racial domination in, 248; racial and ethnic composition of, as unrecorded, 310n57; racial inequality in, 238, 257, 263; racial makeup of, at midcentury, 163; two-tier approach of, criminal v. noncriminal track, 240, 243; Willie Hortonization of, 242

Juvenile Justice Act (1977), 240

The Juvenile Justice Century (Watkins), 242

Juvenile Justice and Delinquency Prevention Act (1974), 253–54

Juvenile Justice and Delinquency Prevention Act (2002), 318n59

juvenile justice reform, 116, 165; and accountability movement, 234; and black

community involvement, 9; and black vote, 170–71; pressure group politics, use of, 170

juvenile justice system, 7, 26, 233; Americanization of, 73; black Americans, freedom dreams of, 60–61; black offenders, and white victims, political dimension of, 51; blacks, and race, significance of on, 6; blacks, as second-class citizens, treated as in, 76; black youths, discrimination of against, 8; chattel slavery, overlap between, 34; court-ordered integration of, 216; and English common law, 48; exclusion, dialectic of, 59; federalism, growing role of in, 231; and nonwhites, 5, 34–35; race-based distinctions of, 45; racial inequality in, 4; racialization of, 49; and racial stratification of, 59; rehabilitation, liberal critique of, 237; and sanctioning, 4; in South, 60, 62; standardization in, 251; whites, as controlled by, 3; and white supremacist notions, 26

Juvenile Offender Act, 240

Juvenile Offender Act (1854), 272–73n37

Juvenile Offender Statute, 315n31

Juvenile Protective Association of Chicago, 111

juvenile reformatories, 52; in South, 60. *See also* black reformatories; houses of refuge

Juvenile Reformatory Association, 83

juvenile rehabilitative ideal, 10, 13–14. *See also* rehabilitative ideal

juvenile social control, 23, 32, 163, 229, 250, 257, 258; as accountability-based, 14; as concern, 19; and integration, 209; and nation-states, 31; racial domination, reassertion of, 246; tightening of, 22. *See also* social control

Juvenile Waiver Law, 253

Kansas, 306n107
Kansas City, 32
Kelley, Camille, 146, 192–93
Kelley, Florence, 140–41, 145, 175
Kennedy, John F., 194–95, 214
Kennedy School of Government, 33
Kentucky, 60, 65–66, 75
King, Martin Luther Jr., 157, 206
King, Wilma, 35